Culture and the Therapeutic Process

COUNSELING AND PSYCHOTHERAPY:
INVESTIGATING PRACTICE FROM SCIENTIFIC, HISTORICAL, AND CULTURAL PERSPECTIVES

A Routledge Book Series
Editor: Bruce E. Wampold, University of Wisconsin

This innovative new series is devoted to grasping the vast complexities of the practice of counseling and psychotherapy. As a set of healing practices delivered in a context shaped by health delivery systems and the attitudes and values of consumers, practitioners, and researchers, counseling and psychotherapy must be examined critically. By understanding the historical and cultural context of counseling and psychotherapy and by examining the extant research, these critical inquiries seek a deeper, richer understanding of what is a remarkably effective endeavor.

Published

Counseling and Therapy with Clients Who Abuse Alcohol or Other Drugs
Cynthia E. Glidden-Tracy

The Great Psychotherapy Debate
Bruce Wampold

The Psychology of Working: Implications for Career Development, Counseling, and Public Policy
David Blustein

Neuropsychotherapy: How the Neurosciences Inform Effective Psychotherapy
Klaus Grawe

Principles of Multicultural Counseling
Uwe P. Gielen, Juris G. Draguns, Jefferson M. Fish

Beyond Evidence-Based Psychotherapy: Fostering the Eight Sources of Change in Child and Adolescent Treatment
George Rosenfeld

Cognitive Behavioral Therapy for Deaf and Hearing Persons with Language and Learning Challenges
Neil Glickman

The Pharmacology and Treatment of Substance Abuse: Evidence and Outcome-Based Perspectives
Lee Cohen, Frank Collins, Alice Young, Dennis McChargue, Thad R. Leffingwell, and Katrina Cook

IDM Supervision: An Integrated Developmental Model for Supervising Counselors and Therapists, Third Edition
Cal Stoltenberg and Brian McNeill

Culture and the Therapeutic Process: A Guide for Mental Health Professionals
Mark M. Leach and Jamie Aten

Forthcoming

The Handbook of Therapeutic Assessment
Stephen E. Finn

The Great Psychotherapy Debate, Revised Edition
Bruce Wampold

Culture and the Therapeutic Process

A Guide for Mental Health Professionals

Mark M. Leach

Jamie D. Aten

Editors

Routledge
Taylor & Francis Group
New York   London

Routledge
Taylor & Francis Group
270 Madison Avenue
New York, NY 10016

Routledge
Taylor & Francis Group
27 Church Road
Hove, East Sussex BN3 2FA

Printed in the United States of America on acid-free paper
10 9 8 7 6 5 4 3 2 1

International Standard Book Number: 978-0-8058-6247-8 (Paperback)

Library of Congress Cataloging-in-Publication Data

Culture and the therapeutic process : a guide for mental health professionals /
   [edited by] Mark M. Leach and Jamie D. Aten.
      p. ; cm.
   Includes bibliographical references and index.
   ISBN 978-0-8058-6247-8 (pbk. : alk. paper)
      1. Psychiatry, Transcultural. I. Leach, Mark M. II. Aten, Jamie D. III. Title.
   [DNLM: 1. Psychotherapy--methods. 2. Counseling--methods. 3. Cultural
Diversity. WM 420 C96785 2009]

RC455.4.E8C8365 2009
616.89'14--dc22   2009017879

Visit the Taylor & Francis Web site at
http://www.taylorandfrancis.com

and the Routledge Web site at
http://www.routledgementalhealth.com

Contents

Series Foreword

This series is devoted to understanding the complexities of the practice of counseling and psychotherapy. As a set of healing practices, delivered in a context molded by health delivery systems and the attitudes and values of consumers, practitioners, and researchers, counseling and psychotherapy must be examined critically. Volumes in this series discuss counseling and psychotherapy from empirical, historical, anthropological, and theoretical perspectives. These critical inquiries avoid making assumptions about the nature of counseling and psychotherapy and seek a deeper understanding of the bases of what is a remarkably effective endeavor.

Unarguably, much has been written about culture in counseling and psychotherapy—indeed, the literature in the area of multicultural counseling has proliferated in the past two decades. The profusion of articles, chapters, and books on this topic signifies its importance. The effective delivery of mental health services to diverse populations is an imperative that cannot be ignored. Yet, the literature is quite ambiguous about how the imperative should be operationalized—what constitutes effective multicultural counseling and psychotherapy? Leach and Aten, in *Culture and the Therapeutic Process: A Guide for Mental Health Professionals*, have created a volume devoted to the pragmatics of delivering mental health services in a cultural context, clarifying how culture should be considered in each step of the therapeutic process. The chapters of this book span the array of therapeutic topics, from intake and assessment to termination. The chapters provide not only procedural guidance but also address the importance of the therapist's cultural awareness, knowledge, and skills, resulting in an effective synthesis of best practices in multicultural counseling and psychotherapy.

Acknowledgments

I would like to dedicate this book to the culturalists who came before me, and those who continue to stretch and develop the field. They are true visionaries and I believe this book to be a practical implementation of their ideas. They have stretched my worldview to make me a better human being.

—Mark Leach

To my parents Pam and Dean Aten. Thank you for teaching me to pursue my interests and for teaching me that it never hurts to try. Most of all, thank you for your ongoing love and support.

—Jamie Aten

About the Editors

Mark M. Leach, Ph.D., is a Professor and Training Director of the Counseling Psychology program at the University of Louisville, Kentucky. He has published numerous articles and chapters with diversity issues as their foundation, and has authored or coedited six books on the topics of suicide, spirituality and religion in therapy, culture and therapy, counseling psychology, and internalizing the psychology curriculum. He is an associate editor of the American Psychological Association Division 36 journal *Psychology of Religion and Spirituality*, cochair of the International Section of Division 17 (Counseling Psychology), and a member of the Executive Committee of Division 16 (Counseling Psychology) of the International Association of Applied Psychology. Dr. Leach's primary research interests include the areas of culture and suicide, forgiveness, comparative ethics, international counseling issues, and spirituality and religion.

Jamie D. Aten, Ph.D., is the Assistant Director of Health and Mental Health for the Katrina Research Center and Assistant Professor of Counseling Psychology at the University of Southern Mississippi. He has published numerous research articles on diversity issues and has presented his research nationally and internationally. He is the coeditor of *Spirituality and the Therapeutic Process: A Comprehensive Resource from Intake through Termination* (American Psychological Association Books). He is also the coeditor of the forthcoming book, *Spiritually Oriented Interventions for Counseling and Psychotherapy* (APA Books). His current research on the role of the African American church in overcoming minority disaster mental health disparities is being supported by grants from the Department of Health and Human

Services, Pew Charitable Trusts, the Red Cross, and the Foundation for the Mid-South, Episcopal Church, and United Jewish Communities. Dr. Aten also serves as the newsletter editor and representative to the Committee on Early Career Psychologists for Division 36 (Psychology of Religion) of the American Psychological Association.

About the Contributors

Benita Belvet is a doctoral student in the counseling psychology program at Virginia Commonwealth University. She received her B.A. in psychology with a minor in African American Studies at the University of North Carolina at Chapel Hill. She is interested in researching the impact of racism-related stress on the quality of life and psychological well-being of African Americans.

Michele C. Boyer, Ph.D., is a Professor of Counseling Psychology and Chairperson of the Department of Communication Disorders and Counseling, School, and Educational Psychology at Indiana State University. She earned her doctorate at the State University of New York at Buffalo and is a licensed psychologist (HSPP) in the state of Indiana. Her teaching, practice, and research interests include the professional training and development of counselors and psychologists, supervisor training, multicultural counseling, religion and spirituality in psychology, feminist theory and practice, sport psychology and performance enhancement, and crisis intervention. Dr. Boyer maintains active involvement in the American Psychological Association (Divisions 17, 35, 36, 44, 45, and 47), the Association for Women in Psychology, and the Council of Counseling Psychology Training Programs.

Allison K. Bradshaw, Ph.D., is a Postdoctoral Resident at the Vanderbilt University Psychological and Counseling Center. Dr. Bradshaw's research interests are diverse and have included cultural competency, social perceptions, and attention deficit/hyperactivity disorder (ADHD) in adults. At Vanderbilt University she conducts individual and couples therapy, assessments, supervision, and engages in administrative activities.

Madonna G. Constantine

Lonnie E. Duncan, Ph.D., is Associate Professor and Co-Training Director of the Counseling Psychology Program, which is a part of the Counselor Education and Counseling Psychology Department at Western Michigan University. He is a licensed psychologist and maintains a small private practice that primarily serves urban families and adolescents. Before arriving at Western Michigan University, Dr. Duncan was a staff psychologist in the Counseling Student and Development Center at Northern Illinois University. His scholarly focus is on cultural factors (that is, race, class, religion, gender, friend network, and so forth) that influence the help-seeking process for historically underserved populations.

Nicole L. Fischer is a second-year student, pursuing her Ph.D. in counseling psychology at Virginia Commonwealth University. She received her B.A. in psychology at the University of Virginia in 2004. She then served 2 years in the U.S. Peace Corps as a community development and education volunteer in Togo, West Africa. Fischer's research interests include acculturation and well-being among West African immigrants, and community health interventions among multicultural populations. She has published work on the influence of cultural orientation on subjective well-being and African-centered psychological constructs.

Lisa Aronson Fontes, Ph.D., has dedicated almost 20 years to making the social service and mental health systems more responsive to culturally diverse people. Her two most recent books are *Interviewing Clients across Cultures: A Practitioner's Guide* (Guilford Press, 2008) and *Child Abuse and Culture: Working with Diverse Families* (Guilford Press, 2005). Dr. Fontes has written widely on cultural issues in child maltreatment and violence against women, cross-cultural research, and ethics. She is on the faculty at the University of Massachusetts, Amherst. She has worked as a family, individual, and group therapist, and has conducted research in Santiago, Chile, and with Puerto Ricans, African Americans, and European Americans in the United States. Dr. Fontes is fluent in Spanish and Portuguese. She completed a Fulbright Foundation Grant in Buenos Aires, Argentina, and volunteered for 3 years with Somali refugees in Springfield, Massachusetts. She is a popular trainer and conference speaker.

Mary A. Fukuyama, Ph.D., received her doctorate from Washington State University in 1981 and has worked at the University of Florida Counseling Center for the past 27 years as a counseling psychologist, supervisor, and trainer. She is a clinical professor and teaches courses on spiritual issues in multicultural counseling. She is an active member of the University of Florida's Center for Spirituality and Health. She coauthored with Todd Sevig a book titled *Integrating Spirituality into Multicultural Counseling* (Sage, 1999), and also published a book with Woodrow M. Parker titled *Consciousness Raising: A Primer for Multicultural Counseling* (3rd ed.; Charles C Thomas, 2006). Another area of interest is "navigating multiple social identities." She recently collaborated with Brent Beam in producing a DVD titled *At the Corner of Me and Myself: Voices of Multiple Social Identities*, available through MicroTraining and Multicultural Development. Dr. Fukuyama is a Fellow in Division 17 (Counseling Psychology) of the American Psychological Association.

Peter A. Gill, Psy.D., is a staff psychologist at the Family Counseling Center of the Massachusetts Society for the Prevention of Cruelty to Children. He received his Psy.D. and M.S. in clinical psychology from Antioch University New England in Keene, New Hampshire, and his M.A. in clinical psychology from the University of Hartford, Connecticut. He is a member of the American Psychological Association. Dr. Gill has a special interest in emotional trauma, attachment theory, and multicultural issues that present in therapy. His clinical work includes treatment with children, adolescents, and adults and psychological and parenting assessments. He also consults at schools, community-based service agencies, and the Massachusetts Department of Children and Families. Dr. Gill has presented workshops on the application of effective treatment approaches to clinicians at the Massachusetts Society for the Prevention of Cruelty. He has coauthored papers published in peer-reviewed scientific journals and has presented papers and posters at professional conferences.

Laura R. Johnson, Ph.D., is an Assistant Professor of Psychology at the University of Mississippi, where she teaches multicultural psychology and supervises doctoral students. Dr. Johnson provides consultation in cultural competence and workshops on intercultural communication for the Croft Institute of International Studies. She founded and supervises the Cultural Connections project for international students and the Lambda support group for gay, lesbian, bisexual, and transgender (GLBT) students. Her research represents a convergence of interests in international, cultural, conservation, and developmental psychology, with a focus on youth development and civic engagement in a global environment. Dr. Johnson has been an international student, Peace Corps volunteer, and Fulbright Fellow. She graduated from the University of Louisville, Kentucky, and completed her internship at the Refugee Health Program of Colorado and Asian Pacific Development Center. She maintains a collaborative research partnership with the Jane Goodall Institute and other community-based organizations. She has written several book chapters on culture in psychology and published articles based on her international research. Dr. Johnson serves on the American Psychological Association's Committee on International Relations in Psychology (CIRP; 2008–2010) and is an APA International Division liaison to Uganda, Tanzania, and China.

Mai M. Kindaichi

Marie L. Miville, Ph.D., is Associate Professor of Psychology and Education and Director of Training of the Ph.D. Program in Counseling Psychology at Teachers College, Columbia University. She has published on multicultural topics, including Latina/o mental health, universal-diverse orientation, and the interrelations of diverse dimensions of identity. Her more recent work focuses on cross-cultural understandings of gender and gender roles and the development of an integrative training model based on the American Psychological Association diversity practice guidelines. Dr. Miville has served as chair of the Council of Counseling Psychology Training Programs and is a Fellow of the American Psychological Association (Divisions 17 and 45).

Delila Owens

Freddy A. Paniagua, Ph.D. (University of Kansas; postdoctoral training at Johns Hopkins University School of Medicine), spent 24 years as a professor in the Department of Psychiatry and Behavioral Sciences, University of Texas Medical Branch at Galveston, where he taught cross-cultural mental health seminars with emphasis on the assessment, diagnosis, and treatment of mental disorders among African American, Asian, American Indian, and Hispanic clients. He is currently a visiting scholar at the U.S. Army Center for Health Promotion and Preventive Medicine (USACHPPM), Aberdeen Proving Ground, Maryland. Dr. Paniagua has published extensively in the area of multiculturalism, including a best-selling textbook titled *Assessing and Treating Culturally Diverse Clients: A Practical Guide* (Sage).

Emma T. T. Phan, Psy.D., received her doctorate at the Florida School of Professional Psychology at Argosy in Tampa. She has worked and trained in a variety of settings including counseling centers, schools, and hospitals, serving patients from ages 8 months to 84 years. She is currently working at Atascadero State Hospital (ASH) as a clinical psychologist. She provides group therapy, individual therapy, behavioral interventions, trial competency preparation, and assessments for mentally disordered offenders in a forensic setting. Her interests include working with the substance abuse population, Asian Americans, and hypnotherapy. Her work at ASH includes translating for and working with the monolingual Vietnamese patients who are unable to receive services in English. She is also involved with Interplast, an international humanitarian organization, as a coordinator/translator, also providing pre- and posthypnotherapy. She is a member of the American Psychological Association, the Asian American Psychological Association, and the Asian American Psychological Association Division of Women.

Charles R. Ridley, Ph.D., is a Professor in the Counseling Psychology program and Director of the Integrated Research, Education, and Training Core, Center for the Study of Health Disparities at Texas A&M University. He received his doctorate from the University of Minnesota. He previously held academic and administrative appointments at several institutions, including 17 years at Indiana University. He is a licensed psychologist and Fellow of Divisions 17 and 45 of the American Psychological Association. His research interests include professional competence and mentoring; multicultural counseling, assessment, and training; therapeutic change; and the integration of psychology and theology. Dr. Ridley consults primarily with religious and nonprofit organizations. He is the author of *Overcoming Unintentional Racism in Counseling and Therapy: A Practitioner's Guide to Intentional Intervention* (2nd ed.; Sage, 2005), and coauthor with W. Brad Johnson of *The Elements of Mentoring* (Rev. ed.; Palgrave MacMillan, 2008) and *The Elements of Ethics* (Palgrave MacMillan, 2008).

Mary Shaw-Ridley, Ph.D., is an Associate Professor in the Health Division of the Department of Health and Kinesiology and Director of the Center for the Study of Health Disparities at Texas A&M University. She received her doctorate in health studies from Texas Woman's University. She previously held academic appointments in the Department of Health Studies at Texas Woman's University and the Department of Applied Health Science at Indiana University. She has more than 16 years of teaching, administrative, and consultancy experience with K–12 learning communities, health organizations, and postsecondary institutions. Dr. Shaw-Ridley's scholarship has focused on health disparities, Black women's health, health literacy, and more recently has included the integration of psychological wellness into diabetes and cancer self-care management therapies.

Gargi Roysircar, Ph.D., is Professor of Clinical Psychology and Director of the Multicultural Center at Antioch University New England. She is a fellow of the American Psychological Association and the editor of the *Journal of Multicultural Counseling and Development*. She is currently writing *Disaster Effects on People, Children, Communities, and Caregivers: Health, Help, and Assessment* and is a coauthor of *Theories and Strategies of Counseling and Psychotherapy: Relevance across Cultures and Settings* (in press, Sage). In her community practice, Dr. Roysircar has been involved in tsunami recovery in Southern India, Hurricanes Katrina and Rita recovery in the Gulf Coast of the United States, and in working with the staff of orphanages in South Africa and Botswana, where HIV/AIDS-infected and -affected orphans and women receive services. Recently, she did postvention psychoeducation in flood-ravaged Villahermosa of Tabasco, Mexico. Dr. Roysircar educates her disaster volunteer teams in disaster trauma, culture-centered response skills specific to communities, and in self-care and resilience.

Daya Singh Sandhu, Ed.D., NCC, NCCC, NCSC, LPCC, is a Distinguished Professor of Research and former chairperson (1996–2004) of the Department of Educational and Counseling Psychology at the University of Louisville, Kentucky. He received his doctor of counselor education degree from Mississippi State University and has taught graduate courses in counseling and counseling psychology for more than 20 years. Dr. Sandhu's interests include school counseling, multicultural counseling, issues relating to international students, and the role of spirituality in counseling and psychotherapy. In addition to more than 50 refereed journal articles and 60 book chapters, Sandhu has authored or edited 12 books. Sandhu has received several distinguished awards including: the Fulbright Senior Research Scholar Award; the Association for Multicultural Counseling and Development (AMCD) Research Award; the President's Distinguished Faculty Award for Outstanding Scholarship, Research and Creativity at the University of Louisville; the Alumnus of the Year Award; and the Kentucky Counselor Educator of the Year Award. Dr. Sandhu is president-elect of the Association for Multicultural Counseling and Development.

Jeffrey D. Strain, Ph.D., is Assistant Professor in the Psychology and Philosophy Department at Texas Woman's University. His research interests include diverse expressions of gender and sexual identity, correctional/prison psychology, underserved populations (for example, sex workers, low-wage workers, people with severe and persistent psychiatric illness), and community/ecological approaches to counseling.

Shawn O. Utsey, Ph.D., is Chair of the Department of African American Studies and Associate Professor of Counseling Psychology in the Department of Psychology at Virginia Commonwealth University. He received his B.A. in psychology from North Carolina A&T State University, his M.A. in rehabilitation counseling from New York University, and his Ph.D. in counseling psychology from Fordham University. He completed his clinical internship at Pace University in New York City. Prior academic appointments include assistant professor of counseling psychology at Seton Hall University from 1997 to 2001 and associate professor of counseling psychology at Howard University from 2001 to 2004. Dr. Utsey's research interests are primarily in two areas, both of which are related to the psychology of the African American experience. First, he is interested in understanding how race-related stress impacts the physical, psychological, and social well-being of African Americans. Dr. Utsey has published on African American psychology in a number of journals, including the *Journal of Black Psychology*, the *Journal of African American Men*, the *Journal of Personality Assessment*, the *Journal of Cross-Cultural Psychology*, *Cultural Diversity and Ethnic Minority Psychology*, and the *Journal of Counseling Psychology*. More recently, however, he has sought to examine how trauma is manifest in the victims of racial violence. Other areas of interest include examining the influence of African American culture (for example, collective social orientation, spiritual centeredness, verve, and so forth) on indicators of health and well-being.

Beverly J. Vandiver, Ph.D., is Associate Professor of Education in the Department of Educational and School Psychology and Special Education at Pennsylvania State University. Prior to arriving at Penn State, she was a staff psychologist in the University Counseling Center at the University of Notre Dame, Indiana, providing services to a diverse clientele. She obtained her doctorate in counseling psychology from Ball State University, Muncie, Indiana, and is a licensed psychologist. Her scholarly focus is on cultural factors and mental health, and various cultural identities and their measurement. Dr. Vandiver is the first author of the Cross Racial Identity Scale, a measure of Black racial identity based on the expanded nigrescence theory.

1

An Introduction
to the Practical Incorporation
of Culture into Practice

Mark M. Leach and Jamie D. Aten

This book largely grew from our own frustration with parts of the literature suggesting that some cultural variable "should be considered" or that
therapists "should be aware of" a cultural factor in order to engage in some
culturally sensitive intervention—but clinical strategies or application guidelines were often noticeably absent. In most cases, these comments were never
followed with specifics of how culture should be considered or developed,
leaving the reader wondering how to practically include culture in counseling. This book was envisioned to include authors who could discuss practical ways of including culture throughout the counseling process, instead of
relying on individuals to just "consider cultural issues." Thus, the goal of
this book is to provide readers with a "start-to-finish" approach to implementing culture into each major component of the therapeutic process. This
book is structured such that each chapter equates to a particular stage of
therapy, beginning with self-awareness and knowledge, and ending with the
inclusion of culture when terminating treatment. It is intended to focus on
the individual (therapist and client), rather than agency or community levels of cultural competence. In the following, we set the stage for the rest of
the book by providing a brief introduction of: (a) defining levels of culture,

(b) cultural salience, (c) the multicultural movement, and (d) the history of multicultural competencies.

Defining Levels of Culture

When the contributing authors were contacted about the applied intent of this book they were given significant leeway regarding cultural factors. In fact, they were explicitly informed that they should not consider only racial or ethnic issues, but a wide range of cultural factors such as sexual orientation, abilities, spiritual and religious issues, gender, and age influences. Because the term *culture* has often been equated with race and ethnicity and has received so many differing definitions, we like the term *diversity*, which supposedly includes the areas previously listed plus many others.

There are almost as many definitions of culture as there are culturalists. Still, it has been suggested that culture can be conceptualized as existing on five levels: (a) anthropological, (b) national, (c) group, (d) within-group, and (e) individual. Because this book is not intended to supplant more detailed texts regarding the nuances of cultural influences on a variety of counseling and psychological outcomes, we will briefly address these five cultural levels. From an anthropological perspective, culture equals country. Epidemiological studies examining suicide rates in Mexico with those in the United States is one example. Another example is the comparison of international ethics codes to examine similar standards across cultural contexts. National definitions of culture are usually large studies that may examine the nuclear family dynamics and then make comparisons with other countries. A group comparison may include general African American and Latino American religious views as they relate to parenting behaviors. Within-group studies may include the level and type of religious behaviors and the ethnic identity level of participants as they relate to parenting behaviors. Finally, the individual level is often reserved for case studies, including the individual client sitting in front of the therapist.

Though all five levels have importance given the context, this book will focus primarily on group, within-group, and individual perspectives. Therapists should be local clinical scientists (Stricker, 2007), meaning that all possible variables are accounted for (as best as possible) during treatment. Further, therapists should continually evaluate their treatments given a client's multiple cultures to which she or he belongs. A client arrives to counseling sessions as a member of multiple cultures, such as possibly identifying closely with both an African American identity and rural identify, for example. The same is true for the therapist, which is why it is important for therapists to be mindful of their own cultural heritages (and influences) and identities.

Part of the difficulty with including culture into treatment is determining the salience of cultural factors at particular points in time during counseling and creating a multicultural mindset with clients. It is hoped that readers will be assisted with both in this book. Determining salience means that therapists make a mental note that a particular behavior, attitude, or value may have important, unique cultural influences that may have to be addressed. For example, assessing the degree to which resistance at a specific point in treatment should not be considered general resistance, but actually cultural resistance, or the idea that the client does not feel comfortable talking with a particular therapist about that topic because of her ethnicity or that her particular cultural group espouses discussing the topic inside the family unit only. Another example may include diagnosing an individual without regard for cultural influences. Studies have shown that people of color are much more likely to get more "severe" diagnoses than European Americans, for example (see Leach & Carlton, 1997).

Determining Cultural Salience

Determining salience takes practice, experience, and time, but also a consistent motivation on behalf of the therapist to develop a multicultural mindset. Becoming multiculturally competent has gained a great deal of attention in the professional literature over the past two decades. Multicultural competence stems from possessing a multicultural mindset, meaning that the counseling (or educational, organizational, etc.) process is embedded within culture. Culturally competent therapists think contextually, always questioning whether the recent comment or behavior has cultural influences. For example, consider a 37-year-old Chinese American woman client who was sexually abused by a stepfather as a teenager and is guarded with a therapist when discussing the abuse. How much of this guard is related to general difficulty in discussing shame, anger, confusion, depression, and the myriad of other emotions found among many survivors? How much is related to cultural influences such as discussing shameful incidents in general? The answer will, in part, be based on the therapist's willingness to consider cultural influences, assessing for cultural influences, and altering treatment interventions to account for cultural influences. Multicultural competence is related to cultural vigilance, including a willingness to consider one's own cultures and the cultures of others. It is not simply a general understanding of cultures, but a value system that says, "I will think of this client as a cultural being and consider both the commonalities among people and also the uniqueness that may be culturally inspired." Guidelines outlining multicultural competencies can offer general areas for consideration, but it will ultimately be up to the therapists and organizations to engage in the constant soul-searching needed to become competent.

Brief Overview of the Multicultural Movement

Over the years there has been an explosion of cultural-specific journals (e.g., *Asian Journal of Psychology, Journal of Black Psychology, Hispanic Journal of Behavioral Sciences*), and cultural-emphasis journals (e.g., *Journal of Multicultural Counseling and Development, Cultural Diversity and Mental Health*). On the whole, practically all journals now welcome manuscript submissions from authors who either include or focus on cultural issues related to their topic. Still, there remain only a small number of practical texts tackling cultural issues in counseling. Several factors likely contribute to the lack of applied works on culture, including: (a) the field of multiculturalism is relatively young; (b) when one talks about multiculturalism, one is really talking about virtues, acknowledged to be difficult to define and facilitate in therapists and students (Fowers & Davidov, 2006); and (c) it is difficult, if not impossible, for individual therapists, educators, and students to always identify specifics when considering cultural backgrounds of individual clients and students.

First, multiculturalism began after the social movements of the 1960s and early 1970s, though it has been only in the past 15 to 20 years that increased emphasis has been placed on diversity within training programs. As with any field and any change in worldview, progress is slow. Research including persons of color is not new, but research examining various aspects of culture as the foundation for studies is relatively new. Prior to the mid-1980s it was rare to read culturally focused research. Before this time, much of the research results considered diversity issues like race and ethnicity as an afterthought. Simplistically, many researchers would combine persons of color into a single category and include results essentially stating, "Oh by the way, differences were noted between Whites and non-Whites."

The field then began to develop by examining between-group differences, followed by increased research on within-group differences. The latter grew from explosions of identity theories and instruments. Racial, ethnic, sexual, religious, and ability identity models (among others) emerged, which allowed researchers and therapists to reconsider the influence of culture on individuals. Many of these models focused on development and included components of views of self, self-reference group, out-groups, and dominant society. We presently have a plethora of information that describe individuals and contribute to good counseling practices. However, this research information is often difficult to translate into practical, daily counseling information.

Second, Fowers and Davidov (2006) integrated Aristotelean virtue ethics into the multiculturalism movement. They indicated that multicultural values such as social justice, inclusion, and respect are central to the movement. However, they also suggested that for the field to truly attain multicultural status, the same values are often difficult for individuals to obtain. It requires personal transformations, true openness to other cultures, and character strengths. They spend a significant amount of time suggesting that transformation requires personal reflections, which can be difficult to personally accept. To move toward multicultural competence, individuals must be willing to examine their own cultural influences and their impact on current practices. Good reflection requires individuals to examine how culture impacts them and realize that their worldview is not shared by everyone. True reflection involves questioning your worldview, and cultural competence can only occur after reflection and acceptance occurs. More of this line of thinking will be discussed in Chapter 2 when considering self-awareness and knowledge.

Third, the field has had difficulty translating the vast multicultural knowledge available to practice. There are growing numbers of culturally specific interventions, but then caveats must always be included indicating that not all individuals of a group may respond to the particular intervention because of individual differences. These differences are the other side of the coin; specific interventions may not be obtainable because of the variability within groups. Many culture-specific interventions are founded on majority interventions but with other cultural considerations. There are certain qualities that we all share regardless of cultural background, but the percentages that are culture-specific warrant greater attention and research. It is the hope of the editors and contributors that we can begin to envision culture throughout the therapeutic process.

History of Multicultural Competencies

Over the past few decades, there has been increased emphasis on mental health professionals obtaining cultural competence to better serve their clients. Arredondo and Perez (2006) have succinctly outlined the history of the multicultural guidelines, beginning with the Civil Rights Act of 1964 and progressing to the implementation within various organizations and divisions within the American Psychological Association (APA), the American Counseling Association (ACA), and others. Arredondo and Perez noted the increase in the number of publications during the 1970s that "highlighted the ethnocentrism of psychology and began to focus in affirmative ways on the particular needs of ethnoracial minority groups" (p. 1). Few publications at the time focused on diversity, and, if examined at all, were typically relegated to a secondary analysis, something considered interesting for future researchers to consider. During this time the overwhelming number of journal articles would be decontextualized, meaning that culture was not included. Essentially, the results would be presented, and discussion sections may have included cultural (often racial) issues almost as an afterthought. It was not unusual to read statements to the effect of "… and there were differences on X measure between Blacks and Whites." There was no theoretical rationale as to why the differences may have occurred and no attempt to explain the differences. They were simply noted, if any mention occurred at all.

Arredondo and Perez (2006) also stated that Sue et al. (1982), at the behest of the then-president of Division 17 (Society of Counseling Psychology) of the APA, wrote a paper outlining 10 multicultural counseling competencies, the first paper of its kind and the one from which others took shape. A decade later the Association of Multicultural Counseling and Development (AMCD; a division of ACA) devised 31 multicultural counseling competencies (Sue, Arredondo, & McDavis, 1992). A few years later the competencies were expanded to include explanatory statements, and resulted in 34 competencies. The APA then approved a 6-point multicultural guidelines document that was published in 2003. The acknowledgments section of this document reads like a who's who of multiculturalists, though many others contributed to multicultural competence development throughout the years and organizations (another useful, yet succinct history can be found in Lum, 2003).

The APA (2003) also developed the *Guidelines on Multicultural Education, Training, Research, Practice, and Organizational Change for Psychologists.*

These guidelines were designed to offer therapists six guiding principles designed to influence psychological practices:

1. Psychologists are encouraged to recognize that ... they may hold attitudes and beliefs [detrimental to working with] individuals who are ethnically and racially different from themselves.
2. Psychologists are encouraged to recognize the importance of multicultural [sensitivity, knowledge, and understanding] of ethnically and racially different individuals.
3. As educators, psychologists are encouraged to employ the constructs of multiculturalism and diversity in psychological education.
4. Culturally sensitive researchers ... recognize the importance of conducting [cultural-centered and ethical] research among persons from ethnic, linguistic, and racial minority backgrounds.
5. Psychologists ... apply culturally appropriate skills in [applied] practices.
6. Psychologists ... use organizational change processes to support culturally informed organizational (policy) development and practices. Each of these principles incorporates general considerations that lead to culturally sensitive and appropriate practices. (pp. 382–392)

Continuing with the increase in cultural competency importance, Constantine and Sue (2005) published an edited text focusing on the application of the guidelines in a variety of settings. Recently, Hansen et al. (2006) identified 52 multicultural counseling competencies and surveyed 149 psychologists about these competencies. Disturbingly, most of these psychologists indicated that they viewed multicultural competence as important but the overwhelming majority of cultural competence items were not actually practiced. The authors pointed out that many competencies require active and intentional efforts outside the therapeutic session, and that passively waiting for cultural issues to arise is not sufficient nor significantly beneficial.

Miley, O'Melia, and DuBois (1998; as reported in Lum, 2003) indicated that cultural competence can be considered on three levels: practitioner, agency, and community. Briefly, at the practitioner level, increasing cultural competencies is considered to be a developmental process of acquiring *awareness* of one's own biases, prejudices, discriminations, and cultural heritage; *knowledge* of different cultural groups; and *skills* related to working with culturally diverse clients. Sue and Sue (1982) presented this tripartite model, and although there have been expanded, alternative models (e.g., Constantine & Ladany, 2001) and critiques of the model (e.g., Mollen, Ridley, & Hill, 2003;

Ridley, Baker, & Hill, 2001), the foundation for cultural competence generally includes these three factors. Thus, therapists are encouraged to consider
their own cultural awareness, identities, privileges, and histories, and to continuously examine the impact of their cultures on clients.

At the agency level, culturally competent therapists promote diversity in
program delivery, hiring practices, evaluation, and structures. The latter can
include the openness to include culturally diverse interventions, interacting
with the community, and focusing on client strengths. Other authors (e.g.,
Sue & Sue, 2007) have also discussed the need for organizational changes
in community agencies, universities, and businesses. In essence, structural
changes are more difficult than individual changes, but organizations at any
level should strive to become more multiculturally inclusive and strive to provide a mental health system that is culturally competent. At the community
level, competence is considered with respect to a promotion of cultural interactions and social justice, the latter of which has been increasing recently in a
variety of fields (e.g., Toporek, Gerstein, Fouad, Roysircar, & Israel, 2006).

Research tends to indicate that cultural competencies can increase over
time when focused on. That is, therapists must be intentional in their efforts
to enhance this knowledge and skill set. Multiple empirical studies have
shown that mental health professionals of color typically score higher than
dominant group professionals on self-report cultural competency inventories
(e.g., Holcomb-McCoy & Myers, 1999; Sodowsky, Kuo-Jackson, Richardson,
& Corey, 1998), yet more outcome studies are still clearly needed.

Chapter-by-Chapter Overview

Each chapter in this book provides practical examples, techniques, and strategies to assist therapists in incorporating culture into each stage of treatment, from the beginning of treatment to the end of treatment. Many of the
examples and strategies are practical, giving the reader new ways to consider
the influence of culture in areas previously not thoroughly considered in the
literature. We recognize that there may be some overlap among a few of
the chapters but also realize that stages within the therapeutic process do
not occur independently; thus, though minimal, some overlap is expected in
order to offer context to the chapters.

In Chapter 2, Leach, Aten, Boyer, Strain, and Bradshaw begin by introducing readers to the need for increasing therapist self-awareness as a cultural
being, and knowledge needed to create and maintain an effective therapeutic

relationship. Self-awareness and knowledge reflect respect for the culturally diverse client, and the authors present an overview of some of the common issues found in the competency triad literature. They present obstacles to developing cultural self-awareness, followed by multiple practical exercises and assessment methods designed to enhance self-awareness and knowledge.

Fontes incorporates a multitude of ways to conduct an intake interview in a culturally competent manner in Chapter 3. She walks the reader through each segment of the intake, offering examples and cultural considerations for therapists. Many practical questions and approaches are described and will assist any therapist hoping to include more cultural expertise into her or his intake procedures.

Paniagua, in Chapter 4, offers alternative means of assessing and diagnosing culturally diverse clients. He begins with a discussion of the impact of acculturation assessment and diagnosis, followed by the influence of racism and cultural identity on these counseling segments. Paniagua then moves to the selection of culturally appropriate tests including the mental status exam, discussion of culture-bound syndromes and cultural variations, and *Diagnostic and Statistical Manual of Mental Disorders* (*DSM*) cultural recommendations.

In Chapter 5, Constantine, Miville, Kindaichi, and Owens illustrate the importance of incorporating cultural issues into case conceptualizations, with the resultant implications for therapy. The authors address how personal biases can impede robust case conceptualizations and offer a case conceptualization highlighting the bias. Readers will also benefit from the taxonomy they present that includes cultural considerations based on the therapist's theoretical orientation.

Johnson and Sandhu present ways to develop treatment plans that embrace a variety of cultural contexts in Chapter 6. They present perspectives of different worldviews and their impact on therapist, client, and professional and theoretical biases. They offer specific skills related to treatment planning and follow with a multitude of specific questions to ask the client, and questions for the therapist to ask herself or himself. All of this is accomplished from an ongoing cultural assessment standpoint based on an explanatory model. Finally, the authors present a checklist for culturally congruent treatment planning and examples of culturally related treatments.

In Chapter 7, Roysircar and Gill highlight cultural issues that arise when establishing a positive therapeutic relationship. The authors focus on cultural encapsulation and decapsulation, using trainee process notes to highlight topics that can arise when developing the relationship. These narrative notes are liberally included throughout the chapter and offer the reader insights into trainee thoughts, transitions, and transformations.

Treatment implementation and recommended approaches to working with clients of diverse sociocultural backgrounds are presented in Chapter 8. Utsey, Fischer, and Belvet begin by discussing how Western worldviews limit the therapeutic possibilities, and how personality development, mental illness, and healthy psychological functioning are influenced by culture. The authors review sociocultural models of therapy, followed by a case study, including brief transcripts of the therapeutic intervention.

Ridley and Shaw-Ridley present a three-stage model of termination within a cultural context in Chapter 9. Culture is often overlooked when considering termination issues and the authors present insight into important factors during their pretermination, active termination, and posttermination phases. They incorporate multiple brief cases from which to accentuate their points. They offer practical means to sustain treatment outcomes and offer readers vast culturally appropriate social support components.

In Chapter 10, Fukuyama and Phan present a case study that includes central cultural variables found in multicultural counseling and therapy. Issues such as acculturation, identity, vocational development, and family relationships are presented. Clinical themes and commentary are provided, as is a liberal use of transcripts of therapeutic sessions. The authors include their own reflections and tie together many of the areas presented in earlier sections of the text.

In Chapter 11, Vandiver and Duncan present best cultural practices in four areas: (a) help seeking, (b) assessment, (c) treatment, and (d) training and supervision. This is accomplished by providing a brief review of clinical research that informs counselors about practicing multicultural counseling and by offering ways that this research can be applied to practice. The authors use a combination of the literature and their own rich experiences to offer practical examples that mental health professionals will find very useful.

Conclusion

When discussions of cultural competence arise, the questions often center on pragmatics. For example, how does one become culturally competent specifically? How can therapists and students provide culturally competent interventions that increase the likelihood of success? Unfortunately, the majority of previous writings discuss issues surrounding culture and cultural competence, but offering means to include culture in each segment of counseling is virtually unavailable. It is the purpose of this book to offer the reader a way of including culture throughout each stage of treatment. Further, an underlying purpose of this book is to help the reader determine where their areas for cultural growth lie, and to offer practical examples that mental health professionals can use to begin or continue their cultural journey.

References

American Psychological Association. (2003). Guidelines for multicultural education, training, research, practice, and organizational change for psychologists. *American Psychologist, 58,* 377–402.

Arredondo, P., & Perez, P. (2006). Historical perspectives on the multicultural guidelines and contemporary applications. *Professional Psychology: Research and Practice, 37,* 1–5.

Constantine, M. G., & Ladany, N. (2001). New visions for defining and assessing multicultural counseling competence. In J. G. Ponterotto, J. M. Casas, L. A. Suzuki, & C. M. Alexander (Eds.), *Handbook of multicultural counseling* (pp. 482–498). Thousand Oaks, CA: Sage.

Constantine, M. G., & Sue, D. W. (Eds.). (2005). *Strategies for building multicultural competence in mental health and educational settings.* Hoboken, NJ: John Wiley & Sons.

Fowers, B. J., & Davidov, B. J. (2006). The virtue of multiculturalism: Personal transformation, character, and openness to the other. *American Psychologist, 61,* 581–594.

Hansen, N. D., Randazzo, K. V., Schwartz, A., Marshall, M., Kalis, D., Frazier, R. et al. (2006). Do we practice what we preach? An exploratory survey of multicultural psychotherapy competencies. *Professional Psychology: Research and Practice, 37,* 66–74.

Holcomb-McCoy, C. C., & Myers, J. E. (1999). Multicultural competence and counselor training: A national survey. *Journal of Counseling & Development, 77,* 294–302.

Leach, M. M., & Carlton, M. A. (1997). Toward defining a multicultural training philosophy. In D. B. Pope-Davis & H. L. K. Coleman (Eds.), *Multicultural counseling competencies: Assessment, education and training, and supervision* (pp. 184–208). Thousand Oaks, CA: Sage.

Lum, D. (2003). *Culturally competent practice: A framework for understanding diverse groups and justice issues.* Pacific Grove, CA: Thomson and Brooks/Cole.

Miley, K. K., O'Melia, M. & Dubois, B. L. (1998). *Generalist social work practice: An empowering approach.* Boston: Allyn & Bacon.

Mollen, D., Ridley, C. R., & Hill, C. L. (2003). Models of multicultural competence. In D. B. Pope-Davis, H. K. Coleman, W. M. Liu, & R. L. Toporek (Eds.), *Handbook of multicultural competencies in counseling and psychology* (pp. 21–37). Thousand Oaks, CA: Sage.

Ridley, C. R., Baker, D. M., & Hill, C. L. (2001). Critical issues concerning cultural competence. *Counseling Psychologist, 29,* 822–832.

Sodowsky, G. R., Kuo-Jackson, P. Y., Richardson, M. F., & Corey, A. T. (1998). Correlates of self-reported multicultural competencies: Counselor multicultural social desirability, race, social inadequacy, locus of control racial ideology, and multicultural training. *Journal of Counseling Psychology, 45,* 256–264.

Stricker, G. (2007). The local clinical scientist. In S. G. Hofmann & J. Weinberger (Eds.), *The art and science of psychotherapy* (pp. 85–99). New York: Routledge.

Sue, D. W., Arredondo, P., & McDavis, R. J. (1992). Multicultural counseling competencies and standards: A call to the profession. *Journal of Multicultural Counseling and Development, 20,* 64–88.

Sue, D. W., Bernier, J., Durran, M., Feinberg, L., Pedersen, P., Smith, E. et al. (1982). Position paper: Multicultural counseling competencies. *The Counseling Psychologist, 10,* 45–52.

Sue, D. W., & Sue, D. (1982). *Counseling the culturally different.* Thousand Oaks, CA: Sage.

Toporek, R. L., Gerstein, L. H., Fouad, N. A., Roysircar, G., & Israel, T. (2006). *Handbook for social justice in counseling psychology.* Thousand, Oaks, CA: Sage.

2

Developing Therapist Self-Awareness and Knowledge

Mark M. Leach, Jamie D. Aten, Michele C. Boyer, Jeffrey D. Strain, and Allison K. Bradshaw

The purpose of this chapter is to bring attention to the role of therapist self-awareness and knowledge to cross-cultural counseling. Emphasis is placed on means and strategies that facilitate cultural awareness. Our hope for the chapter is that the reader will begin to gain a deeper understanding into his or her own attitudes, worldview, and heritage.

Self-Awareness and Knowledge

When considering multicultural competence, therapists and trainees typically follow the awareness–knowledge–skills triad originally advanced over 25 years ago (Casas, Ponterotto, & Gutierrez, 1986; Pedersen, 1988; Sue, Arredondo, & McDavis, 1992; Sue et al., 1982). Though it can be used in a myriad of ways (e.g., individual, organizational), the fundamental components are easy to understand. It is incorporating them into practice where the difficulty lies.

Awareness is reserved for self-awareness, meaning that therapists should seek to understand their own cultural influences and what it means to be a cultural being. Interaction models (e.g., McIntosh, 2001; Pedersen, 1994; Smith, 2004) suggest that therapists examine their own: (a) worldviews, (b) privilege, (c) race, (d) defensiveness, (e) values, (f) power, and (g) sociopolitical issues (Roysircar, Gard, Hubbell, & Ortega, 2005). The rationale for self-examination is that multicultural therapists will evaluate the client through their personal lens, and alternate between the client's culture and their own culture (Arredondo & Arciniega, 2001; Daniel, Roysircar, Abeles, & Boyd, 2004).

Knowledge is reserved for knowledge of other cultural groups. The impossibility of being knowledgeable about all other cultures quickly becomes evident when one considers the possible combinations of cultures and cultural influences. However, there are ways to begin to learn about other cultural groups without becoming consumed by the myriad combinations of cultural variables. Though it is understood that therapists cannot know all other cultures completely, developing openness, respect, and empathy toward other cultures is obtainable. Knowledge is not equated with expertise, but rather represents a willingness and openness to learning about other cultures and how cultural factors may influence counseling and potentially interact with the lack of, or comfort with, one's self-awareness.

Skills constitutes the culturally appropriate interventions necessary to maintain a strong and productive therapeutic relationship, leading to positive therapeutic outcomes. Though the focus of this chapter rests on awareness and knowledge, readers will note that all three components are embedded throughout the rest of the chapters, and hopefully they will develop new sources of self-understanding, knowledge, and skills. The information will be interspersed with increasing knowledge and it is hoped that the reader will begin to understand his or her attitudes related to the information.

Importance of Understanding Cultural Heritage and Background

Therapists must become aware that they possess a cultural heritage regardless of ethnic background, comprised of multiple identities, which may influence work with clients (who also have multiple identities). Embedded within the first component is the idea that therapists should begin to understand other worldviews to assist them with understanding their own worldviews. When therapists enter into a culturally different situation, they must engage in a "self-reflective orientation" (Roysircar, 2004) in which they become introspective to understand their own motivations, and cultural projections and transferences. Unfortunately, this self-reflection can be a difficult task for some. The old adage that "a fish doesn't know it's in water" comes to mind, as it takes getting out of a comfort zone to begin to understand personal values and attitudes. The fish is surrounded by water and does not consider anything outside the water, and it is only when the fish is pulled out of the water does it begin to understand its own culture. Likewise, therapists are surrounded by their cultures and many rarely consider how their cultures may influence their attitudes and behaviors.

One of the first introductions to the authors' multicultural courses was the statement, "Tell me what your culture is." It is difficult to answer, as we all possess multiple cultures (Pedersen, 1994), but the authors have found an interesting trend: students of color are more readily able to respond to the statement than majority students. A reason for this difficulty by majority students is that they are part of the dominant culture and, by definition, dominant cultures often dictate norms and subsume other cultures. Therefore, as part of a dominant norm culture it becomes difficult to self-reflect to determine how the norm influences the non-norm. Of course, readers who have taken courses in multicultural issues understand that much of the course is often, either directly or indirectly, related to cultural self-awareness.

Cultural self-awareness does not automatically lead to interpersonal cultural knowledge, but is an initial step into understanding culturally different clients. It is a continuous process and is not something that ends once the therapist and client have a good working relationship. Self-reflection should be continual regardless of the stage of therapy. Different beliefs arise in counseling and it is imperative that the therapist considers personal cultural influences as a possible explanation for such differences. If cultural differences do occur, it does not mean necessarily that counseling becomes prohibitive, but rather that it could be a factor influencing treatment.

Cultural self-awareness is also reflective of mutual respect for culturally diverse clients. In our courses, we frequently encounter students who equate respecting a client to agreeing with a client's cultural beliefs. This is not necessarily equivalent and more often than not very different. One can still disagree with a client and have difficulty with a client's cultural beliefs, traditions, means of expressing oneself, or any of a myriad of other cultural issues. The emotional difficulty should not detract from the respect for a client. Nor should it obfuscate the similarities found between the therapist or client simply because the client is human, has anxieties, fears, joys, families, and friends, and needs assistance and expertise.

Much of the cultural literature assumes and discusses ethnic differences, such as a European American therapist treating a Latino American client. Certain cultural assumptions are made that the therapist must become aware of personal issues that may limit therapeutic effectiveness. What is also discussed, though much less so, is that all counseling is multicultural (Pedersen, 1994). Therefore, that same European American therapist seeing a European American client cannot assume that their cultural backgrounds are similar. Perhaps there are religious differences, or a degree of physical abilities, or sexual orientation differences, or perhaps no overt religious (or other) differences but differences in ideation.

Sue (2001) presented a multidimensional model of cultural competence that "allows for the systematic identification of cultural competence in a number of different areas" (p. 790). At the individual level, Sue provides an assumption of the model that none of us are motivated at birth to be biased or prejudiced. Instead, biases and prejudices are learned, and by definition, are something that can be unlearned (Ponterotto, Utsey, & Pedersen, 2006). Once these biases and prejudices are brought into conscious awareness most therapists will initially experience resistance. This form of personal resistance can also lead to resistance to cultural competence. However, the journey to breaking the barriers of resistance is possible, though the introspection involved is a challenging process for many. In a special issue of the *Journal of Counseling and Development* in 1999, multiple authors discussed their personal struggles to reducing their own biases and prejudices through self-awareness and analysis, often resulting in an emotional toll. Reducing biases may be only one of the goals of self-awareness. Another goal for therapists may be to understand how their cultural background has influenced their attitudes and values. By understanding one's background, even when devoid of prejudices in specific areas, it gives the therapist a more robust understanding of herself or himself, thus making one more mindful of cultural perspectives in counseling. However, as noted, attempting to understand the self is complex and difficult, and may present obstacles.

Obstacles to Developing Self-Awareness and Knowledge

Sue (2001) has outlined four obstacles that impede cultural awareness that can reduce the likelihood of cultural competence. First, most therapists view themselves as moral, respectful, and decent people. It is difficult to acknowledge biases because the results may be counter to therapists' self-identity. Through our training programs we have noted instances when therapists-in-training have difficulty identifying biases because "we're all therapists," which somehow implies that they are supposed to be bias-free. This attitude is compounded by early theoretical positions suggesting that value-free counseling was optimal. Therapist development theories (e.g., Stoltenberg, McNeill, & Delworth, 1998) would argue that the difficulty in identifying personal biases is consistent with early therapist development because therapists-in-training have not fully integrated their personal and professional identities.

A recent example includes the following from a student in the first author's microskills course, "I was raised Baptist and think that gay people are sinning, but I can work with them in counseling." Another example can be found in a recent statement by another student. When asked about her cultural background and how it may influence clients she reported, "I'm an army brat and have lived all over, so I can work with anyone." The implication is that experience alone allows one to be cognitively flexible and unbiased. Of course this is not the case and throughout the semester her anxiety level increased when counseling a culturally different client whom she initially assumed would cause her no value-based concerns. Through supervision into her own previously hidden values and biases did she realize that the bias was being transferred from one army base to the next.

Second, identifying and discussing social and personal biases in public is generally not acceptable. Outward discussion of bias can lead to challenges that may end with presenting the therapist in a different light than he or she wants to portray. Ideally, training programs would allow for public discussion of biases (which requires developing a safe environment with understood boundaries), but these discussions can still be risky, especially when working closely with colleagues for multiple years. For example, when the student mentioned that lesbian, gay, bisexual, and transgender (LGBT) individuals are committing a sin, another student in class took offense, as might be expected and expressed her own opinion. Third, once some insight is gained, personal responsibility for one's past and present behaviors must be acknowledged. Additionally, this insight can lead to an understanding of how a therapist may have contributed to cultural problems rather than helped alleviate them.

Finally, the emotions surrounding this realization are often difficult to experience, and most individuals are unwilling to consider facing their emotional selves. It is much easier to acknowledge and become concerned with inequities on a social level, but to examine personal beliefs for inequities and personal responsibilities can become burdensome. Explained another way, Harrell (1995, as cited in Mio, Barker-Hackett, & Tumambing, 2006) discusses the "Five D's of Difference" to explain reactions individuals have when they feel different: (a) Distancing, (b) Denial, (c) Defensiveness, (d) Devaluing, and (e) Discovery. Readers will note some overlap among the D's though they are a useful way to conceptualize awareness obstacles. Everyone has felt different at points in their lives and our means of handling the dissension involved with "differentness" is often driven by these Five D's.

Reactions to Difference

Distancing means that if we avoid situations, physically, emotionally, and intellectually, we will not have to confront them. Related, if we distance ourselves from ourselves, then we can remain culturally encapsulated (Wrenn, 1962, 1985) and never push ourselves to a new level of cultural and personal awareness. Some trainers have had students or supervisees who indicate that they will work with some cultural group while in a training program, but will not when working in the community. Other than being a naive statement, it reflects the idea that distancing reinforces the stereotypes and individuals do not have to take responsibility for their own biases.

Denial means that one minimizes or ignores the differences between individuals. The issue of colorblindness is relevant here. *Colorblindness* is a term used for well-intended individuals attempting to look past race or ethnicity to the "universal" aspects of human behavior, but with unforeseen consequences. Frequently one hears comments such as, "I don't see you as (a member of a particular group) but as a person." The concern is that it negates the meaning associated with the particular minority group to which the person identifies. Essentially, the statement takes away part of the person's identity.

Often, a quick exercise in our multicultural courses highlights the concern. If the statement is simply rephrased as "I don't see you as a woman but as an individual," it often leads to immediate insight (at least to the women in the audience) about the importance of being a woman as part of her identity. We have found that once we substitute gender for some previous cultural statements (for example, racial, ethnic, sexual orientation), then the identity denial of the initial statement often becomes obvious and increases understanding. Another concern with colorblindness is that social psychologists have determined that it does not lead to the desired outcome of unbiased treatment across groups (American Psychological Association [APA], 2003). The APA (2003) article highlighted some of the research literature indicating that taking a colorblind approach actually perpetuated stereotypes and social inequalities, and resulted in a less accurate view of others than incorporating a multicultural approach (see Brewer & Brown, 1998; Schofield, 1986; Wolsko, Park, Judd, & Wittenbrink, 2000).

Defensiveness is associated with protection. When therapists feel threatened culturally they may answer with what they believe to be justifiable responses. "I am not homonegative, my cousin is gay" is the type of response that can often be heard in the community, in counseling sessions, and within the supervisory relationship. "I'm not racist but ..." may be another. White individuals making the latter statement may fall into the "conflictive racial attitude" category of the "White racial consciousness" model (LaFleur, Rowe, & Leach, 2002; Leach, Behrens, & LaFleur, 2002). In this model individuals holding this racial attitude are conflicted, often justifying positive attitudes to themselves and the community, but harboring less positive attitudes. From a psychodynamic perspective, individuals might deny through a variety of defense mechanisms such as sublimation, rationalization, and reaction formation. Working through the defenses through counseling, deeper personal reflection, or discussions with others is needed to overcome defensiveness.

Devaluing is represented when we diminish the worth of something or someone we find threatening. When therapists engage in devaluing, whether unintentionally or unconsciously, they become at risk for viewing others negatively. "*They* always act that way" may be a general statement mentioned to justify a manner of thinking while simultaneously belittling another group. Unfortunately, the they–us dichotomy diminishes introspection and understanding of relationships to the self.

The final *D* is Discovery, or dealing with the anxiety associated with confronting culturally different values, attitudes, behaviors, and individuals. Discovery creates the opportunity to grow and learn from new experiences, increasing the likelihood of further introspection and possibly better therapeutic outcomes.

Characteristics of Culturally Competent Therapists

To become culturally competent, therapists must be willing to increase their self-awareness. Through self-awareness therapists begin to understand how biases (or even lack thereof in some instances) influence the way they conduct counseling sessions, assess and diagnose, conceptualize cases, plan interventions, create a therapeutic alliance, implement treatments, and terminate with clients. Therapists approach clients with a collection of attitudes that influence perceptions of others, the same as would any other individual. These worldviews were created and modified through years of training and are so embedded that many therapists are typically unaware of them. Therapist awareness also helps clients, as it helps therapists to consider the client's culture and how it influences who they are and perhaps why they are seeking treatment. Cultural self-awareness can also create cultural empathy (Ridley & Lingle, 1996), contributing to more culturally sensitive treatment.

The awareness–knowledge–skills triad (Sue & Sue, 2007) suggests that all three are intertwined and necessary for good, culturally competent interventions. Unfortunately, one can read textbooks, attend workshops, and even present research and teach diversity issues without assessing how the information relates to the self. However, that individual would not be considered culturally competent. It is through learning the information, incorporating it, and relating it back to the self that becomes critical. For example, most introductory multicultural textbooks include a chapter on Native Americans (American Indians, First Nations), including historical wrongs imparted on them by European Americans. They often include historical events such as the Native American holocaust, governmental land grabs, and treaty breaks leading to discussions about majority member mistrust and other issues. White therapists, for example, will often state that they had nothing to do with these historical events, yet culturally aware therapists will understand how their current status and ethnicity may impact willingness to seek counseling and trust. Related, non-Native American therapists can reflect on their views on related topics like: (a) modern tribal rights, (b) gaming privileges and their relationship to the tax structure, (c) views of typical U.S. holidays such as July 4 and Thanksgiving, and (d) perhaps personal privilege. Responses may help highlight their understanding of historical issues.

Constantine, Melincoff, Barakett, Torino, and Warren (2004) conducted a qualitative study in which they examined the experiences of 12 cultural scholars in 6 areas. They wanted to determine the traits of culturally competent individuals. Three of the most relevant areas for our purpose include aspects of multicultural counseling competence (e.g., personality characteristics, self-awareness, knowledge, skills), awareness of and interest in cultural issues, and multicultural counseling competence (e.g., exposure to other cultures, experiences with discrimination, cultural issues addressed at home).

Results indicated that culturally competent therapists had various personality traits such as open-mindedness, commitment to cultural competence, and actively listening to how their clients construed their world. They also found that culturally competent therapists understand the client's cultural context, including cultural history, and how that influences the client. The history includes not only the client's history but the history of the particular groups (e.g., racial, socioeconomic, religious) to which the individual belongs. For example, the first author received an education about the history of the Church of Jesus Christ of Latter Day Saints (LDS) while working as an intern in Utah many years ago. The history of violence against them and eventual exile due to a belief system has been handed down through the church history. To this day, the LDS church is often misunderstood and vilified. In multicultural courses and religion courses therapists-in-training often subtly discuss biases against faith traditions like the LDS church, potentially influencing their counseling work.

Many of the participants in the Constantine et al. (2004) study also indicated that self-awareness is an important component of cultural competence. Therapists should be aware of their own value systems, including their stereotypes and biases, and their own cultural history. An important piece of self-awareness and knowledge is understanding the components that make up one's identity (gender, ethnic). For example, an understanding of gender, racial, and ethnic identity models, and where individual therapists fall within those models, significantly contributes to attitudes toward out-groups. Additionally, understanding these models helps understand and normalize some client biases, which can be addressed in session. Theoretically, this discussion could lead to decreased premature termination. A previously suicidal African American client of the first author informed him that he would involuntarily commit her to the state hospital, though she was not currently in danger to herself. When asked the reason for her belief she stated, "Because I'm Black and you're White." This statement may have caused some therapists to be taken aback or try to defend themselves. However, given the client's Black racial identity status in which she distrusted practically all Whites, it helped the author to understand her perspective and simultaneously his own perspective, leading to a fruitful therapeutic discussion and her eventual return for extended treatment.

Other areas discussed that may increase cultural competence, through awareness, are exposure to different cultures, identifying personal variables that are salient to the individual therapist, and noting personal experiences with discrimination. For example, salient variables that have impacted the lives of the first two authors include being male, European American, Protestant, and having grown up middle class. The privileges associated with these variables are incredible, and have been addressed in many other resources (e.g., Paniagua, 2005; Schlosser, 2003). Many Protestant therapists do not consider themselves as having privilege, until one talks with others who are Catholic in many parts of the country, LDS, Muslim, or Jewish. For example, readers interested in understanding their own Christian privilege could read Schlosser (2003). Reading his list of 28 Christian privileges allows Christian readers to become more self-aware of stressors they do not have to endure simply because of their religious faith.

Strategies for Increasing Therapist Self-Awareness and Knowledge

We now turn to specific strategies for increasing therapist self-awareness of culture. There are multiple ways to evaluate one's own culture, including values, attitudes, and general worldviews. As a professional or professional-in-training, most therapists have probably been involved with a multicultural course or engaged in continuing education credits that include cultural components geared toward knowledge. Likewise, most therapists will have likely received training, though perhaps to a lesser degree, on counseling skills for working with a culturally different client. Rarely are workshops designed to evaluate the self. Thus, the following offers several methods for facilitating therapist self-awareness and knowledge by highlighting cultural assessment strategies, interpersonal strategies, and training strategies.

Cultural Assessment Strategies

There are a number of instruments designed to assess multicultural competencies, including awareness, knowledge, and skills, and they are all self-report measures. Because of their self-report design they possess the usual concerns of self-report instruments, namely, self-report bias. Examples of general instruments designed to measure awareness, knowledge, and skills include (a) Multicultural Awareness, Knowledge, Skills Survey (MAKSS-CE-R) (D'Andrea, Daniels, & Heck, 1991), (b) Multicultural Counseling Inventory (MCI) (Sodowsky, Taffe, Gutkin, & Wise, 1994), (c) Multicultural Counseling Knowledge and Awareness Scale (MCKAS) (Ponterotto, Gretchen, Utsey, Rieger, & Austin, 2002), and (d) Cross-Cultural Counseling Inventory-Revised (CCCI-R) (LaFromboise, Coleman, & Hernandez, 1991). Questions from these and other inventories usually attempt to tap general multicultural competency. Other instruments therapists can respond to, assess specific cultural areas such as tolerance and prejudice (e.g., Quick Discrimination Index) (Utsey & Ponterotto, 1999) or homosexuality (e.g., Attitudes Toward Lesbians and Gay Men) (Herek, 1984), and can also be completed and offer insights into previously underevaluated biases. Next, we turn our attention to two specific examples of cultural assessments, the Intercultural Development Inventory and cultural genogram.

Intercultural Development Inventory (IDI)   IDI (Hammer & Bennett, 2001a, 2001b) is an assessment tool that we have found to be particularly useful in cultural awareness and cultural competence training. The measure is theoretically based and designed to provide information about an individual's cultural competency by providing an indication of one's sensitivity to, or awareness of, cultural differences. Bennett's (1986, 1993, 2004) Developmental Model of Intercultural Sensitivity (DMIS) provides the underlying theoretical structure for the IDI. Bennett proposes that as individuals' experiences of cultural difference become more complex, their potential for competence in intercultural relations increases. Intercultural competence is reflected in the ability to effectively generate perceptions, shift perspectives, and adapt behavior appropriate to varying cultural contexts.

The DMIS is developmental in nature and contains six stages, worldviews, or orientations toward difference (Denial of Differences, Defense against Difference, Minimization of Difference, Acceptance of Difference, Adaptation to Difference, and Integration of Difference). Each stage is associated with identifiable cognitions, emotions, and behaviors that build on or are in reaction to those that characterize the preceding stages or orientations. Bennett asserts that knowing the underlying cognitive orientation toward cultural difference provides information to (a) make predictions about attitudes and behaviors, and (b) design educational or experiential interventions to facilitate development toward greater cultural sensitivity and competence.

The IDI (Hammer & Bennett, 2001a), currently in its second revision, provides a reliable and valid measure of cultural awareness, or intercultural competence. It is culture-general in nature, which provides the potential for wide application in educational, business, interpersonal, and therapeutic settings where sensitivity to ethnic and nonethnic differences is important. IDI scores are not systematically affected by social desirability, age, education level, or gender (Hammer, Bennett, & Wiseman, 2003). The IDI is a 50-item self-assessment measure that can be taken in paper-and-pencil or electronic formats.

An IDI profile provides a visual bar graph representation of the test taker's Intercultural Sensitivity, Worldview Profile, and Developmental Issues. The "Intercultural Sensitivity" section of the profile plots overall Developmental Intercultural Sensitivity (on the ethnocentric–ethnorelative continuum) and overall Perceived Intercultural Sensitivity (how one sees oneself) across the theoretical dimensions of the DMIS and the actual scales of the IDI. The "Worldview Profile" and "Developmental Issues" sections of the profile indicate the degree to which (unresolved, in transition, resolved) the individual or group has dealt with the developmental tasks associated with the particular worldview being assessed by the various scales (denial/defense, reversal, minimization, acceptance/adaptation, encapsulated marginality). The IDI profile provides a snapshot of how an individual or group experiences difference. This information together with knowledge of the DMIS and the "Interpreting Your Intercultural Development Inventory (IDI) Profile" handout from the *IDI Manual* (Hammer & Bennett, 2001b) provide the foundation upon which a person or group can develop a personalized, developmentally appropriate educational plan to enhance sensitivity to cultural difference and cultural competency. The "Interpreting Your Intercultural Development Inventory (IDI) Profile" resource describes attitudes, beliefs, behaviors, strengths, and developmental tasks associated with each of the measured IDI worldviews that test takers can use to identify activities and opportunities to stimulate their intercultural awareness, given their current way of approaching cultural differences.

Cultural Genogram   A genogram is a map or a chart of one's lineage, similar to a family tree (McGoldrick, Gerson, & Schellenberger, 1999). It uses symbols to denote a number of family members' personal characteristics, as well as overarching patterns within a family system. More specifically, a cultural genogram illustrates cultural aspects of family patterns and structures, such as family values, family member ethnicities, education achievement levels, or socioeconomic status (Hardy & Laszloffy, 1995). Spiritual histories and intercultural marriages may also be depicted (Frame, 2004). In this way, a therapist-in-training is able to visually display and examine his or her own family's cultural patterns, as well as reflect upon the meanings of these patterns in his or her life.

Hardy and Laszloffy (1995) state that to begin a cultural genogram, therapists must first identify their culture(s) of origin or the central group(s) from which they have descended. Next, therapists should identify aspects of their cultures that have positive or negative connotations, such as high educational attainment (a pride issue) or low socioeconomic status (a shame issue). Using the information gathered, the therapist then creates symbols for pride/shame issues and selects colors for each culture represented on the genogram. Finally, a three-generation genogram is constructed, along with a key that reveals the meanings of the colors and symbols. The end goal of creating a cultural genogram is to examine one's culture(s) of origin and to learn from reflections based on this experience.

Cultural Interpersonal Interactions

Culturalists are the first to state that experiences with other cultures and/or interactions with individuals from other cultural groups can significantly increase awareness and knowledge, and, perhaps, skills. Attending local festivals, attending cultural events outside of one's comfort zone, and eating new foods are relatively easy ways to increase awareness and knowledge. Becoming more familiar with a different culture over time is more difficult yet yields tremendous benefits. For example, traveling to different regions of the country or perhaps international travel can be effective, even if for only a short time. However, anyone can travel if they have the time and money. The difficulty lies in becoming observers of culture and interacting with culture as opposed to merely being a tourist. Most people are tourists, but some are willing to evaluate their experiences and consider the cultural nuances instead of the obvious. Though there are too many nuances to list, when traveling some examples may include noticing speech patterns, emotional ranges, time orientations, connections and closeness, reactions to foreigners, family interactions, and level of contextualism. Critical incidents, cross-cultural interviews, and cultural immersion will now be highlighted as examples of cultural interpersonal interaction strategies.

Critical Incidents   Cushner and Brislin (1996) were one of the first to include critical incidents as a means for practitioners, and those in training, to become more culturally aware and knowledgeable. Critical incidents have been used in training formats for decades and began as culture assimilators (Fiedler, Mitchell, & Triandis, 1971), sometimes called the "cultural sensitizer." They are brief scenarios, usually one to three paragraphs, in which the reader is asked to respond to a dilemma based on cultural differences. They typically include some miscommunication or problematic interactions among differing cultural group members, and the reader must choose from multiple options (usually four) to determine the culturally appropriate outcome. They were initially designed for those preparing to live in another culture (usually country) and for those encountering another nondominant group in their own country. The incidents were designed to increase knowledge of other cultures, though they would also influence cultural self-awareness. Discussions of the correct response would occur, including expectations, norms, values, and beliefs of both the new culture and the individual's culture. Critical incidents could easily be included in courses or with individual therapists. A related alternative includes multicultural and cross-cultural dialogues, such as those found in Storti (1994). These dialogues are very brief conversational interactions in which the reader is instructed to determine where the understanding breakdown occurred. Group discussions can occur prior to reading the correct responses, which are included in these books.

Cross-Cultural Interviews   The cross-cultural interview is another way for therapists to continue their self-reflection by beginning to familiarize themselves with a new worldview. According to Hammer and Bennett (1998), seeking cultural difference and learning to shift perspectives, both cognitively and behaviorally, characterizes the ethnorelative point of view that is necessary for a therapist-in-training to be effective when working with culturally different clients. In other words, participating in this exercise should aid in the discovery of differences and similarities between oneself and others (Fuller, 2005).

Cross-cultural interviews are similar to informational interviews that are commonly used in career counseling. According to Reed (1984), the purpose of an informational interview is to "learn about the realities of the job from the persons involved in that career" (p. 174). In the same way, a cross-cultural interview, for the purposes of this chapter, gives therapists-in-training a way to learn about a new and different culture from a person who actually belongs to that cultural group. Just as an informational interview is conducted with a person whose job an interviewer would like to know about, a cross-cultural interview should be conducted with a person whose culture the interviewer would like to understand better. Thus, it is important for the interviewer to choose someone for this exercise who appears very different from him or her. For example, a 24-year-old Caucasian female therapist-in-training may seek to interview a 55-year-old Hispanic female immigrant to learn how the woman's cultural background is different from and similar to her own.

Although a cross-cultural interview may be completely unstructured, Berg-Cross and Chinen (1995) present the Person-in-Culture Interview (PICI) that may be used for just such a purpose. (The PICI can be used in an intake with a client, but may also be used simply for the purpose of multicultural learning.) The goal of a therapist who uses the PICI is to gather information about a person's broad cultural values as well as his or her individual and personal values. It consists of 25 open questions that are based on Psychodynamic, Humanistic, Systems, and Existential factors and, therefore, covers a variety of topics. Sample questions that could be used in a cross-cultural interview from the PICI include "What are the most enjoyable activities in your life?" and "What kinds of things make you angry?"

Cultural Immersion   Yet another way of seeking difference and becoming more familiar with diversity is engaging in a cultural immersion experience. This experience can be used to build off the cross-cultural interview or may become completely separate and unrelated. For the purposes of this exercise, the immersion experience should be individualized, emotionally grounded, well planned, and include self-reflective activities. Thus, according to Wilson (2001), a vacation to a different country with a travel group will not likely fit the criteria for an immersion that will foster cultural competence. Wilson further stipulates that participants in an immersion should enter the experience as a learner, not a helper. So, for example, people engaging in missionary work will not likely be in a true immersion situation as the goal of missionary work is usually to change the existing culture and not simply experience it as it is.

This being said, an immersion may include any number of activities, so long as the time spent immersed is within a culture that is very different from one's own and fits the previously mentioned criteria. Thus, the immersion experience could occur in a different country but could also easily take place within one's own town. For instance, a therapist-in-training may choose to attend a church or worship service that is unfamiliar, engage in a cross-cultural meal with a culturally different family, or participate in a specific festival or ceremony. In any of these experiences, opportunities for learning and challenges will be presented that will lend themselves to later reflection. For instance, Wood and Atkins (2006) describe working through language barriers, using different communication styles, and working with unfamiliar resources as being just a few of these possible challenges.

Cultural Training Strategies

Trainers have sought to provide learning experiences that can help therapists develop the skills and techniques necessary for effective cross-cultural counseling. In addition to the acquisition of specific skill sets, many trainers have also sought to influence therapists' professional identity by emphasizing multiculturalism. Numerous training approaches have evolved with the intent of enhancing therapist cultural self-awareness and knowledge. We will now highlight exercises, personal assignments, portfolios, progress notes, a triad training model, and multiculturally infused supervision as examples of cultural training strategies.

Exercises There are numerous books that provide recommendations for providing insight into our and other cultures. However, most do not offer practical, structured exercises. Notable exceptions include Pedersen's (2004) *110 Experiences for Multicultural Learning*, which provides a section on self-awareness with over 30 exercises, and Hetherington's (1995) *Celebrating Diversity: Working with Groups in the Workplace*. Pedersen, Draguns, Lonner, and Trimble also provide a student workbook with self-awareness exercises that accompany the 1989 third edition of their text, *Counseling Across Cultures* (as cited in Pedersen & Hernandez, 1993). Finally, exercises are included in Pedersen's (1988) *A Handbook for Developing Multicultural Awareness*. Although there are other texts that include structured exercises, these have been used extensively and offer good insights.

Personal Assignments One of the more difficult assignments in the authors' graduate-level multicultural course is for students to "discuss how their cultural history may and/or currently impacts their clinical treatment." It is essentially a self-awareness exercise because the students' first issue is to understand how their culture is actually comprised. Because of the difficulty in the assignment, we inform them on the first day of class that this assignment will count as their final exam. Thus, they can consider their cultural attitudes, history, and values as the semester includes topics such as racial identity, sociopolitical histories, sexual orientation, religious background, and acculturation.

During the semester, questions may arise that have direct influence on their self-awareness, such as the role of Islam in the United States, the genocide of American Indians, immigration issues, and rights of the disabled.

Portfolios   Roysircar (2004) discusses a self-awareness assessment curriculum (C-SAA) that occurs over an academic semester and includes a variety of exercises designed to enhance self-awareness. For example, she includes the use of portfolios with trainees to examine cultural-awareness progress throughout an academic semester. Portfolios are individualized assessment tools where individuals can include materials from a variety of sources to show their best work. While Roysircar has students evaluate themselves based on recent APA guidelines (e.g., "Professional Practice Guidelines for Psychotherapy with Lesbian, Gay, and Bisexual Clients"; "Guidelines on the Multicultural Education and Training, Research, Practice, and Organizational Change for Psychologists"), practitioners can do the same. We find that these guidelines are important places to begin, yet guidelines are often worded generally. It is the intent of culturalists to help move students and practitioners beyond these generalizations. For example, guidelines will often begin sentences with, "Culturally skilled therapists should be aware of (or have an understanding of ...)." Unfortunately, cultural defenses often assist us in convincing ourselves that we have an awareness or understanding of a particular cultural issue when in reality it is limited or actually potentially nontherapeutic. As mentioned earlier, self-awareness is a constant exercise in which good, culturally aware therapists are continually examining their own cultural reactions both inside and outside the treatment room.

Progress Notes   Another exercise that Roysircar (2004) (Roysircar et al., 2005) recommends is weekly progress notes in which her trainees describe their attitudes and beliefs surrounding clients from other cultural groups. Though not necessarily combined, she also mentions that case conceptualization papers can include client cultural issues such as cultural histories, spiritual influences, sexual orientation influences, and the role of socioeconomic status.

Triad Training Model   Pedersen's triad training model (1994, 2000; Irvin & Pedersen, 1995) is designed to make cultural conversations concrete rather than have them maintained in the abstract. In this training model (let's assume one therapist is sitting with one client), two other individuals are in the room with the therapist–client dyad, one representing the pro-therapist and one representing the anti-therapist, both of the same ethnicity as the client. The four goals of the training model are to: (1) express the problem from the client's cultural perspective, (2) recognize specific instances of resistances that may be culturally bound, (3) reduce the therapist's defensiveness, and (4) practice recovery skills when the therapist has trouble.

As the mock counseling session begins, the pro-therapist and anti-therapist begin to add comments as if they represent the thoughts of the client. For example, the pro-therapist may state, "I think he really meant to say this …," whereas the anti-therapist might say, "He really has no idea where you are coming from." Therapists must then respond to the changing counseling session and develop skills that help them recover from mistakes made, eventually becoming more comfortable with difficult culturally diverse situations. After the mock session, discussions of the process, including gaining a cultural understanding of the client's concerns, recognizing specific instances of resistances and culturally protective defensiveness, and recovery skills, lead to therapist awareness and knowledge that can lessen the anxiety and increase counseling effectiveness.

Multiculturally Infused Supervision   The cross- and multicultural literature related to counseling and supervision is replete with examples of the sweeping effects multiculturalism and the pursuit of cultural competence have had on the ways therapists and mental health professionals are trained (D'Andrea, 2005; Locke & Faubert, 2003). To aid in the development of multiculturally infused supervision, Robinson, Bradley, and Hendricks (2000) developed a four-step model of training. The four steps are (1) developing cultural awareness of the counseling supervisor, (2) exploring the cultural dynamics of the counseling supervisory relationship, (3) examining the cultural assumptions of traditional counseling theories, and (4) integrating multicultural issues into existing models of supervision. Because the focus of this chapter is on building one's cultural awareness, we will focus on those steps (i.e., 2, 3, 4) over which the supervisee has direct control.

First, cultural dynamics of the counseling supervisory relationship should be explored. The process by which supervisors are matched with supervisees often depends on the structure of one's training program. In spite of the procedures one's program uses for matching supervisors with supervisees, cultural differences between supervisor and supervisee will certainly emerge. We recommend that cultural dynamics be discussed and appropriately processed throughout supervision. Recognizing that it can be difficult for supervisees, especially new ones, to initiate discussion about potentially sensitive topics (e.g., race, ethnicity, sexuality, religion), we have included some suggestions to help the supervisee begin what will hopefully be an ongoing dialogue.

1. Using self-disclosure or discussing aspects of one's cross-cultural identity could positively affect the supervisory relationship, as it is likely to increase trust and intimacy. Self-disclosing aspects of diversity may also prompt one's supervisor to reciprocate. For example, coming out in supervision as a gay man may prompt the supervisor to disclose her or his sexual orientation. This could lead to a rich discussion about how one's sexual orientation affects both the supervisory and therapeutic relationships. One should be aware, however, that this suggestion does not mean that all supervisors are willing to disclose personal information. Several supervisors, for personal, theoretical, or institutional reasons, avoid self-disclosure. In these instances, it is best to respect the supervisor's boundaries while continuing to push oneself to increase cultural awareness.

2. Sometimes, when working with a supervisor who does not create a space in supervision to discuss cross- and multicultural dynamics, one should consider consulting with peers and other clinicians to raise their self-awareness. In doing so, we should seek out peers or colleagues who share a commitment to being culturally competent clinicians, and with whom we have developed a trusting relationship. These meetings, whether incident specific and sporadic, or permanent and ongoing, should be focused on how one's cultural identity affects their ability to effectively provide mental health services to their clients. To that end, example topics that may be discussed are: (a) personal biases and cultural limitations, (b) expectations of clients whose cultural identity appears to be similar, (c) expectations of clients whose cultural identity appears to be different, (d) where to go to learn about different aspects of diversity and culture, and (e) how to approach and discuss topics related to culture with one's clients.

3. The third suggestion is self-reflection. To get an accurate sense of one's values and beliefs about diversity and culture, we suggest keeping a record or journal of one's thoughts and feelings. This is designed to be a deeply personal memoir, in which one writes their fears and misperceptions regarding cross- and multicultural concepts. Please know that everyone has personal biases and limitations, and that it can be scary to write them down. Nevertheless, until one becomes aware of these shortcomings, it is difficult, if not impossible, to achieve an elevated level of self-awareness.

Second, the cultural assumptions of traditional counseling theories also need to be examined. There are numerous methods used to teach students to use existent counseling theories. In most instances, cross- and multicultural limitations receive only minimal attention or are ignored entirely. According to Robinson et al. (2000), each theory should be carefully examined, as they are all based on a set of beliefs or assumptions that may not accurately reflect the values of cross- and multicultural competent therapists. Consequently, it is important to discuss the limitations or shortcomings of selected theories with one's clinical supervisor. For example, if a supervisee were learning to use multigenerational family therapy, the supervisee would need to be aware of the patriarchal values upon which the theory is based. A multiculturally competent therapist would be mindful not to perpetuate Bowen's early belief that mothers/women should assume a weak and passive parenting role (Luepnitz, 2002).

Third, multicultural issues should be integrated into existing models of counseling supervision. Similar to the point made by Robinson et al. (2000) in the previous paragraph, not all models of supervision were designed to address the multitude of multicultural issues that exist in therapeutic practice or that emerge over the course of clinical supervision. As a result, supervisees are responsible for pushing themselves by asking about multicultural topics that are novel or foreign to them—supervisees should regularly ask their supervisor about cross- or multiculturally related therapeutic issues.

Conclusion

Understanding one's own cultural background is an imperative first step to understanding and empathizing with people from other cultures. According to Fuller (2005), identifying the pieces of one's own cultural background allows therapists to become more effective when working with those who are culturally different in therapeutic relationships. Thus, it is our hope that the strategies described here will be used to help increase therapists' self-awareness and knowledge of their own culture, and, ultimately, that of their clients.

References

American Psychological Association. (2003). Guidelines on multicultural education, training, research, practice, and organizational change for psychologists. *American Psychologist, 58*, 377–402.

Arredondo, P., & Arciniega, M. (2001). Strategies and techniques for counselor training based on the Multicultural Counseling Competencies. *Journal of Multicultural Counseling and Development, 29,* 263–273.

Bennett, M. J. (1986). Towards ethnorelativism: A developmental model of inter-cultural sensitivity. In R. M. Paige (Ed.), *Cross-cultural orientation: New conceptualizations and applications* (pp. 27–69). New York: University Press of America.

Bennett, M. J. (1993). Towards ethnorelativism: A developmental model of intercul-tural sensitivity. In R. M. Paige (Ed.), *Education for the intercultural experience* (pp. 27–71). Yarmouth, ME: Intercultural Press.

Bennett, M. J. (2004). Becoming interculturally competent. In J. Wurzel (Ed.), *Toward multiculturalism: A reader in multicultural education* (2nd ed., pp. 62–77). Newton, MA: Intercultural Resource Corporation.

Berg-Cross, L., & Chinen, R. T. (1995). Multicultural training models and the per-son-in-culture interview. In J. G. Ponterotto, J. M. Casas, L. A. Suzuki, & C. M. Alexander (Eds.), *Handbook of multicultural counseling* (pp. 333–356). Thousand Oaks, CA: Sage.

Brewer, M. B., & Brown, R. J. (1998). Intergroup relations. In D. T. Gilbert & S. T. Fiske (Eds.), *The handbook of social psychology* (4th ed., Vol. 2, pp. 554–594). New York: McGraw-Hill.

Casas, J. M., Ponterotto, J. G., & Gutierrez, J. M. (1986). An ethical indictment of counseling research and training: The cross-cultural perspective. *Journal of Counseling and Development, 64,* 347–349.

Constantine, M. G., Melincoff, D. S., Barakett, M. D., Torino, G. C., & Warren, A. K. (2004). Experiences and perceptions of multicultural counseling scholars: A qualitative examination. *Counselling Psychology Quarterly, 17,* 375–393.

Cushner, K., & Brislin, R. W. (1996). *Intercultural interactions: A practical guide.* Thousand Oaks, CA: Sage.

D'Andrea, M. (2005). Continuing the cultural liberation and transformation of counseling psychology. *Counseling Psychologist, 33,* 524–537.

D'Andrea, M., Daniels, J., & Heck, R. (1991). Evaluating the impact of multicul-tural counseling training. *Journal of Counseling & Development, 70,* 143–150.

Daniel, J. H., Roysircar, G., Abeles, N., & Boyd, C. (2004). Individual and cultural diversity competence: Focus on the therapist. *Journal of Clinical Psychology, 25,* 255–267.

Fiedler, F. E., Mitchell, T., & Triandis, H. C. (1971). The culture assimilator: An approach to cross-culture training. *Journal of Applied Psychology, 55,* 95–102.

Frame, M. W. (2004). The challenges of intercultural marriage: Strategies for pastoral care. *Pastoral Psychology, 52,* 219–232.

Fuller, J. O. (1995). Getting in touch with your heritage. In N. A. Vacc, S. B. DeVaney, & J. Wittmer (Eds.), *Experiencing and counseling multicultural and diverse populations* (4th ed., pp. 9–27). Levittown, PA: Taylor & Francis.

Hammer, M. R., & Bennett, M. J. (2001a). *The intercultural development inventory (v. 2).* Portland, OR: The Intercultural Communication Institute.

Hammer, M. R., & Bennett, M. J. (2001b). *The intercultural development inventory (IDI) manual.* Portland, OR: The Intercultural Communication Institute.

Hammer, M. R., Bennett, M. J., & Wiseman, R. L. (2003). Measuring intercultural sensitivity: The intercultural development inventory. *International Journal of Intercultural Relations, 27,* 421–443.

Hardy, K. V., & Laszloffy, T. A. (1995). The cultural genogram: Key to training culturally competent family therapists. *Journal of Marital and Family Therapy, 21,* 227–237.

Harrell, S. P. (1995). *Dynamics of difference: Personal and sociocultural dimensions of intergroup relations.* Paper presented at the annual meeting of the American Psychological Association, New York.

Herek, G. M. (1984). Attitudes toward lesbians and gay men: A factor analytic study. *Journal of Homosexuality, 10,* 39–51.

Hetherington, C. (1995). *Celebrating diversity: Working with groups in the workplace.* Duluth, MN: Whole Person Associates.

Irvin, R., & Pedersen, P. (1995). The internal dialogue of culturally different clients: An application of the Triad Training Model. *Journal of Multicultural Counseling and Development, 23,* 4–10.

LaFleur, N. K., Rowe, W., & Leach, M. M. (2002). Reconceptualizing white racial consciousness. *Journal of Multicultural Counseling and Development, 30,* 148–152.

LaFromboise, T. D., Coleman, H. D., & Hernandez, A. (1991). Development and factor structure of the Cross-Cultural Counseling Inventory–Revised. *Professional Psychology: Research and Practice, 22,* 380–388.

Leach, M. M., Behrens, J. T., & LaFleur, N. K. (2002). White racial identity and white racial consciousness: Similarities, differences, and recommendations. *Journal of Multicultural Counseling and Development, 30,* 66–80.

Locke, D., & Faubert, M. (2003). Cultural considerations in counselor training and supervision. In F. D. Harper & J. McFadden (Eds.), *Culture and counseling: New approaches* (pp. 324–338). Boston: Allyn & Bacon.

Luepnitz, D. A. (2002). *The family interpreted: Psychoanalysis, feminism, and family therapy.* New York: Basic Books.

McGoldrick, M., Gerson, R. L., & Schellenberger, S. (1999). *Genograms: Assessment and intervention.* New York: Norton.

McIntosh, P. (2001). White privilege and male privilege: A personal account of coming to see correspondences through work in women's studies. In M. L. Andersen & P. H. Collins (Eds.), *Race, class, and gender* (4th ed., pp. 95–105). Belmont, CA: Wadsworth/Thompson.

Mio, J. S., Barker-Hacket, L. & Tumambing, J. (2006). *Multicultural psychology: Understanding our diverse communities.* New York: McGraw-Hill.

Paniagua, F. A. (2005). *Assessing and treating culturally diverse clients: A practical guide* (3rd ed.). Thousand Oaks, CA: Sage.

Pedersen, P. B. (1988). *A handbook for developing multicultural awareness.* Alexandria, VA: American Counseling Association.

Pedersen, P. B. (1994). Simulating the client's internal dialogue as a counselor training technique. *Simulation and Gaming, 25,* 40–50.

Pedersen, P. B. (2000). *A handbook for developing multicultural awareness* (3rd ed.). Alexandria, VA: American Association for Counseling and Development.

Pedersen, P. B. (2004). *110 experiences for multicultural learning.* Washington, DC: American Psychological Association.

Pedersen, P. B., Draguns, J., Lonner, W., & Trimble, J. (1989). *Counseling across cultures* (3rd ed.). Honolulu, HI: University of Hawaii Press.

Pedersen, P. B., & Hernandez, D. (1993). *Teaching counseling across cultures in the classroom.* Honolulu, HI: University of Hawaii Press.

Ponterotto, J. G., Gretchen, D., Utsey, S. O., Rieger, B. P., & Austin, R. (2002). A revision of the Multicultural Counseling Awareness Scale. *Journal of Multicultural Counseling and Development, 30,* 153–180.

Ponterotto, J. G., Utsey, S. O., & Pedersen, P. B. (2006). *Preventing prejudice: A guide for counselors, educators, and parents* (2nd ed.). Thousand Oaks, CA: Sage.

Reed, J. G. (1984). Career planning and exploration: An exercise for use in industrial psychology courses. *Teaching of Psychology, 11,* 174–175.

Ridley, C. R., & Lingle, D. W. (1996). Cultural empathy in multicultural counseling: A multidimensional process model. In P. B. Pedersen, J. G. Draguns, W. J. Lonner, & J. E. Trimble (Eds.), *Counseling across cultures* (4th ed., pp. 21–46). Thousand Oaks, CA: Sage.

Robinson, B., Bradley, L., & Hendricks, C. (2000). Multicultural counselling supervision: A four-step model toward competency. *International Journal for the Advancement of Counselling, 22,* 131 141.

Roysircar, G. (2004). Cultural self-awareness assessment: Practice examples from psychology training. *Professional Psychology: Science and Practice, 35,* 558–666.

Roysircar, G., Gard, G., Hubbell, R., & Ortega, M. (2005). Development of counseling trainees' multicultural awareness through mentoring English as a second language students. *Journal of Multicultural Counseling and Development, 33,* 17–36.

Schlosser, L. Z. (2003). Christian privilege: Breaking a sacred taboo. *Journal of Multicultural Counseling and Development, 31,* 44–51.

Schofield, J. W. (1986). Causes and consequences of the colorblind perspective. In J. F. Dovidio & S. L. Gaertner (Eds.), *Prejudice, discrimination, and racism* (pp. 231–253). San Diego, CA: Academic Press.

Smith, T. B. (2004). *Practicing multiculturalism: Affirming diversity in counseling and psychology.* Boston: Pearson and Allyn & Bacon.

Sodowsky, G. R., Taffe, R. C., Gutkin, T. B., & Wise, S. L. (1994). Development of the Multicultural Counseling Inventory: A self-report measure of multicultural competencies. *Journal of Counseling Psychology, 41,* 137–148.

Stoltenberg, C. D., McNeill, B., & Delworth, U. (1998). *IDM supervision: An integrated developmental model for supervising counselors and therapists.* San Francisco: Jossey-Bass.

Storti, C. (1994). *Cross-cultural dialogues: 74 brief encounters with cultural difference.* Yarmouth, ME: Intercultural Press.

Sue, D. W. (2001). Multidimensional facets of cultural competence. *Counseling Psychologist, 29,* 790–821.

Sue, D. W., Arrendondo, P., & McDavis, R. J. (1992). Multicultural counseling competencies and standards: A call to the professions. *Journal of Counseling and Development, 70,* 477–486.

Sue, D. W., Bernier, J. E., Durran, A., Feinberg, L., Pedersen, P., Smith, E. J., et al. (1982). Position paper: Cross-cultural counseling competencies. *Counseling Psychologist, 10,* 45–52.

Sue, D. W., & Sue, D. (2007). *Counseling the culturally diverse: Theory and practice.* Hoboken, NJ: John Wiley & Sons.

Utsey, S. O., & Ponterotto, J. G. (1999). Further factorial validity assessment of scores on the Quick Discrimination Index (QDI). *Educational and Psychological Measurement, 59,* 325–335.

Wilson, A. H. (2001). Cross-cultural experiential learning for teachers. *Theory Into Practice, 21,* 184–192.

Wolsko, C., Park, B., Judd, C. M., & Wittenbrink, B. (2000). Framing interethnic ideology: Effects of multicultural and color-blind perspectives on judgments of groups and individuals. *Journal of Personality and Social Psychology, 78,* 635–654.

Wood, M. J., & Atkins, M. (2006). Immersion in another culture: One strategy for increasing cultural competency. *Journal of Cultural Diversity, 13,* 50–54.

Wrenn, C. G. (1962). The culturally encapsulated counselor. *Harvard Educational Review, 32,* 444–449.

Wrenn, C. G. (1985). Afterword: The culturally encapsulated counselor revisited. In P. Pedersen (Ed.), *Handbook of cross-cultural counseling and therapy* (pp. 323–329). Westport, CT: Greenwood Press.

3

Considering Culture in the Clinical Intake Interview and Report[*]

Lisa Aronson Fontes

The intake interview provides a crucial platform that supports future ongoing clinical work and establishes the relationship with a new client, often determining whether the client will return for subsequent sessions. This intake session is particularly crucial with clients from ethnic minority groups, who are more likely than others to quit therapy after the first session, especially when paired with counselors who are unlike them culturally (Sue, 1998).

What are we trying to accomplish with a clinical intake interview? We are trying to gather information that will help us chart the course for the rest of therapy, including matching clients with the counselor and therapy modality that suit them best. Intake clinicians often set the groundwork for case conceptualization, enter a diagnosis into clients' charts, and get clients "into the system" by establishing contact with insurance agencies and third-party payers. Unfortunately, cultural differences between the intake clinician and client often contribute to biases and errors, sometimes with far-reaching consequences. This chapter aims to help counselors conduct intake interviews that are fair and culturally competent.

[*]This chapter is adapted from *Interviewing Clients across Cultures: A Practitioner's Guide* by Lisa Aronson Fontes, 2008. (Used by permission of Guilford Press.)

The intake session has to produce information that is accurate and relevant, which requires a productive working relationship. Most of the time, we are trying to do this efficiently in a single session. Often, we are expected to produce reports and make decisions quickly based on the intake meeting. We do not have time to be careless, as every moment and every word should count. For cross-cultural interviews, we need to be especially focused and well prepared. The people we meet with in a clinical intake may differ from us in small and large ways. This difference may be so significant that we need to plan carefully to adjust our tactics, demeanor, approach, tone, seating arrangements, body language, and so forth to get the job done right.

How Intake Interviews Differ from Other Kinds of Conversations

Although intake interviews may appear to differ little from other kinds of conversations, they do have important distinguishing characteristics:

1. The conversation has a definite purpose. The interviewer has particular goals in mind. The client may share the same goals or perhaps may be hoping for a completely different outcome. (For example, the client may hope the counselor will say she is "fine" and "does not need therapy after all," whereas the counselor may assume that "everyone needs therapy" and therefore not even consider dismissing the client after the intake.)

2. The counselor and client have a defined relationship. This relationship usually involves some kind of hierarchy, and the intake counselor is more powerful. The counselor determines which questions will be asked and when, and how the results will be presented. The stakes are ordinarily much higher for the client than for the counselor.

3. Information flows primarily in one direction, from the client to the counselor. Certainly during many intakes, counselors inform clients about matters such as services available, expectations for therapy, and finances. However, the primary purpose of the intake is to gather information from the client.

4. The counselor plans and organizes the interaction, directing the conversation with specific goals in mind.

5. The counselor follows guidelines concerning confidentiality, but clients are usually free to reveal to others as much as they want about what transpired. That is, while clients can tell anyone they want about what

was said during the intake, the counselor is restricted by ethical guidelines and legal mandates to severely limit what he or she communicates about the interview, and to whom.

6. While an intake interview may be therapeutic in the sense that many people experience relief by reaching out to a skilled and caring professional who instills them with hope, this is not the goal of an intake session. Rather, the goals of the intake are to obtain the information and establish the relationship necessary for therapy to happen in the future.

Preparing for and Beginning the Intake Interview

The suggestions given in this section are not intended to be exhaustive. Rather, they call attention to those interview preparations that are most influenced by culture.

Prior Information

Depending on your context, if you have access to previous mental health or other records, it is usually helpful to review these documents before meeting the client. At the same time, you should expect to be surprised by clients and *not* assume that the information contained in their files is correct. Other professionals may have been careless or prejudiced, had inadequate linguistic interpretation, been confused, or failed to establish the necessary rapport to obtain truthful information. In one particularly vivid study, half a community sample of Puerto Rican children was rated as mentally ill according to the *Diagnostic and Statistical Manual of Mental Disorders* (3rd ed.) when the assessments were not conducted in a culturally competent way (Bird et al., 1988). Imagine how these children's diagnoses could follow and haunt them throughout their lives! All too often, one erroneous note in a file is perpetuated indefinitely as subsequent professionals elaborate upon that initial incorrect impression. Counselors should consider a case file with previous information as simply one source of data, which they will confirm, disconfirm, or elaborate upon during subsequent conversations with the client and collateral contacts.

Individuals' and families' prior records and reputations can influence counselors outside their awareness. All of us are subject to confirmatory bias, which is the tendency to notice things that confirm the ideas we already hold, and fail to notice things that disconfirm them. Once aware of this bias, counselors should try to identify aspects of the interview that *disconfirm* or contradict earlier notes in a file. The intention is *not* to disrespect the work of colleagues. Rather, remaining open to the client's current presentation is a way to acknowledge that people grow and change. Prior records help orient counselors to some of the areas worth inquiring about, but do not necessarily provide a complete or accurate portrait of the person who arrives for the intake appointment.

Assuring Initial Cultural Comfort

We will never know how many people decide not to seek our services, refuse our services, or decline to cooperate fully because they do not feel at ease in our agencies. My recommendation is that we err on the side of being as warm, welcoming, and inclusive to as many people as possible; therefore patriotic, political, and religious symbols are not appropriate in most counseling workplaces.

We should remember that people who are less familiar with our work setting will be at a distinct disadvantage when meeting with us. It would be important to convey as clearly as possible the intentions of the intake and whether the relationship will be ongoing or just a one-time contact. Even if we have discussed some of these issues previously on the telephone, they are worth reiterating in person. People who do not speak English fluently or who are hard of hearing may have a particularly difficult time absorbing information gleaned on the phone.

The counselor's goals may match or differ from the goals of the client, the client's family, the client's cultural group, and the referral source. Often interviews begin with crossed signals. Mental health clinicians think they are doing an intake for psychological help while the client wants to buttress an asylum, disability, or child custody claim. These misunderstandings occur all the time and can be partially averted through carefully preparing the clients.

Counselors should inform clients of the likely and possible outcomes of the intake. One psychologist was called by a Puerto Rican mother 5 days after a 20-minute intake interview at a mental health clinic complaining that her child had not changed yet. The mother thought the interview would be like a simple medical appointment—one visit and the cure would be imminent (Margarita O'Neill, personal communication, June 2007).

Handling Initial Paperwork

We should make sure we have on hand all the appropriate forms in the client's preferred language. All clients who are not native speakers of English should be offered the services of a bilingual therapist or interpreting services. (For more information on interpreting in clinical interviews, see Fontes, 2008a.)

Some settings require that the client fill out extensive forms prior to the intake meeting. Others require the clinician to ask the client a series of questions to fill out initial paperwork when they meet together. Although filling out the paperwork may be required and pro forma, even this procedure needs to be approached tactfully and with cultural awareness. In many Middle Eastern countries, a person's word or a handshake is considered more valuable and more honorable than a written signature on a document. Therefore, when a counselor hands a recent immigrant from some Middle Eastern countries a series of documents requiring that they affirm their intention to pay for sessions, for instance, or their understanding of the confidentiality rules, or their consent to treatment, and so on, this may be interpreted as doubting the client's word. The client may smile and hand the stack back to the counselor, saying, "Of course, doctor, you have my word, this is fine." Alternatively the person may sign the forms without reading them, believing that reading them would convey mistrust to the professional. Many American Indians are quite skeptical of written agreements because of United States history of breaking treaties, and will dismiss the paperwork as unimportant while looking carefully for *interpersonal* signs as to whether the counselor can be trusted. Finally, people who have concerns about confidentiality are unlikely to truthfully answer questions about sensitive family matters prior to establishing a trusting relationship with a counselor.

Even when clients would rather not handle paperwork, counselors may need to insist that the documents get filled out. It may help to admit gently that the paperwork is a burden, but we need to complete it as part of our job. Counselors should also be aware of the possibility that the person does not read, does not read English, does not read well enough to understand the forms, has visual impairments, or has forgotten his or her reading glasses and therefore needs verbal help with the paperwork. If the paperwork appears to cause conflict and stress, counselors should limit themselves at the outset to those forms that are absolutely necessary, and consider either postponing or forgoing altogether the less essential paperwork.

Gathering Background Cultural Information

Counselors should gather information about the client's cultural background before the conversational part of the intake, whenever possible. Helpful facts include the person's age, religion, household composition, country of origin, and, where relevant, date and circumstances of immigration and degree of English fluency. Racial information is not enough, since culture is not defined by skin color. For instance, the culture of a Black person from the Dominican Republic is different from that of an African American person who grew up in New York City. A little background reading on the person's ethnic, cultural, and religious group can enhance our understanding before the first meeting. For Native Americans, inquire as to whether they are affiliated with a tribe and if they were raised on or off a reservation. Also ask if they adhere to cultural or tribal traditions and practices, and if they form part of a community with other members of their tribe where they are living now. Assessment of the person's level of acculturation will help you understand how comfortable the client feels in the dominant culture, and therefore how much of an adjustment you need to make to the standard intake process (see Chapter 4 on assessment).

Respecting Values, Negotiating Meanings, and Avoiding Professional Ethnocentrism

When counselors step into the clinical role we do not suddenly cease to be cultural beings. Rather, we bring along with us our own personal attitudes about what is normal, natural, and "the way things are and should be," even though many of these viewpoints may have cultural underpinnings. This attitude is called *ethnocentrism*. Because schools and the media generally reflect majority values and norms, people who come from the dominant groups (in the United States this translates as White, mainstream Christian, born in the country where they live, middle class, and heterosexual) are particularly likely to see the way they act as "normal" and to see others who act in different ways as strange, abnormal, or in need of intervention. In Western countries the values of European groups have tended to be regarded as standard or as "not cultural," whereas values of other groups have historically been considered "ethnic" and a deviation from normality (McGoldrick, Giordano, & García-Preto, 2005).

The dominant culture is so pervasive that it can be taken for granted as easily as the air we breathe. Therefore, it is especially incumbent on members of the dominant culture (and all who have received training in that culture) to be self-reflective and respectful when working with people who may have a different set of values and beliefs. Ethnocentrism is a particular danger during the intake process, where it is all too easy to pass judgment hastily on clients' behaviors, life decisions, and predicaments that may seem strange to counselors simply because of lack of familiarity. Consider the following examples of differences between the professional and the client that are due to ethnic culture, religion, or social class:

- An African American mother, Vernell, holds her 5-year-old son firmly by both arms, looks him in the eyes and says, "You sit down in your chair and answer her questions politely now, you hear?" before she gives him a kiss and leaves him alone with the intake interviewer at their first meeting. The White counselor is upset by the mother's tone, feeling that it is overly stern, harsh, and serious. The mother has an authoritative and loving parenting style, which is common in African American families (Boyd-Franklin, 2003).
- When trying to set up an intake appointment, a counselor suggests to a Latina woman, Blanca, that she come into the office on Wednesday morning. Blanca replies that she cannot—she does her laundry then. The counselor assumes that Blanca is both rigid and relatively uninterested in therapy—otherwise she would simply do her laundry on another day. But the counselor is ignorant about the context. Wednesday morning is the day Blanca's brother, José, has off from work. José picks up Blanca and her young children and brings them to his house so she can do the laundry in his machines—Blanca does not have laundry facilities in her apartment. Blanca and her sister-in-law love their Wednesday morning routine, where they watch out for each other's toddlers, chat, and share a family meal. Giving up a Wednesday morning would imply giving up far more than a rigid schedule.
- An intake clinician notes that a Russian immigrant couple rarely spends time together due to working different shifts. The clinician notes this arrangement as a sign of family estrangement and distance, rather than as a way the parents cope with raising children in an area where they lack extended family members to care for the children during working hours, and do not trust nor can they afford childcare centers.

The more we know about a family's background and their cultural traditions, the less likely we are to condemn practices simply because they are unfamiliar.

It is not always easy to differentiate, however, between practices that are unfamiliar but harmless and practices that are problematic or in need of intervention. For example, a counselor may observe a Malaysian wife deferring consistently to her husband and son in a family intake session. Is this a culturally rooted practice that is oppressing the wife and mother, and causing conflict in the family, shutting down the mother's ability to live life in the way she chooses? Or is this a culturally rooted practice that feels natural and unproblematic to the mother? Or does this arrangement reveal some form of pathology in this particular family, such as a husband and son who physically or emotionally abuse the mother? And how should the counselor describe this dynamic in a report? The counselor who has information about Malaysian families in general as well as this family in particular will be better able to make these determinations.

If an intake counselor has but brief contact with a family, the counselor may be able to do little more than describe what is observed, without drawing conclusions, leaving it to the ongoing clinician to decide how to proceed. For example, counselors who insist that a Haitian father attend the intake session may see the father as distant and uninvolved. The father is not apt to participate voluntarily nor divulge a great deal. The wife may appear more in charge and the father may look quite passive. This is because raising children is considered primarily the mother's responsibility. However, despite appearances, the father may be listening attentively and fully committed to the therapy process (Michelle Clodimir, personal communication, October 9, 2008).

It can be extremely challenging to conduct an intake session with a person who has radically different values from the counselor's. The topics that create the most controversy in society can create similar conflict in the intake, including: family violence, child custody, sex roles, abortion, war, discipline, religion, drugs, alcohol, money, and politics. It can be hard to put aside one's own values and concerns, so the interview remains a forum for getting to know the client, rather than converting it into a forum for the counselor to express his or her own personal values. Some elements of the client's values will be relevant to the topic of the interview, and therefore merit exploration, whereas others are irrelevant and serve as a distraction.

Conveying Interest, Warmth, and Respect

The nonverbal behaviors that communicate interest in a client have been termed *attending behaviors*. These include making appropriate eye contact, nodding, and leaning forward. But if these actions are imposed too mechanically from the outside without inner feelings, they will be insufficient. I encourage counselors to do more than simply demonstrate certain actions to look as if they care. I encourage them, rather, to try to open their heart and their humanity to the clients so they actually *do* care about them. Whether the client is attractive or repulsive, the quantity and quality of the information garnered will improve if the counselor can connect on a level of true feeling.

Counselors continue to build rapport throughout an intake as they raise new topics and the relationship deepens. Many people become cold and distant when they step into their professional roles. I encourage counselors, instead, to appear warm, relaxed, supportive, and nonjudgmental, particularly in cross-cultural intakes where the client may need substantial reassurance. Counselors should show the client a personal and specific caring for him or her as an individual, not merely a generalized empathy. This can be achieved by starting intakes with time to socialize, remembering details about the clients' specific situation and mentioning these during your time together, and truly listening to clients' concerns. Mothers from many cultures will be far more interested in seeing how a counselor interacts with her child than in learning about the counselor's qualifications or theoretical approach. The intake clinician's behavior shows the mother "what the agency is like," similar to the first impressions created by an individual.

The personal relationship is key to interviewing with people from most cultures. In Korean the concept *jeong* expresses a "combination of empathy, sympathy, compassion, emotional attachment, and tenderness, in varying degrees, according to the social context" (Kim & Ryu, 2005, p. 353). A Korean will be observing a clinician for signs of jeong, which may be demonstrated by showing concern for another person's comfort and by revealing one's own humanity. We have no word that is the exact equivalent of jeong in English. Regardless, clients sense this quality and respond well when it is present.

The intake may be routine for the counselor or unusually important for some reason. However, counselors should try to keep in mind that the intake session is apt to be vastly more central to the client's life than to theirs. Intakes may portend life-changing repercussions for clients, and this can make them frightened, defensive, nervous, angry, or overly compliant. Counselors must take extra care to put clients at ease, to increase the likelihood that clients will speak openly.

How rare it is for people to listen to each other with full attention! So often when we speak to each other in our personal and professional lives, we are doing other tasks at the same time, whether driving, washing dishes, listening to music, checking e-mail, or thinking about our plans for that evening. The intake session presents the requirement, and opportunity, to pay full attention to the client, to tune into this person with our full being. When we give them our full attention, people are more likely to speak with us openly. (The exception being interviews with young children, who sometimes prefer if we draw with a crayon or in some other way help them feel less on the spot.)

As much as possible, we should avoid interruptions during our interviews. Interruptions such as answering a phone or even checking a cellular phone to see who called, eating lunch, filing nails, opening a package of gum, or drinking cold or hot beverages without offering them to the client might be considered rude to people from a variety of cultures. Scratching an itch and yawning might similarly be seen as inappropriately personal behaviors, almost like picking one's nose would be seen in the United States.

Counselors will probably want to avoid having a desk between themselves and clients unless they deliberately want to intimidate and create distance. Counselors who take notes may wish to sit across the corner of a table. This arrangement allows the counselor to rest the notes on the table and permits easy eye contact as well as the option of looking away comfortably. Sitting at a table corner is less confrontational than sitting or standing across from clients and facing them directly.

Counselors who take notes during an intake should explain what they are writing and why. They can say, "What you are telling me today is really important. I am writing it down so I won't forget any of it and so I'll remember it all correctly." Especially for people who do not read or write well themselves, the act of taking notes may seem strange and off-putting. Clients will sometimes want to glance at our notes, even if they cannot read English or decipher our handwriting, just to feel that they have some control. I recommend that we write our notes in such a way that if the person we are interviewing does ask to read them, we can feel comfortable handing over the notes during or after the interview. This degree of transparency requires making sure our notes are written respectfully and accurately. Even in situations where we are reluctant to hand our notes to a client, the client could probably, ultimately, have access to them through an attorney.

Experiences with discrimination lead many immigrants and people from ethnic, racial, or religious minority groups to be acutely sensitive to possible demonstrations of disrespect. For example:

> When Jackie, an African American woman, arrived for her intake session the White receptionist greeted her warmly and asked her a question that made Jackie realize that the receptionist thought she was someone

else. Jackie scowled and said, "I guess you must have another Black client because whoever you're thinking of, that's not me." While some might suggest that Jackie is being overly sensitive here and is responding too harshly to an innocent case of mistaken identity, others will identify with Jackie's sense that some people from the majority culture cannot distinguish among persons from a minority ethnic group and don't bother to learn who they truly are.

When experiences of invisibility or negative first impressions are repeated over time it can produce a strong response, like an ill-fitting shoe eventually leading to a blister. (People from the majority group infrequently experience situations like this as well, where all "White people" or all blonde and blue-eyed people are assumed to have the same opportunities, attitudes, and personalities, which is certainly not the case.) After multiple experiences of being overlooked or discriminated against, some people from minority groups vary between feeling weary, angry, determined, defensive, hopeful, and paranoid. They bring these feelings with them to subsequent encounters, including our intake sessions.

Immigrants who come from the lower social classes in the Caribbean, Asia, Latin America, and Africa were probably downtrodden and discriminated against in their countries of origin as well as the United States. They may continue to suffer in the United States, even at the hands of people who are from their same nation. Some will assume the role of acting "inferior" even when they are being treated with respect, coming across as overly obsequious, flattering, or ingratiating (Michelle Clodimir, personal communication, October 9, 2008).

People who blend into the majority group and have not experienced discrimination themselves may underestimate how constant, far-reaching, and distressing this discrimination can be. One Puerto Rican psychotherapist described the multiple burdens of her Latino clients in this way:

> The client is responding to a system which is totally unfair, responding to a really unfair and apathetic system in the school—that because he's in bilingual classes, he's stupid. Or because he speaks two languages but he doesn't speak English so well, he's stupid. And so you have to understand that ... this, too, prevents him from getting ahead. The concept of hope [is difficult], when you have a whole oppressive system on top of you. (Fontes, 1993, p. 24)

Becoming involved with certain agencies is often embarrassing and even humiliating for clients. By doing our utmost to convey respect, we can thwart these shameful feelings, and help clients maintain and recover their dignity.

How do we know if we are behaving in a way that is respectful? We pay careful attention to what we say and how we present ourselves, and then try to figure out how clients hear us. To be able to try on the clients' shoes, we need to accept the idea of a mismatch between the way we want to be seen and heard, and the image we are actually conveying. We must examine our demeanor when we pose questions, explain procedures, look over case files, and fill out forms, and we should explore how these activities may feel from the clients' perspective. As we catch ourselves conveying any trace of disrespect, we must have the courage to try something new. In our professional roles we may still need to do things that clients would rather we did not do; but a respectful manner will make these actions easier to accept.

We should also check in regularly with the people we're interviewing, asking versions of "How are you doing?" "How is it going?" "Are you okay?"

In most cultures, directions will be better received if they are preceded by a nicety such as "Please," or "Would you please" or "Be kind enough to." Direct orders such as "Follow me" or "Fill out this form" may be seen as rude and disrespectful.

One Puerto Rican client I interviewed suggested that professionals aim to communicate the following:

> I'm not here to judge you. I am not God. I am just a human being, just like you are. Whatever you've gone through, I'm here to help. And I'll let you know if I can help and I'll let you know if I can't help, but we'll try. And if we both work at it, we're going to get some place. ... We have to both be together and be honest with each other, not try to pull one over on the other. (Fontes, 1992, p. 92)

Counteracting Shame

While minority group characteristics are a source of pride at some moments, they can be a source of shame at others. Shame is thought to have two components: the feeling of lack of *self*-worth and the feeling of lack of worth *in others' eyes* (social worth). Intake interviews for psychotherapy often stir up feelings of shame as one exposes to another's gaze private aspects of oneself, often for the first time.

Members of ethnic and religious minority groups typically feel empowered by their identities in some contexts and delighted to be from cultures that are distinct from the mainstream. However, most members of minority groups have also experienced moments when they were shamed by others for not conforming to the dominant ideal. An African American student told me about the first racial incident she could remember, when a White kindergartener refused to hold her hand because it was brown. At the age of 6, my daughter (who is Jewish) was approached by another 6-year-old and told, "I don't want to hurt your feelings, but if you don't start believing in Jesus Christ you're going to go to hell." These instances get tucked away into a well of shame inside members of oppressed groups. Additionally shaming experiences, like being followed by security guards in the supermarket or getting harassed or teased by classmates or coworkers, can bring this shame to the surface.

Numerous writers from ethnic minority cultures have described feelings of shame related to the negative connotations attached to their skin color, hair texture, eye shape, social status, accent, or name. In her novel about a Korean adoptee's search for her birth mother, for instance, Lee (2005) described endless taunting by Minnesota schoolmates including children pulling their eyes to the side and saying, "Chinese, Japanese, Dirty Knees," "Ching-Chong Chinaman," and other insults (p. 18). The protagonist wanted so much to blend in with her Minnesota classmates, she was shocked at times to see herself in a mirror and rediscover that she did not have blonde wavy hair.

In another example, let us consider all the layers of shame that might be experienced by a low-income Mexican American man:

> Diego has family members who are undocumented, and he lives in fear and shame that their status might be discovered. He knows that his skin color, black hair, short stature, accent, and country of origin make him a target for members of hate groups. He works as a painter; and his clothes and hands often reveal his trade, which embarrasses him. He takes pride in dressing up neatly whenever he can. He finished high school in Mexico but was never able to resume schooling in the United States, so he feels ashamed when he returns to Mexico and meets with his former classmates who now have professional jobs. He wants to make sure his children attend college, and so he sends them to a parochial school; and he knows they are ashamed to reveal his profession to their classmates.
>
> When anti-foreigner sentiment intensifies, such as following the September 11, 2001, World Trade Center attacks, Diego is called names on the street and he's even had people spit at him. He is apt to feel ashamed of the issues that bring him to a psychotherapy intake as well. Counselors need to understand and work through many layers of shame before Diego will reveal himself openly in an interview.

- "Because we don't have a lot of time today, I'm going to have to focus our conversation."
- "I can see this means a lot to you. It will be important to tell your ongoing clinician about that."
- "Does that fit in with what we were discussing about, or is this a different direction?"
- "Let me return to …"
- "I want to make sure we at least touch on all the important topics today. Please forgive me if I ask you to fast forward to …"
- "I see we only have 15 minutes left, and I …"

Some conflicts over time can be avoided if counselors make explicit at the beginning of the interview the time constraints involved. For example, "We'll have 45 minutes to talk today, and it won't be enough. But you will have more time with the ongoing clinician who will be assigned to work with you" or "This process usually takes about an hour." Counselors can also set up the expectations by saying something like, "I am going to be asking you a lot of questions today, and sometimes I might have to interrupt you so I can be sure to cover all the areas we need to cover. I hope I won't hurt your feelings if I do that." It is important to remember, however, that people from many cultures talk in more of a roundabout way than the linear kinds of conversations usually heard in Western industrialized countries. It would be a shame to interrupt what appears to be a digression if, in fact, the client was making his or her best effort to answer the question posed.

Setting the Tone through Questions

Most intake interviews begin with asking questions; yet we rarely consider the overwhelming impact of the questions themselves. Whatever our intentions, questions are not neutral. Questions convey values and exert influence. Questions establish the professional relationship. Questions determine the scope of the discussion: what topics will be included or excluded. Questions establish power relations. They determine the exact nature of "the problem" and how you and the client will refer to it. Questions embody intentions, and they arise from certain assumptions (Tomm, 1988).

Our questions and our style of questioning reflect who we are as people. We need to look in an imaginary mirror as we ask our questions. Do we convey not only skillful professionalism but also respect and caring? Only if we succeed in conveying this impression will people answer our questions openly and provide the information we need.

Clearly, the questions we ask throughout an interview will depend, in large part, on the purpose and context of the intake and the client's age. The initial questions may range from those that appear to require a simple answer (e.g., "How old are you?") to slightly more complicated ones, (e.g., "How are you feeling today?") to ones that may require the client to make some complex decisions before responding (e.g., "What would you like me to know about you?").

Questions are a particular way to obtain information in an interview, but certainly are not the only method. Posing questions is a directive mode of communicating because questions tell the client what to talk about at that moment. When a counselor asks a question, the counselor is taking control of the conversation (Sommers-Flanagan & Sommers-Flanagan, 2003). In some circumstances, this may be desirable. For instance, sometimes the counselor needs detailed information about a particular issue at a given time, or the counselor will want to limit the ramblings of a particularly verbose client. Questions are a way of focusing an interview or a portion of an interview.

Questions can also be comforting to a person in crisis. I worked on a psychiatric crisis team early in my career. My supervisor suggested that asking very detailed questions about a person's symptoms, thoughts, behaviors, and feelings would be reassuring, just as it can be reassuring when a physician asks detailed questions during a medical consultation. It conveys that the professional will be able to determine what is wrong and provide some relief. Asking detailed questions and listening carefully to the answers also conveys to the client that the counselor is paying close attention.

Questions are sometimes problematic in interviews, however, because when one question is posed after another, clients feel as if they are being interrogated. Questions also place the client in the passive position of being the provider of information that will then be collected and acted upon by the interviewer. This passivity may be advantageous in certain circumstances such as the emergency assessment discussed earlier, where a person in crisis needs to know that he or she will be kept safe. However, inducing passivity in a client can be highly undesirable in other situations. For instance, if a counselor begins an intake with many focused questions, clients are apt to appear quite passive and depressed. They may not be able to demonstrate their full capacity for initiative, curiosity, and resourcefulness.

One psychology professor I know challenged his interns to conduct entire intake interviews without a single question. The students became fluent in other, less formal ways of gathering information, such as, "So your doctor suggested that you come see me," instead of "Why did your doctor suggest that you come see me?" and "I notice you look sad as you discuss your children" rather than "How do you feel about your children?" These are sometimes called *implied* or *indirect* questions, and they can seem less pushy and interrogatory than direct questions.

Sometimes we are tempted to deviate from our usual interview process because of a hunch or an instinct that tells us to pursue a new topic. We must be careful here, because asking questions impulsively may lead us into areas that are unethical or, to put it plainly, simply none of our business. If we are seen as prying unnecessarily or overly curious, we may damage our working alliance with a client. For instance, we might be tempted to inquire about a person mentioned by a client because we think we may know him or her, or we may tempted to ask more questions about sexuality than we need to ask because we find it exciting, or we may want to ask about a cultural practice because we are curious, although it has no bearing on the intake. We must be sure we are asking questions to accomplish our professional goals and with concern for the client, not to satisfy our own interest.

Sometimes clients think we are asking questions for our own prurient reasons, when in fact there is a rationale. Prefacing our questions with, "Now I'm going to ask you about X because ..." may help clients understand our motives.

Questions should be seen as one technique among many for soliciting information. In most intake situations, questions are among our best and most essential tools. In this next section we will look at ways to begin interviews that maximize the free exchange of information.

Eliciting Narratives

Many counselors find it helpful to start intakes by asking open-ended questions that elicit the client's own words (e.g., "Tell me a little about yourself"), rather than by starting with closed questions (e.g., "How old are you?"). Encouraging a free narrative may be especially important when working with people who are not accustomed to speaking freely and openly for long periods of time. In many cultures people do less speaking, in general, than in Western industrialized nations, and particularly the United States. Also, in most cultures people in subordinate positions, such as women, children, and people with a low income or social status, do less speaking when meeting with people of a more dominant status. If you are hoping the client will speak at length about his or her issues, it is important to set up clear expectations from the get-go. However, we should also be careful not to push people into speaking in a way that is uncomfortable for them. If our efforts at eliciting a free narrative fail, we can switch to more focused and direct questions. The ongoing clinician may be better able to encourage the client to speak more freely at subsequent meetings.

The Intake Report

Most clinicians receive little training in writing the report on an intake interview, although the report is likely to remain in a case file for years if not decades, and may have great impact on a client's future. In this next section I will discuss ways to consider culture in writing the intake report.

Recording Behavioral Observations or Presentation

The intake counselor may be expected to write about the client's behavior during the intake. Without a videotape, a person who reads the report relies entirely on what is written to understand what transpired. If the client cries, sighs, moans, or laughs; responds sarcastically, sweetly, or angrily; sits rigidly, slumps, or rocks wildly; wears rags or a suit or a uniform; has needle marks, scars, or bruises, or other unusual physical characteristics that might be relevant—all this will be lost in the report unless the counselor finds an effective way to record it. The behavior displayed in the intake is assumed to be in some way representative of the client's behavior in other situations.

As a counselor observes clients in the waiting room and as the counselor builds rapport at the beginning of an intake, the counselor is assessing the clients' baseline demeanor, the gestures, postures, and ways of speaking that the person displays while relatively relaxed. This baseline demeanor is helpful so the counselor can note any significant changes that occur once more sensitive topics are raised. For example, people who are restless or tense by temperament may fidget constantly. If these are constant habits, they should not be mistaken for indicators of deception or stress.

Our perceptions of people we interview cannot be entirely pure or neutral because we bring our biases into the intake. We see people through our own eyes, and we hear them through our own ears. Exactly what we see and hear depends on which factors stand out enough for us to notice them. Our biases and expectations filter our perceptions and memory in ways that may escape our awareness. For example, people have much greater difficulty remembering and distinguishing faces of people from a different race than their own (Anthony, Cooper, & Mullen, 1992). Beyond what we actually perceive, our expectations and biases also help determine what we consider worth recording and what we leave out.

When writing about an observation that is largely speculative, counselors should be sure to state it as such. For example, an odor of alcohol might also be attributable to other sources, and unless the client has been tested with a Breathalyzer, conclusions about alcohol use can only be described as speculations. Similarly, if a counselor sees scar tissue on the underside of a person's forearm, the origin of the scar could include self-mutilation, suicidal gestures, cooking burns, scratches from an animal, or injuries sustained in a work environment. Counselors should record the observation of the scar, without a description of its source, unless the counselor is certain of it

Reporting the Client's Attitude, Demeanor, and Affect

Counselors often report on a client's general demeanor and attitude toward the intake. Some dimensions that are commonly discussed include open/closed, cooperative/uncooperative, and friendly/hostile. Please remember that these elements may not be stable personality characteristics but rather induced by the demands of the situation. That is, if the client perceives the intake as shameful or threatening in some way, the client will behave in an atypical and less optimum way.

Counselors should not ignore or disregard what they see in the intake—it is, after all, a sample of behavior. But the counselor may not know the significance of the behavior. Rather, counselors should describe as much as possible rather than drawing conclusions or using overly general summarizing words. So, for instance, a counselor might write, "Mr. Luong asked many questions before he signed the form" rather than that he was "uncooperative" or "suspicious." Further, if the counselor thinks Mr. Loung's reluctance stems from his difficulty understanding the form, the counselor could ask him about this and make a note of it in the report.

Intake clinicians are frequently expected to comment on a client's affect. Words that are used commonly include *labile*, *flat*, and *inappropriate to content*. These kinds of conclusions need to be drawn with caution in cross-cultural interviews because of the varied norms concerning emotional expression across cultures (Fontes, 2008b).

It is misleading to comment on whether a person is responding "appropriately" to an event without knowing what that event means to the person involved. For instance, some Christians may respond to a loved one's death with rejoicing because they see heaven as a glorious, welcoming place. Similarly, some Hindus and Sikhs will respond to the death of a loved one with equanimity because they believe the soul remains alive and immortal even when the body dies (Zakariah, 2005). A Lebanese father may seem overly despairing or angry when he finds out that his young daughter has engaged in sex play with a neighbor's similar-aged child because in his community she and the entire family will be seen as disgraced if the word gets out. If a family's emotional, verbal, or behavioral response to an event seems unusual, be sure to ask what the event means to them.

How was the eye contact? (A counselor can note this, even if the counselor is not entirely sure what it means at first.) At what point in the interview did the client display nonverbal changes such as hesitating, blushing, sweating, or averting the eyes? Did the client display any unusual mannerisms or other nonverbal behavior? Remember that many aspects of what a counselor notices may also be culturally based, including what the counselor considers unusual.

Notational Bias

Bias can manifest in reports much as it does in other phases of the interview process. Notational bias refers to ways in which the instruments we use for measuring, our terms, categories, and even our forms can bias our findings. This bias is introduced when the available notation used to describe something influences our ability to describe and approach it. For instance, if there are a limited number of categories for race included in a form, a person who thinks of himself as Black and Filipino may be forced to describe himself or herself as "other" or "biracial," which clearly omits important information.

Notational bias is also introduced when we use shorthand ways of identifying problems, which may have limited validity. For instance, in a study we may use "receives special education services" as a shorthand way to describe a child who has a learning disability. However, of course, there are many factors influencing whether children receive special education services including their parents' attitudes toward such services, the availability of screening programs in schools, greater funding levels for special education as compared to bilingual education, and so forth. So when we have only two categories for learning disabilities, stating that someone receives or doesn't receive special education services, we may be missing the categories of those who once received such services but no longer do, those who should receive such services but do not, those who will receive such services in the future, those who have been identified as needing such services but whose parents refuse it, and so on.

Our forms often do not allow the reporting of shades of gray. We must record the father as either living in the home or not; there is nowhere to record his sporadic presence. We may have to check one box only to describe a person's profession, although that person engages in a number of different jobs. We may be forced to give a person a diagnosis who does not fit neatly into a category. The forms and categories used in our report may themselves introduce unintentional errors. We can guard against this by working to improve our forms and noting the complex reality in the narrative portions of our reports.

Word Choice

We inevitably make choices about which elements of an interview to highlight or play down, and the order for presenting the information. For example, notice the words available to describe a client who taps his feet and fingers as he speaks: agitated, restless, impatient, jittery, fidgety, hyper, high-strung, anxious, and nervous. Each of these words conveys a tone that would influence the readers' perception of the client. The most accurate description and the one with least bias, of course, would be to record simply, "The client tapped his fingers and feet throughout our conversation." The slight valences of meaning contained in our word choices can influence the conclusions readers reach about the person described in the report. We need to make sure words are chosen without prejudice.

Our choice of words can evidence ethnocentrism or multicultural understanding, and can contribute to unfair or just outcomes. It is important to eliminate biased word choice from our reports. This is hard to do, since much of the language we use on a daily basis contains biases that we may not even be aware of. For example, the word *gyp* meaning "to cheat or swindle someone" comes from the word *gypsy*, and so is an unacceptable ethnic slur.

We especially need to be cautious in describing people. When referring to their clothing, write that "Jean wore all black clothes, ripped lacey stockings, heavy black eye liner, and black lipstick," rather than that she was "dressed like a Goth." Or write that James wore "baggy pants that he had to hitch up several times during the interview, a baseball cap on backward, a thick gold chain and several large rings on his fingers," rather than that he was "dressed in gangsta style."

Sometimes individuals or their caretakers who are not very sophisticated, or who are not comfortable with English, may provide inaccurate or confusing information about their own or their child's condition. They may not be able to articulate, for instance, the type of "disability" a child suffers from, confusing a learning disability with mental retardation or a lack of motivation. A counselor may want to use the individual's own terms ("John's mother reported he obtained extra time for formal testing in school") even as [the] counselor seeks more complete and accurate information from other sources.

Referring to Race, Ethnicity, and Other Identity Groups

Counselors often wonder how they should refer to the client's race, ethnicity, or other identity group characteristics. In some situations counselors have no choice—they are required to check a box with a limited number of categories. Data on birth and death certificates, population studies, and health research have all too frequently been found to be inaccurate because of misclassifications. For instance, people are often misclassified as White who, when questioned directly, identify themselves as Native American, Asian, Pacific Islander, multiracial, or "other" (Wilson & Williams, 1998).

In general, it is best not to guess about a person's race or ethnicity. A counselor may be interviewing a child who appears White and whose mother is White, but actually the child is biracial. How should a counselor categorize someone whose family is of Japanese origin but who grew up in Brazil? A counselor may see that someone's name is Roberto Sanchez and therefore assume the person is Latino, but he might come from the Philippines instead. I recommend that counselors proceed as sensitively as possible without making assumptions. I like to ask, "How would you like me to identify your race or ethnicity?" Or, if a limited number of choices are available, I might read the categories to the person and ask how they identify themselves. Bi- or multiracial people often object to having to choose "other"; it can make them feel "other than" human. Many demographers and activists are advocating for the inclusion of the category multiracial, for people whose parents come from more than one of the four official racial groups (Wilson & Williams, 1998).

We all have ideas about race and ethnicity that may be outside of our immediate awareness, but can shape the way we respond to a client and write up the intake. The more we can become aware of these ideas and responses, the less apt we are to inject bias into our interviews or our reports.

In regard to race, the American Psychological Association manual recommends that we respect current usage, which changes periodically. At the time this book is being written, in the United States *Black* and *African American* are both considered acceptable although not identical terms, while *Negro* and *Afro-American* are not considered acceptable. The terms *Black* and *White* should be capitalized when they are used as adjectives or proper nouns to describe or refer to a person or a group. Color words such as yellow, brown, or red should not be used to describe other groups.

The terms *Hispanic* and *Latino* are preferred by different groups. Because the word *Latino* is a Spanish word, whereas the term *Hispanic* was invented in English by the U.S. Census, the word *Latino* is gaining popularity. Whenever possible it is best to use more precise geographical references to say that "Ramón identifies as Cuban American and was born in Miami" and "Wong is from Hong Kong," for instance, rather than using less specific terms such as Latino or Asian.

Most Native Americans in the United States would rather be referred to by their tribe, as Navajo or Ojibwa, for instance, rather than by the catchall terms *Native American* or *American Indian*. The terms *Native American* and *American Indian* are both considered acceptable to refer to the indigenous peoples of North America. *Native American* is a slightly broader term encompassing the native peoples of Hawaii and Samoa. The term *First Nations* is currently gaining use to refer to the original people of Canada. The term *Asian* is preferred over *oriental*, which is considered overly exoticizing. The terms *White* or *European American* are preferred over *Caucasian*, because the latter term is rooted in biological models of race that we now know are largely inaccurate.

As with race and ethnicity, we allow clients to describe their religion. *Latter-Day Saints* usually prefer this term over *Mormon*; Jews strongly prefer to be called *Jewish* rather than *Hebrew*, and so on. When in doubt and when it is relevant, ask. We should be careful not to confuse the term *Muslims* (describing people who practice the religion Islam) with the term *Arabs*, which broadly describes an ethnic group. It is also important to remember that simply knowing a person's religion without knowing how observant the person might be in regard to practicing that religion, or which branch of that religion the person practices, will probably not reveal much about how the person lives.

Some intake reports require synthesizing and analyzing vast quantities of information, and therefore necessarily include the interviewer's perspective. For instance, diagnostic interviews by psychologists and psychiatrists often include a "case formulation." This case formulation may be written in a variety of ways. One format includes a brief restatement of the case history, a differential diagnosis, a best or most likely diagnosis, contributing factors and strengths, additional information that is still needed, a treatment plan, and prognosis (Morrison & Anders, 1999).

Clearly, there is extensive room for personal opinion and judgments in intake reports. Care must be taken to be fair at all times, reporting strengths in addition to weakness, and avoiding a tendency to assign certain diagnoses or treatment plans to people from certain ethnic groups, for instance, based on their group membership. Unfortunately, the client's ethnic or racial identity has been found to unduly influence legal, medical, mental health, and educational decision making (DelBello, 2002).

In their reports, counselors should make sure they preserve a feeling of the humanity of the client, even if this person has been involved in objectionable activity (e.g., sexual offending) or is suffering from an ailment that might make him or her seem "less than" others (e.g., mental retardation). The person is not simply a case, a patient, a client, a problem, a depressive, a victim, or a suspect; the person is a human being with many facets. When in doubt, we should err on the side of professionalism and respect, asking ourselves, "How would I want to be referred to if I was in this person's shoes?" Or, "How would I want my mother (or my daughter) described if she was in this position?"

Contributing Factors, Recommendations, and Prognoses

In the report, the counselor may include a section on contributing factors. Here, we should be sure to mention cultural, linguistic, socioeconomic, and religious factors, or environmental changes that may be important, including but not limited to concerns about deportation, incidents of racial or other forms of harassment or discrimination, recent or upcoming religious rituals, and changes of residence or immigration. For example, Felipe, who worked as an accountant in his native Guatemala, has become a Spanish teacher in the United States. At his intake session he states that his physician referred him to therapy because he was having "nerve attacks" with no medical findings. Contributing factors here could include emigration, change of profession, change of language, distance from extended family, change of diet and climate, and other aspects of culture shock.

We need to conclude many intake reports with a (provisional) diagnosis and a set of recommendations, such as a treatment plan. If the data is incomplete and insufficient to provide a diagnosis, we should provide the least stigmatizing diagnosis possible and recommend gathering more information.

Although this may not be the ideal outcome, it is far better than making decisions based on inadequate information. The intake interview and the report undoubtedly will still have helped complete the picture and identified the gaps that need to be filled. Cross-cultural intakes often *are* incomplete, because of difficulties building rapport or linguistic misunderstandings, among other causes.

Counselors should be careful about employing code words such as "high risk," or negative, gloomy predictions. Many pathways can lead to the same outcome, and a single event might have many outcomes down the road. Counselors can indicate how the client is doing now and give some kind of indication about the future based on the past; but we should be extremely careful in conveying too much certitude about our predictions, especially those concerning the distant future.

If the data is inconsistent, be extremely careful in drawing conclusions. Inconsistent data suggest avenues for further exploration (Sattler, 1998). If "objective measures" such as the results of standardized tests are available, the counselor may be expected to include these in the intake report. However, it is important to remember that many of these instruments have not been normed around people from minority ethnic groups, or for whom English is not their native language, and so their accuracy may be questionable with certain populations (see Chapter 4 on assessment).

When we interview a person only one time and in one location, we obtain a snapshot of that person at that time and in that place. It is necessarily just one limited picture, and our ability to draw inferences about the person from just one contact is severely limited. We should be appropriately modest in our conclusions and the certitude with which we state them. This humility is especially indicated in cross-cultural intake interviews where rapport may be harder to achieve, and where we may be more likely to misinterpret what we see and hear.

Conclusion

We set the foundation for successful psychotherapy at the beginning of the intake session by making clear the process and goals of the intake interview. The more information we can provide about the context of the communication, the better it will be for the client. In simple terms, we need to tell them about the role and position of the intake clinician and how the information will be used. We should tell them as much as we can about the procedures governing the conversation, such as the time frame and expectations. We need to let them know if this is a one-time intake or the beginning of a long-standing relationship. And we need to allow them to ask questions.

As the intake continues, we build rapport with clients by addressing them appropriately, conveying respect, speaking with them in a welcoming tone of voice, and choosing our questions carefully. Of course, a respectful atmosphere is not limited to the first few minutes of an intake. Rather, respect must be sustained over time through listening compassionately, keeping our word (not promising what we cannot deliver), and allowing clients to establish the pace as much as possible. We show that we are listening to and remember what the person said by returning to topics discussed earlier in the interview. We demonstrate appreciation of the person's language and cultural traditions, where we can, and try to engage in appropriate nonverbal behavior (see Fontes, 2008b). Once the groundwork for a productive therapeutic relationship has been established through the intake, the next steps will be easier for the ongoing clinician.

References

Anthony, T., Cooper, C., & Mullen, B. (1992). Cross-racial facial identification: A social cognitive integration. *Personality & Social Psychology Bulletin, 18,* 296–301.

Bird, H., Canino, G., Rubio-Stipec, M., Gould, M., Ribera, J., Sessman, M., et al. (1988). Estimates of the prevalence of childhood maladjustment in a community survey in Puerto Rico. *Archives of General Psychiatry, 45,* 1120–1126.

Boyd-Franklin, N. (2003). *Black families in therapy* (2nd ed.). New York: Guilford.

DelBello, M. (2002). Effects of ethnicity on psychiatric diagnosis: A developmental perspective. *Psychiatric Times, 19*(3). Available at: http://www.psychiatrictimes. com/Mood-Disorders/showArticle.jhtml?checkSite=psychiatricTimes& articleID=175801706

Fontes, L. A. (1992). Considering culture and oppression in child sex abuse: Puerto Ricans in the United States. *Dissertation Abstracts International, 53*(6-A), 1797.

Fontes, L. A. (1993). Disclosures of sexual abuse by Puerto Rican children: Oppression and cultural barriers. *Journal of Child Sexual Abuse, 2,* 21–35.

Fontes, L. A. (2008a). Beyond words: Nonverbal communication in interviews. In *Interviewing clients across cultures: A practitioner's guide* (pp. 80–110). New York: Guilford.

Fontes, L. A. (2008b). The interpreted interview. In *Interviewing clients across cultures: A practitioner's guide* (pp. 140–166). New York: Guilford.

Givens, D. (2005). *Love signals.* New York: St. Martin's Press.

Heredia, R. R., & Brown, J. M. (2004). Bilingual memory. In T. Bhatia & W. C. Ritchie (Eds.), *The bilingual handbook* (pp. 225–248). Malden, MA: Blackwell.

Kim, B. L. C., & Ryu, E. (2005). Korean families. In M. McGoldrick, J. Giordano, & N. Garcia-Preto (Eds.), *Ethnicity and family therapy* (pp. 349–362). Guilford: New York.

Lee, M. M. (2005). *Somebody's daughter*. Boston: Beacon Press.

McGoldrick, M., Giordano, J., & García-Preto, N. (Eds.). (2005). *Ethnicity and family therapy* (3rd ed.). New York: Guilford Press.

Morrison, J., & Anders, T. F. (1999). *Interviewing children and adolescents: Skills and strategies for effective DSM-IV diagnosis*. New York: Guilford Press.

Sattler, J. M. (1998). *Clinical and forensic interviewing in children and families*. San Diego, CA: Sattler.

Sommers-Flanagan, J., & Sommers-Flanagan, R. (2003). *Clinical interviewing* (3rd ed.). New York: Wiley.

Sue, S. (1998). In search of cultural competence in psychotherapy and counseling. *American Psychologist, 53,* 440–448.

Tomm, K. (1988). Interventive interviewing: Part III. Intending to ask lineal, circular, strategic, or reflexive questions? *Family Process, 27,* 1–15.

Wilson, L. C., & Williams, D. R. (1998). Issues in the quality of data on minority groups. In V. C. McLoyd & L. Steinberg (Eds.), *Studying minority adolescents* (pp. 237–250). Mahwah, NJ: Lawrence Erlbaum.

Zachariah, R. (2005). East Indians. In J. G. Lipson, & S. L. Dibble (Eds.), *Culture and clinical care* (pp. 146–162). San Francisco: University of California at San Francisco School of Nursing Press.

4

Assessment and Diagnosis in a Cultural Context

Freddy A. Paniagua

In 1994, the American Psychiatric Association (APA) made a major decision regarding the importance of considering cultural variables in the assessment and diagnosis of psychiatric or mental disorders. This decision resulted in the inclusion of many cultural variables across most (but not all) psychiatric disorders in the *Diagnostic and Statistical Manual of Mental Disorders* (*DSM–IV*) (Paniagua, 2000; Paniagua, Tan, & Lew, 1996). In 2000, the APA published a text revision of the *DSM–IV,* and although nothing new was added regarding cultural variables across mental disorders, cultural variations continued to be a critical addition in the *DSM–IV.* The *DSM–IV,* however, is only a preliminary step in the application of culturally sensitive strategies to minimize biases and prejudices in the assessment and diagnosis of mental disorders among clients from the four major racial/ethnic groups in mental health services, namely, African Americans, American Indians, Asians, and Hispanics (Cuellar & Paniagua, 2000; Paniagua, 2000; Santiago-Rivera, Arredondo, & Gallardo-Cooper, 2002). Examples of additional steps clinicians should consider in the present context include:

1. Clinician's self-assessment of potential biases and prejudices.
2. An assessment of the potential impact of acculturation on both assessment and diagnosis of mental disorders.
3. The role of racism and cultural identity of the client in assessment and diagnostic practices.
4. Selection of culturally appropriate psychological tests to assess intellectual functioning and psychopathology.
5. Formulation of culturally appropriate questions.
6. Use of the mental status in a cultural context.
7. Selecting the least biased assessment strategy.
8. Distinguishing culture-bound syndromes from cultural variations.
9. Guidelines for the cultural formulation.

The main goal of this chapter is to provide an overview of critical issues clinicians should consider across each of these steps leading to an accurate assessment and diagnosis of mental disorders among clients from racially or ethnically diverse communities. It should be noted that although this chapter illustrates the applicability of the aforementioned nine steps in clinical practices with the four major culturally diverse groups in the multicultural society of the United States (i.e., African Americans, American Indians, Asians, and Hispanics), similar steps could also be applied, with some stipulations, in the case of clients from other racial/ethnic groups including, for example, subgroups of Anglo-Americans residing in this country such as Greek, Italian, Irish, and Polish Americans, clients from West Indian or Caribbean islands (e.g., Jamaica, Barbados, Trinidad), and clients from Middle Eastern (e.g., Arab Americans) and Asian Indian (e.g., Hindu Americans) families (Abudabbeh, 1996; Allen, 1988; Almeida, 1996; Jalali, 1988).

Clinician's Self-Assessment of Unintended Biases and Prejudices

Before conducting an assessment and diagnosis of mental disorders among clients from the four culturally diverse groups cited earlier, clinicians are strongly encouraged to conduct a self-assessment of *unintended* biases and prejudices. This recommendation is particularly important to consider in those cases when the clinician does not share the racial/ethnic background of the client. It should be noted that the term *unintended* is emphasized because most biases and prejudices in clinical practices are generally the results of clinicians' and supporting staff's lack of cultural competence training. In this context, Ridley (2005) points out that "many well-meaning counselors are likely to discover that, despite their efforts to treat all clients equitably, they are *unintentional* racists" (p. xi; italics added).

A self-assessment of biases and prejudices could be achieved with the *Self-Evaluation of Biases and Prejudices Scale* suggested by Paniagua (1994, 1998, 2005). This scale includes 10 items inquiring about respondents' experiences with specific issues involving African American, American Indian, Asian, Hispanic, and Anglo-American communities. Examples of items in that scale include, "Would you date or marry a member from the following groups?" and "Would you expect favorable therapy outcome with (e.g., African American)?" Each item is scored on a scale ranging from 1 (very much) to 3 (not at all). The maximum bias-prejudice score is 3.0.

Preliminary results with this scale were reported by Paniagua, O'Boyle, Tan, and Lew (2000) with a group of professionals including counselors, teachers, social workers, psychologists, school principals, education diagnosticians, and administrators of community services. Overall, the alpha coefficient was .87, suggesting acceptable internal consistency for the items. In terms of the mean score of participants' responses to the 10 items, participants reported less bias–prejudice toward clients from their own racial/ethnic background, relative to their response in the case of client–professional racial/ethnic differences. Similar results were found when comparisons were made across participants in relation to clients from their own racial/ethnic background versus participants–clients racial/ethnic differences: in each case, participants sharing the same race/ethnicity of the client tended to show less bias–prejudice toward these clients, relative to their level of bias–prejudice toward clients from a different racial/ethnic background. Additional instruments designed to assess multicultural competence leading to the prevention of unintended biases and prejudice among clinicians resulting from lack of cultural competence, with modest reliability and validity results, include the *Cross-Cultural Counseling Inventory–Revised, Multicultural Counseling Awareness Scale-Form B: Revised Self Assessment, Multicultural Counseling Inventory,* and the *Multicultural Awareness –Knowledge–Skills Survey.* A review of each of these instruments can be found in Ponterotto, Rieger, Barrett, and Sparks (1994) and Pope-Davis and Dings (1995).

Assessment of the Potential Impact of Acculturation on Both Assessment and Diagnosis of Mental Disorders

Definition of Acculturation

Acculturation is a crucial variable that must be considered during the assessment and diagnosis of mental disorders among the four major racially or ethnically diverse groups discussed in this chapter (Buki, Ma, Strom, & Strom, 2003; Cuellar, 2000; Dana, 1993; Sue & Sue, 2007). Acculturation is generally defined in terms of the degree of integration of new cultural patterns into the original cultural patterns (Buki et al., 2003; Grieger & Ponderotto, 1995). As noted by Buki et al. (2003), "the concept of acculturation generally refers to the process by which immigrants adapt to a new culture" (p. 128). I have termed this process *external* (Paniagua, 1994), which differs from the *internal* process of acculturation (Paniagua, 1994) generally absent in the acculturation literature (Casas & Pytluk, 1995; Cuellar, 2000; Witko, 2006a).

In the *external process of acculturation* (Paniagua, 1994, 1998, 2005), a person moves from his or her country of origin into another country. This is the acculturation process generally applied to immigrants who move into the United States from Caribbean (e.g., Dominican Republic, Cuba), Central American (e.g., Panama, El Salvador), South American (e.g., Bolivia, Colombia), and Asian countries (e.g., Japan, China, Vietnam). The effects of the external acculturation process are less dramatic when immigrants move into the United States and reside in cities that resemble their norms, cultural patterns, and values of their home cities. This is the case of most Hispanics or Latinos from Cuba, Dominican Republic, and Puerto Rico residing in New York City and Miami, as well as Mexicans who move to the four major cities in Texas along the U.S.–Mexican border (i.e., Edinburgh, Brownsville, Harlingen, and McAllen). Hispanics residing in such U.S. cities not only encounter people who can understand their language but also find people from their countries of origin who share many of their cultural values (e.g., folk beliefs, customs, music).

The effect of the external acculturation process is more dramatic when a person moves into the United States and resides in a city with little similarity to that person's original cultural patterns (Cuellar, 2000). In this situation, symptoms resembling mental disorders would be expected, particularly in the case of anxiety, mood, and adjustment disorders. The clinician's main goal in this context would be to carefully screen symptoms of mental disorders that appear culturally based rather than clinically based (this is further discussed in the section "Culture-Bound Syndromes and Cultural Variations").

In the *internal process of acculturation* (Paniagua, 1994, 1998, 2005), changes in cultural patterns may occur when members from the culturally diverse groups discussed in this chapter move from a U.S. region to another region in the United States (e.g., from one city to another within the same state or across states). For example, when American Indians living in Arizona, New Mexico, and other states with a large number of reservations move from their reservations to urban cities or non-Indian environments, they experience the impact of a societal lifestyle quite different from the societal lifestyle they experienced on the reservations. For example, competition and individualism are two values with little relevance among American Indians who reside on reservations (Paniagua, 2005; Witko, 2006a). These values, however, are extremely important for anyone who resides outside a reservation. In the present case, American Indians simply move from one area to another within the United States; and the assimilation of new values and lifestyles in the new area is a function of the process of internal acculturation. The impact of the internal process of acculturation would be minimal if an American Indian were to move from one reservation to another reservation in the United States.

The internal process of acculturation is further illustrated by Hispanics residing in certain areas of New York City who move to certain areas in Florida (e.g., Miami). The impact of acculturation as an internal process would be minimal in comparison with a move from New York City to another city, such as Lawrence, Kansas, with few shared cultural patterns between the Hispanics and other residents. Another example is Mexican Americans who reside on the U.S.–Mexican Border (particularly in the Lower Rio Grande Valley of Texas). Mexican Americans who move from this region of the United States to another region resembling little of Mexican American cultural patterns (e.g., Washington, DC) would experience a difficult internal acculturation process. Mexican Americans who move from the U.S.-Mexican border into San Antonio, Texas, though, would not experience that internal process of acculturation (or its impact would be minimal) because many Mexican Americans residing along the U.S.–Mexican border and Mexican Americans residing in San Antonio share similar cultural patterns.

An emphasis on the internal process of acculturation would allow clinicians to prevent using the term *acculturation* only in those cases when the clinical population under consideration is "external" (i.e., representative of a country different from the United States such as clients from Caribbean, Central, or South American countries), and instead to also consider the applicability of that term when the target clinical population is inherent to the United States. For example, through the internal process of acculturation many African Americans tend to embrace cultural identity patterns (e.g., styles of dressing, language, music) associated with the Anglo-American community and to move away from the African American culture (Dana, 1993; Paniagua, 2005). In the case of American Indians, Witko (2006b) provides an excellent discussion regarding the "attempts of the boarding schools and missionaries to assimilate the American Indian people into the mainstream culture" (p. 159) through the internal acculturation process and how this process has led many American Indians residing in urban areas to believe that they are living "in a world that does not truly accept their cultural beliefs" (Witko, 2006b, p. 160).

Levels of Acculturation

It is also important to determine the potential impact of different levels of acculturation upon the assessment and diagnosis of mental disorders involving clients from the aforementioned culturally diverse groups. These levels are generally defined in terms of *number of years* in the internal or the external acculturation process, *age* at which the client enters such processes, and *country of origin*. The general assumption is that younger clients are more easily acculturated than older clients, and that as the number of years in the process increases the level of acculturation also increases. In terms of the country of origin, the main assumption is that a racial group tends to show a higher level of acculturation depending on its country of origin. For example, a client from the Dominican Republic residing in New York City is more easily acculturated than a client from Vietnam residing in the same city because the Dominican experienced (in his or her country of origin) a great deal of U.S. cultural values prior to entering the United States including dressing style, music, language (many of them speak English prior to entering the United States), and a competitive approach to achieve social and political goals.

Table 4.1 includes examples of acculturation scales recommended with multicultural groups. If the therapist does not have enough time to conduct a thorough screening of acculturation using the scales in Table 4.1, the *Brief*

TABLE 4.1		
Acculturation Scales		
Name of Scale	*Group*	*Reference*
Abbreviated Multidimensional Acculturation Scale	Caribbean, Central and South American populations	Zea et al. (2003)
Acculturation Questionnaire	Vietnamese, Nicaraguan refugees	Smither & Rodriguez-Giegling (1982)
Acculturation Rating Scale for Mexican Americans	Mexican Americans	Cuellar et al. (1980, 1995)
Acculturative Balance Scale	Mexican Americans, Japanese	Pierce et al. (1972)
Behavioral Acculturation Scale	Cubans	Szapocznik et al. (1978)
Brief Acculturation Scale for Hispanics	Mexican Americans, Puerto Ricans	Norris et al. (1996)
Children's Acculturation Scale	Mexican Americans	Franco (1983)
Cuban Behavioral Identity Questionnaire	Cubans	Garcia & Lega (1979)
Cultural Life Style Inventory	Mexican Americans	Mendoza (1989)
Developmental Inventory of Black Consciousness	African Americans	Milliones (1980)
Ethnic Identity Questionnaire	Japanese Americans	Masuda et al. (1970)
Multicultural Experience Inventory	Mexican Americans	Ramirez (1984)
Multicultural Acculturation Scale	Southeast Asians, Hispanic Americans, Anglo-Americans	Wong-Rieger & Quintana (1987)
Racial Identity Attitude Scale	African Americans	Helms (1986)
Rosebud Personal Opinion Survey	American Indians	Hoffmann et al. (1985)
Suinn-Lew Asian Self-Identity Acculturation Scale	Chinese, Japanese, Koreans	Suinn et al. (1987)

Source: Adapted from Paniagua (2005).

Acculturation Scale in Box 4.1 is suggested as a preliminary screening of levels of acculturation in clinical contexts. This scale emphasizes three variables in the process of acculturation, namely, generation, language preferred, and social activity (Burnam, Hough, Karno, Escobar, & Telles, 1987; Cuellar, Harris, & Jasso, 1980; Suinn, Rickard-Figueroa, Lew, & Vigil, 1987). For example, family members in the fifth generation are considered highly acculturated, in comparison with members in the first generation. In terms of language preferred, the client should be asked a general question covering most situations in which a certain language is preferred (e.g., with children, with parents, with coworkers). In the case of social activity, a similar approach is recommended. For example, a Mexican American client may be asked "When you listen to music and go to a restaurant to eat, would you do these

BOX 4.1: BRIEF ACCULTURATION SCALE

Instruction: Please check only one item from the group of Generation items, Language Preferred items, and Social Activity items.

My generation is:

First   Second   Third   Fourth   Fifth
 (1)   (2)   (3)   (4)   (5)

The language I prefer to use is:

Mine   Mostly   Both mine   Mostly   Only
only   mine   and English   English   English
 (1)   (2)   (3)   (4)   (5)

I prefer to engage in social activity with:

Only   Mostly   Within/   Mostly with   Only with
within   within   between   a different   a different
racial group racial group racial groups racial group   racial group
 (1)   (2)   (3)   (4)   (5)

Total Score: _____

Number of Items Checked: _____

Acculturation Score (Total Score/Number of Items Checked): _____

The Level of Acculturation for this client is (circle one):

Low   Medium   High

Source: Adapted from Paniagua (1994, 1998, 2005).

things with Mexican Americans only, mostly with Mexican Americans, with Mexican Americans and other racial groups mostly (e.g., African Americans, Whites, Asians, American Indians), with a different racial group of your own (e.g., Whites), or only with a different racial group?"

The following acculturation scores (suggested by Burnam et al., 1987) are recommended in the Brief Acculturation Scale: 1 to 1.75 = low acculturation, 1.76 to 3.25 = medium acculturation, and 3.26 to 5 = high acculturation.

It should be noted that the *Brief Acculturation Scale* in Box 4.1 is a general screening instrument that could be used to quickly assess the level of acculturation with clients from all culturally diverse groups described in this chapter, whereas acculturation scales in Table 4.1 target specific groups or multiple groups. For example, in Table 4.1 the *Abbreviated Multidimensional Acculturation Scale* (Zea, Asner-Self, Birman, & Buki, 2003) could be used to screen the acculturation level of Hispanic or Latino clients born in Central and South American counties, Caribbean countries, and in the United States (that is, the Hispanic Americans). By contrast, the *Acculturation Rating Scale for Mexican American* targets this particular group (Cuellar, Arnold, & Maldonado, 1995), and the *Suinn-Lew Asian Self-Identity Acculturation Scales* is recommended with Chinese, Japanese, and Korean clients (Buki et al., 2003; Suinn, Ahuna, & Khoo, 1992; Suinn et al., 1987).

The assessment of levels of acculturation is particularly recommended in those cases when the focus of clinical attention involves parent–child relational problems and partner relational problems (APA, 2000). In the first case, the formulation of the case would include "a pattern of interaction between parent and child (e.g., impaired communication, overprotection, inadequate discipline) ... associated with clinically significant impairment in individual or family functioning or the development of clinically significant symptoms in parent or child" (APA, 2000, p. 737). In this context, different levels of acculturation between parent and the child may result in parent–child relational problems leading to symptoms of mental disorders. For example, oppositional defiant disorder (APA, 2000) among Hispanic adolescents may be the result of parent–child disagreements regarding adolescents' assimilation of beliefs and attitudes in the mainstream culture, including customs (e.g., dressing) and lifestyles (e.g., dating) Less acculturated Hispanic parents, relative to their more acculturated Hispanic children, would perceive "dressing" among Anglo-American adolescents as a custom that is not in accord with the way Hispanic adolescents should dress. Similarly, dating among many Hispanic families is a very elaborate process in which parents and relatives from both sides are expected to be invited when the boyfriend and girlfriend decided to go out for a date (e.g., a movie, to the mall, amusement game rooms, etc.). More acculturated Hispanic adolescents would disagree with their less acculturated parents regarding who should be present during that dating process. In the case of adolescents, they would argue that their friends are welcome, but that parents and older relatives (e.g., uncles, aunts) should be excluded from that dating process; the opposite is true from the perspective of Hispanic parents and older relatives (i.e., relatives should not be excluded).

In the case of partner relational problems resulting from different levels of acculturation, the focus of clinical attention would be "a pattern of interaction between spouse or partner characterized by negative communication (e.g., criticism), distorted communication (e.g., unrealistic expectations), or noncommunication (e.g., withdrawal) ... associated with clinically significant impairment in individual or family functioning or the development of symptoms in one or both partners" (APA, 2000, p. 737). For example, if one of the partners (e.g., Vietnamese, Hispanic, or Asian wife) has been residing in the United States for several years whereas the other partner stays in the country of origin (e.g., Vietnam, Colombia, or China, respectively), different levels of acculturation would be expected between the two partners when the second partner also moves into this country. This difference in levels of acculturation could result in severe marital difficulties requiring counseling from a clinician with expertise in assessing and diagnosing couples from the respective countries.

Models of Acculturation

Clinicians should also be aware of models of acculturation in the current literature and how each one of these models may impact on the assessment and diagnosis of mental disorders among culturally diverse clients. Four models of acculturation have been identified in cross-cultural literature, namely, *assimilation, separation, integration,* and *marginalization* (Cuellar, 2000; Gurung & Mehta, 2001; Paniagua, 2005; Sue & Sue, 2007).

In the *assimilation* model of acculturation, a highly acculturated client would strongly identify with only the dominant or host culture. This client would not value behaviors and beliefs shared by members of his or her own culture. Examples of those behaviors are forms of dressing, listening to native music, forms of dance, native food preparation, and dating process. Examples of such beliefs include the role of evil spirits and unnatural events explaining medical complications or emotional problems, expected submission of women to the expected authority of men in a marital relationship (particularly among traditional Hispanic families), and the belief in cultural traditions when celebrating significant events in the family such as birthdays and marriages. In this assimilation process of acculturation, children and adolescents who refuse to follow the cultural norms of their own culture but agree to follow the norms of the dominant culture would be diagnosed with oppositional defiant disorder (APA, 2000). Clients who are expected to display behaviors and beliefs culturally sanctioned in the original culture but avoid following these expectations because of the effect of that assimilated process of acculturation would be diagnosed with avoiding personality disorder (APA, 2000) by clinicians not aware of the potential role of that assimilation process of acculturation in shaping over time behaviors resembling symptoms of mental disorders. Another example is diagnosing a client with an adjustment disorder because he or she reports great difficulty adjusting to behaviors and beliefs expected in his or her own culture after being exposed to that assimilation process of acculturation for many years.

In the *separation* model of acculturation, the client would only value behaviors and beliefs of the traditional culture. The client would maintain his or her cultural/ethnic identity, and refuse to adapt or identify with elements of the host (dominant) culture in the working environment and social interactions. This model of acculturation should be particularly explored when children and adolescents are brought to the clinic because they are not displaying behaviors and beliefs expected by their parents. This situation would lead to parent–child relational problems (APA, 2000). In this case, a culturally effective clinician would conclude that conflicts between adolescents and their parents, for example, are probably the results of parents enforcing or demanding adolescents to only value the behaviors and beliefs expected in the traditional culture and to reject adaptation to the dominant (host) culture (see Sue & Sue, 2003, pp. 160–161).

The separation model of acculturation could also negatively impact the psychological state of clients who report occupational problems in the working environment (APA, 2000). Among such problems, job dissatisfaction, a feeling of being rejected by peers, and difficulty interacting with other peers in the working environment may be the result of the client's rejection to adapt or identify with elements of the host (dominant) culture in the working environment. For example, the client may avoid participating in social events where employees are expected to attend (e.g., office celebration of birthday parties, baseball games scheduled by the particular company, etc.), because the client believes that those social events are coordinated and planned by the dominant culture (e.g., most participants are Anglo-Americans, with few participants from the client's own race or ethnicity). Clients experiencing the impact of the separation model of acculturation in this context would come to the clinic for symptoms suggesting a mental disorder (e.g., adjustment problems, depression). In this situation, the central clinical goal would involve a careful assessment of that separation model of acculturation and then to explain to the client in language he or she could understand the reason for the presence of symptoms suggesting a mental disorder and what the client should do to minimize the negative impact of this particular acculturation process on the client's emotional states.

In the *integration* model of acculturation, the client would display behaviors and beliefs from both the traditional and host (dominant) culture. This client would maintain his or her cultural and ethnic identity, and at the same time integrate mainstream values from the host culture. This process of acculturation is also termed *biculturalism* in the sense that the individual would combine behaviors, beliefs, or values from two different cultures in his or her social interactions with individuals from the traditional and dominant culture (see Sue & Sue, 2003, pp. 160–161). That combination may result in conflicts between the integrated client (i.e., sharing elements of both cultures) and those individuals who reject mixing elements of their own culture with elements in the dominant culture. The nature of such conflicts should be particularly important to explore in those cases when the client's reports of specific conflicts (e.g., marital problems, conduct problems among children and adolescents, and so forth) involving either family members assimilated into the dominant culture (i.e., only practicing and valuing behaviors and beliefs of the host culture) or family members separated from the host culture (i.e., adherence to behaviors, beliefs, and norms of the traditional culture, and rejection of all elements of the host culture). That is, whereas a client influenced by the integration model of acculturation would feel comfortable displaying behaviors and beliefs from both the traditional and dominant cultures, he or she would experience conflicts in normal activities of daily living (e.g., rituals and traditions associated with marriage, celebration of significant anniversaries) and emotional difficulties (e.g., depression) when interacting with family members who either only accept the behaviors and values of the host culture (assimilated individuals) or only accept the behaviors and values of the traditional culture (separated individuals).

In the *marginalization* model of acculturation, the client would reject behaviors and beliefs associated with either the traditional culture or the host (dominant) culture. During the initial clinical assessment of this client, clinicians would have great difficulty pointing to the cultural/ethnic identity of this client because he or she would not report behaviors, beliefs, and cultural norms generally associated with either the traditional culture or with the dominant (host) culture. As noted by Cuellar (2000, p. 52), a marginalized client would be more "susceptible to psychological and adjustment disorders than persons who have adopted ... assimilated, integrated or separation modes of adjustment [i.e., acculturation]." The client with *less susceptibility* to psychological and adjustment disorders would be "one in which he or she lives a comfortable existence in the host culture retaining as much of the home culture as he or she likes, together with parts of the host culture's values and behaviors" (Gurung & Mehta, 2001, p. 141). That is, the acculturated individual with minimal reports of conflicts or emotional difficulties in clinical settings would the one who displays behaviors and beliefs corresponding with the integration or biculturalism model of acculturation, and avoids cultural/ethnic identification with only one culture (i.e., either the traditional or host/dominant culture).

An important point to consider in the case of clients experiencing the impact of the marginalization model of acculturation is that they could easily be diagnosed with either schizoid personality disorder or borderline personality disorder (APA, 2000). In the first case, the marginalized (culturally speaking) client would show "a pattern of detachment from social relationships and a restrictive range of emotional expressions" (APA, 2000, p. 685), whereas in the second case the marginalized client would show "a pattern of instability in interpersonal relationships, self-image, and affects, and marked impulsivity" (APA, 2000, p. 685). To avoid misdiagnosing clients affected by the marginalization process of acculturation, clinicians are advised to carefully screen this model of acculturation against clinically based symptoms associated with the aforementioned personality disorders in the *DSM–IV* (APA, 2000).

In summary, diagnosis of mental disorders among clients from culturally diverse backgrounds should not be made without taking into account both the client's level of acculturation (using scales in Table 4.1, for example) and the model of acculturation that appears most applicable during the assessment of the patient's characteristics and symptoms. This recommendation is particularly important in those cases when a discrepancy in the level of acculturation among family members may be in itself the focus of clinical attention (see APA, 2000, p. 741).

The Role of Racism and Cultural Identity of the Client in Assessment and Diagnostic Practices

Definition of Racism and Its Implications in Clinical Practice

In the provision of mental health services to clients from the four major culturally diverse groups discussed in this chapter, the term *racism* is often interpreted in two ways. First, this concept is often used to explain why these clients behave they way they do. For example, intelligence test results are generally lower among African Americans, American Indians, Asians, and Hispanics in comparison with scores derived from White subjects (Jenkins & Ramsey, 1991). In the case of an African American client, the diagnosis of schizophrenia is frequently used with these clients in comparison to White clients (Wilkinson & Spurlock, 1986). The explanation of these results in terms of differences among races is termed *racism* (Paniagua, 1998, 2005). The second usage of *racism* is the reference to "racial prejudice and discrimination used to the advantage of one race and the disadvantage of other races" (Okun, 1996, p. 210). As noted by Miller (1992) and Klonoff, Landrine, and Ullman (1999), prejudice and racial discrimination are in themselves stressful situations that could lead to emotional difficulties among members from the culturally diverse groups discussed in this chapter. For example, clients from these groups may display low self-esteem and symptoms of depression when they sense that they have been racially discriminated (e.g., see Paniagua, 2001, pp. 166–167, for a clinical case illustrating this point).

During the assessment of the culturally diverse clients described here, it is important to determine whether symptoms reported by the client suggest either *personal prejudice, individual racism, cultural racism,* or *institutional racism* (Okun, 1996).

Personal prejudice deals with beliefs and attitudes "that are not acted out behaviorally" (Okun, 1996, p. 217) including, for example, the sense that one has been excluded from social activities (e.g., birthday celebrations) and that someone moves away from people who do not share his or her color. In the case of biracial children, they "may experience personal prejudice from the racial group of both parents," including the use of racial discriminative labels such as "oreos" and "zebras" (see Okun, 1996, p. 217).

Individual racism is the opposite of personal prejudice in that the individual would display overt racial discrimination against a given culturally diverse group. Examples of this form of racism include African American children harassed by White children in school and the fact that, regardless of having many White friends in the neighborhood or school, the African American child is never invited into the homes of these White children (e.g., see Paniagua, 2001, pp. 45–53).

Cultural racism "is based on the assumption that White is the norm, that people of color are inherently inferior, less intelligent … [and considered] as uncivilized, emotional labile, and prone to violence" (Okun, 1996, p. 218). When members from the aforementioned culturally diverse groups "manage to achieve upward mobility [they are considered] as exceptions and are accepted by the dominant white culture as 'You're OK, you're different'" (see Okun, 1996, p. 218; Paniagua, 2001, pp. 45–53).

Institutional racism "is represented by the double standards, and differential treatment inherent in our justice, education, medical, government, housing, and other social systems" (Okun, 1996, p. 220). For example, when culturally diverse individuals (e.g., African Americans, Hispanics) are hired to meet affirmative action quotas but are given less significant or powerful responsibilities in the job, this is a case of institutional racism. A similar case of institutional racism is that in which the school system assumes, for example, that African American children would perform "less well on academic tasks, tracking them in lower levels and creating a self-fulfilling slow learning prophecy" (see Okun, 1996, p. 221). Each of these forms of racism could result in significant emotional difficulties in the individual experiencing them (e.g., see Paniagua, 2001, pp. 45–53 and 166–167).

Definition of Cultural Identity and Its Implications in Clinical Practice

Marsella and Yamada (2000) define *cultural identity* (or ethnocultural identity) as the "extent to which an individual endorses and manifests the cultural traditions and practices of the particular group" (p. 13). A cultural identity conflict would arise when the individual struggles to identify with his or her own culture but at the same time displays a strong sense of cultural identification with a different culturally diverse group (Casas & Pytluk, 1995; Dana, 1997). This conflict is particularly important to assess in the case of biracial children and adolescents. For example, Gibbs (2003) suggested that biracial adolescent females sometimes experience a racial identity problem when they feel uncomfortable with their physical traits, relative to the physical traits in the dominant culture. This would be the case of a biracial adolescent female with Black physical traits (e.g., African American father and Anglo-American mother) who would feel uncomfortable with her facial features, curly hair, and dark skin when socially interacting with adolescents from the Anglo-American (dominant) culture. Similarly, newly arrived clients to the United States from the Asian community and not yet affected by the assimilation acculturation process would feel afraid of losing their racial and ethnic identity by being forced to adapt to values and norms of the dominant culture (Nguyen, 1992). The importance of considering the cultural identity of the client during the assessment and diagnostic processes is recognized in the *DSM–IV* in the section dealing with the cultural formulation of the case (see APA, 2000, pp. 897–903). Examples of reliable and valid instruments for the assessment of the cultural identity of the client include: *Multigroups Ethnic Identity Measures* (Phinney, 1992), *Multiethnic Climate Inventory* (Johnson & Johnson, 1996), *Self-Identity Inventory* (Sevig, Highlen, & Adams, 2000), and *Racial Identity Attitude Scale* (Helms & Parham, 1996).

Selection of Culturally Appropriate Psychological Tests to Assess Intellectual Functioning and Psychopathology

In the case of the assessment of intellectual functioning and psychopathology among culturally diverse groups, it is important to select psychological tests in which the person's relevant characteristics are represented in the standardization sample of the test or by employing an examiner familiar with the aspects of the individual's ethnic or cultural background. This point is particularly important to consider in clinical practices during the assessment of mental retardation, learning disabilities, and communication disorders among children and adolescents (Bernal, 1990; Canino & Spurlock, 1994). Table 4.2 shows examples of tests recommended during the assessment of intellectual functioning and psychopathology among culturally diverse clients. It should be noted that many clinicians (particularly psychiatrists who are not generally trained to use psychological tests) are not expert in the use of these tests. But the issue here is not expertise in cross-cultural testing procedures, but knowledge of culturally sensitive psychological tests appropriate for the particular client and the clinician's efforts to seek appropriate consultation from mental health professionals with expertise in the use and interpretation of such tests.

	Reference
Tests to Assess Intellectual Functioning	
Culture-Fair Intelligence Test	Anastasi (1988)
Kaufman Assessment Battery for Children (K-ABC)	Kaufman et al. (1985)
Leiter International Performance Scale	Anastasi (1988)
Progressive Matrices	Anastasi (1988)
System of Multicultural Pluralistic Assessment (SOMPA)	Mercer & Lewis (1978)
Tests to Assess Psychopathology	
Center for Epidemiologic Depression Studies Depression Scale (CES-D)	Radloff (1977)
Draw-A-Person Test (DAP)	French (1993)
Eysenck Personality Questionnaire (EPQ)	Eysenck & Eysenck (1975)
Holtzman Inkblot Technique (HIT)	Holtzman (1988)
Psychiatric Status Schedule for Asian Americans	Yamamoto et al. (1982)
Schedule for Affective Disorders and Schizophrenia (SADS)	Spitzer & Endicott (1978)
Tell-Me-A-Story Test (TEMAS)	Costantino et al. (1988)
Vietnamese Depression Scale	Kinzie et al. (1982)

TABLE 4.2
Tests Recommended with Culturally Diverse Groups

Source: Adapted from Paniagua (2005).

When seeking cultural consultation in the use of tests to assess intellectual functioning and mental disorders, clinicians should be aware of the potential negative impact of the examiner–client racial/ethnic dissimilarity on an accurate assessment of the case. For example, African Americans often obtain lower scores on intelligence tests when such tests are administered by White practitioners rather than by African American clinicians (Jenkins & Ramsey, 1991). Other studies have shown that African Americans tend to alter their responses on self-report measures when the race of the examiner changes (Lineberger & Calhoun, 1983). In addition, Marcos (1976) suggested that when bilingual Hispanics clients are interviewed in English rather than in their native language (that is, Spanish), the probability of errors in assessment and diagnosing of psychiatric disorders may increase (Arroyo, 1996). Thus, to minimize biases in the assessment of intellectual functioning and mental disorders among culturally diverse groups using psychological tests, the consultation process should include strategies to minimize the sociocultural gap between the examiner and the client (see Paniagua, 1998, pp. 106–125).

Formulation of Culturally Appropriate Questions

Another important issue in the prevention of cultural biases during the assessment and diagnosis of mental disorders is the use of culturally appropriate questions during the clinical interview to enhance a culturally sensitive assessment of psychopathology among clients from the culturally diverse groups discussed in this chapter. For example, the following question is not appropriate with Asian clients: "What is your opinion of yourself compared with other people?" The reason to avoid this question is that many Asians do not like to compare themselves with other people (Yamamoto, 1986). In the specific case of Southeast Asian refugee clients, it is extremely important to avoid questions that deal with the traumatic events those clients experienced during the Vietnam War because it is very difficult for such clients to discuss the nature of such events during their first meeting with a therapist (Paniagua, 2005). In the case of biracial clients, it is also very important to avoid questions dealing with the client's biracial status such as, "Do you feel okay with an African American father and an Anglo/White mother?" This question is not culturally appropriate during the first encounter with biracial clients because it implies the presence of a cultural identity problem in the absence of additional findings to confirm the existence of that potential (biracial/ethnic identity) problem (Gibbs, 2003; Paniagua, 2000, 2005).

Use of the Mental Status Exam
in a Cultural Context

Despite the fact that the mental status exam is not a reliable or valid assessment tool in clinical practices, the exam is extremely important in those cases when it is critical to carefully assess suicidal ideation or attempts (Rosenthal & Akiskal, 1985). An important aspect of culturally sensitive assessment and diagnosis of mental disorders is to prevent or at least to minimize biases when using the *mental status exam* with culturally diverse clients discussed in this chapter. In this context, biases would be prevented or minimized by emphasizing cultural variations that might explain the results of that exam beyond commonly accepted clinical observations during the assessment of the mental status of the client.

The mental status exam makes the assumption that a series of "normal" behaviors and cognitive processes are shared by "normal" people, *regardless of cultural background.* This assumption, however, could lead to misdiagnosis of psychopathology in such clients (Hughes, 1993; Mueller, Kiernan, & Langston, 1992; Westermeyer, 1993). For example, clients who fail the serial 7s test (a client is asked to subtract 7 from 100) may be experiencing anxiety, depression, or early symptoms of schizophrenic disorder. If reliable and valid psychological tests used with these clients (see Table 4.2) also show signs of a given mental disorder, the assumption is that this serial 7s test was a good test under this circumstance.

Aside from the fact that the validity of the serial 7s test is regarded as questionable by many researchers (Hughes, 1993), many members of multicultural groups would fail this task because they are not versed in the area of counting either forward or backward. In addition, prior studies indicate that normal subjects can make between 3 and 12 errors with this test (Hughes, 1993). Therefore, one should not be surprised if that client fails the same test, particularly in a stressful environment such as a clinic with busy clinicians trying to conduct the entire assessment in less than 1 hour to fulfill managed care requirements. A better (culturally sensitive) strategy would be to instruct the client to select a given number (for example, 25; it does not need to be 100) and then to subtract whatever individual number the client wants to subtract from that number. In this case, the client is given the opportunity to use his or her level of math skills rather than someone imposing such skills on the client's knowledge of the subject.

The assessment of *orientation* allows clinicians to assess negativism, confusion, distraction, hearing impairment, and receptive language disorders. This test emphasizes the assessment of the self (the person), place, and time. For example, a clinician would ask, "What is your last name?" "What is the name of this month?" and "Where are you right now?" In response to the first question, an Hispanic client, for example, may look "confused" and "distracted" because he or she would have to decide which last name to report between the two last names often used by Hispanics, which often include one last name for the father (e.g., Castillo) and another for the mother (e.g., Ramos) like in *Miguel Antonio Castillo Ramos.* If the client is not familiar with the name of that month in Standard American English, or is not familiar with the name of the building (or cannot remember that name), and he or she appears to provide incorrect answers in the presence of these situations, the client would show "negativism," "hearing impairment," or "receptive language disorder." In these examples, a culturally sensitive approach would be to say "You're Hispanic, so you probably have one last name for your father and another for your mother … could you tell me these names?" "Do you know the name of this month in English … if not you can say it in Spanish." "At this moment, do you know that you are in a hospital and not in your house?"

The assessment of *general knowledge* could be used to assess poor educational background, severe deterioration in intellectual functioning, and the ability to assess remote memory. For example, a clinician would ask: "What are the colors of the American flag?" "What are the names of three countries in Central America?" "Who is the president of the United States?" or "Who was the president before him?" "What is the total population of the United States of America?" and so forth. As noted by Hughes (1993), the answers to such questions imply geographical and public knowledge and many members of culturally diverse groups discussed in this chapter do not have this kind of knowledge for two reasons. First, they are too poor to travel (this is one way to answer some of these questions). Second, many members in such groups are illiterate (Westermeyer, 1993). Examples of a culturally sensitive mental status exam in this case would be: "What are the colors of your country's flag?" "Tell me the name of three cities in your country." "Who is the president in your country?" "Who was the president in your country before him?" "Could you tell me the approximate number of people living in your country today?"

The assessment of *thought process* is a crucial area in the mental status exam. For example, "thought blocking" is a sudden cessation of thought or speech, which suggests schizophrenia, depression, and anxiety (Mueller et al., 1992). Clients who are not fluent in English would show thought blocking. As noted earlier, Hispanic clients with little command of Standard American English would spend a great deal of time looking for the correct word, phrase, or sentence before answering a question from the therapist and this could create anxiety resulting in thought blocking (Martinez, 1986). African American clients who use Black English in most conversational contexts would also spend a great deal of time looking for the construction of phrases or sentences in Standard American English when they feel that Standard American English is expected in certain circumstances (Smitherman, 1995; Yamamoto, Silva, Justice, Chang, & Leong, 1993). In these examples, a culturally sensitive approach would be to interview Hispanic clients using their native language, and African American clients would be told that they could use Black English when answering questions during this exam.

Appearance is another important element in the mental status examination. For example, lack of eye contact, failure to look directly into the therapist's eyes, and careless or bizarre dressing and grooming could point to signs of psychiatric disorders (Hughes, 1993). Many clients from culturally diverse groups discussed in this chapter would purposely avoid eye contact in clinical encounters. For example, Asian Americans generally avoid eye contact and looking directly into people's eyes during social interactions (Sue & Sue, 2007), partially because in such groups it is impolite to maintain eye contact or to look directly into the eyes of other people. Therefore, eye contact as a measure of appearance should not be part of this exam. The definition of what is normal dressing and grooming in the mind of a clinician may not be shared by a client who always comes to the therapist right after finishing a long-working day in a grocery store, for example, and without enough time to go home to take a shower and change clothes. This client will probably look "dirty," with "a soiled face, hands, and nails," and "careless appearance." Lack of self-care skills (e.g., days without taking a shower or changing clothes) is a critical behavior to consider when assessing certain mental disorders (e.g., major depression, alcohol intoxication). Under this circumstance, however, the issue is not to assume that the absence of self-care skills is in itself a sign of mental disorder but to assess the absence of such skills in terms of environmental variables preventing a given client from displaying such skills under normal (and expected) conditions. The way a client presents himself or herself in the clinic could be a significant point to consider in the assessment and diagnosis of mental disorders (e.g., a client with severe symptoms suggesting major depressive disorder might dress carelessly during the first evaluation); but the point here is to also consider environmental variables with the potential of impacting on the way that particular client is expected to dress when visiting the clinic (e.g., the hypothetical case with the employee who just finished a long working day at the store).

Selecting the Least Biased Assessment Strategy

Clinicians working with culturally diverse clients should make an effort to first use the least biased assessment strategies in a series of available strategies. It should be noted that despite efforts to control bias in the assessment of culturally diverse clients discussed in this chapter, an assessment strategy that is not biased against specific culturally diverse groups is not yet available (Anastasi, 1988; Rogler, 1999). For this reason, Paniagua (1994, 1998, 2005) recommended that rather than looking for unbiased assessment strategies, a better approach would be to learn how best to select and use these strategies with African American, American Indian, Asian, and Hispanic clients (see Yamamoto, 1986, p. 116).

For example, the question is not whether to avoid the mental status exam but how to use materials that are culturally related to the tasks the client is being asked to solve during this exam. In the assessment of *DSM–IV* criteria for major depression (APA, 2000), self-report of psychopathology measures such as the *Minnesota Multiphasic Personality Inventory* (MMPI) and the *Beck Depression Inventory* (Dana, 1993, 1995; Zalewski & Green, 1996) are often recommended. The results obtained with these tests could be enhanced with the design of an assessment strategy in which the client could record actual behaviors indicative of "depression" (e.g., did not attend church or any social activities during the past 2 weeks) and this self-monitoring of actual behaviors could be combined with direct observations made by others (e.g., family members, trained observers in clinical settings) to assess the reliability of the client's self-assessment of symptoms. In this example, self-monitoring is less biased than assessment procedures with the MMPI, for example, direct behavioral observations (e.g., family members recording actual presence versus absence of the client in social activities) would be the least biased assessment method, relative to the MMPI, Beck Depression Inventory, and self-monitoring.

Distinguishing Culture-Bound Syndromes from Cultural Variations

Overdiagnosis, underdiagnosis, and misdiagnosis of psychopathological conditions among culturally diverse groups discussed in this chapter might result from a lack of understanding of the presence of culture-bound syndromes resembling psychopathology (Castillo, 1997; Dana, 1993; Ivey, Ivey, & Simek-Morgan, 1996; Paniagua, 2000; Paris, 1992; Pedersen, 1997; Pedersen, Draguns, Lonner, & Trimble, 1996; Ponterotto, Casas, Suzuki, & Alexander, 1995; Smart & Smart, 1997). Smart and Smart (1997) point out that the glossary (Appendix I) of culture-bound syndromes included in the *DSM–IV* (see APA, 2000, pp. 899–903) "are descriptions of 25 forms of aberrant behavior that are referred to as locality-specific troubling experiences that are limited to certain societies or cultural areas" (p. 394). These "locality-specific aberrant experiences" have been given specific names in the cross-cultural literature. Table 4.3 shows examples of culture-bound syndromes

TABLE 4.3
Summary of Culture-Bound Syndromes

Name	Group/Country	Description
Ataques de nervios	Hispanics	Out-of-consciousness state resulting from evil spirits. Symptoms include attacks of crying, trembling, uncontrollable shouting, physical or verbal aggression, and intense heat in the chest moving to the head. These *ataques* are often associated with stressful events (e.g., death of a loved one, divorce or separation, or witnessing an accident including a family member).
Amok, mal de pelea	Malaysia, Laos, Philippines, Polynesia, Papua New Guinea, Puerto Rico	A dissociative disorder involving outburst of violence and aggression, or homicidal behavior at people and objects. A minor insult would precipitate this condition. Amnesia, exhaustion, and persecutory ideas are often associated with this syndrome.
Brain fag	African Americans	Problems with concentration and thinking among high school and university students experiencing the challenges of schooling. Symptoms include head and neck pain, blurring of vision, burning, and heat resembling somatoform, depressive, and anxiety disorders.
Boufee delirante	Haitians	Sudden outburst of aggression, agitation associated with confusion, psychomotor excitement, and symptoms resembling brief psychotic disorder (including visual and auditory hallucinations, paranoid ideation).
Colera	Hispanics	Anger and rage disturbing body balances leading to headache, screaming, stomach pain, loss of consciousness, and fatigue.
Dhat	India, China, Sri Lanka	Extreme anxiety associated with a sense of weakness, exhaustion, and the discharge of semen.
Falling-out	African Americans	Seizure-like symptoms resulting from traumatic events such as robberies.
Ghost sickness	American Indians	Weakness, dizziness, fainting, anxiety, hallucinations, confusion, and loss of appetite resulting from the action of witches and evil forces.
Hwa-byung	Asians	Pain in the upper abdomen, fear of death, and tiredness resulting from the imbalance between reality and anger.
Koro	Asians	A man's desire to grasp his penis (in a woman, the vulva and nipples) resulting from the fear that it will retract into his body and cause death.
Latah	Asians	A sudden fright resulting in imitative behaviors that appear beyond control including imitation of movements and speech. The individual often follows commands to do things outside his or her wish (e.g., verbal repetition of obscenities).

(continued on next page)

**TABLE 4.3 (continued)
Summary of Culture-Bound Syndromes**

Name	Group/Country	Description
Mal de ojo	Hispanics	Medical problems such as vomiting, fever, diarrhea, and mental problems (e.g., anxiety, depression) could result from the mal de ojo (evil eye) the individual experienced from another person. This condition is common among infants and children; adults might also experience similar symptoms resulting from this mal de ojo.
Ode-ori	Nigeria	Sensations of parasite crawling in the head, feelings of heat in the head, and paranoid fears of malevolent attacks by evil spirits.
Pibloktog	Arctic, Subarctic Eskimos	Excitement, coma, and convulsive seizures resembling an abrupt dissociative episode, often associated with amnesia, withdrawal, irritability, and irrational behaviors, such as breaking furniture, eating feces, and verbalization of obscenities.
Kyofusho	Asians	Guilt about embarrassing others; timidity resulting from the feeling that their appearance, odor, facial expressions are offensive to other people.
Mal puesto, hex, root work, voodoo	African Americans, Hispanics	Unnatural diseases and death resulting from the power of people who use evil spirits.
Susto, espanto, miedo, pasmo, wacinko	Hispanics, American Indians	Tiredness and weakness resulting from frightening and startling experiences. Feeling of anger, withdrawal, mutism, suicide from reaction to disappointment, and interpersonal problems.
Wind/cold illness	Hispanics, Asians	A fear of the cold and the wind; feeling weakness and susceptibility to illness resulting from the belief that natural and supernatural elements are not balanced.

Source: Adapted from Paniagua (2000).

often considered specific to a given cultural context or society (Castillo, 1997; Griffith & Baker, 1993; Levine & Gaw, 1995; Westermeyer, 1985).

The same cross-cultural literature, however, suggests that symptoms associated with a given mental disorder may be related to a particular cultural context but the disorder is not considered an example of a culture-bound syndrome *per se* (e.g., Table 4.3). In this case, clinicians are advised to consider specific cultural variations, which might explain symptoms suggesting the disorder under consideration. Although the *DSM–IV* (APA, 2000) did not explicitly emphasize this point, a review of the way the *DSM–IV* discusses cultural variants across several disorders suggests a distinction between culture-bound syndromes (e.g., Table 4.3) and the cultural variables contributing to symptoms in a given *DSM–IV* disorder. Several examples are provided next to illustrate the impact of cultural variations that might lead to symptoms resembling a mental disorder (see Paniagua, 2005; Paniagua et al., 1996).

Recent immigrants might display symptoms suggesting adjustment disorder with anxiety (APA, 2000) because of difficulty getting adjusted to drastic changes from the original environment to the new setting, in which the new environment serves as a critical stressor leading to symptoms. This is the case among many Hispanic immigrant children who encounter difficulties getting adjusted to the demand of American classrooms where instructions are more structural, relative to classrooms in most Hispanic countries.

In the case of attention deficit/hyperactivity disorder (APA, 2000), Barkley (1990) suggests that the prevalence of this disorder appears higher in developing countries (e.g., United States), relative to underdeveloped countries (for example, Caribbean, Central America, and South American countries) because of increases in the "cultural tempo" in developing countries that lead to parallel increases in environmental stimulation and significant increases in impulsivity, inattention, and overactivity among children exposed to that cultural tempo. In the case of conduct disorder (APA, 2000), clinicians are advised that this diagnosis should not be applied in those cases when immigrant youth come from countries with a history of aggressive behaviors that are necessary for their survival in such countries and associated with long history of wars.

Another example of cultural variations is the abundance of food and the linkage of attractiveness with being thin as potential explanations for the high prevalence of anorexia nervosa and bulimia in developing countries (APA, 2000; Castillo, 1997), relative to underdeveloped countries. Furthermore, among many Hispanic families, the cultural variable known as *marianismo* (the opposite of *machismo*; see Paniagua, 2005, pp. 55–57) may result in diagnosing Hispanic women with dependent personality disorder (APA, 2000), because a key characteristic of marianismo is that Hispanic women are expected to be obedient, dependent, timid, and submissive to the authority of the Hispanic husband who is generally perceived as "machista" (see Paniagua, 2005, pp. 55–57, for further discussion on the distinction between marianismo and machismo in the Hispanic community).

Recent immigrant children into the United States may display symptoms resembling selective mutism (APA, 2000), because they are unfamiliar or uncomfortable with the new language (English). In this case, the *DSM–IV*

(APA, 2000) explicitly recommends that this diagnosis should not be applied and to consider language barrier as the main variable leading to immigrant children's refusal to talk to strangers in the new environment.

Visual and auditory hallucinations (e.g., seeing the Virgin Mary, hearing God's voice) and delusional ideas (e.g., beliefs in witchcraft) could be considered "abnormal" in one culture but completely "normal" in other cultures (APA, 2000; Castillo, 1997). For example, many Hispanics believe that it is possible to have "visual contacts" with the Virgin Mary or to "hear" God's voice, and these beliefs are commonly accepted and promoted by the Catholic Church; but in clinical practices such beliefs would be considered as examples of hallucinations. In the Nigerian culture, fears of evil attacks by spirits are part of the local beliefs, but these fears may be considered as examples of delusional ideas (Kirmayer, Young, & Hayton, 1995). Clients displaying these cultural beliefs may be misdiagnosed with schizophrenia and other psychotic disorders (e.g., delusional disorder). Additional examples of cultural variations across other mental disorders in the *DSM–IV* (APA, 2000) can be found in Castillo (1997), Gaw (1993), Paniagua (2005), and Paniagua et al. (1996).

Guidelines for the Cultural Formulation

The previous discussion would assist clinicians with the cultural formulation of the clinical case following guidelines established in the *DSM–IV* (APA, 1994, 2000). In their clinic notes, clinicians would first summarize the following findings: (1) identifying information (e.g., name, age, gender, race/ethnicity of the client); (2) present mental disorder using *DSM–IV* diagnostic criteria (e.g., major depressive disorder); (3) the history of the present mental disorder (depression as a single episode resulting from a recent divorce); (4) family history of present mental disorder (e.g., depression reported among siblings and parents, or relatives); (5) psychosocial and environmental problems (e.g., history of sexual and physical abuses, unemployment, extreme poverty); and (6) use of the *DSM–IV* multiaxial classification (Axes I–V; APA, 2000). The *DSM–IV* recommends that these findings should be followed by the cultural formulation of the case across *five steps* (see APA, 2000, Appendix I, and Paniagua, 2001, for the illustration of this formulation across many clinical cases involving children, adolescents, and adults with diagnoses of mental disorders).

In the first step, the cultural identity of the client should be recorded, including the client's racial/ethnic-cultural references group (e.g., African

American, Hispanic, etc.), immigration status (e.g., recent arrival from a Caribbean island versus from Central or South American countries), and language preference (e.g., the client could speak English but he or she prefers to speak Spanish, or the client cannot speak English at all).

Second, it is important to record how the client explains the origin of the mental disorder in a cultural context. For example, some Hispanic clients may report that the reason for their symptoms of depression is that that they were exposed to a *mal puesto* (hexes, root work; see Table 4.3), or that "possessing spirits" are responsible for such symptoms. In the case of children experiencing anxiety disorders, particularly acute stress disorder (APA, 2000) that occurs within one month after the experience of an extreme stressor, some Hispanic parents would explain symptoms in terms of the *mal de ojo* (evil eye) culture-bound syndrome (see Table 4.3). These culturally based explanations of mental disorders would result in the client's help-seeking behavior with emphasis on either healers (e.g., curandero/a among Hispanic families, and the medicine man/woman among American Indian families) or witch doctors (brujo/a) in those situations when the solution of the particular mental problem requires the removal of "evil spirits."

Third, cultural factors related to the psychosocial environment of the client should also be recorded, including the client's perception of the role of the church and the extended family (both biological and nonbiological members such as parents, siblings, friends, godparents, etc.) in the assessment, diagnosis, and treatment of the particular mental problem.

Fourth, clinicians are expected to explain in their clinic notes cultural elements of the relationship between the client and the clinician that may impact on the assessment and diagnosis of a given mental disorder. For example, if the race/ethnicity variable are not shared by both the client and the clinician (e.g., the client is African American but the clinician is White, Hispanic, etc.), this difference should be noted in the clinic note because the client–clinician racial/ethnicity difference could result in misdiagnosing or underdiagnosing mental health problems, as well the client's refusal to return for further assessment required to reach a final diagnosis for a given mental disorder (Arroyo, 1996; Paniagua, 2005).

The final (fifth) step in the cultural formulation is an overall cultural assessment in which the clinician would summarize major findings, such as that symptoms reported by the client appear to be culturally related, or that acculturation or religious problems should be the focus of clinical attention.

It should be pointed out that clinicians may be prevented from recording the steps in the cultural formulation because of economical and policy-made reasons. In terms of economical reasons, managed care insurance companies do not reimburse the assessment of elements of the cultural formulation. Therefore, clinicians would not spend a significant amount of time dealing with that formulation during the initial diagnostic evaluation of the case. A major policy-made decision in the *DSM–IV* was to include the cultural formulation in Appendix I, which would suggest to clinicians that they are not actually required to consider cultural variables during the assessment of the case following the guidelines in the cultural formulation. That is, anything that is included in the appendixes of the *DSM–IV* is not required to be considered during the assessment and diagnosis of the clinical case, and this observation would clearly inform clinicians that the inclusion of the cultural formulation (APA, 2000, Appendix I) in their clinic notes is a matter of their own choice. This situation would result in an ethical dilemma among clinicians who believe that an assessment of cultural variables potentially impacting on the final diagnosis of the case should always be considered when serving clients from the African American, American Indian, Asian, and Hispanic communities, as well as clients from other culturally diverse groups (i.e., Italian, Irish, and Polish Americans; West Indian Islanders; and Middle Eastern and Asian Indian communities). Prior to reaching a final diagnosis of mental disorder, however, clinicians would not assess those variables and summarize them in the cultural formulation because of economic reasons or the lack of a clinical directive from the *DSM–IV* enforcing the use of the cultural formulation.

Conclusion

This chapter emphasizes the importance of considering cultural variations during the assessment and diagnosis of mental disorders with emphasis on the four major culturally diverse groups generally encountered in clinical practices in the United States, namely, African Americans, American Indians, Asians, and Hispanics. Culturally appropriate assessment is not only necessary to ensure that the diagnosis of mental disorders is not culturally determined, but attention to cultural variables in this context is also strongly recommended prior to the development and implementation of treatments that are sensitive to the race and ethnic background of clients in both outpatient and inpatient clinical settings.

Clinicians, however, should be careful not to place too much emphasis on such variables during the assessment and diagnosis of the case. Too much emphasis on such variables may prevent clinicians from diagnosing the client with a true mental disorder that may be unrelated to cultural variations. In addition, too much emphasis on such variables may result in the assumption that the client should be referred to a folk healer because the mental health professional who initially evaluated the case concluded that culturally related symptoms are not manageable with the help of established mental health professional practices (see Paniagua, 2001, pp. 27–28).

References

Abudabbeh, N. (1996). Arab families. In M. McGoldrick, J. Giordano, & J. K. Pearce (Eds.), *Ethnicity and family therapy* (pp. 333–346). New York: Gilford Press.

Allen, A. (1988). West Indians. In L. Comas-Diaz & F. E. H. Griffith (Eds.), *Clinical guidelines in cross-cultural mental health* (pp. 305–333). New York: John Wiley.

Almeida, R. (1996). Hindu, Christian, and Muslim families. In M. McGoldrick, J. Giordano, & J. K. Pearce (Eds.), *Ethnicity and family therapy* (pp. 395–423). New York: Gilford Press.

American Psychiatric Association (APA). (1994). *Diagnostic and statistical manual of mental disorders*. Washington, DC: Author.

American Psychiatric Association (APA). (2000). *Diagnostic and statistical manual of mental disorders* (4th ed., text rev.). Washington, DC: Author.

Anastasi, A. (1988). *Psychological testing* (6th ed.). New York: Macmillan.

Arroyo, J. A. (1996). Psychotherapist bias with Hispanics: An analog study. *Hispanic Journal of Behavioral Sciences, 18*, 21–28.

Barkley, R. A. (1990). *Attention-deficit hyperactivity disorder: A handbook for diagnosis and treatment* (2nd ed.). New York: Guilford.

Bernal, E. M. (1990). Increasing the interpretative validity and diagnosis utility of Hispanic children's scores on tests of achievement and intelligence. In F. C. Serafica, A. I. Schwebel, R. K. Russell, P. D. Isaac, & L. B. Meyers (Eds.), *Mental health of ethnic minorities* (pp. 108–138). New York: Praeger.

Buki, L. P., Ma, T.-C., Strom, R. D., & Strom S. K. (2003). Chinese immigrant mothers of adolescents: Self-perceptions of acculturation effects on parenting. *Cultural Diversity & Ethnic Minority Psychology, 9*, 127–140.

Burnam, M. A., Hough, R. L., Karno, M., Escobar, J. I., & Telles, C. A. (1987). Acculturation and lifetime prevalence of psychiatric disorders among Mexican Americans in Los Angeles. *Journal of Health and Social Behavior, 28*, 89–102.

Canino, I. A., & Spurlock, J. (1994). *Culturally diverse children and adolescents: Assessment, diagnosis, and treatment*. New York: Guilford.

Casas, J. M., & Pytluk, S. D. (1995). Hispanic identity development: Implications for research and practice. In J. G. Ponterotto, J. M. Casas, L. A. Suzuki, & C. M. Alexander (Eds.), *Handbook of multicultural counseling* (pp. 155–180). Thousand Oaks, CA: Sage.

Castillo, R. J. (1997). *Culture and mental illness*. Pacific Grove, CA: Brooks/Cole.

Costantino, G., Malgady, R. G., & Rogler, L. H. (1988). *Technical manual: The TEMAS Thematic Apperception Test*. Los Angeles: Western Psychological Services.

Cuellar, I. (2000). Acculturation and mental health: Ecological transactional relations of adjustment. In I. Cuellar & F. A. Paniagua (Eds.), *Handbook of multicultural mental health: Assessment and treatment of diverse populations* (pp. 45–62). New York: Academic Press.

Cuellar, I., Arnold, B., & Maldonado, R. (1995). Acculturation rating scale for Mexicans–II: A revision of the original ARSMA scale. *Hispanic Journal of the Behavioral Sciences, 7*, 275–304.

Cuellar, I., Harris, L. C., & Jasso, R. (1980). An acculturation scale for Mexican American normal and clinical populations. *Hispanic Journal of the Behavioral Sciences, 2*, 199–217.

Cuellar, I., & Paniagua, F. A. (2000). *Handbook of multicultural mental health: Assessment and treatment of diverse populations*. New York: Academic Press.

Dana, R. H. (1993). *Multicultural assessment perspectives for professional psychology*. Boston: Allyn & Bacon.

Dana, R. H. (1995). Culturally competent MMPI assessment of Hispanic populations. *Hispanic Journal of Behavioral Sciences, 17*, 305–319.

Dana, R. H. (1997). *Understanding cultural identity in intervention and assessment*. Thousand Oaks, CA: Sage.

Eysenck, H. J., & Eysenck, S. B. S. (1975). *Manual for the Eysenck Personality Questionnaire*. San Diego, CA: Educational and Industrial and Testing Service.

Franco, J. N. (1983). An acculturation scale for Mexican American children. *Journal of General Psychology, 108*, 175–181.

French, L. A. (1993). Adapting projective tests for minority children. *Psychological Reports, 72*, 15–18.

Garcia, M., & Lega, L. I. (1979). Development of a Cuban ethnic identity questionnaire. *Hispanic Journal of the Behavioral Sciences, 1*, 247–261.

Gaw, A. C. (Ed.). (1993). *Culture, ethnicity, and mental illness*. Washington, DC: American Psychiatric Press.

Gibbs, J. T. (2003). Biracial and bicultural children and adolescents. In J. T. Gibbs & L. N. Huang (Eds.), *Children of color: Psychological interventions with culturally diverse youth* (pp. 145–182). San Francisco: Jossey-Bass.

Grieger, I., & Ponderotto, J. G. (1995). A framework for assessment in multicultural counseling. In J. G. Ponterotto, J. M. Casas, L. A. Suzuki, & C. M. Alexander (Eds.), *Handbook of multicultural counseling* (pp. 357–374). Newbury Park, CA: Sage.

Griffith, E. E. H., & Baker, F. M. (1993). Psychiatric care of African Americans. In A. C. Gaw (Ed.), *Culture, ethnicity, and mental illness* (pp. 147–173). Washington, DC: American Psychiatric Press.

Gurung, R. A. R., & Mehta, V. (2001). Relating ethnic identity, acculturation, and attitudes toward treating minority clients. *Cultural Diversity and Ethnic Minority Psychology, 2*, 139–151.

Helms, J. E. (1986). Expanding racial identity theory to cover the counseling process. *Journal of Counseling Psychology, 33*, 62–64.

Helms, J. E., & Parham, T. A. (1996). The Racial Identity Attitude Scale. In R. L. Jones (Ed.), *Handbook of tests and measurements for Blacks populations* (pp. 167–174). Hampton, VA: Cobb & Henry.

Hoffmann, T., Dana, R., & Bolton, B. (1985). Measured acculturation and MMPI performance of Native American adults. *Journal of Cross-Cultural Psychology, 16*, 243–256.

Holtzman, W. H. (1988). Beyond the Rorschach. *Journal of Personality Assessment, 52*, 578–609.

Hughes, C. C. (1993). Culture in clinical psychiatry. In A. C. Gaw (Ed.), *Culture, ethnicity, and mental illness* (pp. 3–41). Washington, DC: American Psychiatric Press.

Ivey, A. E., Ivey, M. B., & Simek-Morgan, L. (Eds.). (1996). *Counseling and psychotherapy: A multicultural perspective.* Boston: Allyn & Bacon.

Jalali, B. (1988). Ethnicity, cultural adjustment, and behavior: Implications for family therapy. In L. Comas-Diaz & E. E. H. Griffith (Eds.), *Clinical guidelines in cross-cultural mental health* (pp. 9–32). New York: John Wiley.

Jenkins, J. O., & Ramsey, G. A. (1991). Minorities. In M. Hersen, A. E. Kazdin, & A. S. Bellack (Eds.), *The clinical psychology handbook* (pp. 724–740). New York: Pergamon.

Johnson, P. E., & Johnson, R. F. (1996). The role of concrete-abstract thinking levels in teachers' multiethnic beliefs. *Journal of Research and Development in Education, 29*, 134–140.

Kaufman, S., Kamphaus, R. W., & Kaufman, N. L. (1985). New directions in intelligence testing: The Kaufman Assessment Battery for Children (K-ABC). In B. B. Wolman (Ed.), *Handbook of intelligence: Theories, measurements, and applications* (pp. 663–698). New York: Wiley.

Kinzie, J. D., Manson, S. D., Do, T. V., Nguyen, T. T., Anh, B., & Than, N. P. (1982). Development and validation of a Vietnamese-language depression rating scale. *American Journal of Psychiatry, 139*, 127–1281.

Kirmayer, L. J., Young, A., & Hayton, B. (1995). The cultural context of anxiety disorders. *Psychiatric Clinic of North America, 18*, 503–521.

Klonoff, E. A., Landrine, H., & Ullman, J. B. (1999). Racial discrimination and psychiatric symptoms among blacks. *Cultural Diversity and Ethnic Minority Psychology, 5*, 329–339.

Levine, R., & Gaw, A. C. (1995). Culture-bound syndromes. *The Psychiatric Clinics of North America, 18*, 523–536.

Lineberger, M. H., & Calhoun, K. S. (1983). Assertive behavior in Black and White American undergraduates. *Journal of Psychology, 13*, 139–148.

Marcos, L. R. (1976). Bilinguals in psychotherapy: Language as an emotional barrier. *American Journal of Psychotherapy, 30*, 552–560.

Marsella, A. J., & Yamada, A. M. (2000). Culture and mental health: An introduction and overview of foundations, concepts, and issues. In I. Cuella & F. A. Paniagua (Eds.), *Handbook of multicultural mental health: Assessment and treatment of culturally diverse populations* (pp. 3–24). New York: Academic Press.

Martinez, C. (1986). Hispanic psychiatric issues. In C. B. Wilkinson (Ed.), *Ethnic psychiatry* (pp. 61–87). New York: Plenum Medical.

Masuda, M., Matsumoto, G. H., & Meredith, G. M. (1970). Ethnic identity in three generations of Japanese Americans. *Journal of Social Psychology, 81*, 199–207.

Mendoza, R. H. (1989). An empirical scale to measure type and degree of acculturation in Mexican-American adolescents and adults. *Journal of Cross-Cultural Psychology, 20*, 372–385.

Mercer, J., & Lewis, J. (1978). *Systems of multicultural pluralistic assessment.* New York: Psychological Corporation.

Miller, F. S. (1992). Network structure support: Its relationship to psychological development of Black females. In A. K. Burlew, W. C. Banks, H. P. McAdoo, & D. A. Azibo (Eds.), *African American psychology* (pp. 105–126). Newbury Park, CA: Sage.

Milliones, J. (1980). Construction of a Black consciousness measure: Psychotherapeutic implications. *Psychotherapy: Theory, Research, and Practice, 17*, 175–182.

Mueller, J., Kiernan, R. J., & Langston, J. W. (1992). The mental status examination. In H. H. Goldman (Ed.), *Review of general psychiatry* (pp. 109–117). San Mateo, CA: Appleton & Lange.

Nguyen, N. A. (1992). Living between two cultures: Treating first-generation Asian Americans. In L. Vargas & J. D. Chioin (Eds.), *Working with cultures: Psychotherapy interventions with ethnic minority children and adolescents* (pp. 204–222). San Francisco: Jossey-Bass.

Norris, A. E., Ford, K., & Bova, C. A. (1996). Psychometrics of a brief acculturation scale for Hispanics in a probability sample of urban Hispanics adolescents and young adults. *Hispanic Journal of Behavioral Sciences, 18*, 29–38.

Okun, B. (1996). *Understanding diverse families: What practitioners need to know.* New York: Guilford.

Paniagua, F. A. (1994). *Assessing and treating culturally diverse clients: A practical guide* (1st ed.). Thousand Oaks, CA: Sage.

Paniagua, F. A. (1998). *Assessing and treating culturally diverse clients: A practical guide* (2nd ed.). Thousand Oaks, CA: Sage.

Paniagua, F. A. (2000). Culture-bound syndromes, cultural variations, and psychopathology. In I. Cuellar & F. A. Paniagua (Eds.), *Handbook of multicultural mental health: Assessment and treatment of diverse populations* (pp. 139–169). New York: Academic Press.

Paniagua, F. A. (2001). *Diagnosis in a multicultural context: A casebook for mental health professionals.* Thousand Oaks, CA: Sage.

Paniagua, F. A. (2005). *Assessing and treating culturally diverse clients: A practical guide* (3rd ed.). Thousand Oaks, CA: Sage.

Paniagua, F. A., O'Boyle, M., Tan, V. L., & Lew, A. S. (2000). Self-evaluation of unintended biases and prejudices. *Psychological Reports, 87*, 823–829.

Paniagua, F. A., Tan, V. T., & Lew, A. S. (1996). A summary of cultural variants in the DSM-IV. *Sociotam: International Journal for the Social Sciences, 6*, 33–57.

Paris, J. (1992). Dhat: The semen loss anxiety syndrome. *Transcultural Psychiatric Research Review, 29*, 109–118.

Pedersen, P. B. (1997). *Culture-centered counseling interventions: Striving for accuracy.* Newbury Park, CA: Sage.

Pedersen, P. B., Draguns, J. G., Lonner, W. J., & Trimble, J. E. (1996). *Counseling across cultures.* Thousand Oaks, CA: Sage.

Phinney, J. S. (1992). The Multigroup Ethnic Identity Measure: A new scale for use with adolescents and young adults from diverse groups. *Journal of Adolescent Research, 7*, 156–176.

Pierce, R. C., Clark, M., & Kiefer, C. W. (1972). A "bootstrap" scaling technique. *Human Organization, 31*, 403–410.

Ponterotto, J. G., Casas, J. M., Suzuki, L. A., & Alexander, C. M. (Eds.). (1995). *Handbook of multicultural counseling.* Newbury Park, CA: Sage.

Ponterotto, J. G., Rieger, B. P., Barrett, A., & Sparks, R. (1994). Assessing multicultural counseling competence: A review of instrumentation. *Journal of Counseling and Development, 72*, 316–322.

Pope-Davis, D. B., & Dings, J. G. (1995). The assessment of multicultural counseling competencies. In J. G. Ponterotto, J. M. Casas, L. A. Suzuki, & C. M. Alexander (Eds.), *Handbook of multicultural counseling* (pp. 287–330). Thousand Oaks, CA: Sage.

Radloff, L. S. (1977). The CES-D scale: A self-report depression scale for research in the general public. *Applied Psychological Measurement, 1*, 385–401.

Ramirez, M. (1984). Assessing and understanding biculturalism-multiculturalism in Mexican-American adults. In J. L. Martinez & R. H. Mendoza (Eds.), *Chicano psychology* (pp. 77–94). Orlando, FL: Academic Press.

Ridley, C. R. (2005). *Overcoming unintentional racism in counseling and therapy.* Thousands Oaks, CA: Sage.

Rogler, L. H. (1999). Methodological sources of cultural insensitivity in mental health. *American Psychologist, 54*, 424–433.

Rosenthal, R. H., & Akiskal, H. S. (1985). Mental status examination. In M. Hersen & S. M. Turner (Eds.), *Diagnostic interviewing* (pp. 25–52). New York: Plenum.

Santiago-Rivera, A., Arredondo, P., & Gallardo-Cooper, M. (2002). *Counseling Latinos and la familia: A practical guide.* Thousand Oaks, CA: Sage.

Sevig, T. D., Highlen, P. S., & Adams, E. M. (2000). Development and validation of the self-identity inventory (SII): A multicultural identity development instrument. *Cultural Diversity and Ethnic Minority Psychology, 6*, 168–182.

Smart, D. W., & Smart, J. F. (1997). DSM-IV and culturally sensitive diagnosis: Some observations for counselors. *Journal of Counseling & Development, 75*, 392–398.

Smither, R., & Rodriguez-Giegling, M. (1982). Personality, demographics, and acculturation of Vietnamese and Nicaraguan refugees to the United States. *International Journal of Psychology, 17*, 19–25.

Smitherman, G. (1995). *Black talk.* Boston: Houghton Mifflin.

Spitzer, R. L., & Endicott, J. (1978). *The schedule for affective disorders and schizophrenia* (3rd ed.). New York: New York State Psychiatric Institute.

Sue, D. W., & Sue, D. (2003). *Counseling the culturally different: Theory and practice* (4th ed.). New York: John Wiley & Sons.

Sue, D. W., & Sue, D. (2007). *Counseling the culturally different: Theory and practice* (5th ed.). New York: John Wiley & Sons.

Suinn, R. M., Ahuna, C., & Khoo, G. (1992). The Suinn-Lew Asian Self-Identification Acculturation Scale: Concurrent and factorial validation. *Educational and Psychological Measurement, 52*, 1041–1046.

Suinn, R. M., Rickard-Figueroa, K., Lew, S., & Vigil, S. (1987). The Suinn-Lew Asian Self-Identity Acculturation Scale: An initial report. *Education and Psychological Measurement, 47*, 401–407.

Szapocznik, J., Scopetta, M. A., Arnalde, M., & Kurtines, W. (1978). Cuban value structure: Treatment implications. *Journal of Consulting and Clinical Psychology, 46*, 961–970.

Westermeyer, J. (1985). Psychiatric diagnosis across cultural boundaries. *American Journal of Psychiatry, 142*, 798–805.

Westermeyer, J. J. (1993). Cross-cultural psychiatric assessment. In A. C. Gaw (Ed.), *Culture, ethnicity, and mental illness* (pp. 125–144). Washington, DC: American Psychiatric Press.

Wilkinson, C. B., & Spurlock, J. (1986). The mental health of Black Americans: Psychiatric diagnosis and treatment. In C. B. Wilkinson (Ed.), *Ethnic psychiatry* (pp. 1–59). New York: Plenum Medical Book Company.

Witko, T. M. (Ed.). (2006a). *Mental health care for urban Indians.* Washington, DC: American Psychological Association.

Witko, T. M. (2006b). A framework for working with American Indian parents. In T. M. Witko (Ed.), *Mental health care for urban Indians* (pp. 155–171). Washington, DC: American Psychological Association.

Wong-Rieger, D., & Quintana, D. (1987). Comparative acculturation of Southeast Asians and Hispanic immigrants and sojourners. *Journal of Cross-Cultural Psychology, 18,* 145–162.

Yamamoto, J. (1986). Therapy for Asian Americans and Pacific Islanders. In C. B. Wilkinson (Ed.), *Ethnic psychiatry* (pp. 89–141). New York: Plenum Medical Book Company.

Yamamoto, J., Lam, J., Choi, W. I., Reece, S., Lo, S., Hahn, D., et al. (1982). The psychiatric status of schedule for Asian-Americans. *American Journal of Psychiatry, 139,* 1181–1184.

Yamamoto, J., Silva, J. A., Justice, L. R., Chang, C. Y., & Leong, G. B. (1993). Cross-cultural psychotherapy. In A. C. Gaw (Ed.), *Culture, ethnicity, and mental illness* (pp. 101–124). Washington, DC: American Psychiatric Press.

Zalewski, C., & Green, R. L. (1996). Multicultural use of the MMPI-2. In L. A. Zuzuki, P. J. Meller, & G. Ponterotto (Eds.), *Handbook of multicultural assessment: Clinical, psychological, and educational implications* (pp. 77–114). San Francisco: Jossey-Bass.

Zea, M. C., Asner-Self, K. K., Birman, D., & Buki, L. P. (2003). The Abbreviated Multidimensional Acculturation Scale: Empirical validation with two Latino/Latina samples. *Cultural Diversity and Ethnic Minority Psychology, 9,* 107–126.

5

Case Conceptualizations of Mental Health Counselors
Implications for the Delivery of Culturally Competent Care

Madonna G. Constantine, Marie L. Miville, Mai M. Kindaichi, and Delila Owens

Case conceptualization and treatment planning are clinical judgment tasks essential to mental health professionals' roles (Eells & Lombart, 2003; Eells, Lombart, Kendjelic, Turner, & Lucas, 2005). Case conceptualization requires clinicians to interpret diagnostic information, client history, anticipated process dynamics, and other salient issues into their treatment decisions and goals (Falvey, 2001). Case conceptualization also offers therapists the opportunity to rely on existing psychotherapeutic theory and research to guide their developing understanding of clients' needs and experiences (Meier, 1999). In addition, this exercise is an information-processing task in which new knowledge structures interface with existing heuristics to synthesize newer and more accurate clinical conceptualizations (Mayfield, Kardash, & Kivlighan, 1999). In light of the increasing cultural diversity of the United States (U.S. Census Bureau, 2004), mental health professionals' ability to recognize, integrate, and synthesize racial–cultural information into conceptualizations of the complex precipitating factors of clients' concerns is paramount to these clinicians' delivery of culturally competent mental health services (Constantine & Ladany, 2000; Roysircar, 2004).

In this chapter, we address the importance of integrating cultural issues into counselors' conceptualizations of clients' presenting concerns and illustrate how these conceptualizations have direct implications for clinical practice. We also discuss how mental health professionals' racial and cultural biases could hinder their clinical conceptualizations of the presenting concerns of clients of color and, thereby, detrimentally affect the processes and outcomes of therapy with clients of color. A case example is provided to illustrate how counselors' racial and cultural biases could affect their clinical conceptualizations of clients of color and to exemplify the importance of integrating salient racial and cultural information into the context of clients' presenting concerns. In addition, we propose a taxonomy that illustrates how various theoretical orientations to counseling might consider and integrate cultural issues into case conceptualizations in a culturally competent manner. Last, implications and recommendations for enhancing mental health professionals' and trainees' culturally competent case conceptualization ability are delineated.

Why Is Integrating Cultural Issues into Case Conceptualizations Important?

Based on our clinical experiences, there are several rationales that undergird the importance of considering and integrating cultural issues into case conceptualizations:

1. Although the majority of counseling and mental health practitioners in the United States are White (e.g., D'Andrea & Daniels, 1997), the landscape of the country's population has become increasingly racially and culturally diverse (Miville et al., 1999; U.S. Census Bureau, 2004). Moreover, given the diversity of social locations and attitudes about cultural group memberships, it can be argued that all counseling and psychotherapy should be considered multicultural to some degree (American Psychological Association [APA], 2003). Therefore, it is likely that mental health professionals and psychotherapy trainees will provide psychological services to clients from varied racial and cultural groups during the course of their professional careers.

It is vital for practitioners, trainees, and supervisors to recognize and address how clients' experiences of race and culture, in addition to their age, religion, gender, socioeconomic status, ability status, and sexual orientation, shape their clinical presentations as well as inform treatment approaches.

2. Racial and ethnic identities may be particularly salient for many people of color, to the extent that these identities take precedence over other aspects of cultural identity and group membership in certain contexts (Miville, Constantine, Baysden, & So-Lloyd, 2005; Miville & Ferguson, 2004). Additionally, race and ethnicity influence how all individuals experience the world and are experienced in it. For people of color, systems of racism have served to elevate the status and privilege of White people and deny people of color, particularly African Americans, equal access to resources. Not only do race, ethnicity, and other cultural variables influence how clients experience and are experienced in the social world, but they also influence how systems of racial privilege implicitly exist within the context of therapeutic relationships. The importance of therapists' attending to racial and cultural issues in their clinical formulations of clients' experiences is an ethical issue (APA, 2003).

3. Clients of color may present with psychological stressors that are endemic to sociocultural factors, such as racial discrimination. These stressors often are masked as psychological concerns, such as depression and anxiety, and even physical symptoms, such as headaches or stomachaches. Indeed, a potential source of tension and stress for clients of color is attributing personal reasons or deficiencies to problems that are systemically induced. Moreover, some clients may be quite knowledgeable about the external causes of their psychological issues and may view therapists who do not share this worldview with skepticism and even disdain. These clients are likely at the highest risk of attrition from treatment leading to the unfortunate outcome that their psychological concerns may go untreated. Finally, clients may overattribute their problems to external causes and minimize their personal responsibility as a potential area for change. Therapists who do not consider the influence of race and culture on their clients' experiences may cause them to feel marginalized and invalidated in a variety of ways, leading to the re-experience of racial–cultural trauma and further psychological distress.

4. The synthesis of racial–cultural information into case conceptualizations could positively shape some therapists' intervention

approaches. By approaching clients in holistic ways, attending to racial–cultural issues relevant to systemic challenges (e.g., discrimination) as well as individual concerns, therapists can help their clients develop a more realistic framework for dealing with problems in their lives.

5. More complex case conceptualizations that are prototypical of experts tend to articulate multiple hypotheses about the origins of clients' presenting concerns and how to attend effectively to those concerns. Racial and cultural information about oneself and others are important sources for developing these multiple hypotheses. Information regarding this area is complex in and of itself, reflecting issues of oppression, such as prejudice and discrimination, belief and values structures, behavioral expectations, and coping strategies and other treatment interventions. Therapists should consider the complex and multiple influences of race and culture in clients' lives and address such complexities in their case conceptualizations.

Racial and Cultural Biases of Mental Health Professionals: Their Influences on Case Conceptualizations

Mental health professionals rely on different sources of information upon which to ground their case conceptualizations, formulations, and clinical diagnoses. These various sources undoubtedly are influenced by racial and cultural biases, as well as attitudinal preferences (e.g., Bowers & Bieschke, 2005; Burkard & Knox, 2004; Gushue, 2004). Although some therapists are mindful of the impact of racial and cultural biases on clinical diagnoses (Mead, Hoenshil, & Singh, 1997), those who fail to recognize the potential effects of misdiagnosing clients (e.g., Gushue, 2004) as a function of these biases provide a disservice to the field and potentially harm their clients.

The expression of racial and cultural biases in the United States has become more covert in present-day society (e.g., Abreu, 2001; Dovidio & Gaertner, 1986). In recent decades, some researchers and theoreticians have suggested the notion of color-blind racial attitudes to describe an individual's belief that race should not and does not matter. Although these attitudes are viewed by some as admirable, they mask the harmful and continuing effects of historical racism (APA, 2003; Neville et al., 2000). The omission of racial or cultural information in case conceptualizations could reflect some mental health professionals' assumptions that race and social location may not be salient to clients' intrapsychic or interpersonal experiences. Regardless of their racial or ethnic group membership, therapists who have not adequately explored racial or cultural issues in their own lives may overlook potentially salient racial issues in the clinical presentations and experiences of their clients of color. This lack of exploration may result in misattributions about the origins or intensity of these clients' concerns. By neglecting to consider issues of race and culture, as well as other social identities, mental health professionals risk misdiagnosing these clients and developing treatment strategies that have limited applicability to and effectiveness with these clients. Furthermore, although mental health professionals may not endorse racial or cultural stereotypes explicitly (Miville et al., 1999), they may unconsciously apply lower standards of psychological adjustment and functioning to people of color and attribute clients' difficulties according to their race (Gushue, 2004).

Therapists with limited exposure to multicultural training might focus on intrapsychic factors contributing to the presenting concerns of clients of color and ignore important social-contextual factors that are essential in understanding clients' clinical symptomatology (Atkinson, Thompson, & Grant, 1993). That is, racial or cultural biases may influence the degree to which mental health professionals hold clients of color responsible for their psychological distress (Burkard & Knox, 2004), despite the fact that external factors (for example, racial discrimination) may be contributing to their clients' presenting problems.

In general, mental health professionals who operate from both conscious and unconscious racial–cultural stereotypes may exhibit response biases that influence their clinical impressions (e.g., Abreu, 1999). For example, Constantine (2007) reported that African American clients who perceived greater degrees of unconscious racism from White therapists also tended to report lower perceptions of the therapeutic working alliance. These negative working alliance perceptions were predictive of lower levels of client satisfaction with counseling. Thus, therapists' unconscious discriminatory attitudes and beliefs can profoundly affect various psychotherapy processes and outcomes.

Multicultural case conceptualization ability, or therapists' skills in integrating salient racial or cultural information into their conceptualizations of etiology and treatment plans for clients, reflects therapists' recognition that racial and cultural factors are central to clients' experiences (Ladany, Inman, Constantine, & Hofheinz, 1997). Several investigators (e.g., Constantine & Ladany, 2000) have examined multicultural case conceptualization ability as an aspect of demonstrated, rather than anticipated, multicultural counseling competence. Further, therapists' participation in multicultural coursework has been shown to positively predict their multicultural case conceptualization ability (Constantine, 2001a, 2001b). Multicultural case conceptualization ability has been positively related to both empathy and tolerance of other ethnic groups (Constantine, 2001b; Constantine & Gushue, 2003). From this body of research, it appears that therapists' ability to integrate cultural concerns into case conceptualizations could be affected by their ability to take the perspective of others and by their attitudes about racial and ethnic differences.

How Racial and Cultural Biases Influence Case Conceptualization: A Case Example

Jennifer is a 46-year-old, recently divorced African American woman who lives with her mother and son in a small two-bedroom apartment. Jennifer works as a legal secretary in a mostly White law firm. Jennifer enjoys her job for the most part, but at times feels indirect pressure to perform better than her peers to show that she can competently do her job. Her son, Leonard, age 15, has been doing poorly in school lately, despite his previous excellent academic performance. Since the death of Jennifer's father 2 years ago, Jennifer's mother, Martha, has been living with Leonard and Jennifer. Jennifer's father had left a small pension for Martha, but not one sufficient for her to live on her own. Jennifer presents in therapy with headaches and irritability, as well as anxiety and depression. She wonders where she has gone wrong.

Etiology Conceptualization   A number of conscious and unconscious biases could affect a mental health professional's conceptualization of Jennifer's case. Some mental health professionals might focus uniquely on gender issues pertaining to Jennifer's situation, minimizing or ignoring the impact that race and racism might have on, for example, her job or Leonard's educational goals. Another potential bias might arise from an assumption that mental health professionals (for example, those who are female or divorced or both) would "understand" racial biases inherent in this case because they understand gender biases. Similarly, mental health professionals might unconsciously perceive Jennifer according to a general stereotype of African American women as "strong" and, thus, not acknowledge her need for emotional support or to process her feelings about divorce and her family. On the other hand, some mental health professionals may approach Jennifer's case from a "color-blind" perspective, particularly because Jennifer only briefly addressed racial issues in her initial presentation. Such an approach would ignore racial issues and focus, for example, on how Jennifer might find friends like herself at work. Moreover, some mental health professionals may operate from a biased perspective that presumes financial difficulties of people of color (i.e., wanting to help "the disadvantaged"). These professionals may offer to see her for a reduced fee without fully assessing her financial situation.

Treatment Conceptualization   Biased conceptualizations regarding the origins of Jennifer's presenting concerns could affect some mental health professionals' treatment choices and suggested goals for Jennifer and her family. For example, Leonard's difficulties in school might be framed within a context of adjustment to changes in the family system. However, an unconscious bias assuming lower academic achievement for young African American men may cause some mental health professionals to perceive his lower academic achievement as unproblematic. A more adaptive approach would include obtaining help for Leonard regarding his school performance so that his future educational and career choices are not harmed or delayed. His feelings about his family and emerging identity also should be explored and treated at the same time.

Another potential bias may emerge from a therapist's Eurocentric framework or value structures regarding what constitutes a "normal" (i.e., nuclear) family. This bias may be subtly expressed during treatment by helping Jennifer explore "options" regarding her mother's presence in the household. The unconscious implication of this exploration is to communicate that there is something wrong or unhealthy about three generations living in one household. Indeed, although Jennifer might be feeling somewhat cramped in her current living situation, fulfilling important family obligations by providing critical support to her widowed mother may actually serve as an important coping mechanism regarding her self-esteem and general self-efficacy.

Mental health professionals also may hold stereotypic assumptions regarding the importance of religion for people of color and, as a result, inaccurately assess its role in the lives of their clients. Counselors may simply ask about churchgoing, indirectly communicating to Jennifer that she should have some attachment to a church group, rather than determining whether she already has a supportive group of family and friends.

Outcomes   Given the racial biases in both etiology and treatment conceptualizations, outcomes based on these biases also are likely. One potential outcome is that Jennifer simply might not return to therapy. Instead of speaking directly to her therapist about her negative reactions, she could choose to drop out and pursue other interventions or, worse, not seek out psychological help from other sources.

A more subtle impact on outcomes might result from less effective, biased interventions. For example, if Jennifer works with a mental health professional who focuses on the impact of divorce on women, she may process gender issues, but not those arising from issues of race and racism (e.g., her on-the-job pressure or even housing discrimination as an African American woman heading a household). If Jennifer accepts her therapist's perception that indeed, "not everything is about race" she may inappropriately blame herself for difficulties she encounters in her work setting. Indeed, Jennifer might come to believe that it is acceptable for her to always work harder than her peers. This potentially maladaptive belief may lead Jennifer to falsely expect greater rewards, such as increased salary and promotions for her performance. Thus, it is critical for therapists to help Jennifer explore the implications of "working hard" within both racial and individual contexts.

Culturally Competent Case Conceptualizations: Issues and Considerations by Theoretical Orientation to Counseling

For most mental health professionals, counseling theoretical orientations form the major frameworks by which to define and establish professional relationships with clients, identify possible goals and treatment interventions, and evaluate subsequent progress or outcomes in therapy. In the past century, a plethora of theoretical orientations have been promulgated in the literature and include psychodynamic, humanistic, and cognitive-behavioral theories (Constantine, 2001b). Unfortunately, many of these theories have been critiqued regarding their general failure to incorporate racial–ethnic issues. For example, Ivey, D'Andrea, Ivey, and Simek-Morgan (2007) identified the following limitations of the traditional counseling theoretical orientations: (1) dichotomizing important developmental aspects into discrete parts; (2) containing culturally biased (Western) perspectives emphasizing autonomy, separateness, and individuality; and (3) underemphasizing social-contextual forces in the lives of most clients that may serve as important resources for change. Despite these limitations, theoretical orientations provide paradigms for conceptualizing clients' presenting concerns and facilitating interventions and outcomes.

In the past decade, several theoretical approaches have been revised to incorporate racial–ethnic aspects that can help professionals more effectively conceptualize their clients. For example, psychodynamic approaches typically emphasize the importance of the past in understanding both the present and the future (e.g., forms of abuse). Recent psychodynamic approaches have begun to explore how past history includes not only events in individuals' lives, but also their families of origin as nested within a larger sociopolitical context (Ivey et al., 2007). This approach might help mental health professionals to more effectively identify cultural aspects of presenting problems. Psychodynamic perspectives also emphasize that early negative experiences with others may lead to attachment problems in adolescence and adulthood, or, more seriously, to the development of personality disorders. Thus, formulating attachment on the bases of both family and communities may help better identify potential causes of presenting symptoms as well as describe possible treatment and outcomes.

Similarly, cognitive-behavioral therapy (CBT) can be used to more accurately identify culturally oriented symptoms associated with presenting concerns. Tucker (1999) suggested that with African American and other youth of color, it may be more effective to simply describe behaviors that may be problematic for self and others, along with socioeconomic and cultural contexts. By doing so, there is lower likelihood of misdiagnosing or erroneously conceptualizing these children's problems. For example, Tucker noted that so-called behavior problems may in actuality be based on behaviors that are protective, as might be the case in threatening or impoverished situations. She further suggests that *not* incorporating social and economic context "renders diagnoses [and case conceptualizations] for African American children suspect" (p. 41). Other cognitive-behaviorists have suggested explicitly identifying cultural issues in the thoughts and attitudes that are the focus of CBT, as well as conceptualizing client thoughts and behaviors in the larger social context. One of the primary leaders of CBT, Albert Ellis, added context (C) to his theoretical approach, REBCT (rational–emotive–behavior–contextual therapy; Ivey et al., 2007).

White (2002) provided a step-by-step approach of how postmodern/narrative therapy techniques might be incorporated with case conceptualization, such that mental health professionals "find a balance" between traditional case conceptualization and "a postmodern skepticism" (p. 271). She also suggested that case conceptualization must necessarily incorporate the social context to be multiculturally sensitive. White proposed that mental health professionals simultaneously conceptualize their clients from their own perspectives, while helping clients to tell their stories. This storytelling loop can help to create a more accurate picture of clients' situations. In addition, clients are asked to identify strengths and resources, both internal and external; this process also can lead to more effective conceptualization.

Some research (Constantine, 2001a, 2001b) has indicated that having an eclectic/integrative theoretical orientation to counseling may be linked with higher multicultural counseling competence and better multicultural case conceptualization skills. Constantine noted that being eclectic might reflect greater flexibility in utilizing multiple theoretical perspectives, which may be helpful in working with clients of color. Ivey and Ivey (1998) described developmental counseling and therapy (DCT) as one integrative theoretical framework that incorporates elements of psychodynamic, cognitive-behavioral, and existential-humanistic theories, and is simultaneously oriented toward multicultural issues: "The culturally centered professional in the DCT ... works *with* rather than *on* the client" (p. 336; italics in the original). Ivey and Ivey suggested that DCT can facilitate a more effective understanding of presenting problems, such as depression, "as a logical response to developmental concerns" in several dimensions (e.g., racism), rather than a pathological illness that is located within an individual. For example, many native populations often are disproportionately viewed as "paranoid," which Ivey and Ivey contended "may be a very logical response to oppressive environmental conditions" (p. 337).

In considering the role of theoretical orientation to counseling with regard to clinical case conceptualization, we offer the taxonomy in Table 5.1 to help guide clinicians from common counseling theoretical orientations in considering and integrating cultural issues into their case conceptualizations.

The taxonomy identifies important constructs from each theoretical orientation and possible relevant cultural considerations. For instance, object relations theory, a modern reformulation of psychoanalytic theory, emphasizes separation and individuation as important aspects of well-functioning, a presumption being the healthy adults must be clearly separated from their parents (Nichols & Schwartz, 2001). Although healthy adult functioning is important cross-culturally, its presumed indicators, particularly separation and individuation, may look different across racial–ethnic groups. Many adult children may house elderly parents, for cultural, economic, and healthcare reasons (as in the case of Jennifer) rather than maladaptive ones. Socioeconomic circumstances as well as immigration and language status also may play a role in the development of multigenerational households that are important to

TABLE 5.1
Taxonomy Guiding Clinicians from Theory to Culturally Inclusive Case Conceptualizations

Theoretical Orientation to Counseling or Therapy	Key Constructs Relevant to Cultural Issues of Presenting Concerns	Pertinent Issues to Consider in Forming Case Conceptualizations	Sample Summary Statements of Cultural Issues Integrated in Case Conceptualizations by Theoretical Orientation
• Psychodynamic, psychoanalytic, and object relations	• Individuation/ separation • Mirroring • Transference • Countertransference	• Cultural norms • Extended or multigenerational family • Race/ethnicity and associated identities of counselor • Race/ethnicity and associated identities of client(s) • Acculturation	• Cultural norms may dictate what appears to be healthy or unhealthy attachment across generations. • Development of both transference and countertransference may be affected by oppression and privilege issues, cultural values and norms, and customs.
• Cognitive-behavioral	• Maladaptive vs. adaptive cognitions and behaviors	• Perspectives of clients (e.g., assess how cognitions or behaviors may be adaptive) • Perspectives of clients' families • Social contexts • Outcomes of behaviors • Acculturation	• What appear as maladaptive cognitions (e.g., hostility toward teachers) or behaviors (skipping school) may mask adaptive or protective behaviors (unsafe or racist school, need to care for sick family members).
• Humanistic	• Genuineness • Active empathy	• Race/ethnicity and associated identities of counselor • Race/ethnicity and associated identities of client(s)	• Genuineness and empathy should be expressed in the context of the counselor's knowledge and willingness to explore impact of race and culture on the therapeutic relationship.
• Systemic	• Triangles • Boundaries	• Extended or multigenerational families • Immigration issues • Language • Impact of discrimination	• Triangles may exist across several generations (including grandparents, uncles/aunts, and godparents). • Cultural norms should be incorporated in establishing healthy boundaries. • Cultural adjustment issues also may frame bases of triangles (e.g., political refugee status differently affecting grandparents and grandchildren).

consider. Moreover, being aware of cultural issues and biases can help counselors better identify potential problems, such as role and boundary violations, among clients and families of color to which, despite their flexibilities and resiliencies, they may be vulnerable (Boyd-Franklin, 2003).

In sum, considering cultural issues from theoretical orientations may help to minimize racial and ethnic biases that may arise, perhaps unintentionally, during case conceptualization. Simply describing behaviors, thoughts, and feelings, rather than attaching a diagnostic label, will help to minimize the possibility of bias in initially diagnosing presenting concerns. Equally important is the emphasis on social context, and exploring stressors in clients' lives that may lead to "logical responses" or personality styles to damaging situations. Exploring contextual variables also may help mental health professionals gain a genuine appreciation for the strength and resilience of their clients of color that may go unnoticed in the face of unexplored negative stereotypes and affective states by mental health professionals (Greene, 2004).

Implications and Recommendations

Promoting the multicultural case conceptualization ability of mental health professionals and trainees is a priority whose importance is underscored by the changing demographics in client populations. Further, research and scholarship has yielded findings that therapists' personal attitudes about race and culture can predict their ability to effectively conceptualize the presenting concerns and subsequent treatment plans of clients of color (e.g., Constantine & Gushue, 2003). Because participation in multicultural training activities consistently has been shown to predict more complex multicultural case conceptualizations (e.g., Constantine, 2001a, 2001b; Constantine & Gushue, 2003), the following recommendations highlight multicultural training experiences as a vital means to enhance therapists' and trainees' ability to integrate racial–cultural concerns into their case conceptualizations:

1. Mental health professionals and trainees should seek continuing education experiences that are designed toward deepening their cultural self-understanding. Through learning how their cultural group memberships have influenced their worldviews and afforded them cultural or racial privileges they may take for granted, they may further develop

their understanding of the myriad influences of race and culture on their clients. Moreover, it is vital that therapists and other psychological service providers identify and pursue ways to help them address possible racist and culturally intolerant attitudes and beliefs, and commit themselves to such exploration as their careers progress (Constantine & Gushue, 2003). Experiential continuing education opportunities are especially important in achieving these goals.

2. Sperry (2005) asserted that case conceptualization can be learned through didactic instruction, supervision, and continued practice. Thus, with regard to multicultural case conceptualization, mental health professionals and trainees may choose to obtain clinical supervision with a senior member of the field who has expertise in working effectively with culturally diverse clients. In the context of supervision, supervisors may engage their clients actively in case conceptualization activities in which specific attention is drawn to how race and culture influence the etiology of clients' presenting concerns, as well as how trainees and therapists appreciate racial and cultural dynamics in therapeutic moments and in determined interventions. Further, trainees and therapists may employ self-awareness about their needs as practitioners, and how their multicultural supervision needs may change as a function of greater experience.

3. Prieto and Scheel (2002) outlined a detailed guide for trainees to use comprehensive case notes and documentation as a foundation for developing case conceptualizations. Goals of their suggested method include increasing trainees' ability to ascertain facts about the client, develop diagnoses or understanding of clients' concerns, form meaningful treatment plans related to the clients' concerns, be aware of in-session dynamics, understand dynamics as they progress across sessions, adjust therapeutic goals and interventions as the relationship builds, and integrate relevant criteria to evaluate the usefulness and effectiveness of counseling for their clients. Represented by the acronym STIPS, the format they developed consists of five major sections: signs and symptoms (i.e., clients' level of functioning, and presence or absence of diagnostic indications), topics of discussion (i.e., major content developments since the previous session), interventions (i.e., strategies employed to address identified concerns), progress and plan (e.g., treatment targets for future sessions as informed by current sessions' developments), and special issues (e.g., "red-flag" concerns, such as abuse or threats of self

harm, that require immediate attention). The STIPS method of case notes reflects a structure and organization that inform longitudinal case conceptualization.

With regard to the integration of race-related and cultural information in case conceptualization, similar attention should be drawn to case documentation such that multicultural case conceptualization does not emerge from a vacuum. Through the integration of racial–cultural information in case documentation, trainees, therapists, and supervisors are encouraged to consider and attend to the influence of cultural factors on clients' histories, experiences, present-day concerns, and therapeutic interventions.

4. Mental health professionals should enhance their multicultural case conceptualization ability by being cognizant about the power of psychological diagnosis. Mental health professionals may rely on heuristics based in clinical orientations and diagnostic references when conceptualizing the etiology and treatment options for clients; the access to such cognitive shortcuts may lead novice therapists and therapists who have not challenged their multicultural competence to neglect consideration about how racial–cultural biases could be operative. Mental health professionals and trainees should seek opportunities to attend hospital grand rounds or case presentations held by institutions that tend to attract communities of color to learn more about the practice and power of diagnoses regarding clients and communities of color.

5. Eells et al. (2005) found that the ability to devise elaborate treatment plans differentiated expert therapists from experienced therapists. Additionally, Constantine (2001b) found that multicultural treatment conceptualizations were significantly predicted by both cognitive and affective empathy. Attending specifically to treatment plan development with clients of color may offer opportunities for trainees to bridge the gap between multicultural knowledge and skills. For example, mental health professionals should strive to build their knowledge of culturally specific therapeutic techniques (e.g., *cuento* therapy; Constantino, Malgady, & Rogler, 1986) and models of cultural worldviews and values (e.g., *Nguzo Saba*; Karenga, 1988), which could inform culturally congruent and relevant treatment approaches with certain clients based on acculturation status, spiritual orientation, or other intragroup variables.

Conclusion

Although multicultural counseling may be viewed by some as a theoretical approach separate from leading schools of psychotherapy (e.g., psychoanalytic, cognitive-behavioral, rational-emotive behavioral therapy, and family systems), it is vital that mental health practitioners, regardless of the primary theoretical orientation that they espouse, integrate salient cultural issues into their conceptualizations and treatment approaches of culturally diverse individuals. Providing culturally competent and responsive service often begins with an initial awareness of the far-reaching impact of clinicians' covert biases evidenced in clinical diagnoses and evaluations. Thus, it behooves clinicians to be mindful of how their assumptions of normality and the origins of psychological malady may reflect Western cultural norms and may have limited application in conceptualizing the treatment concerns of individuals across racial–cultural groups. The taxonomy and recommendations presented in this chapter underscore how mental health professionals could effectively integrate racial–cultural information into case conceptualizations. Because comprehensive case conceptualizations inform treatment plans and expectations for the course of therapy, clinicians must consider the primary influences of racial, cultural, and environmental forces in clients' lives so as to provide optimum care to these individuals.

References

Abreu, J. M. (1999). Conscious and nonconscious African American stereotypes: Impact on first impression and diagnostic ratings by therapists. *Journal of Consulting and Clinical Psychology, 67,* 387–393.

Abreu, J. M. (2001). Theory and research on stereotypes and perceptual bias: A didactic resource for multicultural counseling trainers. *The Counseling Psychologist, 29,* 487–512.

American Psychiatric Association. (2000). *Diagnostic and statistical manual of mental disorders* (4th ed., text rev.). Washington, DC: Author.

American Psychological Association (APA). (2003). Guidelines for multicultural education, training, research, practice, and organizational change for psychologists. *American Psychologist, 58,* 377–402.

Atkinson, D. R., Thompson, C. E., & Grant, S. K. (1993). A three-dimensional model for counseling racial/ethnic minorities. *The Counseling Psychologist, 21,* 257–277.

Bowers, A. M. V., & Bieschke, K. J. (2005). Psychologists' clinical evaluations and attitudes: An examination of the influence of gender and sexual orientation. *Professional Psychology: Research and Practice, 36*, 97–103.

Boyd-Franklin, N. (2003). *Black families in therapy: Understanding the African American experience* (2nd ed.). New York: Guilford.

Burkard, A. W., & Knox, S. (2004). Effect of therapist color-blindness on empathy and attributions in cross-cultural counseling. *Journal of Counseling Psychology, 51*, 387–397.

Constantine, M. G. (2001a). Independent and interdependent self-construals as predictors of multicultural case conceptualization ability in counsellor trainees. *Counselling Psychology Quarterly, 14*, 33–42.

Constantine, M. G. (2001b). Multicultural training, theoretical orientation, empathy, and multicultural case conceptualization ability in counselors. *Journal of Mental Health Counseling, 23*, 357–372.

Constantine, M. G. (2001c). Theoretical orientation, empathy, and multicultural counseling competence in school counselor trainees. *Professional School Counseling, 4*, 342–348.

Constantine, M. G. (2007). Racial microaggressions against African American clients in cross-cultural counseling relationships. *Journal of Counseling Psychology, 54*, 1–16.

Constantine, M. G., & Gushue, G. V. (2003). School counselors' ethnic tolerance attitudes and racism attitudes as predictors of their multicultural case conceptualization of an immigrant student. *Journal of Counseling and Development, 81*, 185–190.

Constantine, M. G., & Ladany, N. (2000). Self-report multicultural counseling competence scales: Their relation to social desirability attitudes and multicultural case conceptualization ability. *Journal of Counseling Psychology, 47*, 155–164.

Costantino, G., Malgady, R. G., & Rogler, L. H. (1986). Cuento therapy: A culturally sensitive modality for Puerto Rican children. *Journal of Consulting and Clinical Psychology, 54*, 639–645.

D'Andrea, M., & Daniels, J. (1997). Multicultural counseling supervision: Central issues, theoretical considerations, and practical strategies. In D. B. Pope-Davis & H. L. K. Coleman (Eds.), *Multicultural counseling competencies: Assessment, education and training, and supervision* (pp. 290–309). Thousand Oaks, CA: Sage.

Dovidio, J. F., & Gaertner, S. L. (Eds.). (1986). *Prejudice, discrimination, and racism.* San Diego, CA: Academic Press.

Eells, T. C., & Lombart, K. G. (2003). Case formulation and treatment concepts among novice, experienced, and expert cognitive-behavioral and psychodynamic therapists. *Psychotherapy Research, 13*, 187–204.

Eells, T. C., Lombart, K. G., Kendjelic, E. M., Turner, L. C., & Lucas, C. P. (2005). The quality of psychotherapy case formulations: A comparison of expert, experienced, and novice cognitive-behavioral and psychodynamic therapists. *Journal of Consulting and Clinical Psychology, 73*, 579–589.

Falvey, J. E. (2001). Clinical judgment in case conceptualization and treatment planning across mental health disciplines. *Journal of Counseling and Development, 79*, 292–303.

Gushue, G. V. (2004). Race, color-blind racial attitudes, and judgments about mental health: A shifting standards perspective. *Journal of Counseling Psychology, 51*, 398–407.

Ivey, A. E., D'Andrea, M., Ivey, M. B., & Simek-Morgan, L. (2007). *Theories of counseling and psychotherapy: A multicultural perspective* (6th ed.). Boston: Pearson.

Ivey, A. E., & Ivey, M. B. (1998). Reframing *DSM-IV*: Positive strategies from developmental counseling and therapy. *Journal of Counseling and Development, 76,* 334–350.

Karenga, M. R. (1988). *The African American holiday of Kwanzaa.* Los Angeles: University of Sankore Press.

Ladany, N., Inman, A. G., Constantine, M. G., & Hofheinz, E. W. (1997). Supervisee multicultural case conceptualization ability and self-reported multicultural competence as functions of supervisee racial identity and supervisor focus. *Journal of Counseling Psychology, 41,* 284–293.

Mayfield, W. A., Kardash, C. M., & Kivlighan, D. M., Jr. (1999). Differences in experienced and novice counselors' knowledge structures about clients: Implications for case conceptualization. *Journal of Counseling Psychology, 46,* 504–514.

Mead, M. A., Hoenshil, T. H., & Singh, K. (1997). How the DSM system is used by clinical counselors: A national study. *Journal of Mental Health Counseling, 19,* 383–401.

Meier, S. T. (1999). Training the practitioner-scientist: Bridging case conceptualization, assessment, and intervention. *The Counseling Psychologist, 27,* 846–869.

Miville, M. L., Constantine, M. G., Baysden, M. F., & So-Lloyd, G. (2005). Chameleon changes: An exploration of racial identity themes of multiracial people. *Journal of Counseling Psychology, 52,* 507–516.

Miville, M. L., & Ferguson, A. D. (2004). Impossible "choices": Identity and values at a crossroad. *The Counseling Psychologist, 32,* 760–770.

Miville, M. L., Gelso, C. G., Liu, W., Pannu, R., Holloway, P., & Fuertes, J. (1999). Appreciating similarities and valuing differences: The Miville-Guzman Universality-Diversity Scale. *Journal of Counseling Psychology, 46,* 291–307.

Neville, H. A., Lilly, R. L., Duran, G., Lee, R. M., & Browne, L. (2000). Construction and initial validation of the Color-Blind Racial Attitudes Scale (CoBRAS). *Journal of Counseling Psychology, 47,* 59–70.

Nichols, M. P., & Schwartz, R. C. (2001). *The essentials of family therapy.* Boston: Allyn & Bacon.

Prieto, L. R., & Scheel, K. R. (2002). Using case documentation to strengthen counselor trainees' case conceptualization skills. *Journal of Counseling and Development, 80,* 11–21.

Roysircar, G. (2004). Cultural self-awareness assessment: Practice examples from psychology training. *Professional Psychology: Research and Practice, 35,* 658–666.

Sperry, L. (2005). Case conceptualizations: The missing link between theory and practice. *The Family Journal: Counseling and Therapy for Couples and Families, 13,* 71–76.

Tucker, C. M. (1999). *African American children: A self-empowerment approach to modifying behavior problems and preventing academic failure.* Needham Heights, MA: Allyn & Bacon.

U. S. Census Bureau. (2004). *Annual estimates of the population by race alone and Hispanic or Latino origin for the United States and States: July 1, 2004.* Retrieved December 6, 2005, from http://www.census.gov/popest/states/asrh/tables/SC-EST2004-04.xls

White, V. E. (2002). Developing counseling objectives and empowering clients: A strength-based intervention. *Journal of Mental Health Counseling, 24,* 270–279.

6

Treatment Planning in a Multicultural Context
Some Suggestions for Counselors and Psychotherapists

Laura R. Johnson and Daya Singh Sandhu

In an increasingly multicultural environment, mental health professionals must develop awareness, knowledge, and skills for creating culturally congruent and effective plans with a broad array of clients. In this chapter we will discuss how clinicians can prepare treatment plans to work effectively with clients from diverse and unique cultural backgrounds, contexts, and perspectives. We will discuss how practitioners can attend to culture as it relates to both the content of the treatment plan as well as the processes involved in developing and negotiating the plan. We have lived, worked, and conducted research internationally, in addition to working with diverse cultural and language groups in the United States. We will draw on our research and clinical work in diverse settings and with diverse individuals to illustrate some of the issues that arise in treatment planning, demonstrate some of the strategies we have used, and also share some of the mistakes we have made in our own efforts toward culturally competent treatment planning.

Culturally Competent Treatment Planning

Treatment plans will ideally flow from a thorough case conceptualization based on the clinician's theoretical orientation that gives due attention to cultural, social, and other contextual factors (including the *Diagnostic and Statistical Manual of Mental Disorders* [*DSM–IV*] cultural formulation; see Chapter 4). Additionally, it is crucial to incorporate the client's goals and expectations into the treatment plan. The question of how, when, and to what extent to *bring in culture* is not easily answered, as culture's role and importance will vary from client to client and from one context to another. Finding the right balance between *mainstream* (i.e., Western European- and American-based) approaches to treatment and nontraditional approaches (i.e., non-Western, culture specific, indigenous) is a delicate and complex process requiring clinician awareness, knowledge, and skills. These are the components of cultural competence (see Sue, Arredondo, & McDavis, 1992), which we will discuss next as they apply specifically to treatment planning.

Awareness for Treatment Planning

To cultivate cultural *awareness* in treatment planning, clinicians must draw their attention to themselves. They must identify and study their own biases and assumptions about "what is best" for their clients. Acknowledging *the self* as a cultural being can help practitioners understand their personal biases, assumptions, and stereotypes about culturally diverse people, and how these beliefs may influence the treatment planning process. Though we strive to become conscious and reduce our own biases, prejudice, and ethnocentrism, as psychologists and other mental health professionals we are not immune to biased and stereotypical views that result from media exposure and a lack of contact with diverse others. When we lack knowledge and personal experiences with diverse others (described as cultural encapsulation; Wrenn, 1962) we tend to fill in these knowledge gaps with stereotypes that are often negative and potentially harmful.

Clinician's Personal Bias   As clinicians, our biases and stereotypes can interfere with our own ability to plan effective treatments, and also our ability to establish the credibility and rapport needed to carry out the plan. For instance, a counselor relying on negative stereotypes about African American adolescent males might have erroneous assumptions about an adolescent referred from the school system. The counselor might jump to the conclusion that the adolescent might have oppositional conduct disorder or that the referred client is poor, comes from an unsafe neighborhood, or lives in a maternal-headed household. These negative stereotypes could result in misdiagnoses and subsequent improper treatment (Barbarin, 1993). Clinicians should avoid making assumptions about a client's background or treatment needs based on stereotypes, as well as group-level cultural norms or stereotypes (for example, the client is a refugee and therefore should be treated for posttraumatic stress disorder [PTSD], or the client is African American and therefore treatment must address racism and spirituality; Paniagua, 2005).

Clients' Personal Biases   In the clinical setting it is also important for clinicians to be aware of biases that our clients may hold about us based on our ethnicity, cultural background, professional status, or other factors such as gender and age (Vasquez, 2005). For example, an ethnic minority client may expect a White counselor to be unable to help with concerns about racism, whereas an elderly client may feel that a young therapist lacks the life experience or wisdom to help him or her face existential or special gerontological issues of life. Some clients may expect us to act rather formally, as "experts" and to provide direct advice, rather than empowering them indirectly through informal or collaborative approaches. Some clients might have racist and stereotyped views against their therapist (whether majority or minority) that can interfere with their expectations for treatment benefit. As clinicians we need to become aware of our own ascribed credibility with the client and if it is low we must work toward enhancing our credibility, for example, through relationship building (see Chapter 7), through addressing cultural concerns and differences, or by adapting our style and approach (Hays, 2001; Okazaki, 2000).

Professional and Theoretical Bias   Awareness in treatment planning demands that we do not only identify our personal assumptions about clients and what treatments they need, but also those biases that are related to our training or theoretical orientation. As clinicians we must continually remind ourselves that our approach to thinking about cases and planning treatments is culturally embedded (Pedersen, 2004a). Generally speaking, our approaches to psychological education, research, training, and practice are based on a Western worldview of individualism.

In treatment planning, this plays out in the following ways: an emphasis on self-awareness, self-discovery, self-actualization, and self-fulfillment;

a focus on internal experiences, such as thoughts and emotions; a focus on intrapsychic concerns and conflicts; a focus on direct communication and expression of feelings; a focus on behavioral change; and a lack of attention to contextual factors. Clinicians will need to identify these and other biases in their training and in their approach to treatment. The majority of people in the world, including most ethnic minority groups in the United States, come from cultural backgrounds that are more collectivist in nature (Vontress, Johnson, & Epp, 1999). As such, clinicians should consider how Western views about treatment (e.g., what should be treated, whether it should be treated, and how it should be treated) as described may frequently be incongruous with the values and norms held by these culturally different clients.

Working against a client's cultural norms and values could result in inappropriate treatment or treatment nonadherence. It is also possible that in some cases, these treatments may produce some emotionally adverse *iatrogenic* effects. In such cases, culturally insensitive counselors might cause their clients more psychological pain rather than ameliorating their problems. Some examples in which collectivist values may impact treatment planning include: a focus on conforming of others' beliefs, attitudes, and expectations; a focus on conforming to and excelling in certain social or family roles; finding happiness through pleasing others; indirect and high context communication; issues of shame stigma or loss of face; expression of feeling that may be different (e.g., indirect, somatic, spiritual); and through a valuing of interdependence. The relationship with the clinician may be viewed with utmost importance (see Table 6.1).

Significant differences exist among cultures regarding the goals of counseling or psychotherapy. For instance, in some cultures, people believe that psychological symptoms must be reduced rather than endured; whereas in some other cultures, it is assumed that the problematic behaviors or situations have some important lessons for humans to learn, these are mostly spiritual lessons (Tseng, 2003). Whereas many Western cultures are oriented toward avoidance of pain through mental health counseling, in Eastern cultures "pain" is regarded as a positive experience and as a prerequisite for the self-actualization and spiritual development of the clients (Sandhu, Portes, & McPhee, 1996). These differences in underlying beliefs may impact the client's goals for treatment. Examples include gaining others' approval, acceptance of a situation or symptoms, developing patience, or simply receiving emotional support (see Table 6.1).

A failure to recognize these basic differences can result in a lack of therapeutic rapport, incongruous treatment plans, and great frustration on the

TABLE 6.1 How Different Worldviews of Individualism and Collectivism May Impact Treatment Planning		
Potential Areas of Influence on Treatment Planning	*Individualism*	*Collectivism*
Treatment expectations	• Talk about problems (including discussion of emotion) • Focus on own needs and goals • Self-awareness, self-discovery • Self-improvement (e.g., behavioral change)	• Social and emotional support • Get advice • Personal relationship with clinician • Holistic focus, spiritual focus • Family involvement
Treatment goals	• Self-actualization, self-understanding • Self fulfillment • Behavior change • Reduce psychological symptoms • Learn new skills	• Happiness through pleasing others • Approval from others • Conforming to others' attitudes • Emotional and social support • Accept social roles, patience • Spiritual healing, community healing
Treatment processes	• Focus on internal processes and intrapsychic concerns (emotions, cognitions) • Direct communication • Direct expression of feeling • Primacy given to individual needs and goals • Collaborative relationship with therapist	• Focus on social relations and social roles • Indirect and high context communication • Expression of feelings may be different (somatic, restrained, or exaggerated) • Impact of trauma may be felt as social • Issues of "face" or shame • Expectation for therapeutic relationship varies (may expect "expert" advice or collaboration)

part of the client and the clinician. For example, the first author (LRJ) has a very active style, which is eclectic but grounded in cognitive-behavioral theory and techniques. In working with an Iraqi woman who was complaining of parenting stress, social anxiety, and sadness, an initial treatment plan was developed that focused on the content of her complaints and also made faulty assumptions about "how best to help." The treatment plan primarily focused on making changes in her situation to resolve contextual problems and reduce stress (e.g., solving daily life problems, skills building) or making changes in her thinking by identifying and decreasing negative thoughts.

However, despite the inclusion of cultural content into the treatment plan (e.g., build social and cultural supports) and extra time spent building rapport, every attempt to "get the client moving" via behavioral tasks or activities failed.

Upon reflection, it is easy to see that the treatment approach was focused on change, rather than providing support and enhancing patient acceptance of her situation. Newer approaches to treatment show promise for broader multicultural applications as they tend to place more focus on contextual factors, acceptance, and working with (and not against) the client's cultural values, for example, acceptance and commitment therapy (Hayes, Strosahl, & Wilson, 1999), eclectic and integrative approaches (e.g., Lazarus, 1997; Norcross, Hedges, & Prochaska, 2002), and multicultural and culture-centered models (e.g., Pedersen, 2003, 2004b; Sue, Ivey, & Pedersen, 1996).

Knowledge for Treatment Planning

Clinicians can cultivate *knowledge* needed for treatment planning by learning about major differences in possible worldviews and perspectives that clients hold. Major, group-level cultural differences have been described, such as individualism versus collectivism (Triandis, 1995); internal versus external locus of control (Sue, 1978); majority versus minority (Mio, Barker-Hackett, & Tumambing, 2006); and contrasts in value orientation dimensions such as being versus doing, linear versus cyclical, past versus present, and time consciousness versus flexibility (Kluckhohn & Strodtbeck, 1961). It is also important that clinicians understand that, with the increase in cultural diversity, we see a concomitant increase in the range and diversity of help-seeking choices and treatment options that exist within this context (Rogler & Cortez, 1992).

In this context, we have found it useful to think about how we would approach a case and then challenge our own dialectical thinking and monoculturally encapsulated view by thinking of complementary, alternative, and, sometimes, contrasting approaches to the same case. This can enhance clinician flexibility, an important skill in culturally competent treatment planning (Hong, Garcia, & Soriano, 2000). Similarly, clinicians can benefit by thinking about treatment as a balance between etic (culturally universal) and emic (culturally specific) approaches (Munroe & Munroe, 1980). That is, approaches that are assumed or considered to be universal or broadly applicable (these would be the mainstream psychological approaches coming from the clinician) and those that are based on a locally derived, culturally specific, or indigenous model coming from the client (Vontress et al., 1999). New attention has been given to indigenous and nontraditional healing, and given the increasing multicultural nature of society, clinicians can expect increased contact with clients who expect or desire traditional, indigenous, or culture-specific treatments (Koss-Chiono, 2000; Moodley & West, 2005; Sandhu, in press).

An *effective* treatment plan for any particular client will depend on a number of interrelated factors and reciprocal influences related to group (social and cultural), person (individual differences, e.g., personality, learning history) and universal factors. Increasing our knowledge of general cultural concepts, theories, models, and treatment approaches can further our treatment planning efforts. Additionally, learning about specific cultural groups (norms for behavioral expression and help-seeking, language and communication style, sociopolitical history, regional differences between groups) is considered important knowledge for treatment planning. Selecting the *right* focus for treatment and developing an appropriate treatment plan will be aided by clinician knowledge of the client's worldview; cultural, ethnic, and racial identity; level, phase, and mode of acculturation; religious or spiritual beliefs; sexual orientation; gender identity; age and generational factors; disability status; and historical and current sociopolitical and ecological contexts (Aponte & Johnson, 2000; Cuellar, 2000; Hays, 2001). These factors combine in a dynamic way to influence symptom presentation, help seeking, and treatment expectations, among other things. The complex intermix of factors also accounts for the fact that there is more within-group cultural diversity than between-group diversity.

The multidimensional and dynamic nature of culture and its many interactions means that treatment planning is necessarily idiographic, even though nomothetic factors cannot be dismissed. In some cases there is too much cultural information to process quickly and because there are no hard and fast rules for application, clinicians can easily feel overwhelmed. Paul Pedersen (2004b) gives counselors some comfort about the opportunities and possibilities for connecting with clients in meaningful ways despite cultural and language differences (Pedersen, 2004b). He notes that if both the client and the clinician each have about 1,000 different cultural influences, surely there are some areas of common ground and ways that they can relate to each other. Reflecting on this universal connection the Dalai Lama has stated, "I hope that you at this moment will think of yourself as a human being rather than as an American, Asian, European, African, or member of a particular country ... If you and I find common ground as human beings, we will communicate on a basic level." Indeed some of our most meaningful relationships have been with clients and other individuals with whom we shared little in common culturally, but shared a great deal in our humanity.

Skills for Treatment Planning

Understanding the importance of cross-cultural and culture-specific knowledge, and learning about these concepts in the abstract are certainly useful but we have struggled, as do many clinicians, with the application of these ideas in practice. Skills for culturally competent treatment require ongoing practice and development. They include but are not limited to:

- Conducting literature searches and accessing specific cultural information.
- Learning how to work with cultural brokers, including interpreters.
- Asking clients about their cultural background.
- Determining the role and importance of various cultural factors (dynamic sizing).
- Being flexible in roles as a therapist.
- Adapting counseling relationship style, communicating effectively.
- Ability to assess client strengths and adapt treatments.
- Knowing when and how to consult or refer the client elsewhere.

Skills in intercultural communication are also important for collaborating with the client to develop and to negotiate a treatment plan (Martin & Nakayama, 2005). These include:

- Mindfulness and awareness of anxiety and defensive reactions.
- Being keenly observant for cultural factors.
- Ability to suspend initial judgments and think critically about assumptions.
- Ability to have and show respect to others.
- Ability to create a nonjudging atmosphere.
- Being realistic about your cultural knowledge and skills.
- Always maintaining some humility in cross-cultural situations.
- Tolerance for ambiguity and uncertainty.
- Sense of humor.

A *tolerance for ambiguity*, for not knowing all of the cultural details yet still being able to move forward with a client, is essential for effective functioning in the context of cultural differences. Skills in intercultural communication are best developed through real-life cross-cultural experiences, such as developing cross-cultural friendships; participating in diverse cultural communities; or living, working, or studying in another country or among a different cultural group. Clinicians can also be assured that basic therapeutic skills in developing and expressing positive regard, empathy, warmth, openness, flexibility, respect, and professionalism will go a long way in cross-cultural communications (Hays, 2001; Okazaki, 2000; Pedersen, 2004b).

Treatment Planning as an Intercultural Process

All psychotherapy occurs in a multicultural context and all psychotherapy is cross-cultural or intercultural to some extent (Pedersen, 1991). The areas of cultural difference between the clinician and client (e.g., ethnicity, race, language, nationality, gender) and the extent of the differences will vary from case to case. Some differences will be readily visible or apparent (such as language, race, or ethnicity), whereas others (such as political affiliation or sexual orientation) may not. It is safe to assume that when the extent of differences is high, there is an increased potential for miscommunication and poorly planned (i.e., culturally incongruent) treatment. However, an apparent lack of social or cultural differences between client and clinician does not discount the importance of explicitly attending to culture. In fact, in the case of no apparent differences, numerous faulty assumptions are made. This is easily illustrated with heterosexual bias in language, such as asking a man if he has a girlfriend or wife, instead of a partner. Each person (therapist included) is a unique individual with multiple, interactive cultural influences and identities.

Moreover, areas of cultural identity salience cannot be assumed. Although racial identity maybe salient for many African Americans, there may be many other factors, such as religious identity, disability status, or profession, that are important to *this* African American. Group norms should thus be held in the clinician's mind as possibilities to consider (as hypotheses) not generically and broadly *applied* to individual clients. S. Sue (2006) calls this important skill "dynamic sizing," referring to the ability to be flexible in fitting our knowledge of cultural factors to each client and situation. Indeed, planning treatments based on the assumed salience of group level could be considered an ethnic slur (Wohl, 2000). Given the complexity of culture, practitioners should think of all clients and themselves as multicultural beings and also look at every client interaction as cross-cultural in nature.

Clients' Unique Cultural Perspectives

In cross-cultural situations, understanding the unique perspectives of our clients is of paramount importance (American Psychological Association [APA], 2003). As such, the first step in treatment planning should be to get a good understanding of our clients' perspectives—of themselves, their problems, their expectations for treatment, and their desired outcomes. If we do not understand "where the client is coming from" then we have little chance for success in our attempts to plan an appropriate treatment, let alone engage our clients in that treatment (Wohl, 2000).

Asking about Culture

Clinicians can integrate open-ended and specific questions about culture as the relationship develops and as treatment proceeds. Examples of questions a clinician could think about asking a person who has emigrated from his country as a refugee or an immigrant might include:

- Would you tell me about your cultural background?
- What was it like to grow up as a boy or girl in your family and culture?
- Would you mind telling me about your religious (or spiritual) upbringing?
- Would you feel comfortable telling me how you came to the United States?
- What are some of the things about America that surprised you?
- What are some ways you stay connected to your traditional culture?
- What are some things that are difficult for you about living in the United States?
- What are some ideas you have about treatment? How is this problem generally handled in your country?
- Do you have a religious or spiritual practice that you would like to bring into treatment?

These questions and discussions about culture are important and should not be ignored by the therapist. However, clinicians need to be attentive to note how the client responds to such topics. By and large, we have found that, when given an opportunity (and permission) to discuss culture and cultural conflicts, clients respond well. For instance, when an international student is asked what are some of the major challenges you face as an international student here, or a refugee is asked what are some of the main differences you see in your culture and American culture, what are some things you like, and what are some things you are not so sure about, we often see clear expressions of relief as clients feel they have permission to discuss their experiences, including their negative views (Johnson & Sandhu, 2007). We have also found that when given a chance to share cultural information, clients may show momentary improvement in mood, exhibit a sense of cultural pride, and, sometimes, feel empowered at the chance to educate others (i.e., the therapist) about a cultural value, belief, or tradition. In fact, we have found that in cases where the cultural differences are extreme, the cultural exchanges can help rapport building and aid in the forming of the therapist–client relationship.

Ongoing Cultural Assessment

In many therapeutic settings and situations, clinicians will not realistically have the time to conduct an initial, in-depth cultural assessment of the client and the client's situation. In other cases, too much focus on culture and cultural assessment could be inappropriate or off-putting to the client. In many cases, clinicians will have to move ahead, developing and preceding with a (at least an initial) treatment plan. For example, working in a clinic for newly arrived refugees, the first author (LRJ) saw clients from a wide range of language and cultural and ethnic backgrounds (e.g., Bosnian, Afghani, Lebanese, Iraqi, Sudanese, Congolese). Oftentimes, these clients were in great psychological distress, experiencing panic attacks, severe depression, or PTSD. They wanted and needed immediate treatment for symptoms that were causing significant interference in their ability to sleep, learn English, find a job, parent effectively, and so forth. Too much time given to the assessment of specific cultural factors before proceeding with a treatment plan could have been problematic in some of these situations.

Moreover, given the multiple cultures and sometimes instantaneous time frame (e.g., in the case of a crisis situation or a psychological consultation in a medical setting) it may be impossible to learn important background information about the client's culture prior to interacting with the client and suggesting a treatment. As such, a behavioral perspective on assessment can be adopted in which cultural assessment is considered an ongoing process. Clinicians should also be observant for other potential indicators of cultural importance. Pay attention to the style and manner of the client's dress (e.g., do they wear traditional, cultural, or religious clothing); manner and style of communicating; ways of interacting; eye contact; and language usage and fluency (Sue & Sue, 2007). Initial hypotheses based on theoretical orientation, cultural group knowledge, and existing knowledge about the case can combine with a clinician's keen observations as an initial starting place. However, think critically about your assumptions and do not make hasty treatment decisions without some cultural assessment. In addition, it is also important to keep in mind several cultural variables such as prejudice, racism, and discrimination; familism; role of children and spouse; and indirect versus direct forms of communication that may affect assessment and treatment of culturally different clients (Paniagua, 2005).

Our approach is grounded in the social constructionist view that the client's perspective on the problem and on treatment is of key importance in treatment planning. As clinicians, we have our own combined professional and personal views, but understanding our clients brings us to a closer understanding of their experiences. In the case of cultural differences, understanding our clients' perspectives can broaden our perspective, enrich our way of seeing, and also maximize our capacity for empathy. The investigation of client beliefs and expectations has become central among efforts of medical anthropologists and mental health professionals to understand how cultural factors affect client beliefs about treatment, patterns of service utilization, and patient outcomes (Fadiman, 1997; Pelto & Pelto, 1996).

The Explanatory Model: A Treatment Planning Tool

The concept of the explanatory model proposed by Arthur Kleinman (1980) is a useful and valuable tool for clinicians. *Explanatory models* (EMs) are beliefs about an illness or psychological problem (e.g., depression) that give meaning to the problem and convey how it is understood or conceptualized by the afflicted person and by other individuals (e.g., family members), and systems that are involved (Kleinman, 1980). EMs provide an excellent starting point because they capture both cultural and personal aspects of the problem from the client's unique perspective. Moreover, understanding the patient's perspective is highlighted in the multicultural guidelines (APA, 2003) and the *DSM–IV* outline for the cultural formulation (Kleinman, 1980; Pelto & Pelto, 1996; Weiss & Kleinman, 1988). It has been further suggested that understanding EMs is particularly important when working in a multicultural context.

Kleinman (1980) distinguished between the disease and the illness: with the disease/disorder being the actual psychological (or biological) malfunctioning, and the illness being the felt or lived experience of the disorder. EMs capture the lived experience of psychological problems in our clients' lives. Unlike popular health beliefs, EMs refer to a particular episode of the disorder or illness (e.g., an episode of major depression). EMs are multifaceted and are construed of several, more or less interrelated, components or domains. They include beliefs about the perceived nature of the disorder, the cause of the symptoms, its severity and probable course, and the type and degree of impairment resulting from the disorder. EMs contain information about the fears associated with the illness, what kind of treatment, if any, should be sought, and what kinds of treatment results are expected or desired (Chrisman & Johnson, 1996; Kleinman, 1980). These aspects, when taken together, present an overall picture of how one views the problem from inception to outcomes.

Assessing the EM can help us better understand both unique and culture-related client beliefs, help-seeking behaviors, and treatment expectations. Kleinman (1980, p. 106) suggests several questions for exploring client EMs:

- What do you call your problem? What name does it have?
- What do you think caused your problem?
- Why do you think it started when it did?
- What does your illness do to you? How does it work?
- How severe is it? Will it have a short or long course?
- What do you fear most about your problem?
- What are the chief problems your illness has caused for you?
- What kind of treatment do you think you should receive? What are the most important results you hope to get from treatment?

A case example of a client EM is presented in Table 6.2. It briefly outlines the EM of a young woman from Sudan, Sara, seen in a refugee clinic. Sara had arrived in the United States just one week prior to her appointment and her symptoms of distress were acute. The therapist (LRJ) elicited the client's EM (after establishing rapport) through relatively relaxed, back-and-forth conversation, with an Arabic interpreter. It is important to note that client EMs will not always address all of the questions posed by Kleinman, and clinician EMs may be more complete and extensive than those of their clients (Gray, 1995). In the case example, we can see that Sara did not report having an idea about the type of treatment she needed stating "you are the doctor." Some of her other responses were also vague.

The amount of internal consistency between EM components may also show wide variation based on the degree to which concepts are borrowed from popular, personal, or biomedical beliefs, and the amount of metaphor

TABLE 6.2
Comparison of Client and Clinician Explanatory Models (EMs)

EM Component	Client (Young Woman, Sudanese Refugee)	Clinician (LRJ)
What is the problem?	Sadness, a broken heart, alone	Depression (*sadness*), PTSD, numerous psychosocial/ environmental problems, acculturation problem (marginalized, acute phase), loss of identity (personal, *social* isolation cultural, national), *loss of primary support*, trauma history (war, slavery, migration, assault), occupational problems, academic problems
What caused the problem?	Coming to United States, leaving my mother	Multiple traumatic experiences associated with Sudanese war and refugee status; 4 years in captivity; most recent precipitating event: *separation from mother, resettlement in United States*
What does it do to you? How does it work?	Lonely, sad, can't eat, can't sleep, tired, guilt, cry, hold knife to abdomen, ask God should I die	*Lonely, sad, can't eat, can't sleep, tired, guilt, cry*, unable to function independently due to recent arrival, symptoms include nightmares, suicidal ideation, and some self-harm
Will it have a short or long course? How severe is it?	Only God knows, maybe forever Very severe	Successful adjustment to United States will factor in greatly; impact will be lifelong; time and treatment could result in symptom remission
Biggest fears?	I won't see my mother again, my sadness won't go away; I won't get married	*Won't see mother; won't get married*
Treatment goals?	Have my mother back; get married	Client safety, reduce symptoms, facilitate adjustment, bicultural connections and competence (*academic/ occupational goals, social/relational goals*)
Type of treatment?	Don't know, "you are the doctor"; get married; get a job	Case management and behavioral approaches (e.g., activity scheduling, graded tasks, problem solving); *get a job*; learn English; pleasurable events; and social connections

Note: Shared areas of the explanatory model between client and clinician are italicized.

and personal or cultural idioms used in describing the EM (Gray, 1995; Kleinman, 1980). In the case example, Sara's EM is reasonably consistent, the name of her problem ("broken heart") was caused by leaving her mother, which is related to her treatment goal (getting her mother back) and her idea about what she needs to be able to accomplish that goal (get a job).

Research suggests that more often than not, clinicians and their clients disagree in their EMs (Chrisman & Johnson, 1996; Gregg & Curry, 1994;

Kleinman, 1980). Kleinman (1980) describes the disparity between patient and practitioner EMs as a reflection of the "cognitive difference" between them. Areas of congruence and incongruence (or unexplored, unknown beliefs) can be seen in the case with Sara (see Table 6.2).

When patients present for treatment, a transaction, usually tacit, occurs between the EM of the patient and that of the practitioner. Kleinman suggests that disparate beliefs, left unexplored, may result in poor patient–practitioner communication and lead to misdiagnosis, inappropriate treatment, treatment nonadherence, early attrition, and poor treatment outcomes (Chrisman & Johnson, 1996; Kleinman, 1980; Wohl, 2000). EMs are considered to be fluid in nature, continually being updated and modified as new information is received and incorporated into the existing EM. This aspect is important, because it means that, as clinicians, we have some leeway in working with clients who may hold unhelpful beliefs (see section titled "Negotiating a Treatment Plan").

Of particular importance for treatment planning and negotiation are the questions, "What kind of treatment do you think you would need?" and "What are the most important results you hope to get from this treatment?" After assessing the client's explanatory model, including the treatment goals and expectations, clinicians should compare it with their own conceptualization looking for areas of agreement and disagreement. Clinicians should begin with what the client presents and make adjustments as appropriate. In the case example of Sara, working on areas of shared agreement provided an initial place to start. The client and therapist agreed to work toward the client's goals of getting a job and reuniting her with her mother. Sara's EM also pointed to the potential importance of religion and social networks in her treatment plan. A client's EM, combined with any other information gained from records or interviews, can point the clinician in a general direction to develop a treatment plan. Ideally, this will be done in collaboration with the client, keeping in mind client sensitivities regarding role expectations for the clinician and for treatment.

Developing the Treatment Plan

In developing the initial treatment plan, clinicians need to pay attention to both the content as well as the process of treatment. Treatment planning, like cultural assessment, can be thought of as an ongoing process that is continually revised and tailored as new information, including treatment adherence and client response, come into effect. The checklist (see Figure 6.1) can help

FIGURE 6.1
Clinician's Checklist for Culturally Congruent Treatment Planning

Pretherapy and Orientation to Treatment:

☐ Client is unaccustomed to Western psychological perspectives.
　　Comments _____
☐ More attention to basics, such as confidentiality, scheduling, and payment.
☐ Client's expectations. Check all that apply.

　　☐ Direct advice　　　　　　☐ Self-improvement　　☐ Acceptance

　　☐ Holistic/spiritual focus　　☐ Family involvement　　☐ Unsure

　　☐ Other _____

Relationship and Roles:

☐ Sufficient rapport and credibility to proceed. Comments _____
☐ Address the role(s) of the clinician with the client. Check all that apply.

　　☐ Psychotherapist　　　　☐ Adviser　　　　　☐ Advocate

　　☐ Consultant　　　　　　☐ Counselor　　　　☐ Other _____

　　☐ Coach　　　　　　　　☐ Change agent

☐ Clarified with the patient? Comments _____

Identify and Address Barriers:

☐ Are there language barriers? Is an interpreter needed? If yes, _____
☐ Present culture stigmas for the client? If yes, identify. _____
☐ Client's style of communication (e.g., direct, indirect) Other _____
☐ Socioeconomic barriers that may hinder treatment (e.g., transportation, payment/income, education, etc.).
☐ Other _____

Areas of Hypothesized Cultural Importance:

☐ Check all that apply.

　　☐ Race/ethnicity　　　　　　　☐ Age　　　　　　　☐ Disability

　　☐ Education/income　　　　　　☐ Language　　　　　☐ Sociopolitical

　　☐ Geographic (national, regional)　☐ Cultural background　☐ Sexual orientation

　　☐ Gender　　　　　　　　　　☐ Religion　　　　　☐ Other _____

Client Strengths Incorporated:

☐ Client possesses personal strengths that will assist in the treatment.
☐ Coping skills. Check all that apply.

　　☐ Cultural beliefs and support　　☐ Recreation/hobbies　　☐ Religious or spiritual support

　　☐ Family or friends　　　　　　☐ Community　　　　　☐ Other _____

　　☐ Exercise

Treatment Focus and Modality:

☐ Acceptable focus of treatment. Comments _____
☐ Appropriate and acceptable type of treatment. Comments _____
☐ Considerations for problems related to culture. Comments _____
☐ Considerations for an array of approaches or cultural adaptations? Comments _____
　　_____

clinicians think about what cultural information might be important with a particular client and also how to work with those cultural aspects in developing a culturally congruent treatment plan.

Is There a Need for Pretherapy or Orientation?

Before developing a treatment plan (in the traditional sense, to address a problem), clinicians need to consider whether the plan should include "pretherapy" to address issues concerning the client's familiarity and orientation to therapy (S. Sue, 2006).

- Is this client accustomed to Western psychological perspectives and modes of treatment (e.g., talk therapy)?
- Has this client been in treatment before?
- What are this client's expectations for how treatment will proceed?
- What are the client's expectations for how the therapist will interact with him or her?

Many diverse clients, such as American ethnic minorities, older adults, or persons from rural areas, will be unfamiliar with Western-based psychotherapy and will not know what to expect. They may hold assumptions that can result in disappointments. For example, if clients expect direct advice or concrete help (e.g., helping find a job), they may be disappointed or even angry if a clinician merely talks to them about their problem without direct intervention or advice.

Clients who are more familiar with seeking help from family members, friends, or respected leaders in a community or church might find the idea of talking to a stranger in an office quite strange. They may have difficulty understanding traditional client–therapist boundaries and may be surprised, embarrassed, or even feel hurt if clinicians maintain personal distance (e.g., do not share personal information or refuse an invitation to a client's home). To avoid confusion, clinicians should educate their clients, early on, about boundaries, roles, and expectations of their clients and themselves (Vasquez, 2005). At the same time, clinicians should critically consider the limits of their current treatment practices, adopted roles, and functions as helpers. The guidelines for multicultural practice, for example, suggest that multiple helping roles may be adopted for more effective service delivery (APA, 2003).

Clinicians may continue to serve in a traditional counselor or therapist role, while also becoming cultural brokers, advocates, case managers, coaches, change agents, and so forth (APA, 2003; Atkinson, Morten & Sue,

1998). For example, in a clinic for newly arrived refugees in which the second author worked, a "case management approach" to therapy was utilized, allowing clinicians to take on multiple roles and serve the multifactorial concerns of clients. This included explaining some American (and psychological) practices; advocating for client access to interpreters; helping clients negotiate social service agencies to get economic assistance; linking clients with volunteers who could provide transportation (e.g., for shopping and to appointments); and providing emotional support and companionship. In this setting, traditional therapist–client relationship boundaries were also relaxed (with proper consultation and supervision in each case) allowing the therapist to share cultural and sometimes personal information, give and receive gifts, and to participate in social gatherings and events in the refugee community.

Is More Time Needed to Establish Rapport?

In considering whether pretherapy would be helpful, clinicians should also pay careful attention to the relationship and assess their level of credibility and trust with the client. Ask yourself:

- Is there an adequate relationship in place to proceed?
- Do I need to spend more time connecting with the client?
- Do I need to spend more time establishing trust, respect, or credibility?
- What have I done to actively attend to the relationship?
- How can I increase my credibility with this client?

Do not underestimate the importance of giving adequate time to the relationship (Okazaki, 2000; see also Chapter 7). Clients unfamiliar with therapy may need to get a better understanding of "where the therapist is coming from," to get some sense of the therapist's context (Hays, 2001). Therapists may choose to engage in small talk, share cultural information, or even disclose some personal information (e.g., "I also have two children"). Giving the client some sort of "gift" (e.g., concrete help, emotional support, a resource, a journal, or something else of practical or symbolic importance) can also aid in establishing the relationship (S. Sue, 2006). Time spent building rapport may also aid in increasing client support for the treatment plan.

In the case of Sara, pretherapy and extra time for building rapport were definitely needed. Sara was literate and very interested in learning about computers. For the first several sessions, LRJ met her 20 minutes before her appointment to show her how to use the Internet. Cultural differences were bridged and a relationship was built by looking things up on the Internet and discussing Sudanese and American food, music, recreation, and geography. This time was also spent explaining to Sara how the client–clinician relationship would be similar and different from the types of helpers she was familiar with (priests and nuns) and the kinds of things that might be done in therapy, such as talk to about her problems, provide emotional support, and try to help her reduce her symptoms and meet her goals.

Beyond building trust and rapport with particular clients, clinicians can increase their own credibility and that of their organization by building a reputation in the community. For example, LRJ (a White therapist) worked in a very small, low-income community in rural Mississippi, with African American clients. This particular town was quite racially divided and mistrust among African Americans for White therapists or clinicians was quite high. Recognizing this, LRJ rented a house locally (as opposed to commuting like the previous therapists) and also volunteered in the community by teaching exercise classes in the Section 8 housing complex. This visibility and the local friendships that grew as a result had a net effect of building LRJ's credibility as a (nonracist) helper, and as more and more potential clients got the word, client referrals increased dramatically.

Are Treatment Goals Culturally Congruent?

The treatment plan should be directed toward achieving the client's stated goals for treatment. Clients generally want some kind of change to occur, either in their environment or in themselves, whether it is focused on symptom reduction or an increase in acceptance, as mentioned earlier. Client goals vary greatly in their clarity; amount of consideration; feasibility; and whether they are broad, global goals or just short-term, objective goals. Clients' treatment goals may reflect their cultural, personal, or family values. Clinicians can help clients identify, clarify, or break goals into manageable steps. They can also help clients explore how their goals fit across multiple contexts and how their lives may change if their goals are met. Clinicians should consider whether they will be able to effectively help the client work toward those goals.

Is the Focus of Treatment Appropriate and Acceptable?

The focus for treatment will depend partly on the client's treatment goals, expectations for treatment, and problem conceptualization (EM).

This will combine with the clinicians' case formulation and orientation to therapy (clinician EM) to prioritize one or more focus areas or targets for treatment. This could be a universal (presumably etic) mental health problem such as depression, panic disorder, PTSD, behavioral or personality disorders, psychosis, developmental and learning disorders, or acquired disability. Problems related to the psychosocial environment and functioning (often listed on Axis IV of the *DSM–IV*), such as those related to poverty, unemployment, lack of social support, and poor environmental conditions, may be important concerns for minorities and persons of color or diverse cultures. Identity concerns, spiritual problems, and acculturation-related difficulties should also be considered as potential foci of treatment.

Despite the presence of a severe Axis I diagnosis, clinicians should not be surprised if their clients believe that their treatment should focus on more contextually related concerns rather than on the symptoms themselves (such as focusing on negative thoughts in cognitive therapy). Some cultures (for example, some American Indian cultures) find direct discussion about thoughts, emotions, or other intrapsychic experiences to be an inappropriate focus of treatment. In the case of the Sudanese refugee, Sara, discussed earlier, direct questions about her thoughts or feelings related to depression or PTSD would often result in the client beginning to cry or attempting to end the session. An interpreter, acting as a cultural broker, explained that the client was not comfortable discussing these topics as they increased her feeling of being stigmatized. In addition to the possibility of focusing too much attention on internal states, failing to address important contextual and ecological factors may reduce clinician credibility and treatment effectiveness.

Can Clinician Roles Be Expanded? Or Treatment Modalities Modified?

Clinicians need to be flexible in their selection of various types of treatments, making the best match between a client and his or her situation. It has been argued that the most effective treatments for diverse individuals should be comprehensive (holistic), seamless, and multifaceted. Family and group approaches are frequently recommended, as are treatments that are community based and easily accessible, such as in schools, churches, or community settings (Aponte & Bracco, 2000; Tewari, Inman, & Sandhu, 2003; Wilson, Kohn, & Lee, 2000). Given an ethical commitment to social justice, systems-level interventions, such as advocating for client services or policy change, should also be considered by clinicians (Hage, 2005). Mainstream, adapted, indigenous, or culture-specific treatments may be utilized depending on the client's level of acculturation, areas of cultural influence and salience, and explanatory belief model.

Are Potential Barriers Addressed?

Treatment plans will be most effective if they are designed with possible cultural barriers in mind. Just as we encourage our clients to consider possible barriers to completing homework assigned in therapy, we too must develop treatment plans that have identified and addressed potential barriers. Issues such as transportation, a lack of financial resources, inadequate childcare, and time constraints are common barriers for ethnic minority and low-income clients. Treatments should be planned with these realities in mind. Language is another potential barrier. For example, a client with limited English proficiency (LEP) is entitled to interpretation services (under Title VI of the Federal Civil Rights Act of 1964) and this will need to be worked into the plan, as working with an interpreter can complicate scheduling. Sessions may need to be longer, due to the time involved in interpreting the session and in pre- and postsession debriefings with the interpreter. Additionally, a clinician must have training in how to correctly use an interpreter, and in the case of some particular treatment techniques, such as exposure therapy or relaxation, interpreters may need additional education or training before being able to interpret the treatment effectively.

Treatment barriers related to client, family, or culturally held stigmas or beliefs about psychological help-seeking can also impede treatment. Unlike in the United States, clients from other countries and cultures frequently believe that seeking psychological help is only appropriate for "crazy" people (i.e., people with psychotic or other acting out disorders), not for "run of the mill" depression or anxiety, which may be considered products of living rather than psychological disorders. Clients may come to us as a last resort and may have self-blame (e.g., a belief in personal or moral weakness) related to their inability to handle the problem. Negative stigmas can be addressed in pretherapy education. Potential treatment barriers related to low socioeconomic status, such as a lack of transportation or income, should also be considered when developing the treatment plan. If the client cannot get to the treatment site, you can be sure the treatment plan will not be effective. When cultural minority clients do seek help, drastic differences in beliefs about mental health and healing may impede treatment. Ethnic minorities in the United States, for example, may hold spiritual or somatic conceptions of mental illness and may not distinguish between the mind and body as Western clinicians do (Angel & Williams, 2000).

Last, but very important, treatment plans should consider the client's level of treatment readiness (Prochaska, 1999). Clinicians often proceed with developing and trying to activate treatment plans without actually assessing the client's motivation and readiness to undertake a treatment or make a change. Questions to consider include: Is my client thinking about making a change (e.g., a behavior change or undertaking treatment)? Would my client like to make a change, but lacks the confidence or skills (wants treatment to work, but not sure it will)? Is my client ambivalent about change? What are the risks of change? (Even positive changes have associated risks and losses.) For example, working with a female client to increase assertiveness could carry social and physical risks related to cultural beliefs and values about women's roles and behaviors. Listen to your client's "change talk" to get a sense of their readiness for treatment and change (stages of change: precontemplation, contemplation, preparation, and so forth). Psychoeducation, environmental re-evaluation, self re-evaluation, and motivational interviewing are some strategies for enhancing a client's motivation to engage in treatment or change a behavior (Prochaska, 1999). Keep in mind that a focus on direct behavioral change may be less congruent with a client's cultural background, values, or current context than a focus on acceptance, tolerance, or support.

Are Client Strengths and Treatment Resources Included?

Treatment plans will have a better chance of success if they draw from, and work with, a client's natural coping strengths and resources. Clinicians should actively seek out information about client strengths and resources that could facilitate, support, or promulgate treatment (Hays, 2001; Vasquez, 2005). These might include family (broadly defined) or community supports; religious or spiritual practices or values; cultural values, supports, and practices; and other natural coping skills, such as exercise, recreation or hobbies, social events, or activities. Involving a client's family in the treatment may be of particular importance and a great asset in working with clients from tightly knit families or those who come from more collectivist cultures (Wilson et al., 2000). For example, in working with a depressed, bicultural (Lebanese and Kuwaiti) immigrant mother of two, LRJ (after discussing it with the client) enlisted the help of the woman's husband in countering her suicidal thoughts. The husband helped the client come up with evidence to dispute the notion that she was a "bad mother" and deserved punishment. The client's husband also supported her by arranging child care so that his wife could engage in recreational activities, encouraging his wife in her treatment goals, and attending periodic treatment sessions. Both the client and her husband reported satisfaction in working together on the client's treatment goals.

Adjust the Therapeutic Frame to Accommodate Culture

Though cultures all over the world may not be familiar with the Western notion of psychotherapy, all cultures are familiar with the concept of talking to a concerned person, be it a family member, friend, community figure, religious leader, or some type of professional practitioner (e.g., a traditional healer or shaman). This basic similarity can be used as a common base from which to proceed with treatment planning with diverse clients.

Adapting Treatments

Clinicians can make a range of different technical, theoretical, and conceptual adjustments to their treatment planning efforts and approach with culturally diverse clients. These might include: (a) minor or single adjustments in mainstream approaches, such as incorporating cultural or religious material into a cognitive-behavioral approach, or translating a treatment manual into another language; (b) adapted treatments that make multiple cultural adjustments across several areas domains (treatment modality, type, location) and use culture as a resource; and (c) culture-specific, traditional, or indigenous approaches in which the focus of treatment, goals of treatment, and process of treatment all derive from a particular cultural (i.e., emic) perspective. The type of treatment and degree of "adaptations" needed will depend on the client's cultural perspective, current cultural and ecological context, and available resources and services (Tseng, 2003).

Clinicians should be flexible in their approach to treatment. Mainstream treatments should be adapted to meet each client's needs and capitalize on cultural strengths. Treatment adaptations might include reducing jargon; providing the treatment in a different language; incorporating cultural, religious, or other alternative healing strategies into treatment (for example, the use of stories or proverbs); or using a complete system of cultural values or frameworks to undergird techniques (Griner & Smith, 2006). Some

TABLE 6.3
Examples of Culturally Related Treatments

Treatment	Target Population	Description
Nguzo Saba (Bishop, 2002)	African American adolescents	The use of Africentric principles guide self-esteem development and behavioral modification. The seven principles of Nguzo Saba (unity, self-determination, collective work and responsibility, cooperative economics, purpose, creativity, and faith) are used to establish a sense of value and meaning.
Cuento therapy (Constantino, Malgady, & Rogler, 1986)	Puerto Rican children	*Cuentos* are stories that express thoughts, feelings, values, and behaviors that best represent the Puerto Rican culture. Cuentos are written to teach moral themes such as social judgment, control of emotions, and social consequences. The use of this folklore and traditional storytelling is used to ease anxiety and increase the acceptance of psychotherapeutic services.
Hero/heroine modeling (Malgady, Rogler, & Constantino, 1990a)	Puerto Rican adolescents	A preventative therapeutic approach designed to teach through social learning and modeling. This therapy helps to increase ethnic identity and reduce stress symptoms. Adolescents are introduced to successful adult role models who have experienced similar hardships in socioeconomics, education, and environment. Through this similar aspect the adolescent is able to easily identify and focus on how the models successfully adapted to the stressful environment.
Bicultural effectiveness training (BET; Szapocznik et al., 1986)	Latino families	The use of family intervention to address acculturation, interculture conflict, and adolescent behavior modification. BET focuses on improving adolescent functioning by focusing on the acculturation-related stresses encountered by two-generation immigrant families. By concentrating on the cultural aspect of family life, families are more likely to participate and continue the therapeutic process.
Network therapy (Galanter, 1999)	American Indians	Through this multimodal rehabilitation approach, family members and friends, also called network members, serve as the basis for emotional and attitudinal encouragement. Network therapy is the combination of individual and group therapy. Psychodynamic and cognitive-behavioral approaches are taught through the individual therapy process while therapeutic support is provided through the network of family and friends.

examples of culturally related treatments are seen in Table 6.3. Additional adjustments may come into play as treatment foci, goals, and processes are selected. Goals should be culturally congruent and contextually relevant. Which behaviors are targeted for change should be considered in light of the client's multiple cultural contexts.

Incorporating Cultural Rituals

The client or the clinician may bring up an issue of cultural importance, either during the treatment planning process or after treatment is already underway. In such cases, clinicians should consider the possibility that a culturally based response, such as a healing ritual or culturally patterned coping response, may be helpful in addressing the concerns of the clients. Although mainstream approaches may be effective and should not be abandoned, cultural rituals and other traditional healing practices can be powerful, natural coping strengths that can be integrated into (or at least used in conjunction with) a client's treatment plan. Some cultural rituals that can be readily incorporated or used as adjuncts to standard treatment include:

- Service work or other behavioral tasks
- Prayer, mediation, chanting, or other type of devotion
- Purification rituals, such as bathing and confession
- Reading or studying cultural or religious texts or materials
- Veneration of God(s), spirits, or ancestors
- Creative and expressive arts, such as drumming, dancing, storytelling, and art and craft making

These rituals can be readily incorporated or used as adjunct to standard treatment. For example, in working with an Asian Indian woman who had immigrated to the United States over 40 years ago, LRJ used a mainstream behaviorally based treatment protocol for panic disorder (as per the client's request for "CBT"). Cultural rituals and natural coping integrated into the treatment included Hindi devotional chanting, yoga, and *prana yama* breathing exercises.

For other clients, engaging in a ritual may be a nice adjunct to the treatment plan and might be considered in particular circumstances. Consider the example of a woman from Afghanistan who arrived as a refugee in the United States approximately 5 years prior. The client, who had lost her husband and most of her family, was struggling to raise two teenage boys who were beginning to push the limits of her authority in the household. She had not learned English and was unable to get or keep a job due to numerous symptoms and complaints, such as depression, anxiety, difficulty concentrating, difficulty sleeping, and numerous somatic complaints, such as head, stomach, and joint pain. Her treatment plan included: building social and emotional support; parenting problem solving; pleasant-events scheduling; and some cognitive work focused on living (behaving) in accordance with her values and beliefs, and also focused on striving toward more balanced thinking and responding to events. Salient aspects of her cultural identity included being a Moslem, an Afghani (Pashto), a woman (widowed), and a refugee. She was, however, somewhat marginalized from the Afghani community.

One day, this client told the therapist (LRJ) about a dream she had about bowls of raw meat. She was very upset about the dream and when asked for more detail, she revealed that it was considered a bad omen meaning that something bad was going to happen. The therapist asked the client more about the meaning of the dream and if there was anything that could be done: "What would someone do at home in Afghanistan? What would you do?" The client replied that, in the case of a dream of raw meat, two things are done: (1) give a loaf of bread and an onion to a homeless person, and (2) sit by a river, tell your worries to the river, and watch them being carried away. This seemed like something that the client could benefit from and something that the clinician could support and help to facilitate. The therapist worked with the client to determine the usefulness and practicality of undertaking this ritual with the client. The client did want to undertake the ritual, but felt fearful about approaching a homeless person with bread and an onion. She decided to forgo that aspect, but she did have her son escort her to a creek where she declared her worries. The client reported that she felt a little silly undertaking the ritual, wondering what someone would think if they saw her there, talking to the creek. She also reported a relief and reduction in worry and anxiety related to the dream.

Working with Religion

Working with religion may be especially important for clients with strong religious beliefs, spiritual or religious conceptualizations of their problem, or conflicts related to religion or spirituality. Clinicians work with religion themselves in treatment or refer clients for simultaneous religious counseling. In one case, LRJ integrated the Moslem "call to prayer" into a client's treatment plan. The client was a deeply religious and well-educated man of multiethnic (Arabic, African, and Indian) heritage. In pretherapy sessions the client brought the Holy Koran to meetings with the therapist, and (since he lived in East Africa) the client was curious about Western psychotherapy and how it would fit with his religious beliefs. The client was empowered talking about his religion and LRJ viewed it as a potential strength. The client talked about stress and worries in his life and also about the psychological process and experience of engaging in prayer. He described that sometimes when he first heard the call to prayer over the loudspeakers, he would have an initial negative reaction, but that as he took off his shoes and lowered his body in prostration, he experienced a powerful feeling of reverence, release, freedom, and comfort as he let go of everything, turning himself and his life over completely to Allah. Given the significance of this ritual to this client, the call to prayer was used as a central feature of a stress education/mindfulness-based treatment plan, both as a practice and also as a "grounding language" for discussions about treatment-related concepts, such as stress reactivity versus stress responsiveness. To this, other strategies were added, such as recreation and socialization (fishing and tennis with a friend), problem solving related to finances and career, and social and emotional support related to family problems.

Collaborating with Traditional and Indigenous Healers

In many cases, our clients will be seeking other means of help (e.g., through traditional or spiritual healers, alternative therapies) either sequentially or simultaneously, with professional mental health care. Clinicians should learn about other services that their clients may be seeking and, to the extent possible, develop respectful relations with such providers (APA, 2003; Myers et al., 2005). In some cases and contexts, clinicians can work collaboratively with religious or cultural healers, by providing or taking referrals, engaging in consultations, and even providing integrated care (Koss-Chioino, 2000; Myers et al., 2005).

   In one example, LRJ was called on to provide consultation in the case of a teenage girl from Rwanda, who was brought to a traditional healing clinic in East Africa by her aunt. The young woman had suffered from war trauma associated with the genocide and had given birth to a child that resulted from a rape. The girl had poor eye contact, was withdrawn, and experienced frightening hallucinations of wild animals attacking her. She also had numerous self-care issues, including frequently wetting and soiling herself. Due to an apparent lack of interest and inability to take care of her baby, the baby had been taken away, and the girl was frequently and harshly punished for soiling herself. Her symptoms increased and her despondence grew, so that she rarely spoke. In this case, the healer was concerned about the nature of the child's problem, how she was being treated, and what should be done. After interviewing the client and the client's aunt (with the help of an interpreter who had psychological training), LRJ shared her conceptualization of the case and treatment recommendations. The client's symptoms seemed to be related to war trauma, exacerbated by postpartum depression, separation from her child, and the harsh punishment she received. The client's stated goal was to be reunited with her baby. LRJ stressed with the utmost importance that the client should not be punished, recommended basic behavioral tasks, and also suggested that the client would benefit from a medical consultation at the psychiatric clinic at the local hospital. The healer agreed wholeheartedly and the plan was presented to the client and her aunt together. The healer, in a kind but firm manner, informed the aunt that the girl should not be punished and that she should abide by our (joint) recommendations of behavioral tasks and reinforcement for self-care; obtain a psychiatric evaluation; and continue with the herbal and spiritual treatments at the clinic (traditional). With the highly ascribed status of both clinicians in this case (the healer, who had a lifetime of experience in medical and psychological healing and was also president of the district healers' association; and LRJ, an American clinician and researcher, and a guest of the healer) and the joint presentation of an integrated treatment reinforced the integrity of the treatment recommendations and, hopefully, the likelihood that they would be followed.

Treatment Planning for Problems Related to Culture

Based on the cultural formulation and the client's own goals, treatment may focus solely on, or include, a problem that is specifically related to culture. Culture-related problems could include culture-bound syndromes, such as *susto, attaques de nervios,* and *koro* (see *DSM–IV,* Appendix I [American Psychiatric Association, 1994] for listing and descriptions); acculturative stress and cultural adjustment concerns; experiences of oppression, racism, or discrimination related to culture, ethnicity, gender, religion, or nationality; identity concerns related to culture, gender, race, minority status, or sexual orientation; and spiritual or religious problems or concerns (Paniagua, 2000).

Addressing Acculturation Problems

A complex but important relationship exists between acculturation and mental health (Berry & Kim, 1998; Cuellar, 2000). Problems related to acculturation are well documented in refugees, immigrants, international students, and others undergoing the process of culture change and related psychological adjustment (Lonner, Wong & Wong, 2006; Prendes-Lintel, 2001; Sandhu et al., 1996). Symptoms of acculturative stress include depression, anxiety, a sense of loss and homesickness, isolation, somatic complaints, and identity confusion (Berry, Kim, Minde, & Mok, 1987; Sandhu & Asrabadi, 1994). In addition, many families experience conflict related to acculturation, as family members respond differently to the demands of acculturation. The types of problems related to acculturation, and their severity, will depend on factors associated with the acculturating individuals, dominant and nondominant cultural influences and attitudes, the phase/stage of acculturation (how long the person has been acculturating), and the strategy with which acculturation is approached (Aponte & Johnson, 2000).

Treatment plans to help ameliorate or prevent acculturative stress will need to first determine some of the factors surrounding the person's acculturation, what accounts for the stress, and how it is experienced. Most treatment approaches to acculturation work to normalize the process and to build bicultural (or multicultural) skills and effectiveness. This may be accomplished through social learning and skills acquisition; identifying and working with cultural conflicts; and building social supports. In helping to alleviate the acculturative stress of international students, for example, we have suggested (and have found) that offering an array of services in an array of formats is helpful, allowing for maximal benefits in a nonstigmatizing way. Examples of treatment modalities that can be combined into a multifaceted approach include psychoeducational information, American cultural values and customs, adjustment groups, social clubs, and multicultural discussion groups and workshops, as well as more traditional group and individual therapy (Johnson & Sandhu, 2007). Treatments should, ideally, be continuous, comprehensive, and culturally congruous.

In addition to acculturation stress experienced at the individual level, many families and couples experience conflict related to acculturation, as family members respond differently to the demands of acculturation. Children of refugee and immigrant families, for example, tend to learn English more quickly and acculturate more easily than their parents. They may also take an assimilation approach that involves losing their cultural heritage (Sourander, 2003). Marital relationships may also be strained, as new and different gender roles (more egalitarian) may emerge when adapting to a new culture (Sandhu, 1997). Successful approaches to working with problems related to the "acculturation gap" are also based on a bicultural (or multicultural) psychoeducation and skills-building approach. Treatments such as bicultural effectiveness training (BET) have shown promise in treatment outcomes studies working with Mexican and Cuban immigrant families (Szapocznik, Santisteban, Kurtines, Perez-Vidal, & Hervis, 1984).

Working with Cultural Identity Problems

Identity concerns may be particularly important for ethnic minorities; immigrants; cultural or religious minorities; gay, lesbian, bisexual, and transgender persons (GLBT); or others who are undergoing the process of acculturation. Many "soft stage" models of identity development have been developed to provide clinicians with a general heuristic of the psychological phases that individuals go through as they become aware of their personal, social, and cultural identity. This can occur as a result of the age/developmental stage or it can be spurred on by an event, such as an act of racism or moving to a new country where one becomes a "minority" for the first time. Treatments for identity concerns usually aim to promote ethnic, racial, or cultural consciousness and awareness, while also resolving conflicts such as internalized racism or homophobia, and learning to find an acceptable integration between (often opposing and conflicting) cultural messages (Fudge, 1996). Education about social, cultural, and historical facts or events may be included, and clinicians might want to consider group-based approaches and those that involve peer or adult mentoring. Clinicians will also want to help establish networks and support for GLBT individuals who may be facing identity concerns and cultural, religious, and social conflicts related to the coming out process. National and local organizations (e.g., Parents, Families and Friends of Lesbians and Gays [PFLAG] and Human Rights Campaign [HRC]) and student and community-based groups can be valuable resources.

Handling Racism, Discrimination, and Oppression

Cultural, ethnic, religious, and sexual minorities continue to face racism, discrimination, and oppression in their daily lives. Many have had personal, direct experiences with racism or oppression, such as direct verbal or nonverbal attacks and threats based on their race, ethnic group, religion, or gender. Others experience it through their interactions with institutions and systems (e.g., legal, educational, health, business) that were not based on their values or designed for their benefit (Marsella & Yamada, 2000).

Still, many others experience the psychological effects of historical oppression, and major social and cultural traumas (e.g., American Indian genocide, African American slavery, Japanese internment camps) that continue to have an impact on both individuals and groups (Sue & Sue, 2007). Approaches to working with racism will depend on many factors, whether it is current or historical, direct or indirect, or individual or institutional (Ridley, 2005; Trepagnier, 2007). Due to the complexity of prejudice and racism, a multipronged (triadic) approach is recommended that includes treating the negative impact of racism at the individual, social, and political levels (Sandhu & Brown, 1996). Some treatment approaches might include gaining a deeper understanding of racism, power, and privilege (information gathering); assertiveness skills; working with pain associated with experiences of racism or oppression; cross-cultural training; intercultural communication training; social justice approaches, such as community action or systems interventions; and racial reconciliation or other approaches to creating cultural and racial harmony (Ponterotto, Utsey, & Pedersen, 2006; Ridley, 2005; Sandhu & Aspy, 1997; Sandhu & Brown, 1996).

Culture-Bound Syndromes, Religious or Spiritual Problems

In the case of a culture-bound disorder, clinicians should consider how the problem is treated within the context of origin, and combine this with information about the client's acculturation level and current context to develop a treatment plan. Culture-bound syndromes and often spiritual and religious problems are emic (specific to each culture) in nature, arising from cultural beliefs or at least conceptualized from a specific cultural or religious framework. As such, traditional or indigenous healing approaches (alone or combined with Western methods) may offer the best option. Consultation, collaboration, and sometimes referral to traditional or religious healers (e.g., curanderos/as, shamans, spiritualists, diviners, root workers, priests, pastoral counselors, etc.) may be needed (Moodley & West, 2005).

For example, a Muslim client of LRJ once asked for specific help with a cultural and religiously based concern. In particular, he wanted to know if it would be okay (according to Islamic teaching) for him to marry a second wife because his first wife suffered from bipolar disorder. In this particular context (East Africa) polygyny (men having multiple wives) is legal and common, so legality was not a concern for the clinician or the client. However, the client wanted to consider his decision for its appropriateness to his situation based on Islamic teachings. The client brought his Holy Koran to the session to share the specifics of the Koranic language and, thus, the basis of his query and conflict. However, being aware of a personal lack of knowledge about Islamic teachings and because this aspect (religious congruence) was of great concern to the client, LRJ referred her client to an imam to further discuss the religious aspects of his concerns. The client had a previously established relationship with a particular imam, whom he respected well, and he agreed that this was the best approach. At the same time, LRJ informed the client that she would be happy to talk with the client about the issue, identifying his thoughts and feelings, weighing the pros and cons of marrying a second wife, and how it might impact his life and that of his family.

Negotiating a Treatment Plan

After developing a treatment plan, clinicians can think critically about their plans by considering the following questions:

- What is the basis of the treatment plan?
- What are the areas of congruence and incongruence between my ideas about treatment and my client's ideas?
- Are there aspects of my client's EM or treatment expectations that I have not adequately considered or addressed?
- Can my model be adapted/expanded to include client beliefs?
- Are there cultural or personal strengths in my client's EM that I could build on to enhance treatment?

After determining the degree of clinician–client congruence, clinicians will want to consider whether further adaptations are possible and appropriate, and then prepare to negotiate differences and devise an agreement about how to proceed with treatment. To negotiate differences, first summarize the client's view of the problem, expectations, and goals for treatment. This can convey to the client that you have an accurate understanding of the problem and possibly bring to the forefront any areas that have been misunderstood (Hays, 2001). Next, share your conceptualization of the problem with your client. In doing so, pay careful attention to the manner in which the information is presented, using the client's own words whenever possible. Emphasize the similarities but do not ignore differences, as these should be explored and reconciled (Wohl, 2000).

Discussing areas of difference may be difficult and result in feelings of unease on the part of the clinician or the client. During this discussion, be mindful about the style of interaction that is common to the client (direct versus indirect; high or low context) and make adjustment accordingly. For example, if the client is used to an indirect style, then clinician frankness about an area of disagreement may cause undue shame or embarrassment to the client (Tseng, 2003). In such cases, clinicians may want to emphasize similarities and discuss differences, not as conflicting or opposing views, but as multiple and complementary ways of thinking about the problem. Even when there are drastic differences clinicians can focus on similarities and work toward shared goals.

Sharing your problem conceptualization and treatment rationale with the client will usually entail a certain amount of psychoeducation. This can be thought of as a kind of culture sharing, where we share our professional conceptualizations and thus invite clients into the world of our professional culture (Hays, 2001; Pedersen, 2004b). It can be helpful or even tactful to present the information, not as ultimate truth, but as originating from a particular perspective. For example, rather than saying, "What you are suffering from is not a heart problem, it is called panic," you might say, "In psychology (or in counseling) we often use the word panic to describe the same symptoms you are experiencing," or even "We could look at and think about your problem in several different ways, one is (summarize clients view) … another way of thinking about the problem is …" This approach allows the clinician to educate the client without resulting in a loss of face or otherwise causing embarrassment for the client who has a different view. Moreover, educating the client in this way can be empowering and may even result in dramatic relief in clients who do not have clear ideas about the nature of their problem and are searching for "expert" answers.

Next, provide your suggestions for treatment that incorporate client goals and treatment expectations. In all cases a clear rationale for the treatment plan should be provided. Recall that client EMs are often incomplete and usually modifiable (Gray, 1995). To the extent that the clinician has built credibility and trust, clients may be more receptive to new ideas or methods proposed by the therapist. Reframing or psychoeducational approaches can be used to present treatments in culturally palatable ways. Strengths-based approaches are also suggested, and because they are congruent with cultural values, may be more likely to garner client and family support for the treatment plan (Hays, 2001). The following steps provide a summary of the treatment negotiation process:

- Start with what the client presents.
- Share the clinician model, using client language when possible.
- Bridge the models by emphasizing similarities and discussing differences.
- Suggest an initial treatment plan with a clear rationale.
- Get client feedback and make adjustments that are culturally salient.
- Agree to work toward shared goals with a specific treatment plan.
- Continue to monitor, seek client feedback, and modify as needed.

Modifying and Revising the Treatment Plan

Included in the previous list is monitoring the implementation of the plan and revising it as needed, to account for client's adherence to the plan, possible barriers, and also treatment successes. In many cases, clinicians will find that treatment plans will need to be modified. Adherence issues may be related to a lack of resources (e.g., transportation, time, money), a lack of clinician cultural sensitivity, culturally incongruent treatment, a lack of client readiness for treatment, or a lack credibility for the treatment plan by the client or client's family.

Making Mistakes

In the multicultural context in which treatment planning occurs, some mistakes will be made. Sometimes we may underestimate the importance of culture, other times we may overestimate its importance. Sometimes we will make the wrong assumptions, say the wrong things, and make the wrong treatment plans. In the case of Sara, the refugee from Sudan, much attention was given to cultural content (e.g., enhancing bicultural effectiveness, use of religion, discussion and education about the acculturation process and cultural differences) in the treatment plan. However, problems soon arose due to some of the *content* of the treatment plan, the *emphasis* of the plan, and also due to some of the *processes* involved in carrying out the plan.

The therapist, for example, viewed Sara's desire to get married as a long-term goal, whereas the client viewed it as immediate. Although empathetic to the importance of marriage in other cultures and the client's worries about not finding a suitable (Sudanese) partner, LRJ still experienced an initial, culturally and personally biased reaction to the client's stated goal of getting married. The clinicians' Western cultural bias and feminist-based views about the needs of young women to be able function independently resulted in a treatment plan that was overly focused on Sara as an individual (i.e., first take care of herself, then she could bring her mother over and get married). Additional treatment planning mistakes included too much focus on the personal impact of her trauma (symptom reduction of depression and PTSD) rather than the social impact of the trauma (the state of her country and people); and use of some assessment and CBT methods (thought monitoring and direct discussion) that focused on internal states (thoughts and feelings). Sara found direct questions unacceptable and also painful. She also reported feeling anxious and fearful when she did not know "the answer."

Recovery and Treatment Plan Revisions

Pedersen (2004b) gives clinicians comfort by suggesting it is considered "a given" that we will make mistakes in the context of cultural differences; what is key is our ability to recover from those mistakes. To the extent that we have nurtured a respectful, working relationship and achieved some level of credibility with our clients, recovery is made easier, provided we are aware a mistake has been made.

In the case of Sara, she stopped coming in for regular therapy but showed up in a medical clinic reporting serious somatic complaints, including a "paralyzed" leg. Her somatic presentation was viewed as a culturally and personally acceptable way for her to express her grief at a recent loss and also to receive care. From that point, the treatment approach shifted. A primary emphasis was placed on positive actions and development toward Sara's goals, which were framed in a values-congruent way as "in service to others." For example, attending an ESL class so she can get a job, so she can send money to her mother, or get an education so she can do something to bring peace to the Sudan. Treatment proceeded with very few direct questions and little direct discussion of symptoms. From time to time, Sara would initiate discussions of symptoms and express her feelings, often by reading her poetry in session. In beautiful Arabic prose, she spoke of birds leaving their nests, fires burning deep, the liberation of Sudan, and words left unspoken. Sara's appointments became more regular and she made gains in terms of symptom reduction, building social support, and regaining a sense of hope and vision for the future.

Conclusion

In this chapter we have discussed some of the ways that culture impacts treatment planning, both in terms of the content of the plan, and the processes used in developing, presenting, negotiating, and implementing the plan. We provided a brief overview of how cultural competence and its interrelated components of awareness, knowledge, and skills can be applied to treatment planning. We introduced the concept of the explanatory model, as a way of aligning with the client and as a good starting place for developing an acceptable treatment plan. We also provided a start-to-finish approach consisting of questions along with a checklist that can be used to ensure that culture is considered and addressed at multiple levels in the treatment plan. We provided specific examples of ways that treatment plans can be adapted to better match a client's expectations, cultural beliefs and values, and ways of interacting, and also discussed the process of negotiating the treatment plan with the client.

Through case examples, we called attention to biases that might negatively affect the content of treatment plans or mistakes made in the process of presenting or enacting the plan. We also highlighted the need for clinicians to expect and recognize treatment-planning mistakes that are bound to occur. Last, we described the potential for clinicians to recover from such mistakes by soliciting client feedback and revising the treatment plan accordingly. Like cultural competence, effective treatment planning in a multicultural society is best considered an ongoing, developmental process in which treatments are continually evaluated and fine-tuned to better match our clients' unique cultural perspective and changing needs.

References

American Psychiatric Association. (1994). *Diagnostic and statistical manual of mental disorders* (4th ed.). Washington, DC: Author.

American Psychological Association (APA). (2003). Multicultural guidelines: Education training, research, practice and organizational change for psychologists. *American Psychologist, 58*, 377–402.

Angel, R. J., & Williams, K. (2000). Cultural models of health and illness. In I. Cuellar & F. A. Paniagua (Eds.), *Handbook of multicultural mental health* (pp. 25–44). San Diego, CA: Academic Press.

Aponte, J. F., & Bracco, H. F. (2000). Community approaches with ethnic populations. In J. F. Aponte, & J. Wohl (Eds.), *Psychological intervention and cultural diversity* (2nd ed.) (pp. 131–148). Needham Heights, MA: Allyn & Bacon.

Aponte, J. F., & Johnson, L. R. (2000). The impact of culture on intervention and treatment of ethnic populations. In J. F. Aponte & J. Wohl (Eds.), *Psychological intervention and cultural diversity* (2nd ed., pp. 18–39). Needham Heights, MA: Allyn & Bacon.

Atkinson, D. R., Morten, G., & Sue, D. W. (1998). Current issues and future directions in minority group/cross-cultural counseling. In D. R. Atkinson, G. Morten, & D. W. Sue (Eds.), *Counseling American minorities: A cross-cultural perspective* (5th ed., pp. 303–359). Boston: McGraw-Hill.

Barbarin, O. (1993). Emotional and social development of African American children. *Journal of Black Psychologists, 19*(4), 381–390.

Berry, J. W., & Kim, U. (1998). Acculturation and mental health. In P. R. Dasen, J. W. Berry, & N. Sartorius (Eds.), *Health and cross-cultural psychology: Toward applications* (pp. 207–236). Newbury Park, CA: Sage.

Berry, J. W., Kim, U., Minde, T., & Mok, D. (1987). Comparative studies of acculturative stress. *International Migration Review, 21,* 490511.

Bishop, C. L. (2002). *Nguzo Saba: An Africentric approach to examining self-esteem, Africentrism, and behavior modification with African-American adolescents.* Unpublished doctoral dissertation, University of Hartford, Connecticut.

Chrisman, N. J., & Johnson, T. M. (1996). Clinically applied anthropology. In C. F. Sargent & T. M. Johnson (Eds.), *Medial anthropology: Contemporary theory and method* (Rev. ed., pp. 88–109). Westport, CT: Praeger.

Constantino, G., Malgady, R. G., & Rogler, L. H. (1986). Cuento therapy: A culturally sensitive modality for Puerto Rican children. *Journal of Consulting and Clinical Psychology, 54*(4), 639–645.

Cuellar, I. (2000). Acculturation and mental health: Ecological transactional relations of adjustment. In I. Cuellar & F. A. Paniagua (Eds.), *Handbook of multicultural mental health* (pp. 45–62). San Diego, CA: Academic Press.

Fadiman, A. (1997). *The spirit catches you and you fall down.* New York: Farrar, Strauss & Grioux.

Fudge, R. (1996). The use of behavior therapy in the development of ethnic consciousness: A treatment model. *Cognitive and Behavioral Practice, 2,* 317–335.

Galanter, M. (1999). Network therapy. In P. G. Ott, R. E. Tarter, & R. T. Ammerman (Eds.), *Sourcebook on substance abuse: Etiology, epidemiology, assessment, and treatment* (pp. 264–271). Needham Heights, MA: Allyn & Bacon.

Gray, D. E. (1995). Lay conceptions of autism: Parents' explanatory models. *Medical Anthropology, 16,* 99–118.

Gregg, J., & Curry, R. H. (1994). Explanatory models for cancer among African-American women at two Atlanta neighborhood health centers: The implications for a cancer screening program. *Social Science Medicine, 39*(4), 519–526.

Griner, D., & Smith, T. B. (2006). Culturally adapted mental health interventions: A meta-analytic review. *Psychotherapy: Theory, Research, Practice, Training, 43,* 531–548.

Hage, S. M. (2005). Future considerations for fostering multicultural competence in mental health and educational settings: Social justice implications. In M. G. Constantine & D. W. Sue (Eds.), *Strategies for building multicultural competence* (pp. 285–302). Hoboken, NJ: John Wiley & Sons.

Hayes, S. C., Strosahl, K. D., & Wilson, K. G. (1999). *Acceptance and commitment therapy: An experimental approach to behavior change.* New York: Guilford Press.

Hays, P. A. (2001). *Addressing cultural complexities in practice: A framework for clinicians and counselors.* Washington, DC: American Psychological Association.

Hong, G. K., Garcia, M., & Soriano, M. (2000). Responding to the challenge: Preparing mental health professionals for the new millennium. In I. Cuellar & F. A. Paniagua (Eds.), *Handbook of multicultural mental health* (pp. 455–476). San Diego, CA: Academic Press.

Johnson, L. R., & Sandhu, D. S. (2007). Isolation, adjustment, and acculturation issues of international students: Intervention strategies for counselors. In. H. D. Singaravelu & M. Pope (Eds.), *A handbook for counseling international students in the United States* (pp. 13–35). Alexandria, VA: American Counseling Association.

Kleinman, A. (1980). *Patients and healers in the context of culture.* Berkeley: University of California Press.

Kluckhohn, F. R., & Strodtbeck, F. L. (1961). *Variations in value orientations.* Evanston, IL: Row, Patterson, & Co.

Koss-Chioino, J. D. (2000). Traditional and folk approaches among ethnic minorities. In J. F. Aponte & J. Wohl (Eds.), *Psychological intervention and cultural diversity* (2nd ed., pp. 149–166). Needham Heights, MA: Allyn & Bacon.

Lazarus, A. A. (1997). *Brief but comprehensive psychotherapy the multimodal way.* New York: Springer.

Lonner, W. J., Wong, P. T. P., & Wong, L. C. J. (2006). *Handbook of multicultural perspectives on stress and coping: International & cultural psychology.* New York: Springer Science Business Media.

Malgady, R. G., Rogler, L. H., & Constantino, G. (1990a). Hero/heroine modeling for Puerto Rican adolescents: A preventative mental health intervention. *Journal of Consulting and Clinial Psychology, 58,* 469–474.

Malgady, R. G., Rogler, L. H., & Constantino, G. (1990b). Culturally sensitive psychotherapy for Puerto Rican children and adolescents: A program of treating outcome research. *Journal of Consulting and Clinical Psychology, 58,* 704–712.

Marsella, A. J., & Yamada, A. M. (2000). Culture and mental health: An introduction and overview of foundations, concepts, and issues. In I. Cuellar & F. A. Paniagua (Eds.), *Handbook of multicultural mental health* (pp. 3–24). San Diego, CA: Academic Press.

Martin, J. N., & Nakayama, T. K. (2005). *Experiencing intercultural communication* (2nd ed.). New York: McGraw-Hill.

Mio, J. S., Barker-Hackett, L. B., & Tumambing, J. (2006). *Multicultural psychology: Understanding our diverse communities.* Boston: McGraw-Hill.

Moodley, R., & West, W. (Eds.). (2005). *Integrating traditional healing practices into counseling and psychotherapy.* Thousand Oaks, CA: Sage.

Munroe, R. L., & Munroe, R. H. (1980). Perspectives suggested by anthropological data. In H. C. Triandis & J. W. Berry (Eds.), *Handbook of cross-cultural psychiatry: Vol. 2. Methodology* (pp. 253–318). Boston: Allyn & Bacon.

Myers, L. J., Ezemenari, M. O., Jefferson, M., Anderson, M., Godfrey, T., & Purnell, J. (2005). Building multicultural competence around indigenous healing practices. In M. G. Constantine & D. W. Sue (Eds.), *Strategies for building multicultural competence* (pp. 109–126). Hoboken, NJ: John Wiley & Sons.

Norcross, J. C., Hedges, M., & Prochaska, J. O. (2002). The face of 2010: A Delphi poll on the future of psychotherapy. *Professional Psychology: Research and Practice, 33*(3), 316–322.

Okazaki, S. (2000). Assessing and treating Asian Americans: Recent advances. In I. Cuellar & F. A. Paniagua (Eds.), *Handbook of multicultural mental health* (pp. 171–193). San Diego, CA: Academic Press.

Paniagua, F. A. (2000). Culture-bound syndromes, cultural variations, and psychopathology. In I. Cuellar & F. A. Paniagua (Eds.), *Handbook of multicultural mental health* (pp. 139–169). San Diego, CA: Academic Press.

Paniagua, F. A. (2005). *Assessing and treating culturally diverse clients. A practical guide* (3rd ed.). Thousand Oaks, CA: Sage.

Pedersen, P. B. (1991). Multiculturalism as a generic approach to counseling. *Journal of Counseling and Development: Special Issue on Multiculturalism as a Fourth Force, 70*, 6–12.

Pedersen, P. B. (2003). Cross-cultural counseling: Developing culture-centered interactions. In G. Bernal, J. E. Trimble, A. K. Burlew, & F. T. L. Leong (Eds.), *Handbook of racial and ethnic minority psychology* (pp. 487–503). Thousand Oaks, CA: Sage.

Pedersen, P. B. (2004a). The multicultural context of mental health. In T. B. Smith (Ed.), *Practicing multiculturalism* (pp. 17–32). Boston, MA: Allyn & Bacon.

Pedersen, P. B. (2004b). *Culture-centered counseling* [APA Psychotherapy Videotape Series II]. Washington, DC: American Psychological Association.

Pelto, P. J., & Pelto, G. H. (1996). Research designs in medical anthropology. In C. F. Sargent & T. M. Johnson (Eds.), *Medical anthropology: Contemporary theory and method* (pp. 293–324). Westport, CT: Praeger.

Ponterotto, J. G., Utsey, S. O., & Pedersen, P. B. (2006). *Preventing prejudice: A guide for counselors, educators, and parents* (2nd ed.). Thousand Oaks, CA: Sage.

Prendes-Lintel, M. (2001). A working model in counseling recent refugees. In J. G. Ponterotto, J. M. Casas, L. A. Suzuki, & C. M. Alexander (Eds.), *Handbook of multicultural counseling* (pp. 729–752). Thousand Oaks, CA: Sage.

Prochaska, J. O. (1999). How do people change, and how can we change to help many more people. In M. A. Hubble, B. L. Duncan, & S. D. Miller (Eds.), *The heart & soul of change: What works in therapy* (pp. 227–255). Washington, DC: American Psychological Association.

Ridley, C. R. (2005). *Overcoming unintentional racism in counseling and therapy: A practitioners' guide to intentional intervention* (2nd ed.). Thousand Oaks, CA: Sage.

Rogler, L., & Cortez, D. (1992). Help-seeking pathways: A unifying concept in mental health care. *American Journal of Psychiatry, 150*, 553–561.

Sandhu, D. S. (1997). Psychocultural profiles of Asian and Pacific Islander Americans: Implications for counseling and psychotherapy. *Journal of Multicultural Counseling and Development, 25*(1), 7–22.

Sandhu, D. S. (Ed.) (in press). *Alternative approaches to counseling and psychotherapy.* Commack, NY: Nova Science.

Sandhu, D. S., & Aspy, C. B. (1997). *Counseling for prejudice prevention and reduction.* Alexandria, VA: American Counseling Association.

Sandhu, D. S., & Asrabadi, B. R. (1994). Development of an acculturative stress scale for international students: Preliminary findings. *Psychological Reports, 75*, 435–448.

Sandhu, D. S., & Brown, S. P. (1996). Empowering ethnically and racially diverse clients through prejudice reduction. Suggestions and strategies for counselors. *Journal of Multicultural Counseling and Development, 24*(4), 202–217.

Sandhu, D. S., Portes, P. R., & McPhee, S. (1996). Assessing cultural adaptation: Psychometric properties of the cultural adaptation pain scale. *Journal of Multicultural Counseling and Development, 24*(1), 15–25.

Sourander, A. (2003). Refugee families during asylum seeking. *Nordic Journal of Psychiatry, 57,* 203–207.

Sue, D. W. (1978). Eliminating cultural oppression in counseling: Toward a general theory. *Journal of Counseling Psychology, 25,* 419–428.

Sue, D. W, Arredondo, P., & McDavis, R. J. (1992). Multicultural competencies and standards: A call to the profession. *Journal of Counseling & Development, 70,* 477–486.

Sue, D. W., Ivey, A. E., & Pederson, P. B. (1996). *A theory of multicultural counseling and therapy.* Pacific Grove, CA: Brooks/Cole.

Sue, D. W., & Sue, D. (2007). *Counseling the culturally diverse: Theory and practice* (5th ed.). New York: John Wiley & Sons.

Sue, S. (2006). Cultural competency: From philosophy to research and practice. *Journal of Community Psychology, 43,* 237–245.

Szapocznik, J., Rio, A., Perez-Vidal, A., Kurtines, W., Hervis, O., & Santisteban, D. (1986). Bicultural Effectiveness Training (BET): An experimental test of an intervention modality for families experiencing intergenerational/intercultural conflict. *Hispanic Journal of Behavioral Sciences, 8,* 303–330.

Szapocznik, J., Santisteban, D., Kurtines, W., Perez-Vidal, A., & Hervis, O. (1984). Bicultural effectiveness training: A treatment intervention for enhancing intercultural adjustment in Cuban American families. *Hispanic Journal of Behavioral Sciences, 6,* 317–344.

Tewari, N., Inman, A. G., & Sandhu, D. S. (2003). South Asian Americans: Culture, concern, and therapeutic strategies. In J. S. Mio & G. Y. Iwamasa (Eds.), *Culturally diverse mental health: The challenges of research and resistance* (pp. 191–209). New York: Brunner-Routledge.

Trepagnier, B. (2007). *Silent racism: How well-meaning white people perpetuate the racial divide.* Boulder, CO: Paradigm.

Triandis, H. (1995). *Individualism & collectivism.* Boulder, CO: Westview.

Tseng, W. (2003). *Clinician's guide to cultural psychiatry.* San Diego, CA: Academic Press.

Vasquez, M. J. T. (2005). Independent practice settings and the multicultural guidelines. In M. G. Constantine & D. W. Sue (Eds.), *Strategies for building multicultural competence* (pp. 91–108). Hoboken, NJ: John Wiley & Sons.

Vontress, C. E., Johnson, J. A., & Epp, L. R. (1999). *Cross-cultural counseling: A case book.* Alexandria, VA: American Counseling Association.

Weiss, M. G., & Kleinman, A. (1988). Depression in cross-cultural perspective: Developing a culturally informed model. In P. R. Dasen, J. W. Berry, & N. Sartorius (Eds.), *Health and cross-cultural psychology* (pp. 179–205). Newbury Park, CA: Sage.

Wilson, M. N., Kohn, L. P., & Lee, T. S. (2000). Cultural relativistic approach towards ethnic minorities in family therapy. In J. F. Aponte & J. Wohl (Eds.), *Psychological intervention and cultural diversity* (2nd ed., pp. 92–109). Needham Heights, MA: Allyn & Bacon.

Wohl, J. (2000). Psychotherapy and cultural diversity. In J. F. Aponte & J. Wohl (Eds.), *Psychological intervention and cultural diversity* (2nd ed., pp. 75–91). Needham Heights, MA: Allyn & Bacon.

Wrenn, C. G. (1962). The culturally encapsulated counselor. *Harvard Educational Review, 32,* 444–449.

7

Cultural Encapsulation and Decapsulation of Therapist Trainees

Gargi Roysircar and Peter A. Gill

When an individual presents problems in therapy, the role of the therapist is to offer interventions that would alleviate symptoms, mediate maladaptive behavior or thinking patterns, and promote well-being. As an agent of change, the therapist's work begins with understanding the nature of presenting problems and the context in which they are manifested. Knowing how to do therapy speaks not only to the therapist's knowledge of psychopathology and interventions, but also to his or her efforts to connect interpersonally with the client by way of establishing a relationship that is warm, empathic, and collaborative. Establishing a positive therapeutic and collaborative relationship is important (Fischer, Jome, & Atkinson, 1998; Roysircar, Hubbell, & Gard, 2003) because it fosters a positive treatment outcome for the client (Constantine, Fuertes, & Roysircar & Kindaichi, 2008; Roysircar, 2009a; Wampold, 2001).

When considering the multicultural counseling competencies (MCC), the therapeutic relationship is understood to draw attention to the manner in which a therapist presents himself or herself as racially and culturally sensitive and as being comfortable with a client's diversity (Sodowsky, Taffe, Gutkin, & Wise, 1994). The multicultural therapeutic relationship is also how the therapist is perceived by minority individuals seeking treatment

(Constantine & Ladany, 2001; Fuertes & Brobst, 2002; Jones & Markos, 1997; Pope-Davis et al., 2002). In mainstream psychotherapy literature, Kottler (1991) describes individuals seeking treatment as those desiring a professional "who is warm and approachable, someone who listens to and understands them," as well as someone "who is competent and confident, [and] who gives them a sense of hope" (p. 1). These common psychotherapy factors, both multicultural and mainstream, represent the recognition of psychotherapists engaging in specific overt interpersonal characteristics that have been shown to impact clients positively (Fischer et al., 1998; Roysircar, 2009a; Wampold, 2001).

However, has there been a common recognition of *implicit, subtle* therapist characteristics, such as *a priori* assumptions and racial attitudes, brought into the therapy session (e.g., Comas-Diaz & Jacobsen, 1991, 1995; Helms, 1990)? Thus far, less attention has been given by psychotherapy literature to the level of awareness that therapists have about the way their values, biases, and assumptions affect the manner in which they engage minority clients. It is crucial that a therapist gain proficiency in cultural and racial self-awareness, the most basic MCC dimension (Roysircar, 2003), before aspiring to other MCC dimensions, such as multicultural knowledge and skills (for the MCC model, see Arredondo et al., 1996; Roysircar, Arredondo, Fuertes, Ponterotto, & Toporek, 2003; D. W. Sue, Arredondo, & McDavis, 1992).

Awareness of one's biases, or lack thereof, can conceivably influence the manner in which a therapist engages with racially and culturally diverse clients. This influence can be measured empirically. For example, Roysircar, Gard, Hubbell, and Ortega (2005) demonstrated therapist trainees' success at writing process notes to reflect on their level of sensitivity to multicultural issues during mentoring sessions with adolescent minority students attending a middle school program in English as a second language (ESL). Trained observer raters used the process notes to identify trainees' disconnection and connection themes in their reflections on their work with ESL clients. Trainee disconnection themes had no relationship with trainee self-reported levels of MCC and positive White racial identity attitudes. On the other hand, trainee connection themes had significant positive correlations with self-reported MCC and positive White racial identity.

Being interested in understanding implicit, subtle therapist *a priori* assumptions, the authors wanted to understand whether therapist trainees are aware of their cultural encapsulation when engaged with culturally diverse individuals. Excerpts from trainees' self-reflection process notes are used to illustrate their cultural encapsulation as well as decapsulation. Encapsulation means to enclose in a capsule, and decapsulation means the removal of a capsule (Oxford University Press, 1989). Biases, values, assumptions, and racial attitudes represent what are enclosed in therapist trainees' thoughts and expressions. Upon becoming aware of their cultural encapsulation, trainees are expected to reveal expressions of decapsulation.

Trainees engaged in a weekly 1-hour mentoring session with the same community member for 10 weeks. Trainees mentored individuals whose demographic characteristics (e.g., age, socioeconomic status, religion, race, ethnicity, regional/national origin) differed from their own on one or more characteristics. Following each session, trainees submitted a one-page process note to the first author on the next scheduled class day. Within a week of submission, the instructor provided written feedback. Written feedback served as a way to point to limitations in trainees' self-reflections that might prevent them from facilitating and achieving enriching mentoring sessions with culturally diverse community members. A sample of 6 cases of 10 process notes each ($N = 60$ notes) was randomly selected from 30 cases collected in two semesters from 2 successive years. These cases were qualitatively analyzed to provide exemplars of cultural encapsulation and decapsulation, which is the topic of this chapter.

Cultural Encapsulation

Conceptual Origins

Wrenn (1962) offered insights on counselors' inevitable practice of sheltering themselves within their own history of beliefs, values, and customs, which inform how they interpret, behave, and interface with clients in the here-and-now. He referred to this sheltering as "a cocoon of pretend reality" (p. 445). Inevitable societal changes and anticipated social threats (Wrenn, 1962, 1985) lead therapists to unconsciously create this cocoon of pretend reality as a way of resisting the idea of change or protecting themselves from social changes perceived as disturbing. Wrenn's purpose was to raise awareness of the human nature of self-preservation, while also calling attention to the detrimental effects of status-quo preservation.

The illusion (Wrenn, 1962, 1985) of counselors using their own personal history, representing stored practices and experiences that serve to keep them psychologically grounded and to make sense of their social world, is their assumption that their own history will directly lead to a precise understanding of clients' personal histories. However, the experiences that have helped counselors understand their world do not necessarily generalize to the same learning of clients, nor do they necessarily facilitate conceptualization of a client's psychological problems. Wrenn (1962) asserted that making such an assumption "is 'cultural encapsulation,' an encapsulation within our world, within our culture and sub-culture, within a pretense that the present is enduring" (p. 445). In relation to this idea, Wrenn argued how beliefs, values, and assumptions are "culture bound" and "time bound" (p. 447). He sought to increase counselors' awareness of the limitation of what they see as truths, including the knowledge counselors acquire through formal training. He asserted, "Whatever we 'firmly' know now may be firm as a principle but not as a law—perhaps we have no laws of behaviors as yet. Because man [sic] changes with knowledge of man [sic], we may never have laws" (p. 447).

In this chapter, the present authors refer to two related cultural encapsulations in Wrenn's (1962) essay because these are relevant to the training of therapist trainees. One is the "the tendency to be surprised or even unbelieving regarding changes in truth" (p. 446; termed *presumed truth* by the present authors). The second one is "the assumption that the counselor may safely draw upon his [sic] own educational and vocational experience in counseling" (p. 448; termed *maintaining the status quo* by the present authors). Presumed truth refers to the idea that counselors tend to develop their own perspective or social reality of what they believe to be true based on their own life experience. Wrenn (1962, 1985) emphasized that sociocultural events that impact the development of a person's perspective evolve with each new generation. For instance, the Civil Rights Movement and the Women's Movement impacted the first author; however, she currently trains doctoral students who have been impacted by 9/11. Thus, a client is likely to hold beliefs or presumed truths that would likely differ from those of the previous generation as well as those of other persons within his or her own generation. Maintaining the status quo speaks to counselors' strict adherence to knowledge borne out of the academic setting and considered gospel while also being difficult to prove as knowledge that accurately reflects the real, changing world. Thus, while academic or other formal settings (e.g., practicum and internship sites) serve as important arenas for generating and acquiring knowledge, counselors are cautioned to not restrict themselves to schools of thought or the dogmatic thinking inherent in these settings. For example, Wrenn (1962) alerted counselors to consider "the tentativeness of our knowledge of human behavior" (p. 447), as such knowledge evolves and changes as new knowledge of human behavior is acquired. These two encapsulations, presumed truth and maintaining the status quo, appear to fall under *knowledge-based cultural encapsulation*, which is given clinical exemplars from trainees' self-reflection process notes. (For a description of procedures for self-reflection process notes, see Roysircar, 2004; Roysircar et al., 2005; Roysircar, Webster et al., 2003.)

Knowledge-Based Encapsulation Exemplified by Trainees

Presumed Truth, Assumptions, and Judgments Presumed truths, assumptions, and judgments were present in all trainees' narratives about their clients. These represented false impressions trainees had about their clients. The impressions were cognitive in nature and appeared to stem from either book knowledge or prior socialization. For example, trainees had assumptions about how their clients perceived their identity, as it related to their culture or ethnicity.

> She began by telling me that for a long time, she didn't think much about being Korean and, in fact, sometimes she even forgot she was Korean. She says that it wasn't until she looked into a mirror that she remembered. I'm not sure if that really was the case or not. Perhaps she was denying or repressing the differences between her and her White adoptive parents like certain individuals deny their minority identity while denigrating their racial group. This is the preencounter stage of Helms's people of color identity model and in Cross' nigrescence model.

Trainees' narratives also typically reflected avoidance or rationalization of the emotional nature of exchanges with multicultural clients. The trainees practiced intellectualism, as in the following case:

> I've gathered from feedback on my session notes that they lack emotional presence and I think this is because I tend to process emotions after classes for the week are over (also after I have written the process notes). These stay sort of bottled up in me until the Wednesday following our sessions. These emotions have run the gamut: happiness, sorrow, exasperation, confusion, sympathy, empathy, and boredom. I am happy to continue meeting with S because I want to learn more about Judaism, communicate with individuals from other cultures. ...

Assumptions about how a client might view religious figures or spiritual practices were sometimes noted: "As I looked around the walls in his house, I noticed a painting of a Black Jesus. Never before had it crossed my mind that Jesus might be Black."

Maintaining the Status Quo   Trainees generally expressed a universalist position with thoughts like "we are all alike" or "we are all different." While there is an obvious truth to universalism, there was underlying argued defensiveness in trainees or a denial of cultural differences. One trainee wrote:

> The turning point in this session came, not when I saw a change in her, but when I saw a change in myself. For the first time, I began to see L *not* from the vantage point of her ethnicity, but instead I began to think of her (and all beings, actually) as something different. Suddenly, her ethnicity wasn't the lens by which I was talking with her.

Another trainee wrote:

> C and I decided to take our mentoring session to a public setting. What prompted us to do so was a previous discussion we had earlier about how I take it for granted that I am a White person. He told me to go out with him in public and see if people acted differently towards me. I didn't quite understand what he meant because even if I was with him, I was still White, regardless.

Interpersonally Based Cultural Encapsulation

Interpersonally based cultural encapsulation appears in majority–minority interactive and communication styles, which reveal issues of implicit racism, stereotype threat, and racial microaggressions in people who hold a dominant or privileged power status. However, racial attitudes that help to explain interpersonally based cultural encapsulation were not present in Wrenn's framework (1962, 1985). The present authors analyzed how trainees' deeply engrained racial attitudes affected their responses to clients, and they discuss three themes in trainees' interpersonally based cultural encapsulation: implicit racism, stereotype threats, and racial microaggression.

Implicit Racism   Research on subtle racism (e.g., Dovidio, Gaertner, & Kawakami, 2002; Dovidio, Kawakami, Gaertner, & Hodson, 2002) bears on the topic of hidden, deeply engrained racial attitudes. Dovidio, Kawakami, et al. (2002) investigated the effects of implicit and explicit racial attitudes on White persons' perception of their interactions with Black individuals. According to Dovidio, Kawakami, et al., explicit racial attitudes influence "deliberative, well-considered responses for which people have the motivation and opportunity to weigh the costs and benefits of various courses of action" (p. 62). Examples of explicit racism are the recent spurt of hangman's nooses and swastika signs that have been placed in educational and work settings (Pignatiello & Roysircar, 2008), with the planned intention to intimidate and humiliate African Americans and American Jews, but at little cost to the perpetrators since such acts have been done anonymously and under cover.

Alternatively, implicit racial attitudes influence "responses that are more difficult to monitor and control [e.g., eye movements, blinking] or responses that people do not view as an indication of their attitude and thus do not try to control" (Dovidio, Kawakami et al., 2002, p. 62). Dovidio, Kawakami, et al. (2002) revealed in their study that explicit prejudice of White participants, as indicated in paper-and-pencil tests, was significantly associated with the rating of their verbal friendliness (less overt prejudice–more verbal friendliness) but not to the ratings of their nonverbal behaviors (eye contact). Implicit prejudice, however, as measured by a response-latency task, was significantly associated with ratings of nonverbal friendliness but not to the ratings of verbal behaviors. For instance, White participants' explicit prejudicial attitudes and verbal behavior were significantly associated with their self-perceived friendliness toward Black confederates. On the other hand, Black confederates' perception of bias in the behavior of the White participants was significantly associated with White participants' implicit racial attitudes and nonverbal behaviors. No relationship was found between White participants' impression of their own prejudice and the impression of prejudice perceived by Black confederates.

The difference in perception of implicit and explicit racial attitudes between White participants and Black confederates spoke to the type of information that White participants relied on compared to the type of information that Black confederates relied on when interpreting their verbal interchange (Dovidio, Kawakami, et al., 2002). The role of social cognition helps to explain this difference. Judgment, memory, and motivation of Whites and Blacks are likely to contribute to how persons in each racial group perceive the intention of the other in interpersonal interactions. Implicit racism was noted in the following trainee response:

> I could sit here and say that spending the day at the mall with C, as part of my ESL mentoring service, didn't bother me—I mean ... after all, I did have a good time. However, I realize now that I would be lying if I said that I didn't feel the least bit uncomfortable laughing and hanging out with a young Black man. The truth is, I did feel uncomfortable at times. I expressed these feelings and the guilt they elicited in me to C and he assured me that this is a natural response, which he said he can sense even if I were not to show or talk about it.

Implicit racism can translate into avoidance of or guilt about issues of how trainees' race and privileged status, as members of the dominant society, might define them. Following is an example:

> I must admit, I became a little envious of close-knit families. I wish I could say that my siblings are my best friends; however, I cannot. I feel guilty that I don't spend much time with my sister or brother or my parents. So, I responded to him by saying how I wished that I grew up in a culture where so many different types of family values were important. I notice that I feel extreme feelings like guilt, jealousy, and even pity when I am with my culturally different client.

Stereotype Threats　　Another racialized behavior is the "stereotype threat." Steele (1997) determined how societal stereotypes influence minority individuals' intellectual functioning, identity development, and achievement. A stereotype threat is a negative stereotype about a group that threatens a part of the group's identity and ultimately influences the ability of the group to succeed within the realm with which the threat is associated. Women and African Americans must contend with negative stereotypes about their intellectual abilities and performance in areas such as math and science. This stereotype can become internalized and influence performance within the pertinent academic domains. The threat associated with negative stereotypes prompts individuals to engage in disidentification. Disidentification causes students to distance themselves motivationally from the academic domain in question, therefore influencing their ability to succeed in that area. When comparing self-esteem and school achievement among African American and White students, it was found that although African American students underperformed in comparison to White students on standardized tests, their overall self-esteem was equal to or greater than that of the White students. Steele (1997) suggests that here, perhaps, was the source of African Americans' overall self-regard: disidentification with domains (e.g., math and science) in which their evaluative prospects were poor and identification with domains in which their prospects were better (i.e., their peers' acceptance).

Some trainee narratives indicated stereotypic attitudes, as reflected by the following:

> I'm going to rent and lend *Driving Miss Daisy* and *Get on the Bus*, both movies that portray Jewish and African-American relationships. I think it would be very interesting to hear S's reaction to both and to ask him how the portrayals relate to his experiences. I have already explained

this idea to S and he is interested in it. As a conversation partner to an elderly Jewish man, who served once as a cantor, his attitudes toward Blacks would make a good discussion.

Racial Microaggressions   D. W. Sue and colleagues (Sue, Bucceri, Lin, Nadal, & Torino, 2007; Sue, Capodilupo, et al., 2007) refer to "The Invisibility of Unintentional Expressions of Bias" (p. 277) by the offender. According to D. W. Sue, Bucceri et al. (2007), microaggressions tend to be indirect and unintentional, and are most likely to emerge not when behavior would look prejudicial, but when other rationales can be offered for prejudicial behavior. Many microaggressions become conditioned and people do not realize that they are engaging in these behaviors. This results in the dilemma of "Clash of Racial Realities" (D. W. Sue, Capodilupo, et al., 2007, p. 277). In this dilemma, there is a question as to whether a racial incident actually happened because Whites believe racism is on the decline. Minorities, on the other hand, have experienced racial microaggressions firsthand. One question that arises is how people with such different experiences of reality can come to any mutual understanding.

Microinsult/microinvalidation or multicultural verbal ineptness/naïveté represents verbal or behavioral microaggressions that are unintentional but nonetheless demeaning, invalidating, or both, as indicated by the following trainee narrative:

> During the 3rd meeting, P and I talked about the Indian marriage rituals. She brought pictures of her sister's marriage to show me and the interaction was going really well until we started talking about the third day of the ceremony. On the third day the wife moves with her husband to his family's home. Before she leaves a ritual is performed in which she is told to be good and to always respect her in-laws. She is also told that she should take all of the abuse that she receives. When P told me this I laughed in disbelief. Coming from my own experience of being taught to stand up for myself and not let anyone walk all over me, this rule seemed absurd. P was offended with my reaction.

While there is evidence that individuals are likely to unknowingly exhibit implicit racial attitudes or microaggressions even if they assert themselves as having no prejudicial beliefs or engaging in behaviors reflecting prejudicial tones (e.g., Dovidio, Kawakami, et al., 2002), there is evidence that writing self-reflection process notes helps psychology trainees increase their self-awareness and understand their level of sensitivity to multicultural issues when working with minority clients (e.g., Roysircar, 2004; Roysircar et al., 2005; Roysircar et al., 2003). It was also expected that trainees would show decapsulation in their self-reflection process notes.

Cultural Decapsulation

The practice of continuously examining a social situation in order to modify or replace knowledge that is presumed to be true is one approach described by Wrenn (1962) that serves to ameliorate cultural encapsulation. This chapter includes an analysis of the continuous efforts over time by therapist trainees to self-examine their encapsulated style of responding. By developing understanding of their cultural encapsulation through reflective self-analysis, therapist trainees determine the specifics of self-awareness that they need with regard to their values, beliefs, assumptions, and racial attitudes about their multicultural clients.

The overall positive outcome of a greater number of cultural decapsulation themes than cultural encapsulation themes in the authors' analyses of trainee self-reflections suggests how trainees might engage actively in a learning process of becoming culturally skilled. Trainees' investment to become culturally competent has led to the emergence of more themes reflecting cultural decapsulation. This finding is similar to the one observed in Manese et al.'s (2001) study on the effect of a predoctoral internship program on the development of interns' multicultural counseling competencies. Manese and colleagues did not generate any finding that would suggest a failure or challenge by interns to developing multicultural counseling competencies. They concluded that study participants appeared to have begun their internship program interested in multiculturalism.

Awareness of clients' worldview, context, and experience of racism and *sizing the client* with regard to understanding the client's group-based affiliations, universalism, and individualism were common themes across all trainee self-reflections. The general occurrence of these themes is important for understanding specific cognitive stimuli in self-reflective process notes that increase trainees' awareness of their clients' worldview.

Awareness-Based Cultural Decapsulation

Awareness of clients' worldview, context, and experience of racism was a theme that was found across all cases. If therapists are to be culturally sensitive and in tune with racial and ethnic minority clients, prescribed interventions should be based on the cultural context of the client, be culturally consistent with the client's worldview and understanding of normality and abnormality (Toporek, 2003), and be acceptable to the client in order to preserve the common factors of psychotherapy (Wampold, 2001). Whatever the clinical activity, a way of understanding the process by which therapists might consciously understand and accept clients' cultural contexts is to consider the role of cultural decapsulation in their responses to culturally diverse clients. One trainee disclosed:

> What she really wants is to be like everyone else and not stand out. However, later in our conversation, she spoke of being proud that she is different. I sense that she is quite ambivalent about her ethnicity and cultural background because she has been teased in the school bus and called "Chinese" when she is not. It will be interesting to see what else she will share with me, now that we have proceeded beyond the first few meetings. I also need to understand better the issues of Chinese and Korean and distinguish their differences.

Another trainee disclosed the following narrative:

> L interrupted the conversation to say that she didn't agree with S's answer. In order to avoid any confusion, I simply posed the question to her. I was hoping that by pulling her into the conversation more actively, we would be able to continue talking from our various points of view.

Roysircar, Webster et al. (2003) found that the connection between therapist trainees and their ESL clients was characterized by trainees' awareness of other people and their reflection on this other-awareness, as well as an intentional exchange of cultural information between the client and the trainee.

Sizing the Client

It was noted in all cases that trainees felt compelled to understand their interviewees' unique needs. Although this approach is similar to that of the initial assessment sessions of therapy (Kottler, 1991), it is a particularly important skill with minority individuals whose individuality may be overlooked by an overemphasis on the group-specific factors of their identity, such as race, ethnicity, or cultural values (Roysircar, 2003). Specifically, within-group difference among minorities should be just as basic to pretherapy information as individual differences are to mainstream counseling, particularly because information about within-group differences and unique client characteristics provide additional knowledge about clients related to favorable outcomes. However, avoidance of stereotypes through attention to within-group differences does not mean ignoring cultural group characteristics that may also affect an individual. Knowing how to appropriately categorize experiences as cultural, knowing when to generalize and be inclusive, and knowing when to individualize and be exclusive is a skill- and knowledge-based multicultural competency. Stanley Sue (1998) called this the "dynamic sizing" of the client.

One student reflected on children of immigrants, as they may differ from their immigrant parents:

> M might be uniquely reflective of the changing face of Islam in America. Having been raised in America and spared the first-generation acculturation process, he feels less pressure to hold any one aspect of his identity at a distance and is comfortably developing his own understanding of what it means to be both an American and a Muslim. It is pinning down how these attitudes translate to the arena of mental health that is at the heart our conversations. What has been the effect of 9/11 on M's potential treatment-seeking behavior and stress levels? Does he stigmatize mental illness or see it as spiritual deficiency, as first-generation Muslim immigrants do?

Social Justice Advocacy

Social justice behaviors found in trainee self-reflections coincided with the more recent social justice literature (Roysircar, 2008, 2009b; Toporek, Gerstein, Fouad, Roysircar, & Israel, 2006). Social justice advocacy had four themes in trainees' narratives. First, *giving access* represented trainees' desire to help their clients access community resources or community information; or it represented trainees' plans to promote cultural change at the community level, thereby facilitating their clients' access to community resources or community information. An example of providing access included:

> It is clear that he joined the Communist Party to become more active and it seems odd that he hasn't joined any type of organization since moving to the area. My hope is to help him find at least a newsletter that may provide him with a consistent link to the "outside world." If he is not interested or seems hesitant I will not pursue this course of action.

Second, *active help* represented trainees becoming proactive in helping their clients fulfill a social need at an individual or community level, or increasing trainees' availability to clients. Here's an example:

> YH had expressed her difficulty talking on the phone. I asked her if she would like to practice talking with me on the phone sometime and she replied that she would very much like to try.

Third, *sharing power* represented trainees' efforts at eliminating any power differential with their clients, as reflected in the following narrative:

> She gave me her phone number and I made the mistake of realizing, after I left, that I had neglected to give her my number. I felt awful, due to the power differential inherent in this arrangement. I am going to call her tomorrow and give her my number with apologies that I forgot today.

Fourth, trainees jointly planning and cultivating their mentoring outreach with their clients resulted in their reflections on *collaboration*:

> I decided to ask her what she would consider important about our sessions that she would like me to incorporate in my final case conceptualization paper.

All four social justice themes—giving access, active help, sharing power, and collaboration—represented the proactive efforts of trainees to enrich the 10-week outreach with their clients by advocating for and empowering them within their community. As such, trainees' advocacy efforts emulated those of culturally minded therapists who endeavor to produce positive social change for marginalized or underrepresented groups through "community outreach, facilitating indigenous support networks, advocacy, and public policy making" (Vera & Speight, 2003, p. 263).

Microcounseling Skills

Microcounseling skills were represented by two themes in trainees' self-reflection process notes. That two themes emerged from trainees' process notes suggested that trainees were striving to exercise general counseling skills, such as *pacing with the client* and *listening/expressing interest*, in addition to their efforts to demonstrate multicultural counseling competencies. An example of pacing with the client included:

I assured her that I could understand, and that I felt she had a very good command of the language. I realized, however, that I needed to be more active in displaying my understanding. I began slightly paraphrasing while answering questions, and I did more verbal and facial expressions to acknowledge her speech. She appeared more at ease with this type of exchange.

For listening and expressing interest, a trainee noted:

I learned in this week's interaction that sometimes silence can be the best gift that you can give a culturally different client. By simply listening, instead of always interjecting one's own thoughts and suggestions, the therapist affirms the client's experiences.

The importance of trainees' capacity to exercise behaviors reflecting one or more microcounseling skills calls attention to the common therapy variables necessary for alliance building (Fischer et al., 1998; Kottler, 1991; Roysircar, 2009a; Wampold, 2001). In fact, demonstrating general counseling competencies is an essential component of multicultural counseling competencies (Sodowsky et al., 1994).

Interpersonally Based Cultural Decapsulation

Themes in interpersonally based cultural decapsulation represented relationship-building strategies that are culturally responsive or sensitive to cultural contexts. One theme included *culturally sensitive self-disclosure* from the therapist trainee:

Even though it seemed strange at first to be sharing my experiences, I realized that it was important to her to know how I felt about ethnicity, culture, and family background: it was as if she wanted to know if she could trust me. I told her a story about my Polish grandmother.

Another theme included *cultural empathy*:

I showed her that I understood why she felt the way she did by saying, "I can see why you get frustrated with the people's stories, being that you come from a family-oriented culture AND have felt the pain of losing a son. It must be difficult to hear people complaining when you are so far away from your parents to talk to them and would do anything for one more moment with your son." In doing this I validated her feelings. I hope that I helped her to see that her thoughts that people here are constantly complaining about not getting this or that (like being selfish) are a natural result of her cultural values and her family serving as a shared resource.

Affective connection with the client emerged as a third theme:

> My second meeting with L was very enjoyable and I actually found myself giggling with her much of the time.

The general occurrence of three themes—presumed truth and judgments; awareness of client worldview, context, and experience of racism; and sizing the client—is important for understanding specific cognitive stimuli in self-reflective process notes that increase trainees' self-awareness and awareness of their clients' worldview. These three themes found in the articulations of all cases provide a preliminary indication of the type of responses and attitudes that training programs could expect from trainees participating in experiential training or community outreach. For instance, these three themes could further elucidate other themes reported in the literature that refer to counseling trainees' barriers to and connections with minority clients (see Roysircar et al., 2005; Roysircar, Webster, et al., 2003). Perhaps the theme presumed truth, assumptions, and judgments discussed here sheds light on other themes on barriers to minority clients, including trainees' frustration with barriers, preoccupation with cultural similarities and differences, and anxiety about progress (Roysircar, Webster, et al., 2003). The other two themes—awareness of client worldview, context, and experience of racism; and sizing the client—on the other hand, could further explicate themes reflecting the process of making connections with minority clients.

See Table 7.1 for a listing of qualitatively analyzed domains, categories, and core ideas from therapist trainees' six self-reflection process notes.

Discussion

Wrenn (1962) stressed that competing ideas of human behaviors among academics precludes the creation of absolute explanations of different behavioral phenomena. Maintaining the status quo speaks to the risk of counselors referring entirely to and generalizing from their past formal experience to address problems that clients present in therapy today and problems that will present in therapy by future clients. The risk lies in believing that one's past experience can sufficiently serve as a reference to a current problem. As Wrenn (1962) stated, "Some of what we have learned may be for tomorrow but most of it remains for yesterday" (p. 448).

TABLE 7.1
Cases Represented in Each Theme within Each Domain across All Six Cases

Domain	Themes	Frequency	Classification[a]
Knowledge-based cultural encapsulation	Presumed truth, assumptions, judgments	6	General
	Denial of differences	4	Typical
	Maintaining the status quo/universalist position	2	Variant
Interpersonally based cultural encapsulation	Stereotypes	3	Typical
	Intellectualizing	3	Typical
	Microinsult/microinvalidated (multicultural/verbal ineptness, naïveté)	3	Typical
	Low cultural self-identification/White guilt	2	Variant
	Implicit racism	1	Nonrep
Awareness-based cultural decapsulation	Awareness of interviewee's worldview/context/racism experience	6	General
	Self-awareness of stereotypes or racist attitudes	4	Typical
	Increased self-awareness of own culture	4	Typical
	Multicultural knowledge	3	Typical
Social justice advocacy	Giving access	3	Typical
	Active help	3	Typical
	Collaboration	3	Typical
	Sharing power	2	Variant
Interpersonally based cultural decapsulation	Cultural empathy	5	Typical
	Affective connection (connecting with clients)	5	Typical
	Culturally sensitive self-disclosure	4	Typical
General microcounseling skills	Sizing the interviewee	6	General
	Pacing with the interviewee	3	Typical
	Listening/expressing interest	2	Variant

[a] Themes were identified as general if they applied to all six cases, typical when applicable to three to five cases, and variant for two cases. Nonrep = Nonrepresentative or one case only.

Note: The consensual qualitative research method of Hill, Knox, Thompson, Williams, Hess, and Ladany (2005) was utilized in the development of this table.

Enculturation

To appreciate the concept of cultural encapsulation, it is necessary to refer to another concept considered to be its precursor, namely, enculturation. According to Berry (2001), a person is enculturated when he or she embraces and exhibits behaviors and attitudes that reflect the norms of a given culture.

Children are enculturated into the society in which they are born and raised. Enculturation occurs through socialization provided by one's parents, school, and peers (Berry, 2001). However, since enculturation occurs outside the person's awareness, it gives way to the development of cultural encapsulation. The meaning of one's own culture is not entirely clear but is, nevertheless, recognized as a correct way of being. When the encapsulated person meets a culturally different person, the encapsulated person is not cognizant of a host of cultural beliefs and practices of the other person, which are different from those of his or her own given culture. This, in turn, leads the encapsulated person to think and behave unintentionally in a manner that minimizes the perplexity and contradictions rising from the interface of two individuals and their different worldviews. Thus, understanding how therapist trainees might be culturally encapsulated would include their examination of their socialization in a particular culture, race, and ethnicity. This understanding, in turn, may help to determine the type of training that may be needed to reduce trainee encapsulation.

Cultural Encapsulation in Treatment

Owing to cultural encapsulation, most therapists might assert that they minimize bias by referring to base rates, group norms, diagnostic criteria, and extensive intake information. Psychological assessment, which is said to minimize bias, is regarded as helping therapists to objectively develop hypotheses about why maladjustments manifest in clients, regardless of clients' racial or ethnic identity. But do practicing psychologists regard their assessment work as a means to control their biases (Roysircar, 2005)? Do they go beyond nomothetic data, such as diagnoses in the *Diagnostic and Statistical Manual of Mental Disorders* (*DSM*) or Minnesota Multiphasic Personality Inventory (MMPI-2) code types, when assessing symptomatology, and consider ideographic and contextual data that speak to the differences of a culturally different individual (Roysircar, 2005)?

Therapists have been told that they can improve clinical judgment that is based solely on interviews by obtaining objective, actuarial assessment (Dawes, Faust, & Meehl, 1989); by adhering to diagnostic criteria; by being systematic and comprehensive when conducting interviews; by following legal and ethical principles; by following scientific standards; by using decision aids; and by describing clients' strengths (Garb, 1998). Although these recommendations are well-taken and should be practiced, Roysircar (2005) questions the generalizability of empirical correlates of *DSM* diagnostic categories and empirical criterion-keyed assessment measures when diagnostic and clinical criterion groups represent native English speakers of White American descent. Roysircar states that clinicians tend to make diagnoses by comparing racial and ethnic minority and culturally diverse clients to typical White American clients, as in the case of the MMPI-2 code types. Garb (1998) refers to the overpathologizing and overshadowing biases of clinicians. It cannot be assumed that therapists will not be influenced by their biases just because they are told to be aware of their biases by their social cognitive theories and their professional ethical codes. A psychotherapist ascribing to a cognitive therapy approach is described as an "active participant," who may adhere to practice guidelines or rules to stay true to a theoretical frame. However, there is uncertainty regarding the extent to which therapists actually succeed at keeping the therapy process from being tainted with their own social reality.

Mahoney's (1991) discussion on the role of social constructivism reflects a growing acknowledgment that people's understanding of themselves, their interpersonal experiences, and their world is a product of their interaction with their environment. What is welcomed about social constructivism is the recognition that the crux of understanding human behavior, especially in achieving positive change, lies in how people's social perceptions influence the type of interactions they will experience in their environment. However, the mechanism of change underlying mainstream therapies, whether it be cognitive, behavioral, or psychodynamic, has never explicitly taken into account how a therapist's worldview or value assumptions play a role in interpreting issues of cultural diversity, although it is understood that the process of change requires the therapist to understand presenting problems from the client's worldview. What contemporary theorists do not seem to communicate is how, if at all, a therapist might keep his or her own worldview, assumptions, and racial biases from influencing the manner in which he or she guides racial and ethnic minority clients.

Mahoney (1991) argued that the mainstream literature shows that practitioners of various schools of clinical practice have converged in their understanding of human behavior. However, he illustrated that various theories of clinical practice fall short when they fail to take into account how the interdependence of their respective concepts helps to elucidate what the individual theories have been unable to explain. Other contemporary theorists, including those representing psychodynamic (e.g., Leary, 1995; Shapiro, 1975) and client-centered (e.g., MacDougall, 2002) therapies, have noted the shortcomings of their respective disciplines as well. For instance, Shapiro (1975) challenged the practice in psychodynamic treatment of viewing resistance in psychotherapy as an internal and dysfunctional process, and suggested that we consider its adaptive features as a situation-based phenomenon. MacDougall (2002) indirectly refers to Wrenn's notion of maintaining the status quo by pointing to client-centered therapists' failure to be open and adaptable to cultural differences by only relying on an empathic listening approach.

Ways to Ameliorate Cultural Encapsulation in Trainees

Consider the study by Roysircar, Webster et al. (2003) where master's- and doctoral-level therapist trainees participated in community service that was intended to help them develop their competencies of cultural awareness and multicultural relationship. Trainees served immigrant students enrolled in a middle school's program in ESL and met with these clients for 10 sessions. To document and examine the interactional processes that took place between trainees and clients, trainees were required to write process notes, reflecting on each encounter with clients. Themes derived from the process notes through qualitative analyses reflected trainees' positive and negative perceptions of their ESL clients and their mentoring service with them. The positive themes were: other awareness and reflection, self-awareness and reflection, empathy and self-disclosure, treatment planning and implementation, analysis of counselor values, and intentional exchange of cultural information. The negative themes were: barriers, frustration with barriers, preoccupation with cultural similarities and differences, and anxiety about progress. Correlations between these themes and trainees' responses on subscales of the self-report Multicultural Counseling Inventory (MCI) (Sodowsky, Taffe, Gutkin, & Wise, 1994), a multicultural competency measure, showed that negative themes were significantly correlated with trainees' lower scores on the MCI compared to higher scores, which had negative significant correlations with the negative themes. Positive themes were significantly correlated with higher scores on the MCI. According to Roysircar, Webster et al., interacting directly with minority clients and writing process notes to reflect on cultural issues in each meeting served as effective tools for helping trainees develop cultural self-awareness. The trainees' responses to the Multicultural Social Desirability Scale (Sodowsky, Kuo-Jackson, Richardson, & Corey, 1998) fell within average norms and had nonsignificant relationships with the derived process notes themes, both positive and negative, as well as the MCI.

In another study, Roysircar et al. (2005) qualitatively analyzed trainees' reactions to ESL clients as stated in trainees' process notes. This sample was different from the sample in the previous study. The negative themes identified were: environmental barriers, frustrations with environmental barriers, unintegrated differences, overgeneralizations of similarities, and stereotypes. These were called disconnection/distance themes. The positive themes were: differences integrated, cultural empathy-cognitive, affective connection with client's subjective culture, counselor self-disclosure, and counselor self-reflection. These were called connection/closeness themes. It is important to note that when trainees expressed themes of disconnection/distance, it was with the motivation to change these reactions, and they later expressed more themes of connection/closeness. Trainees' connection/closeness themes were related to their positive White racial identity attitudes of pseudoindependence and autonomy (Helms, 1990).

Another way to evaluate the development of cultural competence is to look at critical incidents. Critical incidents involve a divergence of perspective between the client and the therapist, in which the correct response is not apparent, but it is clear that the wrong response by the therapist would have negative effects on the client (Roysircar, 2004). In analyzing critical incidents in their multicultural interactions, trainees focused on their observable behaviors (Roysircar, 2004). Trainees then reflected on these incidents, examined their worldviews and biases, and learned from their experiences.

Many educators agree that multicultural training should be experiential and process oriented (e.g., Kim & Lyons, 2003; Manese et al., 2001) so that trainees can have live experiences in cultural awareness and practice. Kim and Lyons (2003) underscored the importance of including games, role-playing, and use of film in the learning process of multicultural competence training. According to Kim and Lyons, experiential activities serve as essential adjuncts to didactic presentation and are ideal for instilling the dimensions of multicultural competence (i.e., belief and attitudes, knowledge, and skills). Particular attention is given to the use of games as a learning tool. The authors describe games as providing "a tool to positively influence the counseling process" (p. 402). Several benefits of using games are identified. For example, games could help counseling students in the following ways: "to sensitize a person to previous behaviors of which he or she is unaware; to allow a person to confront feelings of powerlessness" and "to offer opportunities to deal with the rules of the game as an analogy to living by norms of society, norms that may be different from personal norms" (pp. 402–403). For multicultural counseling training, the authors describe specific ways that games can instill multicultural competence in counselor trainees for each of the dimensions of cultural competence. For example, counseling trainees can increase their sense of safety through the use of games with low-risk potential for analyzing the dimension of their negative beliefs. Games that enable counseling students to explore accurate and inaccurate perceptions and that will not make them suffer retribution could be used for the dimension of knowledge. Finally, games that involve role-playing and perspective-taking can help counseling students develop competency for the dimension of skills.

Conclusion

This chapter emphasized the understanding of cultural encapsulation and decapsulation experienced by therapist trainees, since one goal of most training programs in psychology is to help trainees become multiculturally competent therapists in their service delivery. The present authors operationalized and expanded on Wrenn's (1962, 1985) thesis of cultural encapsulation with exemplars from therapist trainees' self-refection process notes. To explain interpersonally oriented cultural encapsulation, the authors referred to and provided trainee narratives on their racial attitudes that lead to implicit racism (Dovidio, Kawakami, et al., 2002), stereotype threat (Steele, 1997), and racial microaggressions (D. W. Sue et al., 2007).

The authors have contributed to the MCC literature by providing evidence of how therapist trainees' thoughts and responses, as reflected in their process notes, are demonstrative of their likelihood to be culturally encapsulated with a culturally diverse person. In addition, the findings are particularly demonstrative of trainees' tendencies to proactively become decapsulated. The authors, in fact, did not expect a greater number of themes on cultural decapsulation, as opposed to cultural encapsulation, to emerge from the content analysis. This unexpected finding points to the authors' own biases as ethnic and biracial persons—assumptions, values, and biases that have developed from their personal experiences of racial prejudice as well as from their socialization as culturally diverse persons.

Overall, it is hoped that the authors have succeeded in giving readers a greater appreciation of how Wrenn's (1962, 1985) thesis from an earlier period in the history of multicultural psychology lends itself to the current theory and practice of multicultural competency training. The content analysis should help trainers to recognize the knowledge that is to be gained from using self-reflective process notes to help therapist trainees have insight into thoughts and responses that reveal cultural encapsulation as well as ways of learning decapsulation.

References

American Psychological Association. (2003). Guidelines on multicultural education, training, research, practice, and organizational change for psychologists. *American Psychologist, 58*, 377–402.

Arrendondo, P., Toporek, R., Brown, S. P., Jones, J., Locke, D. C., Sanchez, J., et al. (1996). Operationalization of the multicultural counseling competencies. *Journal of Multicultural Counseling and Development, 24*, 42–78.

Berry, J. W. (2001). Contextual studies of cognitive adaptation. In J. M. Collis & S. Messick (Eds.), *Intelligence and personality: Bridging the gap in theory and measurement* (pp. 319–333). Mahwah, NJ: Lawrence Erlbaum.

Comas-Diaz, L., & Jacobsen, F. M. (1991). Ethnocultural transference and countertransference in the therapeutic dyad. *American Journal of Orthopsychiatry, 61*, 392–402.

Comas-Diaz, L., & Jacobsen, F. M. (1995). The therapist of color and the White patient dyad: Contradictions and recognitions. *Cultural Diversity and Mental Health, 1*, 93–106.

Constantine, M., Fuertes J., & Roysircar, G., & Kindaichi, M. M. (2008). Multicultural competence. Clinical practice, training, and research. In B. Walsh, N. Fouad, R. Fassinger, B. Wampold, & R. Carter (Eds.), *Biennial review of counseling psychology* (pp. 97–128). Mahwah, NJ: Lawrence Erlbaum.

Constantine, M. G., & Ladany, N. (2001). New visions for defining and assessing multicultural counseling competence. In J. G. Ponterotto, J. M. Casas, L. A. Suzuki, & C. M. Alexander (Eds.), *Handbook of multicultural counseling* (2nd ed., pp. 482–498). Thousand Oaks, CA: Sage.

Dawes, R. M., Faust, D., & Meehl, P. E. (1989). Clinical versus actuarial judgment. *Science, 243*, 1668–1674.

Dovidio, J. F., Kawakami, S. L., Gaertner, K., & Hodson, G. (2002). Why can't we just get along? Interpersonal biases and interracial distrust. *Cultural Diversity and Ethnic Minority Psychology, 8*, 88–102.

Dovidio, J. F., Gaertner, K., & Kawakami, S. L. (2002). Implicit and explicit prejudice and interracial interaction. *Journal of Personality and Social Psychology, 82*, 62–68.

Fischer, A. R., Jome, L. M., & Atkinson, D. R. (1998). Reconceptualizing multicultural counseling: Universal healing conditions in a culturally specific context. *The Counseling Psychologist, 26*(4), 525–587.

Fuertes, J. N., & Brobst, K. (2002). Clients' ratings of counselor multicultural competency. *Cultural Diversity and Ethnic Minority Psychology, 8*, 214–223.

Garb, H. N. (1998). *Studying the clinician: Judgment, research and psychological assessment.* Washington, DC: American Psychological Association.

Helms, J. E. (1990). *Black and White racial identity: Theory, research, and practice.* New York: Greenwood.

Hill, C. E., Knox, S., Thompson, B. J., Williams, E. N., Hess, S. A., & Ladany, H. (2005). Consensual qualitative research: An update. *Journal of Counseling Psychology, 52*, 196–205.

Jones, W. P., & Markos, P. A. (1997). Client rating of counselor effectiveness: A call for caution. *Journal of Applied Rehabilitation Counseling, 28*, 23–28.

Kim, B. S., & Lyons, H. Z. (2003). Experiential activities and multicultural counseling competency training. *Journal of Counseling & Development*, *81*, 400–408.

Kottler, J. A. (1991). *The compleat therapist*. San Francisco: Jossey-Bass.

Leary, K. (1995). "Interpreting in the dark": Race and ethnicity in psychoanalytic psychotherapy. *Psychoanalytic Psychology*, *12*, 127–140.

MacDougall, C. (2002). Roger's person-centered approach: Consideration for use in multicultural counseling. *Journal of Humanistic Psychology*, *42*, 46–65.

Mahoney, M. J. (1991). *Human change processes*. New York: Basic Books.

Manese, J. E., Wu, J. T., & Nepomuceno, C. A. (2001). The effect of training on multicultural counseling competencies: An exploratory study over a 10-year period. *Journal of Multicultural Counseling and Development*, *29*, 31–40.

Oxford University Press. (1989). *Oxford English Dictionary Online* (2nd ed.). Oxford, UK: Author. Retrieved April 30, 2007, from http://dictionary/oed.com.proxy.ohiolink.edu:9099/cgi/

Pignatiello, V., & Roysircar, G. (2008, August). *Another noose hanging: Events following Jena 6*. Paper presented at the Annual Conference of the American Psychological Association, Boston, MA.

Pope-Davis, D. B., Toporek, R. L., Ortega-Villalobos, L., Ligiero, D. P., Brittan-Powell, C. S., Liu, W. M., et al. (2002). Client perspectives of multicultural counseling competence: A qualitative examination. *The Counseling Psychologist*, *30*, 355–393.

Roysircar, G. (2003). Counselor awareness of own assumptions, values, and biases. In G. Roysircar, P. Arredondo, J. N. Fuertes, J. G. Ponterotto, & R. L. Toporek (Eds.), *Multicultural counseling competencies 2003: Association for Multicultural Counseling and Development* (pp. 17–38). Alexandria, VA: Association for Multicultural Counseling and Development.

Roysircar, G. (2004). Cultural self-awareness assessment: Practice examples from psychology training. *Professional Psychology: Research and Practice*, *35*, 658–666.

Roysircar, G. (2005). Culturally sensitive assessment, diagnosis, and guidelines. In M. G. Constantine & D. W. Sue (Eds.), *Strategies for building multicultural competencies in mental health and educational settings* (pp. 19–38). Hoboken, NJ: John Wiley & Sons.

Roysircar, G. (2008). Social privilege: Counselors' competence with systemically determined inequalities. *Journal for Specialists in Group Work*, *33*(4), 377–384.

Roysircar, G. (2009a). Evidence-based practice and its implications for culturally sensitive treatment. *Journal of Multicultural Counseling and Development*, *37*(2), 66–82.

Roysircar, G. (2009b). The big picture of social justice advocacy: Counselor heal society and thyself. *Journal of Counseling and Development*, *87*, 288–295.

Roysircar, G., Arredondo, P., Fuertes, J. N., Ponterotto, J. G., & Toporek, R. L. (Eds.). (2003). *Multicultural counseling competencies 2003: Association for Multicultural Counseling and Development*. Alexandria, VA: Association for Multicultural Counseling and Development.

Roysircar, G., Gard, G., Hubbell R., & Ortega, M. (2005). Development of counseling trainees' multicultural awareness through mentoring ESL students. *Journal of Multicultural Counseling and Development*, *33*, 17–36.

Roysircar, G., Hubbell, R., & Gard, G. (2003). Multicultural research on counselor and client variables: A relational perspective. In D. Pope-Davis, H. L. K.
Coleman, W. M. Liu, & R. L. Toporek (Eds.), *Handbook of multicultural competencies* (pp. 247–282*)*. Thousand Oaks, CA: Sage.

Roysircar, G., Webster, D. R., Germer, J., Campbell, G., Lynne, E., Palensky, J. J.,
et al. (2003). Experiential training in multicultural counseling: Implementation
and evaluation of counselor process. In G. Roysircar, D. S. Sandhu, & V. B.
Bibbins (Eds.), *Multicultural competencies: A guidebook of practices* (pp. 3–15).
Alexandria, VA: American Counseling Association.

Shapiro, D. (1975). Dynamic and holistic ideas of neurosis and psychotherapy.
Psychiatry, 38, 218–226.

Sodowsky, G. R., Kuo-Jackson, P. Y., Richardson, M. F., & Corey, A. T. (1998).
Correlates of self-reported multicultural competencies: Counselor multicultural social desirability, race, social inadequacy, locus of control racial
ideology, and multicultural training. *Journal of Counseling Psychology, 45,*
256–264.

Sodowsky, G., Taffe, R. C., Gutkin, T. B., & Wise, S. L. (1994). Development of
the multicultural counseling inventory: A self-report measure of multicultural
competencies. *Journal of Counseling Psychology, 41,* 137–148.

Steele, C. M. (1997). A threat in the air: How stereotypes shape intellectual identity
and performance. *American Psychologist, 52,* 613–629.

Sue, D. W., Arredondo, P., & McDavis, R. J. (1992). Multicultural counseling
competencies and standards: A call to the profession. *Journal of Multicultural
Counseling and Development, 20,* 64–68.

Sue, D. W., Bucceri, J., Lin, A. I., Nadal, K. L., & Torino, G. C. (2007). Racial
microaggressions and the Asian American experience. *Cultural Diversity and
Ethnic Minority Psychology, 13,* 72–81.

Sue, D. W., Capodilupo, C. M., Torino, G. C., Bucceri, J. M., Holder, A. M. B.,
Nadal, K. L., et al. (2007). Racial microaggressions in everyday life: Implications
for clinical practice. *American Psychologist, 62*(4), 271–286.

Sue, S. (1998). In search of cultural competence in psychotherapy and counseling.
American Psychologist, 53, 440–448.

Toporek, R. L. (2003). Counselor awareness of client's worldview. In G. Roysircar, P.
Arredondo, J. N. Fuertes, J. G. Ponterotto, & R. L. Toporek (Eds.), *Multicultural
counseling competencies 2003: Association for Multicultural Counseling and
Development* (pp. 39–50). Alexandria, VA: Association for Multicultural
Counseling and Development.

Toporek, R. L., Gerstein, L. H., Fouad, N. A., Roysircar, G., & Israel, T. (Eds.).
(2006). *Handbook for social justice in counseling psychology: Leadership, vision,
and action.* Thousand Oaks, CA: Sage.

Vera, E. M., & Speight, S. L. (2003). Multicultural competence, social justice, and counseling psychology: Expanding our roles. *Counseling Psychologist, 31,* 253–272.

Wampold, B. E. (2001). *The great psychotherapy debate: Models, methods, and findings.*
Mahwah, NJ: Erlbaum.

Wrenn, G. (1962). The culturally encapsulated therapist. *Harvard Educational
Review, 32,* 444–449.

Wrenn, G. (1985). Afterword: The culturally encapsulated counselor revisited. In P.
Pedersen (Ed.), *Handbook of cross-cultural counseling and therapy* (pp. 323–329).
Westport, CT: Greenwood Press.

8

Culture and Worldview in Counseling and Psychotherapy

Recommended Approaches for Working with Persons from Diverse Sociocultural Backgrounds

Shawn O. Utsey, Nicole L. Fischer, and Benita Belvet

Power and liberty are of course never given; they are demanded, taken, and assumed. For if and when "given," they are at best conditional, often superficial, and readily "taken away."

—Hussein Abdilahi Bulhan, 1985, p. 276

The theoretical and empirical literature documenting the importance of considering culture and worldview in psychological counseling are voluminous and continues to grow. There is little debate among graduate training programs in psychology and counseling as to whether they should include multicultural counseling theories and techniques in the curriculum or the importance of evaluating their trainees for cultural competencies. Despite this awareness, many professional psychology training programs continue to adhere to a *generic* framework that assumes the universal application of psychological theory to all human beings without regard to culture (Helms &

Cook, 1999; Ponterotto, Utsey, & Pedersen, 2006; Richardson & Molinaro, 1996; Sue, Ivey, & Pedersen, 1996; Utsey, Grange, & Allyne, 2006). Given the increasing cultural diversity of the United States, psychology training programs must redouble their efforts to give their trainees the tools they will need to enter the profession in which the cultural backgrounds of their clients will likely be different than their own.

Most traditional counseling and psychotherapy techniques/approaches are culturally encapsulated in a Eurocentric theoretical framework and worldview (Sue et al., 1996; Utsey, Bolden, & Brown, 2001). As such, when counselors apply these techniques in their work with individuals who are not of European descent they risk imposing an alien cultural reality structure to understanding the values, beliefs, behaviors, and worldview of their clients. In an effort to check the cultural hegemony of Western science on the provision of psychology services to persons from diverse racial/ethnic/cultural/linguistic groups living in the United States, the American Psychological Association (APA) prescribed a set of guidelines for multicultural education, training, research, practice, and organizational change (see "The Guidelines on Multicultural Education, Training, Research, Practice, and Organizational Change for Psychologists," APA, 2003). The guidelines provide praxis for the provision of culturally relevant psychological services to individuals from diverse racial/ethnic/cultural/linguistic backgrounds.

The importance of culture and worldview in the provision of psychological services to individuals from diverse racial and cultural backgrounds cannot be overstated. Culture is a framework for understanding reality, and establishing values, beliefs, and behaviors that shape the lives of individuals who share a common reality (Chung & Bemak, 2002; Nobles, 1990). Worldview, on the other hand, is a set of interrelated beliefs and assumptions about human nature, the universe, and one's existence in the world (Koltok-Rivera, 2004). The counseling and psychotherapy process requires the counselor to formulate clinical impressions that they will use to guide them in the diagnosis and treatment of their clients. Moreover, the counselor's clinical impressions will dictate the selection and use of specific diagnostic and assessment tools, intervention strategies (i.e., individual, group, family), and counseling orientations (e.g., cognitive-behavioral, psychodynamic, client-centered). Clinical impressions are generated from face-to-face interviews, testing and assessment, and behavioral observations. The counselor uses the data gathered during the evaluation period to formulate hypotheses as to the origin and nature of the client's presenting problem. These hypotheses will also be used to formulate treatment plans, including the specific interventions to be used. All of the activities involved in formulating clinical impressions require counselors to consider the culture and worldview of the client. Moreover, the ethically responsible counselor also seeks to understand and acknowledge the role of their own cultural worldview as a lens with which they view their clients (APA, 2003; Utsey et al., 2006).

The literature on culture, worldview, and multicultural counseling is sizable and it would be impossible to do justice to the topic in this limited space, therefore, we will limit our focus to a more manageable range of topics. First, we discuss Western psychology's perpetuation of scientific racism and how this limits its utility with people from historically marginalized social and cultural groups. Part of this discussion focuses on the axiological, ontological, and epistemological framework of Western psychology and its cultural encapsulation in a Eurocentric cultural worldview. This section also discusses how culture influences personality development and what, in a cultural context, constitutes mental illness and healthy psychological functioning. Finally, we review several models of culturally congruent approaches to counseling and psychotherapy, and provide a case study to illustrate the application of one approach. The chapter concludes with a summary of main points and recommendations for future directions.

Culture, Worldview, and Psychology

The cultural hegemony of Western psychology has a long and nefarious history (for a review, see Guthrie, 1998; Thomas & Sillen, 1972). Some of the earliest forensic evidence of psychology's crimes against humanity can be found in the 1800s in the antebellum south, where Dr. Samuel Cartwright, a Louisiana physician, first coined the term *drapetomania* (or "the flight from home madness") to describe slaves who attempted to run away (Thomas & Sillen, 1972). He later coined the term *dysaesthesia aethiopica* (or "insensibility of nerves") to describe slaves who caused problems for their overseers or failed to perform their duties (Thomas & Sillen, 1972). Further evidence of psychology's malfeasance toward humanity is Carl Jung's statement that the "childlike" and "primitive" nature of the Negro was a consequence of having less brain matter (Guthrie, 1998). Arrah Evarts would publish *Dementia Praecox in the Colored Race* (1914), asserting that slavery allowed Blacks to develop their full potential as a race (Thomas & Sillen, 1972). William McDougall, in his influential work *Introduction to Social Psychology* (1908), asserted that Blacks were instinctively submissive.

The development of complex statistical procedures and the advent of mental abilities testing converged to launch the pseudoscience of IQ and hereditability (Ponterotto et al., 2006). Lewis Terman was among the first to promote the hereditability of low intelligence in certain races (i.e., Native Americans, Mexicans, and Negroes; Guthrie, 1998; Thomas & Sillen, 1972). He provided the impetus for the likes of Edward Thorndike, Robert Yerkes, William Shockley, Audrey Shuey, Arthur Jensen, Hans Eysenck, and others who would devote their entire careers to proving that Blacks are innately less intelligent than Whites (Guthrie, 1998). This very brief review of psychology's sinister past was intended to demonstrate how its history is indicative of the discipline's current worldview.

Beyond the scientific racism entrenched in Western psychology's past and present, its theories, methods, and models are culturally encapsulated in a Eurocentric epistemological, ontological, and axiological framework (Ani, 1994; Kambon, 1998; Nobles, 1986, 1990; Utsey & Bolden, 2008). Relying on positivist philosophical assumptions (i.e., reality is objective and independent of those who observe it; unbiased observations of this reality constitute scientific knowledge), the culturally encapsulated counselor attempts to construct the physical, social, psychological, and spiritual reality of his or her clients, oftentimes doing more harm than good.

Culture, Worldview, and Personality Development

Western psychology developed out the philosophical interpretations of Greek culture (Ani, 1994). The general axiological thrust of Western psychology is to rank-order, assign value, and count behaviors (Ani, 1994). The epistemological imperative of Western psychology is based on "rational" and "logical" thought and observable and quantifiable behavior (Ani, 1994; Nobles, 1986). The ontological orientation of Western psychology is grounded in the material nature of the world and is structured through a misinterpretation of physics that ignores and denies the presence of spirit as part of the human reality. Given this culturally encapsulated worldview, Western psychology is ill-equipped to adequately address the social, psychological, and spiritual needs of persons who are not of European descent. In fact, based on the empirical evidence concerning psychotherapy outcomes, it is questionable as to whether individuals who are of European ancestry benefit from traditional approaches to counseling and psychotherapy.

Sociocultural Models of Counseling and Psychotherapy

Liberation Psychology and Psychotherapy

Liberation psychology is a contemporary theory within the multicultural counseling and therapy framework that examines self-exploration through social awareness and cultural acceptance (Bulhan, 1985; Comas-Diaz, Lykes, & Alarcon, 1998; Ivey, 1995; Utsey et al., 2001). The primary intent of this approach is to create an opportunity to observe, analyze, and act to promote social changes that improve the material, spiritual, and psychological lives of persons previously denied power and resources. Liberation psychology—inspired by liberation theology—is a theory of psychology that utilizes emotional liberties as a catalyst for justice, peace, human rights, psychological well-being, and humanity (Slattery & Corbett, 2002). Liberation psychology utilizes the client's cultural context as a means for self-reflection, thereby accounting for environmental influences and inherent circumstances. This way, clients may view difficulties as a consequence of social context and history, rather than of innate pathologies.

Liberation psychology aligns with cultural identity theory (Ivey, 1994), which states that the most significant strategy used to achieve critical consciousness, or self-awareness, is to examine oneself as a racial and ethnic being (see Cross, 1971; Helms, 1985, 1990; Jackson, 1975, 1990; Sue & Sue, 1990). Understandably, the liberation that comes from self-awareness will lead to a broader form of self-concept, or reference group orientation (Cross, 1991).

Theory   The purpose of liberation psychology is to enable clients to view difficulties in a social and historical context, highlighting multiculturalism and social justice (Comas-Diaz et al., 1998; Ivey, 1995). Based on this model, clients are led to understand that conflicts and resolutions are contingent upon self-awareness within a respective culture. Theoretically, when a client recognizes his or her own culture, then he or she is able to examine that culture more closely, and in turn is able to distinguish discrepancies between one's culture and another. This describes a progression from mere experience, to conscious reflection and critical analysis. The liberation ideal of liberation psychology is contingent upon understanding one's situation in comparison to another, in an attempt to bring about more adequate awareness of oppression and social justice issues (Ivey, 1995). Overall, liberation psychology is a grassroots approach to analyzing and understanding the perspective of disadvantaged groups and individuals. It is a modest approach to understanding the circumstances of others and how to address difficulties within a cultural framework.

Application　Liberation psychology applies a social justice orientation that requires greater attention to outreach, prevention, community service, and advocacy, in conjunction with multicultural competencies. The techniques that are used are performed with the intent to expand self and cultural awareness, such as group consciousness-raising programs. Traditional cognitive and behavioral psychological theories are also useful when they are culturally appropriate.

The most significant challenge of liberation psychology is self-exploration within a cultural framework. Fromm (1976) describes the liberatory process as the ability to identify the cultural norms that one's identity encompasses, and how this affects views of selfhood, development, psychopathology, and healing. It is a matter of enabling the cultural unconscious to become conscious.

NTU Therapy

The NTU approach to psychotherapy is one of many therapeutic models that stems from an Africentric view of healing. This is a spiritually oriented approach that blends Eastern philosophies and practices and Western counseling techniques with the aim of guiding the client toward natural balance and harmony both intrapsychically and interpersonally (Phillips, 1990). The central principles of NTU therapy are harmony, balance, interconnectedness, and authenticity. NTU is a central African (Bantu) concept that refers to the primal universal force, or energy, that is the essence of all being (Gregory & Harper, 2001; Phillips, 1990). In this form of therapy, the therapist works intimately with the client to reconnect with this spiritual energy, work in harmony with it, and allow healing to occur naturally as the goals of therapy are achieved. This approach views each client as emotionally and spiritually bound to his or her family, and thus strives to treat not just the individual, but focuses on the entire family, even if only the individual is physically present for therapy (Gregory & Harper, 2001). The focus on the enhancement of family and community is essential in this model. NTU therapy also focuses on the interconnectedness between mind, body, and spirit, and according to this holistic model, healing cannot be complete until these systems are in harmony (Gregory & Harper, 2001; Phillips, 1990).

Theory   The seven principles of Kwanzaa serve as the sacred values of NTU healing, to which both client and therapist adhere (Gregory & Harper, 2001; Phillips, 1990). These principles are: Umoja (unity), Kujichaguila (self-determination), Ujima (collective work and responsibility), Ujamaa (cooperative economics), Kuumba (creativity), Nia (purpose), and Imani (faith). Along with instructing the client to apply these principles to his or her life, another central goal of NTU therapy is to help the client to discover the truth within himself or herself and live authentically according to that personal and spiritual truth (Phillips, 1990). The therapist aids the client in experiencing life and relationships with authenticity and balance. During the course of therapy, the focus is not only on balancing the client's internal systems (mind, body, and spirit) but also the client's external systems (family, work, and other relationships) so that the client learns to allow his or her life to move with the flow of the NTU (Gregory & Harper, 2001; Phillips, 1990).

Application   There are five phases of NTU therapy that guide both client and therapist in the process of working toward optimal psychological functioning: harmony, awareness, alignment, actualization, and synthesis (Gregory & Harper, 2001; Phillips, 1990). Harmony refers to the spiritual, therapeutic relationship between client and therapist. In the implementation of this phase, NTU therapy builds on the humanistic model of counseling in that the working alliance, therapeutic ritual, and the concepts of genuineness, authenticity, and empathy are of prime importance in achieving harmony (Phillips, 1990). Harmony is key in building initial rapport, and it remains critical throughout the entire process. The awareness phase entails clarifying the actual problem or issue that has prompted the client to seek counseling and then deconstructing the issue, making it easier to arrive at a workable solution (Gregory & Harper, 2001). The goal of the alignment phase is to achieve congruence in the client's internal and external systems. This phase is particularly aimed at achieving compatibility of thought, focus, and energy across the different members of the client's family (external system) (Gregory & Harper, 2001). In the actualization phase, the client is charged with actually making the necessary life changes to bring about the balance, harmony, and authenticity he or she has been seeking. The synthesis phase involves the client reflecting on and examining his or her therapeutic experience. Throughout the therapeutic process, the therapist uses a pluralistic combination of modern Western counseling methods as well as nonmainstream techniques such as herbal therapy, meditation, affirmations, and visualization (Phillips, 1990). Various other techniques such as acupuncture and spiritual readings may be used, depending on the skills of the therapist (Gregory & Harper, 2001).

Feminist Approaches to Psychotherapy

Feminist therapy is a unique application of multicultural awareness and understanding of behaviors related to the diverse and complex experiences of women, including race, class, culture, sexual orientation, religion, and environment (Ballou, 1990; Brown, 2006). The purpose of this approach is to empower women and encourage them to self-reflect, with the intent to raise consciousness and understanding of personal circumstances (Brown, 2006). This approach accounts for the restrictions, limitations, and special concerns of women as an oppressed group. Awareness of such factors distinguishes feminist therapy from traditional therapy, which presumably accommodates the majority population, (that is, White, middle-class, male, Western culture). Similar to proponents of multicultural counseling, feminist therapists believe that behavior must be understood within the broader social context. Therefore, the impact of external realities on internal and unconscious processes must be factored into interpretations of behaviors (Brown, 2006).

Theory   Feminist therapy suggests that the overarching goal of treatment is that clients develop *feminist consciousness* (Brown, 1994). This is defined as awareness that one's own suffering arises not from individual deficits but rather from the ways in which one has been systemically invalidated, excluded, and silenced because of one's status as a member of a nondominant group in the culture (Lerner, 1993). Although feminist therapy recognizes the disadvantages of the group, therapy is intended to enhance livelihood rather than dwell on social hardships. Similarly, a commitment to social justice is integral among feminist therapy, examining politics through the perspective of gender (Brown, 2006).

Application   The relationship between a feminist therapist and client is imperative to the success of therapy; this is repeated throughout the literature. Similar to the humanistic approach to therapy, the therapeutic relationship among feminist therapy is a primary consideration, intended to be mutually egalitarian and supportive. This image of a collaborative, competence-based treatment is a primary value for feminist practice (Brabeck & Brown, 1997; Brown, 1994).

Although the primary objective of feminist therapy is to encourage social productivity and stabilize self-awareness among women, the approach may be applied by either male or female psychologists. The sex of the therapist is irrelevant, in comparison with his or her intent to sustain the feminist ideals throughout therapy. The egalitarian aspect of feminist therapy is the creation of a relationship between the therapist and client that values one another's expertise and competence, and power hierarchies are irrelevant. Feminist therapy is intended to emphasize the strengths and abilities of the client, rather than disadvantages or a lack of capabilities (Brown, 2007). This highlights the egalitarian nature of feminist therapy.

Feminist therapy is an additional approach to apply among a nontraditional group, namely, women. This approach holds firm its social advocacy initiatives and purpose of well-being among female clients and the issues that surround them.

Integrative Model

The integrative model of psychological assessment and intervention was originally proposed in counseling Asian American adolescents (Huang, 1994), but has beneficial applications across cultures. The integrative approach entails gathering and assembling information regarding the individual client; his or her family, school, or work environment; and involvement with peers and other relationships. An ethnocultural component of the assessment plays an essential role in this model, especially in cases involving clients who may be experiencing acculturative stress because they themselves or their family members (especially parents) have trouble adjusting or adhering to American customs and value systems due to migration status or cultural disparities.

Theory   This approach considers the importance and the impact of the client's culture of origin on the four key areas of the assessment (individual, family, school, and peers). For example, what are the client's feelings about his or her ethnicity and how does this affect his or her self-concept? What impact do the client's language abilities or accent have on his or her social adjustment? If the client migrated to the United States, when and under what circumstances? What is the composition of the client's family, and what is the client's role? Are there any generational conflicts present? How does the client's view of culture and ethnicity compare with the views of the family? How do cultural factors impact the school or work environment? How do the values of the client's peers match with his or her own values? What is the role of the peer group in the client's life? How does the client adjust to the demands of each of these different aspects of life and what conflicts arise? Socioeconomic status is also considered. This thorough assessment is meant to uncover the main sources of conflict and difficulty in resolving various demands and expectations imposed on the individual.

Application   In many cultures, there is distrust or embarrassment around seeking counseling with a mental health professional. The integrative approach to therapy values awareness and sensitivity to cultural issues such as this, and aims to reframe the idea of therapy as a process that will enhance important aspects of life (such as work performance and family harmony), rather than a process that is meant to identify and repair what is "wrong" with the client. The goal of the integrative intervention is to address and attempt to resolve the presenting problem by bringing in other key individuals, such as family members and teachers, and discussing the key issues in a culturally relevant way. It may initially be challenging to engage other relevant individuals into the intervention, especially when cultural mistrust is a factor in a reluctance to participate, which makes it even more important to convey genuineness, empathy, and warmth in building rapport and trust. Establishing a common goal and explaining the intervention as a tool that is meant to optimize functioning for everyone involved are also critical elements of this approach. The issue at hand should be explained in a way that everyone finds to be important, and unfamiliar or culturally inappropriate terms should not be used during therapy. It may be necessary to provide education, giving everyone a clear explanation of the unique challenges that the client faces that are in need of resolution. There may be differing cultural viewpoints that need to be expressed, explained, and addressed, for example, in situations where a more "Americanized" client is in conflict with other members of the family who feel that following American customs is a denial of the culture of origin. It is helpful for the therapist to reassure the people involved in the intervention that the issues at hand are not abnormal or uncommon. This may serve to assuage any embarrassment and encourage a more open dialogue.

Sociocultural Approaches to Intervention: A Case Study

Olufemi is a 25-year-old immigrant from Nigeria, West Africa, who came to the MLK Community Mental Health Service Center complaining of anxiety, inability to sleep, excessive worry, and severe headaches. He immigrated to the United States 6 years ago and currently lives in a two-bedroom apartment with his wife and three children. Olufemi works full time as a short-order cook at a restaurant in Harlem, New York. He was referred to the center by a coworker who noticed a sudden and dramatic change in his otherwise jovial demeanor.

Reason for Referral

Olufemi reports having just experienced the death of his grandmother, with whom he was very close, just 2 weeks ago. Beyond the grief that would be anticipated from the loss of a close relative, Olufemi was quite distressed that his financial situation would not allow him to return home for a very important funerary rite (known among the Igbo as Okwukwu). Olufemi explained that there are both social and spiritual consequences for his failure to perform certain rituals required by his cultural group. As a consequence, for the past 2 weeks he has experienced increased levels of anxiety, insomnia, and somatic complaints (that is, severe headaches). Olufemi interprets these symptoms as an indication that his grandmother's spirit is not at peace and that he will not be at peace until he returns home to perform the appropriate rites.

Family History

Olufemi is the eldest child in a family consisting of six siblings, his mother and father, and both of his father's parents. His father works for a housing contractor in the capital city of Lagos in Nigeria. His mother is a homemaker and cares for his younger siblings, ages 4 to 16. Although Olufemi's parents have no formal education, he and all of his siblings have attended private school. Olufemi graduated at the top of his class and received a scholarship to study in the United States. He immigrated to the United States with his then fiancée, whom he has since wed. Olufemi and his wife have two sons ages 2 and 3 and a daughter 14 months. Prior to Olufemi's departure, his grandmother fell ill and required medical attention. Because of a dispute the family had with neighbors, they believed the grandmother's illness was caused by a curse from a *juju* man (practitioner of witchcraft or sorcery). Since his grandmother's illness the family has sought the assistance of a *dibia* (a traditional healer, medicine man/woman or priest).

Cultural Context

Olufemi belongs to the Igbo ethnic group of Nigeria. The Igbo are a small but influential (politically and economically) ethnic group. More important, the Igbo are deeply connected to their cultural traditions. The Igbo believe that good and ill health are determined by the relationships one has with family, community, the material and spiritual worlds, and the ancestral cult spirits (Iroegbu, 2005). Among the most important traditions are the funeral rites and ceremonies to honor the deceased. Okwukwu is the funeral rite of the Igbo of Southern Nigeria that continues to be practiced by the majority of Igbos living in Nigeria and abroad (Ogbonna, 2001). The Igbo believe that the soul of the deceased cannot enter the ancestral afterlife until Okwukwu is performed, preferably by the eldest male child. Okwukwu is performed in elaborate ceremonies that take on a carnival-like atmosphere with participants engaged in dancing, drumming, singing, masquerades, and other forms of celebration (Ogbonna, 2001). Moreover, traditional healers perform acts of wonder for the people to witness. The festivities are accentuated with lots of food and drink for family and friends to share. If Okwukwu is not performed, the deceased cannot become an ancestor and their soul is stuck in a state of perpetual limbo. Being unable to enter the ancestral realm, the deceased cannot rest in peace and is displeased with the living family (Ogbonna, 2001). Olufemi's belief that his symptoms are the result of his requirement to perform Okwukwu for his recently deceased grandmother is grounded in his cultural belief system and must be considered in formulating any diagnostic impressions.

Diagnostic Impressions

During the initial interview, Olufemi was oriented in time and space. His level of insight was keen and he clearly expressed his thoughts and emotions during the interview. Olufemi denied any suicidal or homicidal thoughts. He does not use alcohol or illicit drugs. Olufemi reported normal sexual functioning and regular relations with his wife. There has not been an increase in the number of arguments at work or home, and church attendance has remained consistent. Olufemi's concerns, and perhaps his symptoms, are likely attributable to his sense of distress over his grandmother's death. His distress appears reasonable for what might be considered the normal grieving process. An extra component to Olufemi's distress is related to his need to perform Okwukwu (burial rite to honor the deceased) to honor his grand-mother as is required by his culture. The requirement to perform Okwukwu has presented Olufemi with some unanticipated challenges that exacerbate the distress he is already experiencing from the loss of his grandmother. First, he must raise the money to pay for the expenses associated with conducting the funeral rites and ceremonies. Second, he will have to leave his wife and children here in the United States while he travels to Nigeria to perform the burial rites; the expense of taking his entire family is prohibitive. Olufemi is concerned about the safety of his wife and children, since he will not be here to protect them. Last, but certainly not the least significant, he will have to confront the suspicion back home that his grandmother's death was the work of a juju man's curse. This situation, if not handled delicately, could result in violence between members of the community. Olufemi is anxious and stressed about this possibility and realizes his responsibility to prevent any violence from occurring in his community.

Intervention

This section describes two face-to-face meetings with Olufemi as well as other interventions that took place outside of the agency. Our first meeting was held in my office at the agency. When Olufemi arrived at the agency, I escorted him to my office where we spent some time talking and getting to know each other. After about 15 minutes of chatting, I asked him to tell me what brought him to the agency. To avoid the possibility of causing embarrassment, I refrained from using words like help, counseling, therapy, mental illness, psychological health, and others that are potentially stigmatizing. The NTU theoretical orientation selected for working with Olufemi. Below are a few excerpts that characterize the exchange:

Counselor: How are you today?
Olufemi: I am well, thanks.
Counselor: Tell me what brings you here today.

Olufemi: We are having some trouble to solve. It is my family I have come to help.
Counselor: What sort of trouble does your family need help with?

Here we can see how the collectivistic orientation of Olufemi is expressed in his concern not for himself but for his family. In this situation it is important for the counselor to acknowledge these important cultural cues or otherwise risk misinterpreting Olufemi's concern for his family as being in denial about his own problems. Consistent with NTU therapy, I attempted to acknowledge the importance of interconnectedness with family. I was careful not to express any value judgment about the focus on Olufemi's concerns.

Counselor: What sort of trouble is your family having?
Olufemi: My grandmother has died and I must return home for the family and perform certain rituals so that she [grandmother] can be OK. So that she can rest and be in a good way.
Counselor: Yes, I can sense the urgency in your voice.
Olufemi: There will be many problems if I do not perform my duties. I worry that I will fail my family. I worry that I will fail my grandmother. I do not want to disgrace myself and my family.
Counselor: What kind of problems will you face if the rituals are not performed?
Olufemi: If I do not perform Okwukwu for my grandmother her spirit will not rest and misfortune will befall the family and community. My family will be disgraced and outcast from the community. Things will be bad and I cannot exist as a man.

Olufemi does not view himself as separate from his family and the community, as an extension thereof. Moreover, despite his grandmother's death he continues to acknowledge the importance of their relationship. It is important to observe the collective cultural orientation that Olufemi is expressing in his desire to uphold the integrity of his family by adhering to the cultural expectations of the group. The unaware counselor runs the risk of interpreting this behavior as dependency or enmeshment, as it might legitimately be considered in the context of a Western cultural orientation. Most important, in African culture the living, once deceased, and given the proper circumstances (lived a righteous life), become ancestors and continue to be active participants in the lives of the living. Ancestors have the power to protect and bring good fortune or to cause mischief and harm (Ogbonna,

2001). Consequently, the counselor is cautioned to not dismiss Olufemi's concerns as mere superstition but to acknowledge the seriousness of the situation and support Olufemi's decision to return home. Consistent with the NTU approach, my focus was on understanding the threat to harmony and balance and how I might assist Olufemi to reduce this threat. His need to perform the proper rituals speaks directly to issues that the NTU approach terms alignment. The NTU counselor must facilitate the individual's alignment with their internal and external worlds (Gregory & Harper, 2001).

Counselor: Will it be difficult for you to return home for the rituals? What type of support do you need for your wife and children so that you can make the trip without concern for their safety?

Olufemi: I am just very concerned to leave my family alone. A good father or husband does not abandon their family. I am not even a human being for doing such a thing. I am not sure if this is something I should do and what will happen to my family in my absence.

Counselor: Would it be possible to bring your family with you for our next meeting? I would like to include them in our discussions as well as any preparations we might make for your trip.

Olufemi: Yes, I can bring them if you like.

Here we again see the theme related to notions of the self in collectivistic cultures. Olufemi, like others from collectivistic cultures, attaches his selfhood to his role as a father and husband. He views himself only in the context of his family, specifically, in his role as father and husband. Western-oriented counselors might interpret Olufemi's concerns as abnormal and reflective of patriarchal attitudes and values. In the framework of an NTU counseling approach, I sought to bring the family in as cocollaborators in the process. As was noted by Gregory and Harper (2001), in NTU counseling the focus in not exclusively on the individual but includes the entire family. Given Olufemi's uncertainty about his planned trip home to perform the required funeral rites for his grandmother, I made the decision that we would consult a *dibia afa*. A dibia afa is a traditional healer who performs divination for the purpose of diagnosis (Iroegbu, 2005). Olufemi was pleased with this decision as it would allow him to ask specific questions of the diviner in relation to his upcoming trip to Igboland, questions he felt were only knowable with the assistance of a traditional diviner.

The diviner was able to answer a number of Olufemi's questions that allowed him to feel comfortable with making the necessary trip to his homeland. The culturally competent counselor must be prepared to consult with indigenous healers in matters of spiritual importance. This case study was intended to provide a brief introduction to working cross-culturally from an NTU theoretical orientation. One goal of the case study was to present the reader with a real-world situation in which the individual's distress is culture-based and to apply a culturally appropriate conceptualization and intervention. A second goal was to highlight the importance of culture and worldview in conceptualizing an individual's presenting problem so as to reduce the potential for the misinterpretation of thoughts, emotions, and behaviors that would result in misdiagnosis.

Conclusion

This chapter was intended to provide an introduction and overview of the importance of culture and worldview in the counseling and psychotherapy process. In addition to reviewing the major concepts needed for competent practice with persons from diverse racial and cultural groups, we presented several culturally based counseling and psychotherapy techniques for consideration by counselors and other mental health practitioners. Counselors are encouraged to deconstruct the culturally encapsulated, ethnocentric, epistemological, ontological, and axiological frameworks that undergird Western psychology. The case study was intended to introduce the reader to the complexities of cross-cultural counseling and psychotherapy.

Many more efforts are needed to improve the quality of training in multicultural counseling and psychotherapy. Most counselor training programs require at least one course in multicultural counseling (Das, 1995; Kiselica, 1998). This is a starting point, but these efforts alone are inadequate to properly prepare trainees to work with individuals from diverse racial and cultural groups. A number of scholars in the area of multicultural and cross-cultural counseling have advocated that issues of race and culture, including ethnicity, gender, class, and sexual orientation, be infused into all aspects of the training curriculum for counselors and psychologists (Das, 1995; Holcomb-McCoy & Myers, 1999). In fact, the accrediting organizations for counselors (Council for Accreditation of Counseling and Related Educational Programs [CACREP]) and psychologists (APA) have incorporated cross-cultural issues into their standards for evaluating the accreditation-worthiness of training programs (Holcomb-McCoy & Myers, 1999). Both CACREP and APA require graduate training programs to go beyond the "single course" approach to cross-cultural therapy (CCT) and insure adequate representation throughout the training curriculum (APA, 2003; CACREP, 2009). In spite of these mandates, many counseling and psychology training programs have been slow in adhering to even the minimal standards set forth by their respective accrediting bodies.

References

American Psychological Association. (2003). Guidelines on Multicultural Education, Training, Research, Practice, and Organizational Change for Psychologists. *American Psychologist, 58*, 377–402.

Ani, M. (1994). *Yurugu: An African-centered critique of European cultural thought and behavior.* Trenton, NJ: African World Press.

Brabeck, M., & Brown, L. S. (1997). Feminist theory and psychological practice. In J. Worell & N. Johnson (Eds.), *Shaping the future of feminist psychology: Education, research and practice* (pp. 15–36). Washington, DC: American Psychological Association.

Brown, L. S. (1994). Boundaries in feminist therapy: A conceptual formulation. *Women & Therapy, 15*(1), 29–38.

Brown, L. S. (2006). Still subversive after all these years: The relevance of feminist therapy in the age of evidence-based practice. *Psychology of Women Quarterly, 30*, 15–24.

Brown, L. S. (2007). Empathy, genuineness—and the dynamics of power: A feminist responds to Rogers. *Psychotherapy: Theory, Research, Practice, Training, 44*(3), 257–259.

Bulhan, H. A. (1985). *Frantz Fanon and the psychology of oppression.* New York: Plenum Press.

Chung, R. C., & Bemak, F. (2002). The relationship of culture and empathy in cross-cultural counseling. *Journal of Counseling and Development, 80,* 154–159.

Comas-Diaz, L., Lykes, M. B., & Alarcon, R. D. (1998). Ethnic conflict and the psychology of liberation in Guatemala, Peru, and Puerto Rico. *American Psychologist, 53*, 778–792.

Cross, W. (1971) The Negro to Black conversion experience. *Black World, 20*, 13–25.

Cross, W. (1991). *Shades of Black.* Philadelphia: Temple University Press.

Das, A. K. (1995). Rethinking multicultural counseling: Implications for counselor education. *Journal of Counseling and Development, 74*, 45–52.

Fromm, E. (1976). *To have or to be.* New York: Bantam Books.

Gregory, W. H., & Harper, K. W. (2001). The NTU approach to health and healing. *Journal of Black Psychology, 27,* 304–320.

Guthrie, R. V. (1998). *Even the rat was White: A historical view of psychology* (2nd ed.). Boston: Allyn & Bacon.

Helms, J. (1985). Toward a theoretical explanation of the effects of race on counseling: A Black and White model. *Counseling Psychologist, 12,* 153–165.

Helms, J. (1990). *Black and White racial identity.* Westport, CT: Greenwood.

Helms, J. E., & Cook, D. A. (Eds.). (1999). *Using race and culture in counseling and psychotherapy.* Boston: Allyn & Bacon.

Holcomb-McCoy, C. C., & Myers, J. E. (1999). Multicultural competence and counselor training: A national survey. *Journal of Counseling & Development, 77,* 294–302.

Huang, L. N. (1994). An integrative approach to clinical assessment and intervention with Asian-American adolescents. *Journal of Clinical Child Psychology, 23,* 21–31.

Iroegbu, P. (2005). Healing insanity: Skills and expert knowledge of Igbo healers. *Africa Development, 30,* 78–92.

Ivey, A. E. (1995). Psychotherapy as liberation: Toward specific skills and strategies in multicultural counseling and therapy. In J. G. Ponterotto, J. M. Casas, L. A. Suzuki, & C. M. Alexander (Eds.), *Handbook of multicultural counseling* (pp. 53–72). Thousand Oaks, CA: Sage.

Jackson, B. (1975). Black identity development. *Journal of Educational Diversity and Innovation, 2,* 19–25.

Jackson, B. (1990, September). *Building a multicultural school.* Presentation to the Amherst Regional School System, Amherst, MA.

Kambon, K. K. (1998). *African/Black psychology in the American context.* Tallahassee, FL: Nubian Nation Publications.

Kiselica, M. S. (1998). Preparing Anglos for the challenges and joys of multiculturalism. *Counseling Psychologist, 26,* 5–21.

Koltko-Rivera, M. E. (2004). The psychology of worldviews. *Review of General Psychology, 8,* 3–58.

Lerner, G. (1993). *The creation of feminist consciousness.* New York: Oxford University Press.

Nobles, W. (1990). African philosophy: Foundation of Black psychology. In R. L. Jones (Ed.), *Black psychology* (pp. 47–63). Berkeley, CA: Cobb & Henry.

Ogbonna, M. S. (2001). *Okwukwu: Psychological imperatives of funeral rites among the Igbo of Nigeria.* New York: Triatlantic Books.

Phillips, F. B. (1990). NTU psychotherapy: An Afrocentric approach. *Journal of Black Psychology, 17,* 55–74.

Ponterorro, J. G., Utsey, S. O., & Pedersen, P. B. (2006). *Preventing prejudice: A guide for counselors, educators, and parents* (2nd ed.). Thousand Oaks, CA: Sage Publications.

Richardson, T. Q., & Molinaro, K. L. (1996). White counselor self-awareness: A prerequisite for developing multicultural competence. *Journal of Counseling and Development, 74,* 238–242.

Slattery, D., & Corbett, L. (Eds.). (2002). *Depth psychology: Meditations in the field.* Einsiedeln, Switzerland: Daimon Verlag.

Sue, D. W., Ivey, A. E., & Pedersen, P. (Eds.). (1996). *A theory of multicultural counseling and therapy.* Pacific Grove, CA: Brooks/Cole.

Sue, D. W., & Sue, D. (1990). *Counseling the culturally different* (2nd ed.). New York: Wiley.

Thomas, A., & Sillen, S. (1972). *Racism and psychiatry.* New York: Carol Publishing.

Utsey, S. O., & Bolden, M. A. (2008). Cross-cultural considerations in quality of life assessment. In L. Suzuki, J. Ponterotto, & P. Meller (Eds.), *Handbook of multicultural assessment* (3rd ed., pp. 299–317). New York: Jossey-Bass.

Utsey, S. O., Bolden, M., & Brown, A. (2001). Vision of revolution from the spirit of Frantz Fanon: A psychology of liberation for counseling African Americans confronting societal racism and oppression. In J. Ponterotto, J. Casas, L. Suzuki, & C. Alexander (Eds.), *Handbook of multicultural counseling* (2nd ed., pp. 311–336). Thousand Oaks, CA: Sage.

Utsey, S. O., Grange, C., & Allyne, R. (2006). Guidelines for evaluating the racial and cultural environment of professional psychology training programs. In M. G. Constantine & D. W. Sue (Eds.), *Addressing racism: Facilitating cultural competence in mental health and educational settings* (pp. 213–232). Hoboken, NJ: John Wiley & Sons.

9

Termination within the Context of Culture
A Three-Phase Model

Charles R. Ridley and Mary Shaw-Ridley

Consider the following scenario:

> A young female athlete, age 19, was referred for 7 weeks of physical therapy after a surgical procedure in which her right shoulder was reconstructed. The young woman was unable to move her right arm to perform simple tasks such as writing, brushing her teeth, or removing a shirt without assistance. The young woman had two, 2-hour sessions per week with the therapist. Therapeutic goals were established at the outset of therapy, and the goals were mutually defined based on the athlete's desire to continue playing her sport. Moreover, the goals were discussed throughout the therapy. The therapist gathered cultural assessment data during the first few visits and came to understand the education values, religious practices, food traditions, and family functions that might influence the goal setting and ultimately the success of physical therapy. During week 4, the therapist began assessment for readiness to terminate the patient at the end of week 7. Both the patient and therapist discussed gains and what was necessary to maintain the gains. The therapist inquired about support systems at home to assist in maintenance, especially prior to returning to her university athletic trainer. The young woman was able to communicate gains in the same language used by the therapist, and explained and demonstrated

what techniques should be used at home to strengthen the muscles and maintain range of motion. Specifically, the young woman was given a prescription of daily exercises and tools for documenting daily exercises to maintain the therapeutic gains. The therapist and patient had a mutual understanding that failure to comply with the "beyond therapy" protocol would result in setbacks, and the setbacks might compromise the therapeutic gains of the 7 weeks of physical therapy.

Although this situation is not counseling or psychotherapy, the processes of rehabilitation and counseling share some similarities. Clearly, mental health professionals might consider the best practices of another profession in preparing patients and clients for termination. The preparation of clients for termination from counseling should begin at the outset. It must be in the conscious thoughts of both the therapist and client. Our discussion describes termination activities that should be occurring in three distinct phases. We have deliberately avoided prescribing a length of time for each phase, as this will be determined by the nature of the presenting problem.

The purpose of counseling and psychotherapy, much like physical therapy's goal of rehabilitation, is to facilitate therapeutic change. Clients seeking the services of counselors and therapists present with a wide variety of issues, problems, needs, and assets. Their concerns range from coping with various physical, social, and psychological stressors to managing major psychiatric disorders. Whatever the nature of the presenting concerns, therapeutic change always should be the preeminent goal of psychotherapy. In the quest to develop culturally competent therapists, however, the profession inadvertently has overlooked the necessity of beginning counseling with this "big picture" frame of reference. The picture must give specific consideration to the client's culture, which is vital for sustaining change. In particular, much of the literature on the multicultural competencies fails to address the issue of treatment outcomes. The beginning reference for counselors and clients should be a view of the ending of counseling, and healthier and more fully functioning clients who eventually separate from counseling.

This chapter describes how the ending of therapy, referred to in the mental health field as termination, ought to contribute to therapeutic change. The gold standard of successful counseling in general and termination in particular is the capacity of clients to sustain positive treatment outcomes. We assert that counselors' effectiveness goes beyond helping clients change. Their competence is most clearly manifested in facilitating the sustenance of positive outcomes. To achieve this end, counselors need a sound conceptual framework to guide their interventions. Therefore, we propose a three-phase model to elucidate the process of termination.

To explain our topic, we organize the chapter into three sections. First, we set forth a philosophical foundation that underlies our conceptualization of termination. In the second section, we describe our three-phase model of termination. We provide a conclusion in the third section.

Philosophical Foundation

In this section, we set forth the philosophical foundation on which we build our model. Seven principles underpin our model. By explicating our foundational principles, we position ourselves to discuss the practical application of termination.

1. *Effective termination is integral to therapeutic change.* Therapeutic change is the ultimate goal of counseling and psychotherapy. By therapeutic change, we mean a qualitative, second-order transformation in which clients adopt more self-enhancing and less self-defeating lifestyles. Nothing should take priority over therapeutic change, and it should drive every aspect of the endeavor. Any aspect of therapy that fails to support this goal is inherently nontherapeutic. Furthermore, any aspect of counseling that is not therapeutic has the potential to undermine and compromise the entire therapeutic endeavor, regardless of the effectiveness of any other aspect of treatment. In light of this principle, termination ought to be purpose driven, executed in ways that are commensurate with the goal of achieving therapeutic change, and vigorously channeled to prevent the compromise of this purpose. This principle implies the seriousness of the responsibility of terminating clients.

2. *Begin counseling with the end in mind.* Effective termination depends on setting goals and treatment planning early in counseling (Berman, 1997). Remember the young woman who had reconstructive surgery; her treatment goals were established at the outset of physical therapy. Of course, human experience is complex, and psychological goals often are not as clear-cut as physical goals. Therefore, unlike physical therapy, more than one session may be required to establish goals for counseling clients. Nevertheless, the complexity of human experience should not obviate the setting of treatment goals as early as possible in

counseling. As the end point of counseling, termination should build on the therapeutic work done throughout the counseling. We posit that the goals set for clients should meet several criteria: (a) They should be holistic in that they reflect change in behavior, affective processes, cognitive processes, spirituality, and relational dynamics; (b) they should be second order in that they represent a qualitative change rather than a surface change in clients; (c) they should be lifestyle oriented in that they reflect clients' commitment to and ongoing engagement in a new way of experiencing the world; and (d) they should be attainable in that while stretching clients and causing them to experience necessary pain, they are within clients' reach.

3. *Incorporating considerations of culture is essential for effective termination.* Culture is ubiquitous in counseling and psychotherapy. Always present, whether counselors and therapists acknowledge its presence or leverage it for therapeutic gains, culture is an entity never to be dismissed, discounted, or overlooked. As Draguns (1989) pointed out, culture is an invisible and silent partner in counseling. Counselors and clients both bring to counseling their cultural experiences, and counseling takes place in a cultural setting. The interaction of the cultural exigencies of client, counselor, and counseling setting adds to the complexity inherent in therapeutic change. Therefore, we take the position that culture is relevant to all aspects and phases of counseling. This means that the only reasonable posture for therapists is to consciously incorporate culture in the termination process.

4. *Termination is a process, and as a process, it consists of phases.* Termination is not a single event. Instead, it is a process that entails a series of successive events and operations that unfold over time and lead to a particular result. Although clients normally do not change in a straightforward and linear fashion, there is a natural sequence to the unfolding of important events in termination. We use the term *phases* to indicate these events. Each succeeding phase is sequel to antecedent phases. In our model, we propose termination as a three-phase process, each phase serving a distinct purpose and consisting of subordinate units of the process. To be maximally effective, therapists must facilitate the entire process, giving each phase its appropriate consideration and doing so in a competent manner.

5. *Termination must be client-centered.* In making this assertion, we are not advocating that termination necessarily follows the protocol of Rogers's (1961) person-centered therapy. In fact, we explain aspects of

termination that are not discussed in the literature of client-centered therapy. We argue that all of the events and operations involved in termination should set a priority on the interest of the clients. Certainly, we understand that the majority of practitioners are altruistic. They are drawn to the mental health professions because of their deep interest in helping people. Despite their altruism, many instances of therapists' "within" therapy behavior are not helpful. Ridley (2005) makes the compelling case that much of the behavior of clinicians, especially in multicultural contexts, amounts to unintentional racism. Armed with the best of intentions, clinicians may sabotage their own efforts by inadvertently engaging in behaviors that lead to aversive consequences for clients. These outcomes contradict the purpose of counseling, which again is therapeutic change. Therefore, it is in the interest of clinicians to become aware of their privileged experiences, unintentional racism, biases, prejudices, and sexism. They must replace these attitudes with a more accepting stance and learn intentional interventions that keep them ostensibly client-centered. What are the perceptions, enablers, and nurturers for the client? From a client's perspective, what are the positive and negative behaviors associated with the presenting problem?

6. *Effective termination requires the mutual participation of therapists and clients in a shared decision-making process.* This approach to termination is a fundamental shift from the hierarchical, medical model practice found in much of counseling. It is collaborative, equitably involving both the therapist and client in a shared decision-making process and recognizing the unique strengths that each participant brings. We frame this operation as *participatory decision making.* Like every other aspect of counseling, termination should draw upon the respective contributions of therapists and clients to the process. Although collaboration should be initiated by therapists, their contribution is no more important than that of clients. Both parties are considered as having expertise. The expertise of therapists should lie in facilitating termination and framing the experience of the client. The expertise of clients lies in their being the most important source in reporting their experiences and taking responsibility for change.

7. *To demonstrate competence in terminating clients, therapists must be motivated to execute all phases and operations of the process.* As a multiphase, multioperation process, therapists are enjoined to execute a multiplicity of operations. In light of this multiplicity, numerous factors potentially can compromise the effectiveness of termination. The motivation of

therapists illustrates this point. On the one hand, therapists may be competent in many aspects of treatment such as building a therapeutic alliance, demonstrating empathic understanding, and even collaborating with clients to establish treatment goals. However, they may be incompetent in some of the operations of termination such as evaluating treatment goals or helping clients identify structured, often cultural, supports outside of therapy. On the other hand, therapists may be competent in many of the operations relevant to termination, but they may be differentially motivated. For instance, they may be highly motivated to evaluate the progress clients make toward their treatment goals, but they may not be motivated to help clients structure their social supports, even though they might be capable in this area.

Termination within the Context of Culture as a Three-Phase Process

We conceptualize culturally appropriate termination as a three-phase process, consisting of pretermination, active termination, and posttermination. As we have postulated, the process assumes that therapists integrate culture throughout all of counseling, which, of course, includes the termination phase. We assert that counselors do not have to be from the same culture as their clients to effectively facilitate the process. Instead, they need to take into careful consideration pertinent cultural issues and determine how best to communicate with clients about these issues. See the model in Figure 9.1. In our opinion, the model is a more culturally comprehensive conceptualization of the events and operations inherent in the process than typically is found in discussions of termination. Although the model has three distinct phases, we believe the dynamic nature of termination suggests the phases are not mutually exclusive.

Phase 1: Pretermination

In one sense, all of therapy, except for its actual ending, is pretermination. In another sense, even though pretermination may exist throughout counseling, four major tasks constitute this phase: (a) preventing premature termination, (b) facilitating mutual understanding of therapeutic gains, (c) evaluating

Figure 9.1
Three-Phase Model of Termination

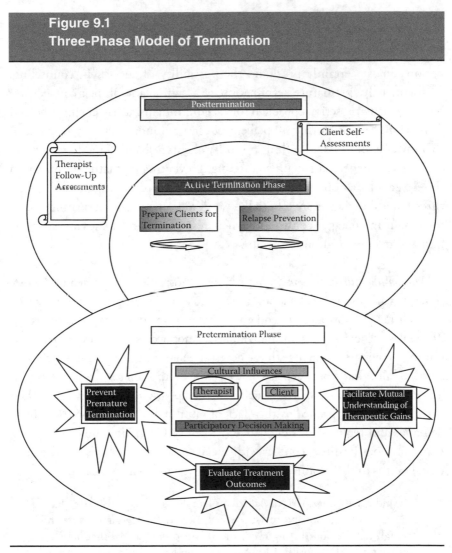

treatment outcomes, and (d) processing clients' emotions and perceptions about the inevitable termination. Collectively, these clinical activities help clients make progress toward their goals, overcome obstacles to reaching their goals, and generally improve the chances that the counseling experience will be successful. Therapists should have an investment in these activities throughout counseling. Therefore, no specific number of sessions is indicated in this phase since the length of therapy depends on a host of factors relative to each case.

Prevent Premature Termination   The longer clients remain in therapy the more opportunity they have for making therapeutic gains. Although remaining in therapy does not guarantee therapeutic change, premature termination almost certainly precludes the possibility of success in counseling. Unfortunately, premature termination is a significant problem in general but a particularly serious problem for racial/ethnic minority clients. Sue and Zane (1987) reported that 50 percent of ethnic minority clients drop out of therapy after one session. Ethnic minority clients also are found to have more dissatisfying experiences with counseling. Preventing premature termination should be the first operation in facilitating effective termination. To this end, three clinical activities are especially useful to therapists—motivating clients to remain in therapy, confronting their resistance, and removing systemic barriers for continuation in therapy.

Motivating Clients to Remain in Therapy   Motivation, as defined in the dictionary, is an "incentive to action." In this sense, it is misleading to suggest that some clients are motivated, and others are not motivated. Everyone is motivated. The real issue here is that some individuals are not necessarily motivated in areas leading to therapeutic change. If the necessary changes are in conflict with their cultural values and norms, clients may lack the motivation to remain in therapy. They may be desirous of the benefits of therapeutic change. However, their desire often is undermined by their lack of motivation to engage in the painful demands and requirements of change (Ridley & Goodwin, 2004). Changing may put them in direct conflict with social, religious, economic, and educational norms in their communities. Consider the following scenario:

> Rashida is a young African American female who has a history of having sex with multiple partners. She has entered counseling because she is high risk for contracting HIV, and she recently learned that her best girlfriend is HIV positive. Rashida is struggling with how to manage her intimate relationships so that she reduces her risk for contracting HIV. She communicates to the therapist that African American men prefer not to use condoms, and they shy away from dating women who insist on using condoms and engaging in safer sex practices. Rashida is torn between holding the line with "no condom, no sex" and yielding to the pressure to have unprotected sex. What matters the most to her is being in a relationship with an African American male. She emphasizes, however, that there is a shortage of eligible Black men because many of them are incarcerated or on drugs. Rashida is not motivated to change her behavior or remain in therapy right now. She does not see how the therapist can assist with her problem.

Cultural context is an important factor to consider in motivating Rashida to stay in therapy. Of course, not every African American male has the expectation of unsafe sex practices, and it would be stereotyping to suggest that this is the cultural norm. Nevertheless, Rashida lives with the pressure for either having unsafe sex or having no relationships with young men. Unless her therapist processes this issue with Rashida, she almost certainly will terminate prematurely from therapy. The therapist must help Rashida face the problem of isolation. If the client is expected to stay in therapy, the therapist must help the client find benefits that will replace the losses for changing her behavior. In light of the importance Rashida places on having relationships with men, the therapist has to work diligently to help the client find alternative sources of fulfillment.

Confronting Clients' Resistance to Change   Even if clients become motivated to engage in therapy, they may encounter a particular aspect of the change process that is particularly painful. Then they begin to resist change. Resistance is counter-therapeutic behavior, which serves the goal of avoiding the painful requirements of change (Ridley, 2005). Here also is where they become more vulnerable for dropping out. Seeking to understand the culturally accepted values and norms of the client is first-order business for confronting resistance. For example, Jaimie is a 17-year-old Hispanic male who expresses interest in becoming a psychologist. He lives in a low-income housing project in a downtown area where he attends a large, urban high school. Jaimie is ashamed that he aspires to do well academically and gets teased by other Hispanic males who live in his community. He expresses confusion over how to be accepted by his peers and not appear to be a nerd. He wants his teachers to know that he is smart, but he does not want his friends to know this. Jaimie's parents are supportive but speak limited English. Jaimie is failing at least one subject and marginally performing in another course because he does not want to be teased or bullied by his friends. *Machismo* is the name of the game. So how does the therapist confront these issues in a culturally appropriate manner?

The therapist recognizes that status and acceptance among peers are extremely important to Jaimie. He would be shattered if his friends rejected him. At the same time, he has ambitious career aspirations. He would be discouraged if he did not make reasonable progress toward his goal. Then the therapist helps Jaimie to see his responsibilities. Sexton and Alexander (2004) stated that motivation to change occurs when clients come to view the presenting problem as one in which they contribute. Of course, the challenge for

Jaimie's therapist lies in helping him see his contribution to the problem but doing so without "blaming the victim." Sexton and Alexander suggest that motivation is most likely to occur in an environment in which therapists create hope, expectation of change, a sense of responsibility, and a positive alliance. Jaimie's therapist might help him reframe his dilemma as an asset, one that prepares him for life by learning how to make difficult choices. The therapist also might help Jaimie see the long-term benefits of working hard to achieve his goals and how this achievement can help him contribute to his community.

Removing Systemic Barriers to Treatment A variety of barriers serve as impediments to consumers continuing in therapy. Five barriers to service are particularly noteworthy. We call them the Five A's: availability, accessibility, affordability, acceptability, and appropriateness. Removal of these barriers requires intervention on two levels: macrosystem and microsystem. On the macrosystem level, mental health reform can target these barriers through social policy, policy management, and funding. On the microsystem level, administrators of agencies and therapists can create environments that are consumer-friendly with special sensitivity to needs and interests of minorities and the medically underserved. What would an agency look like or feel like if it was culturally responsive to minorities and medically underserved persons? Consider asking a client this basic question. It might help the therapist and agency to identify systemic barriers to treatment.

Facilitate Mutual Understanding of Therapeutic Gains Based on the principle of participatory decision making, the practical question is: How should counselors facilitate understanding of therapeutic gains to clients? A sidebar to this question is: How should counselors assess for mutual understanding of the therapeutic gains? And can counselors and their clients explain the therapeutic gains in a similar manner. We present eight steps to assist counselors in creating a shared decision-making culture in which clients develop an understanding of the therapeutic gains and become empowered to apply the gains in their daily living.

1. *Inspire* a shared vision. Help clients envision the future beyond therapy.
2. *Foster* collaboration by promoting cooperative goals and building trust.
3. *Recognize* the assets that clients and therapists bring to the table.
4. *Engage* clients in conversations about the therapeutic gains.
5. *Communicate* important milestones (gains) to clients; check for their understanding of the milestones.

6. *Encourage* clients to describe their perceptions of therapeutic gains.
7. *Celebrate* the values and victories of clients and their support systems, specifically as they relate to sustaining the therapeutic gains.
8. *Expect* clients to evaluate their counseling experience (effectiveness of the counseling as it relates to mutually established goals).

Evaluate Treatment Outcomes   The success of counseling hinges on clients reaching their treatment goals. Ideally, termination should not take place until clients reach all of their goals. Therefore, verifying that clients reach their goals is critical to the success of counseling. Otherwise, by not verifying goal attainment, counselors can draw erroneous conclusions about clients' progress. They may assume clients are making more progress than is actually the case. To verify clients' progress, counselors should conduct an evaluation. Lauver and Harvey (1997) proposed two types of evaluation: process and outcome. Process evaluation means that therapists continually monitor clients' progress along the way to the expected outcomes. Outcome evaluation is a determination of the extent to which clients reach their treatment goals. We believe that both process and outcome evaluations are essential in effectively terminating clients from counseling.

Baruth and Huber (1985) recommend five strategies for measuring clients' progress in therapy: verbal self-reports, frequency counts, duration counts, rating scales, and checklists. Some of these measures are quantitative, and some are qualitative. Each one has its strengths and limitations. We propose that the most valid way of evaluating treatment outcomes is to utilize a combination of these strategies such that the weaknesses of the various strategies are compensated by the strengths of other strategies.

Processing Clients' Emotions and Perceptions about the Inevitable Termination   Although every aspect of counseling is emotionally laden, termination itself can conjure up intense feelings and new perceptions in clients. Clients may find themselves having to grapple with this new challenge in addition to the emotional challenges that led them to counseling. Evans, Hearn, Uhlemann, and Ivey (2008) commented on this experience:

> Termination may involve the experience of a variety of emotions including gratitude, loss, and issues associated with separation and autonomy. The interviewer needs to assist the client to talk openly and to resolve any feelings associated with termination. (p. 232)

The importance of processing clients' emotions and perceptions about termination cannot be overstated. In the context of making significant therapeutic gains, the relationship clients develop with their therapists often takes on special meaning. The special meaning to the client may entail powerful emotions about the relationship. Yet, termination in counseling is inevitable. To terminate therapy without processing these feelings with clients potentially is to set them up for another traumatic experience, one that might involve deep loss, anger, and undermining of the gains made in therapy. Therefore, in the interest of client-centeredness, therapists can prepare clients for termination by helping them work through the emotional issues pertaining to ending the relationship.

The first author supervised a doctoral student in an advanced practicum. The student is an African American woman, and one of her clients was a White, middle-aged man. Initially, the client was apprehensive about therapy and disgruntled about having an African American woman as a therapist. He acknowledged his racist upbringing. During the course of counseling, a strong therapeutic alliance was established, and the client made a complete shift in his attitude toward the counselor. After 8 months of counseling, the counselor had to transfer the client to a new counselor because she had finished her practicum. The client demonstrated strong feelings and disappointment that the relationship was ending. The supervisor had to move the counselor from indirectly dealing with the client's emotions to directly processing termination as a significant loss.

Phase 2: Active Termination

During this phase of termination, counselors prepare clients for the actual ending of regular counseling sessions. Like the other phases of termination, no specific number of sessions is specified since a variety of factors can influence the amount of time needed for active termination. Certainly, by this time in counseling, clients are expected to be functioning at a higher level. As the major objective is sustaining treatment outcomes, transferring therapeutic gains and preventing relapse are key strategies of this phase. The two psychosocial resources most useful for achieving this objective are the clients as individuals and structured support systems.

Sustaining Treatment Outcomes   Transferring the gains made in therapy and preventing relapse actually are interdependent strategies. Successful implementation of one depends on the successful implementation of the other.

Transferring Gains   Once clients terminate from counseling, they face a new challenge: extending their therapeutic gains beyond counseling. The important question here is this: Will clients carry over into other settings the changes they made in the counseling setting? The extension of positive treatment outcomes into new situations, settings, and circumstances is critical. Otherwise, the gains clients make in therapy amount to nothing more than an exercise in futility. Kazdin (2001) provided a perspective on the *transfer of training* in therapy:

> We do not want clients to be adjusted, less anxious, and free from serious problems (severe anxiety, drug abuse) merely in the therapy sessions while under the influence of a mental health professional. We want any changes to be maintained and to extend well outside of the session. (pp. 370–371)

The point of transfer is that the positive outcomes achieved by clients in counseling will be manifested in their homes, workplaces, leisure venues, religious establishments, educational institutions, and communities. In other words, neither counselors nor clients can assume that the positive outcomes of counseling automatically will transfer to other settings. Transferring treatment outcomes requires intentionality and preparation. Therefore, instituting a plan to transfer therapeutic gains increases the likelihood that the treatment outcomes will occur in relevant situations, settings, and circumstances in the client's life (Miltenberger, 2008). If counselors fail to collaborate with clients to develop a plan, the chances are that clients will not effectively transfer their therapeutic gains.

Preventing Relapse   Therapeutic change seldom progresses in a straightforward or linear fashion. In fact, clients may have some success in transferring their therapeutic gains to other settings, but the initial transfer does not mean clients will sustain their gains indefinitely. The important question here is this: Will the gains clients transfer to other settings continue over the long term? The extension of positive treatment outcomes over the long term, in addition to across settings, completes the overall objective of sustenance of outcomes.

Because therapeutic change can be demanding and painful, clients may have lapses en route to achieving their treatment goals. A lapse occurs when clients engage in behavior they are trying to overcome (Watson & Tharp, 1993). Metaphorically, a lapse is like taking two steps forward and one step backward. However, the larger problem for many clients is that their lapses become relapses. A relapse occurs when clients go back to their full-blown patterns of dysfunction (Watson & Tharp, 1993). Although lapses are to be expected, therapists still equip clients with skills to prevent their lapses from becoming relapses. Along these lines, Ridley (2005) stated:

> Changing problem behavior is one accomplishment; maintaining constructive change is another. The real test of termination's effectiveness lies in whether or not therapeutic gains last long after counseling is over. Competent counselors attempt to help their minority client avoid the relapse of problem behaviors. (p. 152)

The point of relapse prevention is that the positive outcomes achieved by clients in counseling will be manifested long after therapy has concluded. Counselors and clients cannot assume that treatment gains automatically will sustain themselves without a plan of action. The challenge clients face after the conclusion of therapy can be difficult, and the rate of relapse for many problems is high (Marlatt & Gordon, 1985).

Psychosocial Resources   The two resources most useful for achieving the objectives of active termination are the individual and structured support systems. Whereas the former is focused on the client as a self agent, the latter is focused on the agency of various social systems of which clients are members and interact. Both resources are essential in sustaining treatment outcomes.

The Individual   Ecological theory reminds us that adaptation is critical to the survival of each living organism. Hence the client who begins therapy must be expected to continually adapt to an ever-changing environment, composed of living and nonliving things. Sustenance of therapeutic gains requires clients to master skills and attitudes that enhance the likelihood of being able to adapt to the dynamic environment in which they experience life on a daily basis. As personal agents for sustaining their positive outcomes, clients possess a variety of cognitive, emotional, spiritual, and behavioral capacities upon which they can draw. Considerable research indicates that individuals are capable of controlling personal habits, health behaviors, professional behaviors, and personal problems (Brigham, 1989; Epstein, 1996; Stuart, 1977; Watson & Tharp, 1993; Yates, 1986). Clearly, individual clients must look to themselves as a key resource for transferring therapeutic gains and preventing relapse. Although it is in their interest to draw upon social supports, they cannot and should not discount the vital role they play in sustaining their personal well-being. Consider this case scenario:

Shonya is a 29-year-old biracial woman who identifies herself with the African American community. Her physician referred her to a psychologist as part of the treatment team to assist in her weight loss. Her current weight puts her at risk for other health problems. In therapy, Shonya claims that her weight is common for women in her community, almost like a cultural norm. She also states that African American men are attracted to heavy-set women. After in-depth sessions with the client, the psychologist determined a couple of secondary gains that were underlying Shonya's unhealthy eating habits and lack of exercise. She had a need to be accepted by other African American women as fully "one of them." She remembers with horror being teased one time by other girls about having a White mother. She also wanted to avoid the possible discovering that she still could not "get a man," even if she lost weight. So staying at an unhealthy weight amounted to playing it safe. Until Shonya comes to terms with her real motivations and beneficially uses her psychological resources, she will always self-sabotage her efforts to lose weight.

As a culturally competent therapist, the psychologist first acknowledges Shonya's view about weight and African American men. He responds to her with deep concern and empathy, reflecting his understanding of the importance of her cultural values. But he does not stop there. He presses the issue to find out if there is more to the story. To ascertain Shonya's secondary gains, those hidden motivations for not losing weight, the psychologist asks what appears to be an unthinkable question: "Shonya, how do you benefit from not losing weight?" He anticipated her resistance. But remaining persistent, she eventually admitted her deep fears associated with losing weight. Then the psychologist engaged in a cultural confrontation (Ridley, Ethington, & Heppner, 2007). He challenged her to see how using this particular culturally based attitude was a self-defeating "smokescreen."

Structured Social Support Systems   The principles of ecology—nonliving and living things interact with each other, adaptation, predator–prey relationships, and survival of the fittest (among others)—are relevant to termination. They underpin the notion that clients must have structured support systems within their culture to sustain therapeutic gains and prevent relapse during the posttermination phase. Structured support systems consist of living and nonliving things (built environments) that enhance the psychological well-being of individuals such that they are able to have healthy, balanced lifestyles. The active phase of termination requires therapists to: (a) assess the

nature of clients' structured support systems, (b) intensify intervention strategies to assist clients with identification of *therapeutic enhancing structured
support systems*, and (c) facilitate clients' assessment of the quality of these
structured support systems.

Clients interact with family members or a close circle of friends who function like family to form an ecosystem. As human ecosystems, families provide biological sustenance, economic maintenance, and psychological and
nurturance functions for their members as well as society in general (Bubolz
& Sontag, 1993). It is within the ecosystem that clients must be able to effectively self-regulate and sustain their therapeutic gains. Consider the following example:

> Azarel, a young Hispanic female, has been attending an all women's
> college on the East Coast. The young woman comes from a family with
> strong traditions and values rooted in Catholic culture. She announces
> that she is lesbian and wants to bring her lover home to the South Texas
> area. The family is shocked and struggles to embrace her new lifestyle.
> Azarel decides that it is not a good idea to return home at this point.
> She decides to seek counseling to help her cope with family and friends
> who are resistant to the new lifestyle. Azarel's cultural identity is rooted
> in her Hispanic Catholic upbringing. She is now faced with a bicultural
> identity crisis; the lesbian culture is very foreign to her family.

This example demonstrates the importance of extending interventions
beyond the individual to the social support system. At some point, Azarel
either must face her family or decide that she will be indefinitely estranged
from her parents, siblings, and old friends. The first option available to the
therapist is to help Azarel begin constructive conversations with her family.
The purpose of these conversations is to openly share the different perspectives, deeply felt emotions, and hopefully move the family to an acceptance
of her lifestyle. The second option, if the first one does not work out, is to
help Azarel to resolve the pain of estrangement and structure social systems
that are more supportive.

Studies of the health-enhancing components of social relationships have
defined several key terms that are important to this discussion of structured
support systems (Berkman, Glass, Brissette, & Seeman, 2000). The term
social integration refers to the existence of social ties. The term *social network*
refers to the web of social relationships that surround clients. The provision of
social support is one of the important functions of social relationships. Social
networks are linkages between people that may (or may not) provide social
support. They also may serve functions other than providing support. In this

sense, the use of the term *social support* may be an oxymoron—an implicit contradiction in terms. In the therapeutic setting, the social networks that provide "real" social support are the ones we characterize as *structured*.

According to House (1981), social support is the functional content of relationships that can be categorized into four broad types of supportive behaviors or acts: (a) *emotional support* involves the provision of empathy, love, trust, and caring; (b) *instrumental support* involves the provision of tangible aid and services that directly assist a person in need; (c) *informational support* involves the provision of advice, suggestions, and information that a person can use to address problems; and (d) *appraisal support* involves the provision of information that is useful for self-evaluation purposes. The information is given in the form of constructive feedback, affirmation, and social comparison.

Four Modalities of Active Termination   By combining the two strategies and two resources of this phase, we can conceptualize four modalities of the active termination phase. See Figure 9.2.

Transferring Gains Using the Individual as a Resource

- *Develop a therapeutic gains checklist.* A therapeutic gains checklist is developed over the course of counseling in collaboration with the client. Therapeutic gains equate to treatment outcomes that are elucidated through the participatory decision-making process. The therapist should facilitate the development of a user-friendly checklist that can be utilized by the client to self-monitor progress and maintenance beyond counseling. The checklist can also be used as an accountability tool by reliable and trustworthy members of clients' structured support systems. Clients should be encouraged to enlist the monitoring support of at least one reliable support person prior to entering the post-termination phase of counseling.
- *Learn self-regulation techniques.* Many behaviors and patterns of behavior are so well established that they occur without people thinking about them. Although behaviors seem to occur automatically, people actually have voluntary control over much of what they do. Making a conscious effort to control one's behaviors is called self-regulation (Watson & Tharp, 1993). Self-regulation is useful for overcoming self-defeating behavior, coping effectively with stressful situations, and resisting temptations. There are a variety of techniques we can use to gain self-control.

**Figure 9.2
Sustaining Treatment Outcomes**

Transferring Gains ⇐ ⇒ Preventing Relapse

	Transferring Gains	Preventing Relapse
Individual	Develop a therapeutic gains checklist Learn self-regulation techniques Verbalize words of self-encouragement Take photographs that show evidence of therapeutic gains in applied settings	Utilize the therapeutic gains checklist Practice self-regulation techniques Develop an emergency preparedness plan for high risk situations Test the emergency plan within a structured support group Develop alternative supportive systems
Structured Social Support	Engage a trustworthy support person(s) Apply new knowledge, skills within selected support systems Identify healthy versus unhealthy social supports (cognitive mapping) Determine positive reinforcers and negative stressors Develop buffers to negative stressors	Identify reliable, trustworthy resources Access the resources in acceptable settings Cultivate healthy relationships within different support systems Develop alternative (back-up) support for crisis situations

RESOURCES (label at left between the two rows)

- *Read or view selected support materials.* There are a variety of self-help resources in diverse media formats to assist the client during the termination phases of counseling. The therapist should determine the client's preferred method of learning, reading, listening, viewing, and so forth before recommending support materials. The authors recommend that at least one reading or visual resource be selected in collaboration with the client and utilized during the active termination phase to begin the formal acceptance that a variety of support materials can help reinforce the therapeutic gains of counseling. Books and video resources may also provide discussion materials that can be utilized within selected support systems to facilitate maintenance of counseling therapeutic gains.
- *Verbalize words of self-encouragement.* Self-encouragement is a powerful tool to counter normal feelings of hopelessness, guilt, shame, and

so forth that may interfere with therapeutic gains. Consider the following scenario: Erica was a 26-year-old Latina who struggled with being obese. She was popular and accepted within the Hispanic community. However, her employment within a diabetes prevention clinic had made her aware of the possible outcomes associated with obesity, the predisposition to Type 2 diabetes. Erica's family emphasized that she was overly concerned about her weight and that she was preoccupied with looking like White women in the United States. Erica encountered counseling to develop some coping skills for managing life in two seemingly different worlds: her work setting and her family home. During counseling, Erica had to learn to verbalize words of self-encouragement. These words included: "I will be loved by my family even if I make healthier food choices"; "It is okay to want to be healthier"; "I feel better when I make healthier food choices, despite what my family thinks."

- *Take photographs that show evidence of therapeutic gains*. It has been stated that a picture is worth a thousand words. Individuals should continually be engaged in assessing their interactions with others. Photographs help to capture and create memories that can serve to remind clients of rewarding and fulfilling experiences. Feelings of isolation and defeat can sometimes be countered when an individual can remember a good experience with friends or a success story. Encourage clients to begin a "Caught in the Act" memory album; that is, caught in the act with various structured social supports (caught laughing, having fun at a party without the significant other who has died; caught in conversation with a person who is typically a source of tremendous stress). Photographs may assist the therapist in understanding more about the clients' culture. Pictures can communicate so much about the lived experiences of our clients.

Transferring Gains Using Structured Social Support as a Resource

- *Engage a trustworthy support person in counseling*. During the early stages of counseling, the therapist should encourage the client to begin the process of identifying a trustworthy support person. The person can be identified through an analysis of the available and acceptable structured support systems of the client. Figure 9.3 presents a model for exploring the possible relationships that a client could consider for identifying a trustworthy support person.

Figure 9.3
Structured Social Supports

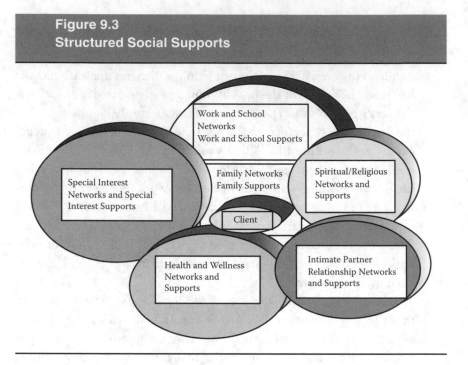

- *Make a realistic assessment of the sources of emotional, instrumental, infor-mational, and appraisal support that are available and accessible to the client.* Employing participatory decision making, the assessment should occur throughout therapy but especially during the active phase of ter-mination. Because therapy seeks to sustain therapeutic gains and prevent relapse, it is imperative that therapists facilitate a collaborative assessment of clients' structured supports as early in counseling as possible. Clearly, one of the mutually agreed upon therapeutic goals should be the devel-opment, enhancement, and restructuring of structured support systems to ensure sustainable therapeutic gains made during counseling.

- *Apply new knowledge, skills within selected support systems.* During this active phase of termination, it is imperative that the client begin to apply newly acquired knowledge and skills within selected structured support systems. For example, the spiritual structured support systems may represent a more viable option to clients who have determined that their family support system and existing family network are dys-functional and distressing. However, clients find encouragement and peace through interactions with members of the structured spiritual community. Hence, clients should be encouraged to seek a trustworthy

support, which we refer to as informed and reliable sources of information and encouragement as opposed to uniformed and unreliable
sources of support (negative stressors).

- *Identify healthy versus unhealthy social support.* The therapist might consider using cognitive mapping techniques to assist clients with determining the "real" support in each subsystem. The purpose of these
activities is to elucidate structured support systems that might be available, acceptable, and accessible to the client during the posttermination
phase. During the active termination phase, it becomes critical for the
client to identify healthy versus unhealthy social support. Figure 9.3
provides a framework for conceptualizing and mapping clients' networks and supports.

- *Determine positive reinforcers and negative stressors.* Positive reinforcers
are best described as the individuals and things that support therapeutic gains. The positive reinforcers should have the capacity to confront
undesirable client cognitions, attitudes, and behaviors—specifically
those that interfere with treatment outcomes. Negative stressors may
be perceived as uninformed, naysayers, criticizers, and generally unsup-
portive of the issues and problems of the client. Many clients may view
negative stressors as self-absorbed individuals incapable of offering
encouragement. The identification of positive reinforcers and negative
stressors is an ongoing dialogue that must occur between the therapist
and client during counseling. Failure to clearly identify these reinforcers and stressors sets a client up for relapse during posttherapy. Consider
the following scenario:

> Rhonda, a 35-year-old HIV positive African American female, partic-
> ipated in 9-week, clinic-based support group intervention facilitated
> by a health educator and social worker. During a group exercise, the
> young woman revealed that she had been living with HIV for 8 years
> and that no one in her family, including her children, knew that she
> was HIV positive. The young woman had determined that there were
> no trustworthy support people in her social network. She was gain-
> fully employed prior to the HIV diagnosis and was actively engaged in
> a Black, Baptist church. She indicated that based on her observations
> of how others with HIV were treated within her family and church,
> she decided it was in her best interest to manage the HIV illness alone.
> She had identified everyone in her family and church family to be a
> negative stressor—they would criticize, question, and generally create
> much more stress for her than she could bear giving the enormous
> challenges she faced living with HIV.

- *Develop buffers to negative stressors.* Buffers are those things, people, places, or events that might serve to neutralize the effects of negative stressors. The therapist should collaborate with the client to develop strategies for managing negative stressors. These might include: thinking about a peaceful place to retreat from the negative stressor, or verbalizing or thinking positive words of encouragement when interacting with a negative stressor.

Preventing Relapse Using the Individual as a Resource

- *Utilize the therapeutic gains checklist.* The therapist should provide the client with the treatment outcomes (therapeutic gains) checklist. The checklist should include the mutually agreed upon outcomes determined earlier in counseling. A user-friendly checklist should be developed by the therapist and discussed with the client during active termination. The client should begin using the checklist outside of counseling prior to the posttermination phase of counseling. This will provide an opportunity for the client to discuss utilization of the checklist outside of the formal counseling setting.
- *Practice self-regulation techniques.* As mentioned, there are a variety of available self-regulation techniques from which clients can employ. Two are particularly useful. Clients can use self-instructions and self-praise statements (Miltenberger, 2008). Self-instructions are statements to oneself concerning what and how to engage in a specific target behavior at the appropriate time and in the appropriate setting. Self-praise are statements to oneself that immediately follow the target behavior and provide positive evaluations.
- *Develop an emergency preparedness plan for high-risk situations.* Emergency preparedness plans for high-risk situations are essential for the client. A culturally competent therapist will facilitate the development of such a plan prior to the posttermination phase of therapy. This conversation requires both the therapist and client to consider cultural values and norms. If the client comes from a culture in which emergency preparedness for life-altering situations has not been part of the lived experience, this may be a difficult counseling topic. Nonetheless, a therapist should consider the cultural context for this conversation. For example, how does the client view time, money, people, possessions, and so forth? A person who only lives for now may be resistant

to an emergency preparedness plan. The competent therapist should have gathered important cultural data through the counseling process that will assist with the development of an emergency plan for high-risk situations.

- *Test the emergency plan within a structured support system.* An emergency plan is only good if it passes the test. Through the process of planning and testing, an individual determines whether a plan will work. An untested emergency plan is doomed to failure. Consider the case of a Hurricane City catastrophe. City officials had developed a plan to evacuate the city if necessary. The plan included buses to evacuate residents. Unfortunately, the plan was never tested and when it became necessary to use the buses, the city determined that there were not enough drivers for the buses; hence buses were available, but the supply of properly licensed drivers was nonexistent. The untested plan caused millions of residents to be stranded in a city that was doomed to flood. A great plan was in place, but it had not been tested.

- *Develop alternative support systems.* The counselor should assist the client in developing strategies to expand the existing support systems to include new ones. For example, the spiritual health of a client may be a wellness dimension in which the client struggled prior to counseling. The client might begin conversations aimed at elucidating the client's perception of available, appropriate, and accessible spiritual or religious supports. The therapist should have explored the relative importance of spirituality to the clients' perception of wellness prior to the active termination phase. If the client has become disconnected from a spiritual structured support system, the therapist could facilitate discussions about ways to reconnect with an acceptable spiritual support system, especially if the client deems spirituality to be an important aspect of well-being.

Preventing Relapse Using Structured Social Support as a Resource

- *Identify reliable, trustworthy resources.* The counselor should facilitate conversations that will help the client to identify at least one or two people within existing structured social support resources. The resources should become an integral part of the client's lived experiences during the course of counseling, especially during the active phase of termination.

- *Access the resources in acceptable settings.* The reliable, trustworthy resources should be accessible to the client in acceptable settings. Acceptable settings should be mutually determined by the therapist and client. The setting should facilitate maintenance of therapeutic gains and not be a high-risk setting for the client.
- *Cultivate healthy relationships within different support systems.* Cultivation of healthy relationships requires active participation from the client. These relationships should develop as the client applies newly acquired knowledge and skills in the "real world," beyond therapy. The client should be encouraged to expand existing and available structured support systems to include new ones that may not have previously existed.
- *Develop alternative (backup) supports for crisis situations.* A culturally competent counselor will encourage the client to consider "what happens when plan A fails." Even the best structured support system may be inaccessible during a crisis. As the movie *Ghostbusters* eloquently asked, "Who you gonna call?" Assist the client with thinking through alternative or backup supports. All of us need a backup plan!

Phase 3: Posttermination

During this phase of termination, the real test of the effectiveness of counseling can be found. As clients terminate from therapy, they not only must sustain their therapeutic gains but do so within the communities and social environments from which they have come. Herein is a challenge. Clients sometimes find themselves in conflict with some cultural values in their social contexts. In fact, the problems that precipitated their need for counseling may relate directly to their cultural conflicts and cultural-specific self-defeating behaviors (Ridley et al., 2007). Take a second-generation Hmong adolescent who has grown up in the United States and in many ways is acculturated to Western values. However, the adolescent is constantly in conflict with his parents and grandparents who endorse the traditional values of their homeland. The conflict is so severe that the adolescent resorts to various forms of externalizing behavior.

To sustain positive outcomes, counseling should assist the client in negotiating cultural values with significant others. The purpose of the negotiation is to garner social support for the client's therapeutic gains. Both the client and the members of the support system must come to terms with the self-defeating consequences of extreme adherence to one's cultural values as well as extreme overreaction to cultural values. Both extremes can be inherently self-defeating.

In posttermination, we assert the importance of follow-up assessment. Two general strategies may be employed: an assessment conducted by the counselor and an assessment conducted by the client.

Counselor Follow-Up Assessment   Culturally competent counselors recognize the inadequacies of traditional procedures in termination. They understand the value of scheduling a follow-up appointment with clients after the active phase of termination. The purpose of the follow-up is to review and assess the client's adherence to the treatment goals. The follow up assessment should occur at some reasonable interval after termination (1 month, 2 months, or 3 months). The counselor should seek an agreement with the client and take the initiative for contacting the client and scheduling the appointment.

Client Follow-Up Self-Assessment   Culturally competent therapists recognize the need to provide a client with some form of self-assessment tool. It is beyond the scope of this chapter to discuss the various formats that this might take. However, an assessment tool kit should include the following: mutually agreed upon counseling goals and objectives stated in terms understandable by the client; clearly stated treatment outcomes, emanating from the measurable counseling goals/objectives; strategies or methods to support sustaining the treatment outcomes (specific to each outcome); a checklist of structured support systems (names, places, and so forth), including contact information; tentative dates to expect follow-up communication with the therapist (postcounseling checkups); and a short relapse prevention reminder card (fact sheet).

Conclusion

In this chapter, we have set forth a culturally centered three-phase model of termination. Our attempt was to demonstrate the complexity of the process and the necessity of integrating culture throughout each phase. To effectively terminate clients, counselors must establish a climate of trust and credibility. Trust and credibility are rooted in communicating an understanding of the client's cultural values. To understand the client's cultural values, counselors must get to know those values. To get to know those values, counselors must facilitate collaboration with the client. In facilitating collaboration, counselors establish mutually acceptable goals for treatment and communicate a culturally tailored message about how to sustain therapeutic gains and prevent relapse.

In writing this chapter, we sought to provoke critical thinking and make a connection between theory and practice that comprehensively considers the client's culture from the beginning until the end. When culture is an integral part of the therapeutic process, sustainable outcomes are more likely to be achieved. Clients may even began to refer to counseling services as more accessible, available, appropriate, acceptable, and maybe even venture to say that they are more affordable. Clearly, this becomes a win–win for our profession and for the clients we serve. We invite the community of mental health professionals to consider our ideas, engage in conversation about our model, and provide constructive criticism. These are the professional activities that help our profession advance and provide the highest possible service to clients.

References

Baruth, L. G., & Huber, C. H. (1985). *Counseling and psychotherapy: Theoretical analyses and skills applications.* Columbus, OH: Charles E. Merrill.

Berkman, L. F., Glass, T., Brissette, L., & Seeman, T. E. (2000). From social integration to health: Durkheim in the new millennium. *Social Science and Medicine, 51,* 843–857.

Berman, P. S. (1997). *Case conceptualization and treatment planning: Exercises for integrating theory with clinical practice.* Thousand Oaks, CA: Sage.

Brigham, T. A. (1989). *Managing everyday problems.* New York: Guildford.

Bubolz, M. M., & Sontag, M. S. (1993). Human ecology theory. In P. G. Boss, W. J. Doherty, R. LaRossa, W. R. Schumm, & S. K. Steinmetz (Eds.), *Sourcebook of family theories and methods: A contextual approach* (pp. 419–448). New York: Plenum Press.

Draguns, J. G. (1989). Dilemmas and choices in cross-cultural counseling: The universal versus the culturally distinctive. In P. B. Pedersen, J. G. Draguns, W. J. Lonner, & J. E. Trimble (Eds.), *Counseling across cultures* (3rd ed., pp. 3–21). Honolulu: University of Hawaii Press.

Epstein, R. (1996). *Self-help without hype.* Tucker, GA: Performance Management Publications.

Evans, D. R., Hearn, M. T., Uhlemann, M. R., & Ivey, A. E. (2008). *Essential interviewing* (7th ed.). Belmont, CA: Thomson Brooks/Cole.

House, J. S. (1981). *Work, stress, and social support.* Reading, MA: Addison-Wesley.

Kazdin, A. E. (2001). *Behavior modification in applied settings* (6th ed.). Belmont, CA: Wadsworth/Thomson Learning.

Lauver, P., & Harvey, D. R. (1997). *The practical counselor: Elements of effective helping.* Belmont, CA: Thomson Brooks/Cole Publishing.

Marlatt, G. A., & Gordon, J. R. (1985). *Relapse prevention: Maintenance strategies for addictive behavior change.* New York: Guildford Press.

Miltenberger, R. G. (2008). *Behavior modification: Principles and procedures* (4th ed.). Belmont, CA: Thomson Wadsworth.

Ridley, C. R. (2005). *Overcoming unintentional racism in counseling and therapy: A practitioner's guide to intentional intervention* (2nd ed.). Thousand Oaks, CA: Sage.

Ridley, C. R., Ethington, L. L., & Heppner, P. P. (2007). Cultural confrontation: A skill of advanced cultural empathy. In P. B. Pedersen, J. G. Draguns, W. J. Lonner, & J. E. Trimble (Eds.), *Counseling across cultures* (6th ed., pp. 373–393). Thousand Oaks, CA: Sage.

Ridley, C. R., & Goodwin, S. J. (2003). *Overcoming resistance to change.* St. Charles, IL: Churchsmart Resources.

Rogers, C. R. (1961). *On becoming a person.* Boston: Houghton Mifflin.

Sexton, T. L., & Alexander, J. F. (2004). *Functional family therapy clinical training manual.* Seattle, WA: FFT LLC.

Stuart, R. B. (1977). *Behavioral self-management: Strategies, techniques, and outcomes.* New York: Brunner Mazel.

Sue, S., & Zane, N. (1987). The role of culture and cultural techniques in psychotherapy: A critique and reformulation. *American Psychologist, 42,* 37–45.

Watson, D. L., & Tharp, R. G. (1993). *Self-directed behavior: Self-modification for personal adjustment* (6th ed). Pacific Grove, CA: Brooks/Cole.

Yates, B. T. (1986). *Applications in self-management.* Belmont, CA: Wadsworth.

10

Looking through a Kaleidoscope
A Case Study

Mary A. Fukuyama and Emma T. T. Phan

> Reality is a kaleidoscopic flux from which we organize through linguistic systems of our minds, make meaningful chunks, and construe experience.
>
> —**Milton Bennett, 2005**

Overview

In this chapter a clinical case example is presented, discussed, and expanded by varying key cultural variables that are salient in multicultural counseling. The demographic descriptors and identifying details have been changed to protect the anonymity of the client. In addition, this case study represents a composite of clinical issues that are typically presented by college students who struggle with issues of assimilation and acculturation, bicultural identity, career development, and family relationships. The reader is advised not to generalize from these materials, but to study the multiple perspectives as a means toward understanding cultural complexity in multicultural counseling.

Introduction

Consider the beauty, complexity, and unpredictability of looking through a kaleidoscope. As it turns, various shapes and colors are featured and perceptions shift. Working in therapy is a similar phenomenon. In this chapter, the experiences of counseling with a Vietnamese American young woman in a university setting will be presented and discussed. The case is based upon clinical work of about 15 individual sessions over a period of about 7 months. The chapter opens with an introduction of three persons: the client, the counselor, and a cultural consultant.

Client

In this case vignette, the demographics and identifying details have been changed to protect the anonymity of the client. The client was a 22-year-old Vietnamese American female psychology senior and prehealth professional major in a public university. She came to counseling because her parents wanted her to go to pharmacy school, but she doubted that this was the right career path for her. However, she believed that she would be seen as a failure if she did not become a pharmacist. In addition, she was in a relationship with a White (Euro-American) boyfriend for 4 years, but had not told her parents because they would disapprove. She felt stressed by leading a duplicitous life and was worried about making major life decisions as she prepared to graduate in a year. She presented with symptoms of depression (sleeplessness, sad affect, helplessness, and hopelessness), anxiety, and anger directed passively toward her father.

Family Background   The client was the second child of four siblings: an older sister age 25 was in medical school, and a younger sister age 17 and a younger brother age 14 lived at home. She was born in Vietnam and came to the United States when she was 9 years old with her parents who fled through a boat lift in the 1980s. Her parents ran a small business. She described her parents as traditional and saw herself as more "Americanized." She described her father as authoritarian and temperamental, her mother as deferent, her older sister as more traditional, her younger sister as "troubled," and her younger brother as the "perfect child." The client reported a history of sexual molestation when she was 5 years old by an adolescent male cousin. She said that she was past "self-blame" on this issue but still had difficulty with trusting males.

Counselor

Mary Fukuyama is a middle-aged woman of a multiracial background. She identifies as both *sansei* (third-generation Japanese American) and Anglo in heritage. She is the second oldest of five siblings and she is the only daughter. Her father was a Protestant minister and her mother a writer and poet. Her father's family was incarcerated during World War II in the Japanese American internment camps. She has worked in university counseling center settings as a counseling psychologist for over 25 years, with a specialization in multicultural counseling and training. Her counseling theoretical orientation is humanistic-existential and she draws from eclectic interventions.

Cultural Consultant

A cultural consultant was enlisted in writing this chapter because of her expertise and psychological insights drawn from her training as a psychologist and her experience as a Vietnamese refugee and immigrant. She was invited to coauthor this chapter to demonstrate the importance of acquiring culture-specific knowledge when working with ethnically diverse clients. The cultural consultant has cultural expertise and life experiences that parallel those of the client.

Emma Phan is a first-generation Vietnamese American in her late 20s. She and her family were part of the wave of Vietnamese boat families who escaped their war-torn country to find a better life in America in the early 1980s. She was born in Vietnam and fled to America at the age of 4. Her family resided in Louisiana for 3 years and then moved to California where they currently live. She received her doctorate degree in clinical psychology in August 2007. Emma considers her orientation to be eclectic. When working with Asian American clients who are dealing with cultural issues, she prefers to take a multicultural approach, asking about family of origin issues, religious or spiritual beliefs, and how important their culture and family are to them.

In her own words, Emma describes what it means to be Vietnamese and tells her story of coming to the United States:

> There is a phrase in Vietnamese, *Con rồng cháu tiên*, that describes how the Vietnamese people originated as children of the dragon and nieces and nephews of the phoenix. The dragon and the phoenix represent beauty and strength. Legend has it that Vietnam's origin lay in the harmonious

union of Lac Long Quan, king of the sea, and Au Co, princess of the mountains. They birthed 100 eggs, 50 of which hatched in the North and 50 hatched in the South. The result was a tight-knit Vietnamese culture and belief that the Vietnamese people all grew out of beauty and strength. This myth reinforces the importance of cultural identity.

Due to my young age during our escape, I do not remember any of the details of floating out in the sea and living in the refugee camps in Indonesia and Malaysia. My memories started in Louisiana and onward. I was completely dependent on my parents to care for me and maintain my safety. They risked life and limb for their children to have a better life in America.

From the perspective of my oldest sister who at the time of the escape was 14, she had the responsibility to care for her younger siblings and set appropriate examples for us to follow. The pressure and expectations came from my parents who would remind her to set the right examples for us. My sister, in retrospect and in my eyes, did everything right. She started finding employment at the earliest age that she could be legally employed in the U.S., she contributed to the family income, she studied hard, she listened to my parents, she cared for all of our well-being and health; she dated a Vietnamese male and married him, and they have three healthy, beautiful kids. Although she appeared to have led a very straight-and-narrow life to outsiders, I have been witness to her disagreements with our parents and the general Vietnamese cultural expectations. No matter how much she seemed to disagree, she would eventually follow the path that was expected of her from my parents and our relatives. A part of me feels that she would cave in partly because she loves and respects my parents and partly because she knows that she has to set a decent example for the rest of her six younger siblings to follow, an example that reflects her love, care, and respect for our parents and our culture. It's the ultimate sacrifice of your own happiness for the happiness of others—sacrificing for the greater good (collectivism).

In writing this chapter together, the coauthors discuss the case and relevant cultural themes. The remainder of the chapter is organized around clinical themes illustrated with culture-specific examples. Counselor reflections will provide a view into the counselor's thoughts and process. The cultural consultant's views are incorporated throughout the chapter by utilizing an interview question-and-answer format. Sample counseling dialogues have been constructed to illustrate key points. Finally, selected cultural variables are altered and implications discussed to illustrate the fluidity and complexity of multicultural counseling.

Clinical Themes and Commentary

In this section, an overview of the therapeutic work will be presented and the following topics discussed: intake (first appointment) issues, establishing the working alliance through demonstrating "credibility and gift-giving," understanding client worldview, working with affect, exploring the meaning of being bicultural, and providing treatment interventions. Counselor–client dialogues have been constructed to illustrate key points, and the coauthors (Mary and Emma) converse in a question-and-answer format about relevant cultural themes. These dialogues and counselor reflections are interwoven throughout.

Intake Appointment

The first hour of the counselor–client dyad is critical, especially when the client and counselor come from ethnically and culturally diverse backgrounds (Parker & Fukuyama, 2006). Multicultural factors influence establishing the working alliance from the very first session (Perez, Fukuyama, & Case, 2005). In the beginning, both client and counselor may experience anxiety related to establishing a relationship, meeting expectations, and being successful. Due to the importance of the first hour of therapy, the inner thoughts of the counselor and client will be explored. This internal and hidden process embodies personal, family, and cultural messages about the efficacy of counseling. For example, potential negative thoughts have been identified as barriers to counseling effectively. An example is demonstrated in the following client inner thoughts during the first session:

- What would my parents think if they knew I came to counseling?
- Is this really confidential? I feel so awkward and ashamed to be here.
- Maybe I shouldn't have come.

Like the client, the counselor may have questions when he or she first encounters a culturally diverse client. Some of those questions might include:

- I wonder what the client thinks of me.
- What if I make a racial/ethnic/cultural blunder?
- I don't know much about Vietnamese culture. Is it okay to ask her to educate me?

Counselors can learn to manage such thoughts by practicing dialogues through role-plays, for example, using Paul Pedersen's (2004) *pro-counselor* and *anti-counselor* triad model training. In this training technique, three persons simulate a counseling session: one plays the counselor, one plays a client from a different cultural background, and the third person articulates the client's cultural messages, either in a supportive role (for) or disruptive role (against) the counseling experience (Neimeyer, Fukuyama, Bingham, Hall, & Mussenden, 1986).

For example, when utilizing the pro-counselor triad model, the pro-counselor expresses support for the counselor, reinforces effective counselor behaviors, and offers cultural information that will facilitate the counseling process. Several examples follow. Imagine these statements being directed to the counselor trainee:

- Taking time to get to know the client will help her to feel more comfortable.
- Offering reassurance about confidentiality is particularly important due to the stigma associated with seeking mental health care.
- Varying the intensity of your eye contact helps to put the client at ease, as she has been taught to defer eye contact with elders.

On the other hand, anti-counselor messages may include some of the following; imagine these statements being directed to the client in the presence of the counselor, as an attempt to disrupt the counseling process:

- You're not supposed to talk with strangers about family business.
- Going to a counselor means you are crazy; people will talk badly about you.
- Seeking help is a sign of weakness.
- If you were emotionally strong, you wouldn't need help.

Using the triad model as a training technique has been shown as an effective way of learning cross-cultural counseling competencies (Neimeyer et al, 1986). A sample *initial session* dialogue follows:

Client: Sits quietly, waiting for counselor to initiate the conversation. She appears somewhat anxious and tired, but pleasant in demeanor.

Counselor (scanning the intake form): I guess this is your first time to come to counseling?

(Client nods yes.)

Counselor: Well, in an intake session, we try to allow time for you to talk about your concerns. But first, I like to get acquainted. Let's see, you are a 4th year psychology major? And how's school going for you?

Client: Well, I like my major but my parents want me to go to pharmacy school. I've applied and been accepted, but I just can't see myself doing it.

Counselor: What would you rather do?

Client: That's the problem, I just don't know, but I do know that filling prescriptions all day just doesn't fit my personality. I'm much more of a people person. But my parents think it's a good profession with job security and good money. My cousin is a pharmacist and they always point out how successful she is.

Counselor: So it's important to have job security and a good salary from your parents' perspective?

Client: Yes, and professional status, like a medical doctor or engineer …

Counselor: It sounds like a good time to think about careers and to learn more about your options. That's something we can do in counseling. I am wondering if there are any other concerns that are important to mention today.

Client: Well, yes, I am worried about graduating in a year and don't know what I will do. I have a boyfriend and we talk about marriage but neither of us is ready for that. And I have not told my parents about him because he is an American, and they wouldn't approve of dating to begin with, but certainly not someone who is not Vietnamese.

Counselor: What a difficult situation for you! That must be stressful.

Client: Yes, I am having trouble sleeping at night …

Counselor Reflections   My primary counseling orientation is humanistic in the sense that I am client-centered and developmentally oriented. I often view college students as going through life struggles with transitions into adulthood. In order to build trust, I tend to begin with empathy and concrete problem solving, such as career exploration, as a bridge into deeper therapeutic work. In part, I look for areas in the client's life where she can begin to build confidence (or ego strength) before dealing with the more difficult issues of cultural conflict and bicultural dissonance. I usually address confidentiality in the first session as well. In terms of conceptualization, I begin with making some working hypotheses about the client's problem. In this case, a variety of themes are presented in the first session, including career decision making, stress and worry about the future, and bicultural dissonance and intergenerational conflict. The client expressed feeling that for her not to study pharmacy is to be a "failure" in the eyes of her family. Her sense of loyalty to family is in direct opposition to her personal desires. It is not unusual for presenting issues to be expressed in polarities that on the surface seem to be insurmountable. Additionally, the client was presenting with symptoms of depression, which seemed associated with loss of connection with her parents due to conflict. I make a mental note that there may be recovery issues from trauma in the family system and a need for healing related to sexual molestation that was noted in the intake form. I conceptualize this case initially as also including acculturation stress due to cultural differences between Vietnamese and U.S. American cultures, which are exemplified in conflict between the client and her parents.

Establishing the Working Alliance

Scott Miller and associates have summarized therapy outcome studies and concluded that clients' ratings of the *therapeutic alliance* are the best predictor of engagement and outcome. In addition, the clients' *subjective experience of change* early in the process is the best predictor of success in therapy (Duncan & Miller, 2000). Sometimes counselors will need to explain how counseling works, clarify limits of confidentiality, and verbalize mutual expectations. These goals are accomplished in the context of managing first impressions and working toward establishing a working alliance.

S. Sue and Zane (1987) summarized two dimensions that are helpful for establishing a working alliance: *credibility* and *gift-giving*. These process variables will be described as one way of defining strategies for a first session, and clinical examples will be offered.

Credibility is defined as when the client views the counselor as an effective and trustworthy helper. Credibility is enhanced through:

- *Ascribed Status*—The counselor demonstrates understanding of the position/role the client is assigned by others (based on race, class, gender, professional titles, and so on).

Example: "Hello, my name is Mary Fukuyama and I am one of the staff psychologists and I'll be doing your intake today. I'm glad to meet you. Please have a seat." Nonverbal cues: Smile in greeting, review intake paperwork as a way of structuring the interview, present in a medical model format initially in terms of asking questions and gathering information, relax into the interview and set file aside when engaging in more informal conversation.

- *Achieved Status*—Through counselor skills, the client comes to have trust, hope, and confidence.

  Example: "What we try to do in an intake is for you to have a chance to talk about the concerns that brought you in today and for me to explain how our counseling services are offered. And hopefully by the end of the hour, we'll come up with a plan together of what to do next."

- *Conceptualization of the Problem*—Counselor's view of the problem represents an integration of the problems and the client's belief system/worldview.

  Example: "As I understand your situation, I hear that you are worried about letting down your parents, and at the same time, wondering if there is any way for you to find a career path that is meaningful for you. At the moment, it doesn't seem like there is any solution to this problem, because your parents want you to go to pharmacy school, which really doesn't work for you."

- *Approach to Problem Resolution*—Interventions toward change are congruent with the client's value system.

  Example: "I can see that you are concerned about your family and your personal life goals, and I believe we can work together to find positive resolution of what at this point might feel like a tough either–or forced choice. I believe in finding both–and solutions, so that both your parents and you can be happy."

- *Therapeutic Goals*—The client feels aligned with the counselor and feels essential aspects of his or her culture are affirmed (humanity/spirit).

  Example: "It seems that as an immigrant family, you have many survival strengths, one of which is your family loyalty and dedication to helping one another get ahead. It seems to me that some of your career goals are to bring honor and respect to your family. And at the same time, being happy in a career path is also an important part of success. This is something we can work on together."

Gift-giving refers to the client's perception that something was received during the therapeutic encounter. Meaningful "gifts" may include cognitive clarity, normalization, reassurance, skills acquisition, and coping mechanisms. For example: "I applaud you for coming in today. I know that it was not easy to make a counseling appointment. I don't see counseling as a sign of weakness. Quite the opposite; I think it takes strength to be vulnerable and open, like you were today."

Clients typically feel nervous in the first counseling session. Sometimes they feel embarrassed to ask for help or associate a negative stigma with mental illness. In this case study, the client had been exposed to counseling graduate students as teaching assistants through her classes and had a favorable attitude toward counseling, seeing it as potentially helpful to her. However, she also felt some initial shyness and appreciated when the counselor provided leading questions and reassurance.

What follows are excerpts from a conversation between Mary and Emma on topics of relevance to counseling with this client. On numerous issues, Emma observed that she has had life experiences similar to the client.

On Careers

Mary: What were your family expectations regarding careers?

Emma: Everybody is expected, not forced, but strongly expected to be within one of those highly respected careers ... doctors, pharmacists; like my older sister is a pharmacist, and so from her we are supposed to fall in line, and if you quit, then you are seen as ... "you are bringing shame onto the family... just make other people proud so that the family has a better position in society." So I myself was expected to follow along, specifically my sister's path, to become a pharmacist ...

And I felt that I was going to drop out if I was going to go into pharmacy. I knew that wasn't my interest, and so I fought against it, and so there was a lot of conflict in that. My parents would say, "Why don't you do it? Your sister already did it. She's already creating a path for you. It should be really simple, if you need notes or anything she has the books, notes, everything is there for you. Just go in there and do it." It became especially strong because I expressed an interest in psychology and it wasn't looked very highly upon.

Mary: What is a Vietnamese view of psychology and social sciences in general?

Emma: They are not "real doctors." So they are like pseudodoctors, especially working with mental illness, which is a huge stigma within the Asian community and specifically within my family also. And so, I got messages like "Why do you want to work as a psychologist? You're not really doing anything like real doctor's work and there are crazy people out there and they're going to follow you home," and [they were] very fearful for my safety. I guess the stereotype was ... "you are working with crazy people and one of these days they might kill you!"

Mary: Tell me about family loyalty.

Emma: And I am almost positive that a lot of our choices that we've made as my parents' children were based on not bringing shame onto the family ... to make them proud and to earn your keep as a daughter or son. It's never explicit that you need to earn your keep but it's filial piety; we want to pay back for what our parents have given us, and for bringing us to America. They worked really hard to immigrate to America. They have gone through a lot. We were boat people. So we have heard all the stories about what we have gone through as a family and the sacrifices, the major sacrifices that my parents have made for us, and so for me personally there is the sense that I would never ever be able to pay back the amount of things that they have given to me.

Another sample dialogue between the counselor and client follows in which the counselor invites a conversation about career exploration with the client:

Client: Asian families want their children to achieve and be in reputable careers.

Counselor: So your parents think you should be ... what?

Client: They want me to become a professional such as a doctor, lawyer, engineer, or most importantly a pharmacist. Pharmacy is seen as accessible, it's easier to get the degree as opposed to medical doctor or engineer. It's seen as a more straightforward track.

Counselor: And for you, I guess what I'm wondering is have you had a chance to explore any other careers that are well regarded and professional?

Client: I have not … honestly, before going to college and during my college years, because the pressure was so great to become a pharmacist. I wasn't encouraged to look elsewhere for a career. And if I did mention others, they would get shot down and I was discouraged …

Counselor: As a psychology major and in the liberal arts, you are prepared for a variety of careers, and I would encourage you to participate in a career fair where you'll get a chance to talk to employers. … Basically we find that students do better in careers and jobs that they have interest in.

Client: Well, I know I'm not interested in pharmacy.

Counselor: I think that … for immigrant families, the younger generation has to educate the older generation that there are more than just three careers. It falls in the hands of the younger generation to educate their parents about these other careers that also have prestige …

Client: I'm willing to try to go to the career fair and see what's out there for me. But a part of me feels that if the occupations I find are not similar to what my parents want me to be, I'll just end up back in square one—disappointing them and stressing myself out.

Counselor: I can hear that you're worried about how your parents are going to handle your decision making and career choice, and my suggestion is that you do the exploration first before discussing it with them.

Client: Yeah, I think that is a good idea because if I discuss anything with them beforehand, I feel like they already have a set mind and idea of what they want for me so I won't have much leeway in my own decisions.

Understanding Worldview

One of the basic multicultural counseling competencies entails understanding the client's worldview (D. W. Sue et al., 1998). Counseling Asian American students and also Asian international college students necessitates understanding the differences between individualistic and collectivistic cultures (Sheu & Fukuyama, 2007). U.S. American culture is one of a few cultures that emphasizes the importance of the individual. In contrast, collectivistic cultures emphasize relationships and group identity and well-being over the individual's.

Many Asian Americans struggle with how to balance the values of individual versus collective. For example, in a fall orientation speech for an Asian American student assembly, the keynote speaker (a successful Asian American journalism professor) encouraged students to pursue their dreams and to fulfill their parents' expectations to be successful, but not necessarily in this order. She told the story of a friend who became a doctor to please his parents and secondly pursued his interest in music.

These stories illustrate the power of cultural identity and the importance of the group. Such strong values often conflict with U.S. American values, resulting in bicultural conflict or dissonance.

Mary and Emma discussed differing cultural expectations on what it means to be an individual in contrast with collectivistic values, that is, putting family wishes first:

Mary: What I might imagine as the template of healthy individuation (U.S. American style) does not "compute" with healthy individuation within a Vietnamese culture …

Emma: Yeah. It looks different. And the stereotype is there also. That the American way is bad, there's too much individualism. There's not enough censorship. It's very unlike Vietnamese culture.

Mary: Not enough censorship?

Emma: Yes, like on TV and in the movies and in public displays of affection, the American way is "bad," so if you start to deviate and start to become more American you are doing something that is bad, "come back to our way." Then there's internal locus of control and external locus of control, too. But I think it's important in terms of how she or anybody else can manage to do the things that they do, and if things are operated by … we just know as professionals, that if it is internal, then there's more likelihood of some kind of success or repetition, or comfort because you are understanding it yourself and you believe it, but if there's external locus of control, there's more likelihood that a problem will arise or some kind of issue will rise again because it is not inherent in you to believe something like that, and I think, for Vietnamese girls living in the U.S. there is a lot of external control forced on you and then here you are in this culture developing a new sense of being okay with having an internal locus of control.

Mary: Mmm ... newly developing, that internal ...

Emma: Yeah, because I think that Vietnamese girls living in Vietnam, the very traditional family, they don't have a sense of internal locus of control. They are doing it because you are supposed to do it; it's not something you want to do, it's just something you are supposed to do and you learn to like it, you learn to love it. My parents had an arranged marriage. So my parents, one of their excuses is "you don't have to love him, you know, you can go with somebody, and you will eventually learn to love him because I learned to love your dad. If I have done it ... [and the external locus of control is okay] ... You can do it too."

Mary: Yet another argument for doing what you are told. (*Laughter.*)

(Emma describes her process of psychological development.)

Emma: In my early 20s, I was at UCSD getting my undergraduate degree in psychology. I believe that with exposure to readings on philosophy, psychology, and social sciences in general, I realized the importance of finding happiness for yourself before you can effectively provide happiness for others. This runs counter to our cultural belief that you should take others into consideration before you take yourself into consideration. I have dealt with this, on countless occasions, where I would take others into consideration before myself and end up feeling miserable, fraudulent (not true to myself), and incomplete. Using this concept of finding inner peace and happiness, I would apply this mindset to decisions that I have made. This serves as a kind of justification for my actions ("I can't make my parents truly happy if I am not happy myself ... who wants to be around a miserable person?"). As more of these statements/ideas came to mind, I became more individualistic in thinking. But since I love, honor, and respect my parents and culture, I still find that there are times when I put my wants and needs behind my family's wants and needs for the greater good of us all. This conflict is something that I still experience but I believe that this is a healthy conflict that keeps me grounded in both cultures. My resolution is picking and choosing my battles strategically.

Mary: That sounds like what Milton Bennett calls "constructive marginality" where one utilizes a process of loose cultural identification to enter and experience different cultural groups, also called "dynamic in-between-ness" (Bennett, 2005).

Emma: I have seen my cousins, aunts, and uncles who are unhappy because of choices that they've made for the greater good (their parents or family) and I don't want that unhappiness for myself. I am willing to give up some of my collectivistic mindset if that means less headaches and conflicts for myself, but I am not willing to give up all of this mindset because I believe it is what makes my family bond strong and resilient and it is what makes me who I am. I am able to live with myself because I still feel true to my Vietnamese culture and true to myself. The strong sense of loyalty to my family also helps me retain some collectivistic thinking.

Mary: What's it like for you to be bicultural?

Emma: And so I can see … hearing other Asian clients who are going through that same struggle with being able to accommodate their parents' wishes and then being more American, living in America, having more time here to adjust and acculturate and having that struggle there, I totally understand it. Just in terms of "You don't want to disappoint them [parents], they have done so much for you." And face and shame and stigma are so huge in the Asian community too, that you have to acknowledge that also.

Mary: Mmhmm, so there is that individualism which is cultivated in American culture in contrast with the family group obligations and shame … that is a real tension point negotiating that …

Emma: Yeah, and it is so alive at any given point in time, both sides are so alive, because you are constantly being reminded when you go home or when you are interacting with your parents or relatives and you are constantly being reminded because you are here immersed in American culture where individualism is encouraged and expression is encouraged, so there's that clash no matter where you going to go, you're going to feel it.

Counselor Reflection The lived experience of being bicultural is difficult to understand for U.S. Americans who have lived in the United States for generations. Nevertheless, it is a reality that shapes worldview and cultural values. Consider the following observations by Thuy Thi Diem Le, a writer and solo performance artist who describes childhood memories of her family who were "boat people," fleeing to the United States in 1978.

> My mother was the one who alerted me to the simultaneity of worlds. She spoke about Vietnam as if it were right around the corner, as alive as were we were, if not more so. While school and mainstream American movies defined Vietnam as a war, from my mother I might have thought there had never been a war, that history hadn't twisted itself around us like a tornado, lifting us up into the heart of it, stomping out our past with a flick of its tail and then depositing us as far from home as possible. She treated the United States like some place we were passing through, made bearable by the belief that no matter how long or how difficult this journey would be, in the end we were still Vietnamese and we would eventually make it back to Vietnam. According to my mother, every ordeal was a test of our strength, meant to build character. Strange, inexplicable things happened. One night, we had boarded a boat in southern Vietnam. One day, we landed by plane in Southern California. That was fate. (Le, 1998, pp. 44–45)

Affective Work with Grief and Loss

Although the client's presenting issues have focused on career concerns, the affective dimension is marked by feelings of depression and anguish, especially related to her family. Here is a sample dialogue that includes expressions of grief:

Client: I'm planning to go home next weekend because it's my father's birthday but I don't want to go. The last time I was home he yelled at me about something, I can't remember now what but he was really mean to me. I just can't talk with my father. And my mother doesn't say anything.

Counselor: That seems like a stressful situation for you and I hear your sadness and anger …

Client: I wish they would accept me as I am but they are so critical, I can't seem to do anything right. But they are my family and they're all I've got.

Counselor: I'm also wondering what it's been like not to be able to talk about your boyfriend to your parents.

Client: Well I would really like to talk to my mother but I know she'll tell my father so I can't do that. I just wish I could be closer. I just feel so disconnected from them.

Counselor: And that's a loss for you …

Client: I guess I've always felt distant from them because in Vietnam I lived with my aunt for a while and I don't know … why … (*Tears.*)

Counselor: I can see from your tears that this is very painful for you. It's possible that there's some early childhood losses from your family that are still affecting your relationship with your family today. Does that resonate with you?

Client: I don't know … I've always felt this way.

Counselor: Have you shared this with anybody yet?

Client: Well, I talk with my boyfriend but sometimes he gets tired of hearing me cry.

Counselor: Sometimes your grief is really tapping into generations of pains/losses and in a way, it's bigger than you are …

Client: So what do I do about that? It's this huge thing. Sometimes I ask myself what's the point.

Counselor: So what is it like for you to share these feelings with me?

Client: I feel a little bit embarrassed but it feels good to be able to let it out. When I try to talk to my older sister she just says something like "life goes on, get over it." And I think I should get over it …

Counselor: Expressing these emotions are a part of healing and it's a normal and healthy thing to do. I think it takes strength to be vulnerable with your feelings.

Counselor Reflection   I'm wondering about grief related to the early childhood molestation, feelings of abandonment, and trauma in the family related to postwar dislocation and stress. At this point, I want to normalize grief and support affective release. I encourage her to learn self-care and self-soothing activities. In addition, I want to be sure to reinforce that immigrant/refugee families have a lot of strength to survive under such incredible difficulties. I see both the client and her family as resilient in the midst of expressing much pain (LaRoce & Maxie, 2003; Portes & Rumbaut, 2001).

On Being Bicultural

In general, people are not aware of cultural values and norms. Similar to the "fish that doesn't realize it is in water," culture is invisible. One counseling strategy is to raise clients' awareness or consciousness about how culture influences identity development. The following dialogue introduces multicultural knowledge, which may be helpful for her identity development.

Client: Well my boyfriend and I have been together for 4 years and he's really my best friend. But it's hard to see into the future whether or not we'll still be together. I can't talk about him to my family because he's not Vietnamese. Sometimes I feel like I'm too dependent on him.

Counselor: In what ways do feel like you're dependent on him?

Client: When he's working late in the lab I get worried about him and want him to call me but he won't or sometimes he wants to be out with his friends and I feel really insecure. Sometimes I feel like I want to talk about my anger toward my parents and I just want someone to listen to me and hear me, not necessarily give me feedback but just be there for me and I rely on my boyfriend a lot for that because I don't tend to ask for these things or expect of these things from anyone else around me.

Counselor: So it seems like you expect him to meet a lot of your needs and it puts a lot of pressure on your relationship?

Client: Yes.

Counselor: Are there any other friends or roommates that you can rely on?

Client: Not many. If I do talk to my friends, I feel that I wear them out and I can tell they don't want to hear me talk about it anymore.

Counselor: It sounds like you feel lonely and I'm wondering from a social point of view, where do you see yourself fitting in or not? For example, have you tried joining the Vietnamese Student Organization?

Client: No I don't feel comfortable around other Vietnamese students. I don't feel like I fit into that group. And the White friends that I do have don't understand the stress that I have with my family.

Counselor: So maybe your discomfort has something to do with being bicultural, that is … your family is from another culture living in this country.

Client: Well I don't know about that. Most of my memories are of growing up in this country.

Counselor: Have you heard about being 1.5 generation?

Client: No.

Counselor: Well that's when someone's born in another country, comes to the U.S. as a child, typically elementary school age, and grows up in this country. So you basically have a mixture of cultural experiences.

Client: No, I hadn't thought about that before. But it is true that when I go home I'm in a different world than when I'm at school. When

I go home, I feel like I have to do an identity switch. I'm a good and obedient Vietnamese daughter and when I am at school I am an American.

Counselor: I think the people who are going to understand you most are those like you in the sense that they're living out a bicultural reality.

Counselor Reflection   I am wondering what it is like for her to be a Vietnamese woman living in America. She may be experiencing what Milton Bennett calls "encapsulated marginality," when one feels isolated and disconnected from identification and participation in cultural groups or feels stuck in between cultures, belonging to neither, with accompanying feelings of alienation and anomie (Bennett, 2005).

In addition, I want to explore what kind of expectations she has for herself, from family, and from peers? Being able to differentiate and be clear on these expectations can help her to decide what is most important, and how to go about achieving it. They also help define context-specific behaviors and norms.

Finally, Emma commented on the significance of the Vietnamese community.

Mary: Do you have any thoughts about the larger … the closeness of the community itself?

Emma: Well, living in San Diego, the Vietnamese community is a lot bigger than it is in Florida, or other places I have been, and even there you would think you get lost in the masses somehow, but everybody seems to know everybody still.

Mary: Everybody knows everybody's business?

Emma: Yeah … so news travels fast, very fast, and so you have to be really careful what you do, or what kind of reputation you bring onto your family because it will travel. And even if it doesn't travel, you have that fear, and your parents would absolutely have a larger fear of that traveling to other adults who are respected in the community.

Treatment Interventions

In addition to career concerns, I conceptualized that the client has to meet developmental tasks (e.g., mastery and intimacy) as she learns how to negotiate cultural differences within her family of origin. I supported her being actively engaged in identity development and utilized Rowe and Marcia's (1980) ego identity model as a psychoeducational tool. In this model, the four identity statuses are *diffuse* (never having engaged in exploration, uncommitted), *foreclosed* (commitment made without exploration, usually based on parental values), *moratorium* (in the process of exploration and not yet ready for commitment), and *achieved identity* (a firm commitment made after a period of exploration and values clarification) (Rowe & Marcia, 1980). This model helped to justify doing things like career exploration in contrast with accepting a predetermined career path. A successful resolution for her career search resulted in her deciding to apply to a physical therapy program, which was more reflective of her personal values. Even though her parents did not understand this career choice, she felt confident enough to pursue this goal.

Returning to the metaphor of the kaleidoscope, therapy evolved over time to encompass a range of issues. In several sessions, we did dream interpretation, and I focused on supporting grief work that was related to the "disconnect" between her parents and her. I introduced guided imagery and breathing practices to help her learn self-soothing. I introduced the concept of the 1.5 generation identity to acknowledge her biculturalness.

Bibliographic references were helpful to support her bicultural identity work (see O'Hearn, 1998) and in addition, I recommended that she view a documentary film available on DVD called *Daughter from Danang*, which contrasts Vietnamese and U.S. American cultures (http://www.daughterfromdanang.com/about/). She reported that she watched it with her family and they discussed differences between U.S. American culture and Vietnamese culture.

Counselor Reflection   My perception was that the client was experiencing the pain of being between two cultures (encapsulated marginality). Clients in this situation can benefit from participating in a support group for Asian American women (see *The Way Home*, a documentary film by Shakti Butler as an example of the benefits from participating in similar ethnic "affinity" groups http://www.Worldtrust.org/videos/home.html).

In summary, I was active in terms of providing psychoeducational interventions and supporting her identity work. She began to feel more empowered by participating in an active job search and career exploration, through which she felt affirmed that she was "worthy." Subsequently, she felt more confident to deal with family differences, and sought emotional support for being bicultural initially through Internet Web sites.

As the Kaleidoscope Turns

Various demographic factors influence the course of therapy, such as gender, sexual orientation, race/ethnicity, socioeconomic status, and so on. In this case study discussion, we wondered how changing a few demographic factors might alter case conceptualization and the course of therapy. For example, what if the client had been a male? How are gender roles constructed and what are the implications for counseling?

Mary: How would traditional Asian or Vietnamese hierarchy with the male at the head of the family influence counseling issues, that is, are there different expectations for males ... for brothers?

Emma: Tasks are very sex oriented ... males, the boys do specific gender roles; boys fix cars, build things for the house, girls wash dishes and cook, and I fought against that too and got yelled at many times. "I don't want to cook, I don't have to cook all the time." "But you are a girl. Your brother is working hard outside and you cook for him." "But why can't he do it himself?" ... I'm very stubborn.

Mary: So you are not only bicultural but sort of a feminist some of the times, willing to challenge the gender roles.

Emma: But I don't think they will ever see me as an adult, and I've talked to other friends who are Asian also and their family does the same thing like they are never treated as adults, especially with females. You are always their child, their little girl, their princess, even if you are 50 years old, you can't make decisions for your own because "you are my child."

    I think a lot of women who are battling between the bicultural recognition ... of just balancing that act ... which one is stronger for you? It kind of dictates how your decisions are going to be made, and how you are going to live your life ... which one is more primary to you? And of course with either one ... you'll still have [the other] ...

What if the client had been dating a man of color?

Emma: I have a feeling about Asians; if you are going to date outside the Asian community, White is better than black. Black is just like the worst of it.

Mary: Because of racism?

Mary: Because of racism, because of color discrimination.

Mary: And that exists within Vietnamese culture?

Emma: Absolutely, because of color. Depending upon the region where you are from, you are either paler or darker, and the people who are darker are usually the ones who are looked down upon more, and even within the Vietnamese culture here in the U.S. there are bleaching creams where you can make your skin lighter. And it's so hard, and at times… you just don't think about it because you just go on with life, but then when you really think about it and you really try to balance and please everybody and yourself too … it's so hard.

Mary: Is it exhausting? … What are clinical dimensions … for example symptoms because of stress?

Emma: Hopelessness, helplessness, sometime you just feel like, you give up, there's no point any more, you just want things to be anyway they can be, just be, some way, you know … just so you don't have this conflict. Stress interferes with school, work, then you always try to reach out for some kind of support … you're not getting that support from your family, so you want support of friends, support of somebody out there who says "Oh, it's okay to date a Black guy"… so you're not holding this all to yourself.

Counselor Reflection   I would want to let the client know I am supportive of interracial relationships (my parents were in one) and connect her to social support, for example, through the Internet, if local resources are not available.

What are some socioeconomic differences?

Emma: There is a discrepancy between having money and education. Speaking personally, my cousins, aunts, and uncles in Louisiana represent a diversity of SES [socioeconomic status]. Some are commercial fishermen, some work in the cosmetology industry doing nails or hair, and some are in college or working as pharmacists. In the Vietnamese community, we tend to value education and status of the career/job. Money is an important aspect of earning respect but the status of the career is more important. Although many of my relatives who are in the fishing industry or cosmetology are millionaires, their jobs are not as highly revered

as the pharmacists or the college graduates who are making sub-
stantially less money. This is probably due to the fact that college
and higher education is seen as a mark of class and prestige. For
example, you wouldn't necessarily need a college education to
become a successful fisherman. Even working-class parents want
their children to be educated though, because children are your
social security. They will take care of you when you are old.

Mary: What about sexual orientation?

Emma: If a Vietnamese American college student is dealing with sexual
orientation, there's no way he or she can come out to family. There
is such a negative stigma associated with being gay or lesbian,
and it is seen as like being an "American" in a derogatory sort of
way. However, I have known of two instances of Vietnamese gay
men who represent different coming out stories. One was seen as
flamboyant and feminine. Everyone was aware that he was gay
but no one, including himself, openly talked about his sexual
orientation or discussed it. He dealt with it by not talking about
it. In a way, his situation was not unlike the U.S. military's policy
of "don't ask, don't tell." His family and friends have not turned
away from him or neglected him, but they just don't bring it up.

On the other hand, I know of a young man who came out
in public in his undergraduate years at a university in Southern
California. His sister refused to talk to him any more and has
stopped any contact with the family. His mother slowly accepted
him being gay, and he is very vocal about LGBT [lesbian, gay,
bisexual, and transgender] issues on and off campus. He has
many friends, and now his mother is fully supportive of him
and his cause. His coming out was seen as an "American success
story," because he was accepted and he is very open and comfortable with himself and his actions.

When considering multiple social identities and multiple oppressions, it is
important to note that traditional LGBT identity development models may
not apply. Identity may be more strongly influenced by social context than as a
personality construct, and there are times when sexual orientation may or may
not be salient (Fukuyama & Ferguson, 1999). Thus, the counselor is advised
not to assume that coming out is the only measure of psychological health and
adjustment, especially when coming out may threaten his or her cultural base
that includes family relationships and basic safety/security needs.

Summary Comments

Counselor Reflection

Multicultural counseling is a multilayered phenomenon. I selected this case study to illustrate the complexity of psychological and cultural issues. In some areas of her life, the client was able to resolve conflicts, and in others, I imagine that she is still working at them. Counseling is seldom finished neatly, and I have learned to live with that sort of ambiguity. When we terminated, the client gave me a thank-you card saying that she appreciated learning to accept herself more. She had increased her self-efficacy and decided to move back home while she pursued the next step in her education.

How am I changed as a result of working with this client? I was impressed with the client's resilience, resourcefulness, and ability to persevere even in harsh circumstances, which I believe also mirrored the family's story of survival in a foreign land. I always have respected immigrant and refugee stories, and they help me connect to my personal ancestry on both sides of my family. I am also sensitive to multiple social roles and multiple oppressions. The larger systemic issues provided a framework within which to help the client form her identity.

Consultant Reflection

Working with Asian American women has been very rewarding to me in many different ways. It has been rewarding to see them go through strife, conflict, and responsibilities that are self-imposed as well as socially imposed and emerge still resilient and motivated. Generally, the Asian women that I have worked with deal with many issues at one time and in every situation; acculturation and or assimilation are factors that either inhibit or encourage their growth. It is exciting and moving to see these individuals realize a need to find internal happiness but also care for their family's happiness. It is rewarding to see these clients be able to gain clarity on their issues and to see relief on their faces as their issues, strife, stressors, and conflicts get validated and heard. Counseling, as I see it, allows these individuals to have a venue to voice their issues, be validated and heard, and have an outlet to process the difficulties of being bicultural.

When working with multicultural clients dealing with struggles related to cultural, family, and career conflicts, sometimes it is enough to allow the client to vent and help them to make sense of their issues. Counseling can allow them to prioritize their concerns while at the same time respect their loved ones' wishes. I do not believe that it is a counseling failure if the client walks away without clearly resolving their issues. Often, client work feels unfinished, especially with the limitations of short-term therapy. I think it is the beginning of a counseling success that the bicultural client has walked through the doors of a counseling center and is asking for help. It is a bigger success if the client can realize that he or she can coexist in two cultures and not have to give up either one to find happiness. In working with Asian American clients dealing with cultural issues, the journey, in my opinion, is truly more important than the destination. Just giving them a voice and acknowledging their stress is already a part of the success.

References

Bennett, M. (2005, July 27). *The developmental model of intercultural sensitivity*. Workshop presentation at the Summer Institute for Intercultural Communication, Forest Grove, OR.

Duncan, B. L., & Miller, S.D. (2000). *The heroic client: Doing client-directed, outcome-informed therapy*. San Francisco: Jossey-Bass.

Fukuyama, M. A., & Ferguson, A. D. (1999). Lesbian, gay, and bisexual people of color: Understanding cultural complexity and managing multiple oppressions. In R. M. Perez, K. A. DeBord, & K. J. Bieschke (Eds.), *Handbook of counseling and psychotherapy with lesbian, gay, and bisexual clients* (pp. 81–105). Washington, DC: American Psychological Association.

LaRoce, M. J., & Maxie, A. (2003). Ten considerations in addressing cultural differences in psychotherapy. *Professional Psychology: Research and Practice, 34*, 180–186.

Le, T. T. D. (1998). California palms. In C. C. O'Hearn (Ed.), *Half and half: Writers on growing up biracial and bicultural* (pp. 38–48). New York: Pantheon Books.

Neimeyer, G. J., Fukuyama, M. A., Bingham, R. P., Hall, L. E., & Mussenden, M. E. (1986). Training cross-cultural counselors: A comparison of the pro-counselor models and anti-counselor triad models. *Journal of Counseling and Development, 64*, 437–439.

O'Hearn, C. C. (Ed.). (1998). *Half and half: Writers on growing up biracial and bicultural*. New York: Pantheon Books.

Parker, W. M., & Fukuyama, M. A. (2006). *Consciousness raising: A primer for multicultural counseling* (3rd ed.). Springfield, IL: Charles C. Thomas.

Pedersen, P. B. (2004). The triad training model. In *110 experiences for multicultural learning* (pp. 153–156). Washington, DC: American Psychological Association.

Perez, R., Fukuyama, M., & Case, A. (2005, April 8). *Integrating multicultural competencies into intakes and initial counseling sessions*. Paper presented at Psychologist Continuing Education Workshops, Gainesville, FL.

Portes, A., & Rumbaut, R. G. (2001). *Legacies: The story of the immigrant second generation.* Berkeley: University of California Press.

Rowe, I., & Marcia, J. E. (1980). Ego identity status, formal operations, and moral development. *Journal of Youth and Adolescence, 9*(2), 87–99.

Sheu, H. B., & Fukuyama, M. (2007). Counseling international students from East Asia. In H. D. Singaravelu & M. Pope (Eds.), A *handbook for counseling international students in the United States* (pp. 173–193). Alexandria VA: American Counseling Association.

Sue, D. W., Carter, R. T., Casas, J. M., Fouad, N. A., Ivey, A. E., Jensen, M., et al. (1998). *Multicultural counseling competencies: Individual and organizational development.* Thousand Oaks, CA: Sage.

Sue, S., & Zane, N. (1987). The role of culture and cultural techniques in psychotherapy: A critique and reformulation. *American Psychologist, 42*, 37–45.

11

Toward Practicing Culturally Sound Counseling
A Synthesis of Current Clinical Research and Experience

Beverly J. Vandiver and Lonnie E. Duncan

Overview

The purpose of this chapter is to summarize best cultural counseling practices in four core areas of mental health treatment with racial–ethnic minorities: (a) help-seeking, (b) assessment, (c) treatment, and (d) training and supervision. These recommended practices are based on existing clinical research in conjunction with the authors' almost 40 years of combined clinical experience in working with diverse populations. It is imperative that helping professionals take *concrete* steps to ensure that cultural aspects are integral to the entirety of counseling, not just at the process level, and that treatment is based on the most current sound knowledge in the field, and that training of practitioners and the treatment of clients reflect both.

Introduction

Helping professionals (i.e., social workers, counselors, psychologists, psychiatrists) are expected to be culturally competent to meet the needs of a diverse society. The importance of cultural competence is reflected in the professional standards and ethical guidelines of various helping professional organizations for their respective members to follow when working cross-culturally (e.g., American College of Physicians, 2004; American Psychological Association, 2002; Association of Multicultural Counseling and Development [AMCD], Arredondo et al., 1996; Lim, 2006; National Association of Social Workers [NASW], 2000; Roysircar, 2005). Two factors make it critical that helping professionals meet the expectation of cultural competence. The Surgeon General Supplemental Report (U.S. Department of Health & Human Services [DHHS], 2001) on racial–ethnic minority health care highlights (a) the disparities for racial–ethnic minorities in mental health services and (b) the lack of research and adequate training of helping professions to serve these populations effectively. Racial and ethnic minorities have less access to mental health services than do Whites; they are less likely to receive needed care; and when they receive care, it is more likely to be poor in quality (DHHS, 1999). These barriers persist even when ethnic minorities are insured at the same level as nonminorities (Zambrana, Carter-Pokras, Nunez, Valdez, & Villarruel, 2004). These needs and obstacles are becoming more evident as the U.S. population becomes increasingly culturally and linguistically diverse. According to the U.S. Bureau of the Census (2004), racial and ethnic minorities will represent 40 percent of the population by 2030 and almost 50 percent of the population by 2050.

Although the aspirations, expectations, and guidelines of the various mental health professions are noteworthy and highlight the importance given to the training and practice of culturally competent practitioners, the implementation of these guidelines in real-world settings has fallen short (Miranda, Nakamura, & Bernal, 2003). Sue (2006) aptly describes the current state of implementing cultural competence into mental health practice:

> Guidelines have been largely aspirational or hortatory in effect (e.g., emphasizing that therapists should consider the cultural background of clients), with less attention given to how cultural competence can be measured, conceptualized in terms of skills, implemented in practice, and trained in others. The most critical problem facing the cultural competency movement is to progress from a philosophical definition to a *practice-* or *research-oriented* one. (p. 238)

Isaacs, Huang, Hernandez, and Echo-Hawk (2005) have echoed similar concerns (lack of definitional clarity, operational framework and strategy) about the challenges of implementing sound cultural mental health treatment. The various mental health professions have addressed cultural competence from a discipline-specific view of mental health treatment and have not worked cooperatively to address the cultural issues faced by underserved populations. This lack of cooperation has complicated the movement from philosophy to practice and uniformity across human service sectors and mental health professional disciplines in addressing cultural issues and developing best practices. Finally, there has been an overreliance on nonvalidating self-assessment protocols and little focus on evaluation and empirical research.

So where do these concerns and challenges about cultural competence leave the helping professionals working with culturally diverse clients on a daily basis? The complexities of working with an indefinite number of cultural factors that may influence the attitudes and behaviors of potential clients have overwhelmed many in the helping profession. Numerous books and articles have been published within the last decade to provide a variety of tools, frameworks, and techniques to help mental health professionals consider contextual variables when treating and diagnosing clients (Hays, 2001), but the issue is which ones are most effective for practitioners to use. Many mental health professionals have developed an increased awareness of cultural beliefs and practice but hinder their work with certain clients by continuing to practice from culture-bound frameworks due to their anxiety and ambivalence in implementing sound cultural practices. According to Marsella and Pedersen (2004), even when mental health professionals recognize that old rules are not working, it is not easy to replace them with new culturally different rules. It is still unclear for many practitioners as to when, where, and how to address cultural issues in the therapeutic relationship (Cardemil & Battle, 2003; Hargrove & Sedlacek, 1997; Hays, 2001). In summary, widespread acceptance of cultural competence in the helping professions seems to have occurred, but cultural competence and its implementation have remained elusive for the reasons noted earlier (Isaacs et al., 2005; Sue, 2006). Without a clear consensus of the components of cultural competence, it has become increasingly difficult to create a set of measurable outcomes for research and evaluation purposes or to provide clear directions for the various mental health professions (Isaacs et al., 2005).

The purpose of this chapter is twofold: (a) to provide a brief review of mental health research that informs the helping professionals about the practice of multicultural counseling and (b) to highlight how this information can be applied into an existing mental health practice. Between the two of us, we have more than 40 years of clinical experience working with diverse clients (young, old, rich, poor, Black, White, Asian, Latino/a, male, female, lesbian/gay, heterosexual, urban, rural, etc.). We have spent almost 20 years talking to each other about the issues we raise in this chapter, challenging each other's thinking and practice as well as discussing the available research about practice with the goal of strengthening the cultural effectiveness of our work. To achieve the objectives of this chapter, we will first provide a set of working definitions to convey as clearly as possible what we mean. Because we want this chapter to be used in mental health practice, we have structured the information in the sequence of a typical practice: (a) starting with the state of help seeking, (b) looking at treatment interventions, including the assessment process and psychotropic medication, and (c) addressing professional training and supervision. At each juncture, concrete recommendations are provided that we believe will aid both the new and experienced helping professionals in developing as well as strengthening their clinical skills in working with culturally diverse clients.

Working Definitions

The definition of multicultural counseling or practice has become quite broad, with multiculturalism defined to be inclusive of all diversity within human beings (that is, age, race–ethnicity, nationality, religion, physicality, gender, social class, language, sexual orientation, and so forth) (Pedersen, 1991). However, due to the limitation of space, we will not be able to cover the clinical utility of research for all possible cultural groups and do adequate justice to each one. Traditionally, the mental health literature has defined underserved populations as those who are representative of the four primary racial–ethnic groups (i.e., African American, Asian American, Hispanic American, and Native American). The historical and traditional underutilization of mental health services by racial–ethnic minorities has driven much of the research in this area, although it too has been limited. As a result, our focus will be primarily on the clinical research of and its application to members of racial and ethnic minority groups, as this area of cultural diversity was one of the first to be addressed in the counseling fields (Jackson, 1995). When possible, we will periodically reference clinical work relevant to members of other cultural groups.

What is child weather

There has been much debate about the terminology used to describe a person's racial or ethnic background. We have decided to use the term *racial/ ethnic minority* to underscore that the phrase reflects the sociopolitical realities of people systematically oppressed and discriminated against due to their pigmentation of skin, cultural background, and power status in society (Sue & Dhindsa, 2006). These macro issues are also reflected in the history of race and ethnicity in social work, psychology, counseling, and psychiatry, and the challenges these applied helping disciplines face in training professionals and treating culturally diverse clients. We will also use interchangeably broad terms such as helping professional, counselor, practitioner, or therapist to describe the helping professionals in psychology, social work, counselor education, and psychiatry.

We use two definitions of culture, one broad and the other narrow, in situating the content of this chapter. There is no standard definition of culture, as various disciplines from anthropology, sociology, history, and psychology characterize culture differently (McAuliffe et al., 2008). Broadly, we adopt the definition of culture as the "thoughts, communications, actions, beliefs, values, customs, and institutions of racial, ethnic, religious, or social groups" (Office of Minority Health [OMH], 2000). We also accept OMH's definition of culture in health care, of which mental health treatment is a component. Culture in health care refers to (a) how health care information is processed, (b) how rights and practices are exercised, (c) how health problems are defined, (d) how symptoms are expressed and interpreted, (e) who is the assigned preferred provider for problems, and (f) what type of treatment should be given (OMH, 2000). We ultimately believe that the helping professions are cultural institutions and the cultural beings in these professions need to constantly assess their role and responsibility in providing effective treatment of diverse clients.

There is no single definition for either multicultural or cultural competence. The terms *multicultural competence* and *cultural competence* have both been used in the literature of helping professionals. Multicultural competence is defined as the ability of counselors to incorporate cultural diversity into their work within the counseling session (Vera & Speight, 2003). Multicultural competency refers also to counselors gaining the necessary knowledge, awareness, and skills to work effectively cross-culturally (Arredondo, 1998). Cultural competence involves integrating and transforming knowledge about individuals or groups into specific standards, policies, practices, and attitudes that are used appropriately in cultural settings to increase the quality of care and outcomes for underserved populations (T. Cross, Bazron, Dennis, &

Isaacs, 1989). These terms have been used interchangeably in the counseling literature as well as in other disciplines in health care. Differences between the two terms appear to be based on the context and stated goal of the article or manuscript. Cultural competence appears to be more widely used in the broader health care literature, whereas multicultural competence seems more unique to certain professions in the mental health field. To reflect that mental health treatment can occur beyond applied psychology, we will use the term *cultural competence* in framing our writing.

The Big Picture of Cultural Competence

Any discussion about providing culturally sensitive assessment and treatment starts with a broader discussion centered on cultural competence. According to Sue (2006), cultural competence encompasses the analysis of three levels of skills. The first level is the provider level, which is characterized by the provider's ability to be interpersonally sensitive, to build rapport, and to establish a therapeutic alliance and credibility. This analysis specifically looks at effectiveness and the cultural appropriateness of the therapeutic intervention. The second level occurs within the context of the agency in which helping professionals work and focuses on the cultural competence of the agency and mental health programs. In essence, are the mental health programs or services culturally competent? Other agency issues that are pertinent to cultural competence include the organizational structure and its hiring practices, programs, evaluations, outreach, access and availability of service, utilization, cost and benefits, and quality of care. All aspects of the mental health agency need to be scrutinized for its cultural effectiveness in reaching into the communities in which many underserved populations reside. The final level deals with systems of care within a community, specifically as it relates to racial/ethnic populations (for example, geographic areas served and collaborations with community agencies, churches, schools, and so forth). Most of the discussion on cultural competence has focused on the provider level. As a result, our focus will be primarily at the provider level, with periodic comments made about the cultural issues within the systems of mental health disciplines, agencies, and community.

Helping professionals have been encouraged to increase their cultural competence through seminars, additional training in serving underrepresented populations, and additional coursework. However, with all of the training that has taken place it is still unclear as to what constitutes cultural competence. Some scholars have advocated that gaining knowledge, awareness, and skills about specific ethnic groups is the best way to increase cultural competence. This point of view is known as the culture-specific perspective (McAuliffe et al., 2008). Those who advocate this position outline specific skill sets related to each of the four main ethnic groups (that is, African American, Latina/o, Asian American, and Native American). This view has been criticized as being too narrow by focusing exclusively on race and ethnicity while avoiding other types of diversity (for example, disability, religion, sexual orientation, gender).

Sue and Sue (2003) delineate three factors that may make racial minorities apprehensive about including other minority groups in the multicultural dialogue. First, those who are uncomfortable with confronting their own racial biases may be able to avoid dealing with them by focusing on nonracial cultural groups. Second, considering all counseling as multicultural makes the concept meaningless and reverts the mental health professionals' focus to traditional counseling—individual differences. And third, disagreements exist among counseling professionals over whether gender and sexual orientation constitute distinct cultures.

On the other end of the spectrum, some practitioners believe that all counseling is multicultural. They contend that individuals see the world through multiple lenses, which include ethnicity, race, social class, gender, religion, and so forth. These multiple lenses constitute cultural groups in which meaning is derived (McAuliffe et al., 2008). Sue and Sue (2003) note that each person is born into a cultural context in which beliefs, values, rules, and practices are already in existence. Furthermore, various contextual variables (e.g., race, ethnicity, and religion) have a powerful impact on individuals' worldviews.

An alternative view of human nature is the tripartite model of human experience. Speight, Myers, Cox, and Highlen (1991) contend that people have both a unique individuality and a common humanity. Thus, it is important to look at individuals through the intersection of culture, universality, and individuality. Culture can be addressed in counseling while including individual and universal explanations for the behavior (Speight et al., 1991).

In summary, helping professionals need to first understand what encompasses their view of cultural competence. Is cultural competence viewed only at the provider's level? What is the position of the profession or the mental health agency? Does it matter? What is the worldview of the provider about cultural competence? Is it race specific or inclusive of all cultures? Knowing this information provides a base from which clinicians can assess and, if necessary, change their approach to working within the profession, within agencies, and within communities.

Culture and Help-Seeking Behavior

Racial/ethnic disparities in access and use of mental health services have been well documented through several national studies and surveys (e.g., DHHS, 2001; Hogan et al., 2003). With few exceptions, findings have been consistent that racial/ethnic minorities experience a higher level of mental health problems than Caucasians due to access and availability of services, and that disparities remain even after adjusting for socioeconomic differences. They are less likely than Caucasians to enter mental health treatment, and if they do enter treatment, they are unlikely to stay until treatment has been completed. Treatment is often also poorer in quality than for Caucasians (DHHS, 2001). Furthermore, racial/ethnic minorities are likely to "seek mental health assistance in emergency rooms, inpatient settings, and through child welfare placement" than through mental health agencies (Snowden & Yamada, 2005, p. 148). We use the term *help-seeking behavior* to capture these myriad aspects of mental health disparities—treatment utilization, premature termination, service-provider preference, and beliefs and expectations about care. The various components of help-seeking behavior are critical in mental health professionals' understanding of how to work with racial/ethnic minority clients. Although culture is not the only factor that influences an individual's help-seeking process, the DHHS (2001) summarized the important role that culture plays in the help-seeking process:

> More often, culture bears on whether people even seek help in the first place, what types of help they seek, what types of coping styles and social supports they have, and how much stigma they attach to mental illness. Culture also influences the *meanings* that people impart to their illness. Consumers of mental health services, whose cultures vary both between and within groups, naturally carry this diversity directly to the service setting. (p. 25)

Treatment Utilization

African Americans, Hispanics, Native Americans, and Asian Americans are least likely to utilize mental health services and experience more barriers than

European Americans. Asian Americans and Pacific Islanders have the lowest utilization rate of mental health services than any other ethnic group, and Mexican Americans have lower utilization rates than European Americans and African Americans (Kung, 2003; Vega, Kolody, Aguilar-Gaxiola, & Catalano, 1999; Wells, Klap, Koike, & Sherbourne, 2001). African Americans and Latinos in comparison to Caucasians are less likely to receive mental health treatment through primary care or specialty treatment (Snowden & Yamada, 2005). Alegria et al. (2002) also found that social position and geographical location influenced access to treatment. Treatment disparity between Latinos and Caucasians was significant among the poor, but disparity in treatment was greatest between African Americans and Caucasians. African Americans who were not poor were less likely to receive mental health specialty treatment in comparison to Caucasians of a comparable socioeconomic status. Furthermore, African Americans living in the South or the West were more likely than Caucasians not to use specialty services. In other studies, disparities have been found to be lowest among the poor as treatment is financed from public sources (Chow, Jaffee, & Snowden, 2003; Snowden & Thomas, 2000). The same pattern is observed for non-White children. African American and other non-White children are less likely than Whites to receive mental health care (Snowden & Yamada, 2005). Research has indicated that individuals of some racial/ethnic minority groups delay seeking mental health treatment until they are in a crisis state, which may explain the increased number of racial/ethnic minorities seeking mental health treatment in emergency rooms and inpatient units (Snowden & Yamada, 2005).

Provider Preference

Few differences exist among African Americans, Latinos, and Caucasians in use of primary care or other sources in the general medical sector (Alegria et al., 2002; Wells et al., 2001). The general public goes to primary medical caregivers for most problems, including mental health issues, but racial and ethnic minorities are more likely than Caucasians, in general, to seek assistance from their primary caregiver (Snowden & Yamada, 2005). African Americans, however, are not as likely to use primary care for mental health issues as Caucasians (Lasser, Himmelstein, Woohandler, McCormick, & Bor, 2002). Within–ethnic group differences also exist in their preference for mental health services. U.S.-born Mexican Americans are more likely to seek help from general medical and specialty caregivers than Mexico-born

Mexican Americans, who preferred assistance form informal providers such as folk healers, spiritualists, and astrologers (Vega et al., 1999). More African American and Asian American adults preferred complementary and alternative medicine (e.g., indigenous healers, informal networks, folk healers, and family and friends; Duncan, 2005; Leong, Wagner, & Tata, 1995; Neighbors, 1991) than Caucasians. Latinos also considered complementary care if prayer was one of the alternative practices. However, the issue is what constitutes alternative or complementary medicine. Individuals have varying definitions of what they are (Snowden & Yamada, 2005). A primary alternative source of mental health treatment is the growing trend of using churches. In some ethnic communities, churches have employed professional mental health providers to meet the mental health needs of their congregants (Adkison-Bradley, Johnson, Lipford Sanders, Duncan, & Holcomb-McCoy, 2005). Faith and spirituality are important components of the lives of African Americans and Latinos. Spirituality, religion, prayers, and religious leaders have been cited by many ethnic/racial minorities as primary sources in coping with their mental health issues. Nadeem, Lange, and Miranda (2003) found in a survey of low-income immigrant (i.e., African, Caribbean, and Central and South American origin) and U.S.-born women (i.e., Caucasian, African American, and Latina) with known emotional problems that the racial/ethnic minority women preferred turning to their faith than Caucasian women.

Finally, even though African Americans have a lower help-seeking pattern, many African American clients indicate that they would consider counseling for mental health problems (Anglin, Alberti, Link, & Phelan, 2008; Nadeem et al., 2007). In fact, African Americans reported preferring counseling to drug therapy (Anglin et al., 2008). This preference for counseling over drug therapy appears to be related to potential side effects, effectiveness, and the potential of becoming addicted (Cooper-Patrick et al., 1997).

Premature Termination

Racial/ethnic minorities who overcome the initial barriers to access and use mental health services do not remain in continuous care but drop out prematurely. African Americans, Latinos, and Asian Americans tend to drop out at a higher rate and attend fewer sessions than Caucasians (DHHS, 2001; Snowden & Yamada, 2005). Many racial/ethnic minority clients do not return after the first session (Bernal & Sáez-Santiago, 2006).

Barriers to Help Seeking

Numerous barriers have been identified to explain the help-seeking patterns of racial/ethnic minorities: (a) language barriers (Sue, Fujino, Hu, Takeuchi, & Zane, 1991), (b) cultural variation in symptom expression (Johnson & Cameron, 2001), (c) bias in diagnosis (Neighbors, Trierweiler, Ford, & Muroff, 2003), (d) lack of culturally sensitive therapy (Hall, 2001), (e) cost of care and limited insurance (Snowden & Yamada, 2005), and (f) degree of acculturation (Snowden & Yamada, 2005). Some barriers are less tangible and reflect internalized qualities due to socialization or borne from discriminatory experiences. For example, researchers have found that racial/ethnic minorities place a higher emphasis on self-reliance (Snowden & Yamada, 2005). This characteristic and other related ones tend to be incompatible to seeking help. Ortega and Alegria (2002) found that low-income Puerto Rican residents who had been assessed as in need of mental health services were less likely to seek such assistance if they reported a high level of self-reliance. In a survey of Chinese Americans in need of mental health services, Kung (2003) found that those who had scored high on a "hardy personality configuration" were not as likely to seek help from medical or specialty mental health sources in comparison to others without such a personality configuration. Anglin et al. (2008) also found that African Americans were more likely than Caucasians to believe that mental health problems would improve on their own.

Furthermore, research on beliefs about counseling has found some unexpected results. Diala et al. (2001) discovered that African Americans with mental health problems had a more positive attitude than Caucasians about seeking care and obtaining effective treatment, findings replicated by Anglin et al. (2008). However, a favorable view about counseling did not translate into an increased number of them seeking mental health service, as African Americans also viewed treatment as being unnecessary. Problems were believed to improve without any assistance.

The stigma of mental illness and treatment has long been an explanation provided about health disparities. Little research, however, has been done on the effects of stigma on services used by racial/ethnic minorities. There is evidence to suggest that ethnic minority groups in the United States exhibit higher levels of stigma than U.S-born Caucasians (Nadeem et al., 2007; Snowden & Yamada, 2005). According to Zhang, Snowden, and Sue (1998) when questioning Asian Americans who live in Los Angeles, only 12 percent of Asians would mention their mental health issues as opposed to 25 percent of Whites who would disclose the same information.

When racial/ethnic minority individuals do seek counseling they have varied experiences with the mental health services. This experience, in part, is influenced by the expectations that they have when entering into the therapeutic process. For the most part, racial/ethnic minority clients do not have different expectations about counseling than their White counterparts, but culture seems to have an influence on counseling preference and on acceptable treatment modalities. For example, racial/ethnic minorities more often perceive through their interactions that mental health professionals treat them unfairly because of their race and ethnicity in comparison to White American clients (LaVeist, Nickerson, & Bowie, 2000; Leong et al., 1995; Neighbors, 1991). As noted earlier, African Americans may have a positive view of mental health treatment even if they do not go (Diala et al., 2001). However, their attitude appears to change. African Americans who received mental health services had negative attitudes about further assistance through mental health agencies. Diala et al. (2001) speculated that unpleasant experiences or ineffective treatment seemed to account for the shift in attitudes more than cultural mistrust or having an aversion to treatment.

This general feeling of being treated unfairly becomes a pervasive issue that is difficult to counteract, despite gains made in the helping profession to address these issues. The pervasive mistrust that has developed between ethnic minority clients and mental health professionals has had direct consequences. Thus, many ethnic minorities would prefer to see mental health providers who are of the same race or ethnicity, seek assistance from other sources (clergy, physician, and so on), or avoid getting any assistance. The preference for a same-race therapist appears to be stronger for African American clients (DHHS, 2001).

Some Recommendations for Overcoming Help-Seeking Barriers

Mental health professionals do not have control over some of the barriers that exist in the help-seeking process, such as the geographical location of their agencies, the cost of treatment or insurance practices, or the cultural beliefs of the community. What happens at the time of contact, however, does have implications for future help-seeking behavior. At the time of the first session, both clinician and client are looking each other over. Whether the cultural interaction is addressed or not, it is present in all clinician–client relationships, be it race/ethnicity, gender, socioeconomic status, religion, age, or sexual orientation. Many racial/ethnic minority clients are fearful, suspicious, and uncomfortable in regard to psychological treatment. They are more likely than European Americans to link causes of mental illness to spiritual failings, lack of willpower, and weaknesses of character (Alvidrez, 1999; Klonoff & Landrine, 1994; Sanchez-Hucles, 2000). Many racial/ethnic minorities are sensitive to nonverbal communication (e.g., eye contact, facial expressions, proximity, and so on) and the possible meanings that may be attached to gestures and body language. Given the perception of the etiology of psychological distress held by racial/minority clients, the first two to three meetings are crucial to establishing a productive therapeutic relationship (Sanchez-Hucles, 2000). Also, a long-held view is that one of the reasons that non-Caucasians do not use counseling is their perception of counselors. Non-Caucasians may not believe that counselors are real or authentic, perceiving them instead as "too perfect, distant and unable to understand" their concerns (Rivera, Phan, Maddux, Wilbur, & Arredondo, 2006, p. 37). So it is important that trust and rapport are established early to increase the likelihood that the client will return to counseling, as many racial/ethnic minority clients do not return after the first session or prematurely terminate (Bernal & Sáez-Santiago, 2006).

We recommend implementing three practices that may increase the help-seeking behavior of racial/ethnic minority clients, improve the interpersonal counseling process, and reduce premature termination: (a) community outreach, (b) precounseling orientation, and (c) organizational and procedural variables.

Community Outreach   Reaching out to the community of racial/ethnic people is crucial in increasing cultural trust and reducing the misperceptions potential clients might have about counseling. Reaching out means working outside the mental health office, symbolically making the broader community the mental health office. Helping professionals need to attend local community meetings once a week, such as neighborhood groups, nongovernmental organizations (NGOs), town hall/borough meetings, health and social services, parent–teacher associations, and public health and disability services. In addition, any volunteer work (e.g., Habitat for Humanity, American Cancer Society, etc.) needs to be done within the community that the practitioner serves. Reaching out means attending special community events on a regular basis such as Chinese New Year, Kwanzaa, Cinco de Mayo, All Saints' Day, and Hispanic Heritage Month. Reading the community newspapers is important to stay abreast of the unique challenges of the community. Equally crucial is connecting to the informal gatekeepers of the community. Many practitioners know the formal gatekeepers (police, juvenile authorities, judges, attorneys, and so forth) but usually do not know the informal gatekeepers (elders of the community, church leaders, well-established leaders of NGOs). While working at one counseling agency, the first author had an opportunity to work with a group of American Indians. To do so in a culturally sound fashion required finding the informal gate-keepers. In asking around, two people were identified as being important to the specific American Indian community. Both were sought out to gain their permission to proceed as well as to gain insights on how to do so. They were supportive, conveying it emotionally and symbolically through gift giving (a feather and wooden serving bowls). The support was tremendous and significant in making it easier in connecting to the American Indians in the area and to increase their level of trust in seeking help at the local counseling center.

Creating community connections is time consuming; thus, it is important that mental health practitioners start small and try not to do everything at once, but be consistent. Making a concerted effort to attend community meetings and events on a regular basis, even if it is monthly, will go a long way in establishing trust and credibility and to realign perspectives about what is normative and dysfunctional in the community. These facets increase the likelihood that some of the help-seeking barriers will recede to the back-ground instead of being the focal point of treatment. Furthermore, being involved in community meetings may result in fostering strong relationships with other community agencies, such as churches, food banks, school systems, and unemployment offices, which may result in strengthening the use of effective interventions across spheres of a client's functioning. To remain in the confines of a mental health office is the surest way for practitioners to maintain the status quo of faulty perceptions between mental health practitioners and potential clients. Initially, going into the community in which the practitioner is unaccustomed to being with the racial/ethnic minority may be difficult and anxiety laden. However, a sustained effort of doing so will serve the practitioner well in the long run. Over time the community and the practitioner will become familiar to each other, but it does take time. The most crucial aspect is that practitioners must find a way to start becoming members of the communities they serve.

Finally, all practitioners need to do community outreach, not just one person designated as the community liaison. Will only one person be working with only racial/ethnic minority clients? Otherwise, the referrals will be disproportionally scheduled with the practitioner who is doing the outreach or the lone racial/ethnic counselor. Thus, when the designated counselor has a full schedule of clients, then the other clients are either placed on a wait list or is scheduled to see another clinician who has little understanding of the client's context to establish a working alliance or to draw informed cultural conclusions about the person's mental health functioning.

Precounseling Orientation   Misperceptions about counseling exist because clients do not know what to expect. As a result, it is important that clinicians take the time to orient clients to the counseling process by being as explicit as possible about what to expect from the first session and subsequent ones. Conducting a detailed orientation session at the time of intake will likely decrease the level of distrust racial/ethnic minority clients might have about the counselor and the process as well as increase the likelihood of the client trusting what the counselor says. Detailed information becomes more crucial for clients who have less than a college education and have had limited interactions with Whites or other racial/ethnic minorities or have had previous negative counseling experiences. Typical questions include the following: (a) Have you been to counseling before? (b) If so, when did you go? (c) What was the experience like? (d) What made it go well or how come it went so poorly? Statements that we have used frequently to newcomers to counseling go like this:

> If you have never been in counseling before, let me tell you what we are going to do today and if you have any questions, please feel free to ask. I want to know what brought you here today, but I am also going to ask a wide variety of questions about you, including your family and other personal aspects about your life. You may wonder why I am asking so many personal questions and what does this have to do with why you are here today. I have just met you now and need to know as much as possible about you in order to understand you and provide you with the best care possible. All that has gone before is related to who you are now and what is happening now. Does this make sense? Do you have any questions before we get started?

Besides sharing with the client what a typical session is like, the clinician will need to inquire about what the client is expecting from the sessions and what concerns the person might have about counseling. Knowing this information will be helpful in personalizing the interventions for the client. For example, a biracial client with identity and alcohol abuse problems returned to counseling and was scheduled for the first time with the first author. When asked, the client freely shared what her previous counseling experience was like, admitting that she wasn't always candid but enjoyed verbalizing her concerns; however, she did not follow through with any behavioral interventions. This information was used to (a) increase the use of behavioral interventions in the session and (b) contract with the client about expectations and follow-through. Continued counseling was contingent on making an effort to comply with directives. Taking into consideration the client's comments resulted in significant improvement during counseling and long-term success later.

Frequently, clients may have difficulty articulating such expectations and concerns, as they may be unsure about their rights as a client. If such difficulties occur, then the clinician may need to increase the structure in the session to assist the client in articulating an answer without clinicians imposing their worldview and expectations. Cultural issues, if appropriate, may need to be raised and initially addressed at the time of orientation. More racial/ethnic minority clients than Caucasians may raise cultural issues in the first session. Subtle questions may be based on cultural decorations in the room or the counselor's background. However, we have raised these similar cultural questions to clients. For example, we have asked clients to elaborate about their ethnic or racial background, share what role race/ethnicity or culture has in their life, or voice any concerns about cultural barriers or concerns they have about counseling.

Stating the obvious is important. Many times counselors assume that the obvious is apparent to the clients, but it is not. The obvious include scheduling appointments, being on time for appointments, calling to cancel or reschedule, making payments, communicating concerns, and knowing explicitly their rights as a client. Counselor behavior and expectations are not obvious and need to be shared. Throughout our careers, we have made a point of being as explicit as possible with all clients. From the time a client enters into counseling until the process ends, we have always kept clients informed, have clarified information, and have followed up with others on behalf of the client. These simple steps increase the client's trust in the counselor and the likelihood of keeping scheduled appointments.

Making client orientation a standard practice is invaluable in removing help-seeking barriers to the counseling process. Information is power and well-informed clients will believe that they have power over their lives to make changes, which start in the counseling sessions. This premise is the essence of liberation psychology (Ivey, 1995) and is also reflective of the work of Paulo Freire (1970). When clients are not oriented to counseling, then the imbalance of power between client and counselor is greater. Clients will not know what to expect, will be uncomfortable with the process, and will be more likely to drop out prematurely from counseling. Everyone wants to feel in control. Clients are no different.

Organizational and Procedural Variables   The culture of mental health agencies and practices and the day-to-day operations are often overlooked. However, the infrastructure of mental health agencies and practice is just as important as the counseling process. When clients enter a mental health facility, they encounter the organization and its infrastructure first. The old saying "you never get a second chance to make a first impression" is applicable to the influence of organizational presentation on the help-seeking behavior of racial/ethnic minority clients. Is the atmosphere welcoming? Are there cultural artifacts and decorations reflective of a diverse clientele? What is the tenor of the administrative staff, such as the receptionist or the finance staff? How much time is taken to orient the client to the paperwork, or is it business as usual, "assembly" style? How has staff been trained in dealing with clients who come at impromptu times? It is not uncommon for some racial/ethnic minority clients to stop in the counseling office unscheduled to share something with the counselor. The typical response is for the receptionist to indicate that the counselor is not available and to take a message. However, counselors need to inform receptionists how to handle this differently. For instance, the receptionist could indicate to the client that the counselor is with someone right now and if the person wants to wait, the counselor will be informed. In essence, the staff in the front office of the mental health center needs to be involved in cultural sensitivity training as much as the practitioners. The atmosphere of the front office staff is reflective of the organizational culture of the mental health profession.

Culturally Sensitive Practice

Those in the helping profession generally accept the idea that culturally sensitive interventions include the following components: (a) awareness of culture, (b) acquisition of knowledge about cultural aspects (i.e., customs, norms, language, and so on), (c) capacity to differentiate between culture and pathology, and (d) capacity to integrate the previous three dimensions in the intervention (Arredondo, 1998; Bernal & Sáez-Santiago, 2006). Culture sensitivity is seen as a dynamic process that changes based on context and time, and involves testing cultural assumptions throughout the therapeutic process. In this section we highlight the essence of culturally sensitive assessment and treatment. Using as our base Sue's (2006) depiction of translating cultural competence into practice, we delineate our overarching approach to culturally sound assessment and treatment. Then, we examine key cultural issues in assessing clients, followed by presenting a clinical research study that reflects best cultural treatment practices.

We agree with Sue (2006) that cultural competency is best viewed as both process and content. As a process, cultural competency is viewed as a multi-dimensional phenomenon that includes therapist characteristics that have been identified as scientific mindedness, dynamic sizing, and culturally specific expertise. These terms sound quite technical and abstract, but really reflect the mental and practical structures that practitioners need to cultivate in moving beyond the conventional socialization of how to see the world and understand the experiences of others. In addition to process characteristics, concrete steps are required, what Sue (2006) calls content, to improve the effectiveness of working with a racial/ethnic minority client. These content areas reflect the range of activities that counselors engage in during the counseling process. Cultural sensitivity must be used in assessing the client, orienting the client to the therapeutic process, and developing and testing hypotheses about the nature of the client and best treatment approach. As the content areas of mental health interventions are distinct, therapists may be proficient in none or a few areas such as assessment or a specific cultural technique. Variations in practitioners' area of competence indicate that becoming culturally competent is an ongoing process—one that the helping professional must continually work at to develop each specific area. We start by summarizing the usefulness of scientific mindedness, dynamic sizing, and culture-specific expertise. Content of sessions permeates the discussion of these process factors.

The Practitioner's Mindset

The structure of client assessment and interventions may vary in that it is the practitioner's decision as to how both should proceed. Regardless of how either is structured, the mindset of the practitioner determines the trustworthiness of the assessment and interventions.

Thus, the practitioner must believe in and operate from a scientific mindset, starting with two premises. Clinical work is not an art. It is a science and should be treated as such. Scientific mindedness refers to the cognitive set that emphasizes critical thinking skills that relate to the functions (e.g., evaluation, accurate assessment of the problem, hypothesis testing, etc.) needed to successfully engage the client during the counseling process (Sue, 2006). It refers to a counselor who can form hypotheses rather than prematurely draw conclusions about the status of clients who are culturally different. For example, a scientifically minded helping professional, in the spirit of a researcher, would listen intently to his or her client while simultaneously developing hypotheses that would guide inquiries as to the validity of the client's functioning.

The testing of these hypotheses would likely lead to questions and possible answers beyond what the therapist may know at a given time. Not knowing is understandable, but filling in the gap is important. A tangible way to view scientific mindedness is for clinicians to develop a decision tree on how to critically assess, conceptualize, and create a treatment plan for all clients. Contained in this decision tree should be general guidelines in forming hypotheses about possible problems to rule in as well as to rule out. Prior to seeing any clients, it is vital that clinicians have an established decision tree about how to engage the client, about the type of areas to assess, and how to proceed based on the answers and presentation of the client. This decision tree will become refined over time as the clinician gains more experience. Practicing conceptualizing all clients by this method allows the counselor to break the natural pattern of seeing the client from the therapist's culture of origin and the associated inherent assumptions.

Related to scientific mindedness and a necessary component to the clinician creating a culturally sound mindset is dynamic sizing. Sue (2006) refers to dynamic sizing as the ability to shift between a cognitive set informed by normative data to an idiographic framework for understanding client behavior. It is developing skills in which the helping professional knows when to generalize and apply skills that may be inclusive to a particular cultural group. Dynamic sizing reflects the balancing of inductive and deductive reasoning and serves as a mechanism for clinicians to check themselves from imposing cultural stereotypes and ignoring individual differences of a culturally diverse client. This process is difficult to do unless the clinicians know the community from which the clients come. For example, reflection of feeling is a skill that is helpful in getting clients to process emotional issues on a deeper level. However, some ethnic groups may view this skill as a deflection by the counselor to hide something and not to be straight with the client. We have found this to be particularly true in urban areas where clients are mistrustful of systems and the people who work in them.

By knowing the community, clinicians are able to establish a base rate of normal and dysfunctional behavior. Base rate refers to the "proportion of actual positives that exist in the total sample" (Wiggins, 1973, p. 244) or in a particular population. For example, what proportion of the community is considered schizophrenic? What proportion of the community is middle class? Or what proportion of the community suffers from anxiety attacks? Clinicians can obtain this information from three sources: (a) the composition of the clients seen at the mental health agency; (b) other gatekeepers' (police, public health, newspaper accounts, other social service agencies, schools, etc.) views or data on the base rate of community functioning; and (c) the views of informal gatekeepers (community watchers). Knowing how a local community functions provides the clinician with the necessary information to evaluate clients for their unique features as well as in relation to what is normative in their community. The biggest challenge counselors have in assessing culturally diverse clients, especially racial/ethnic minorities, is not to overpathologize them. Knowing the community will assist the clinicians to think twice about appropriate diagnoses and as well as provide sources to consult about normative behavior.

Culture-Specific Expertise

Culture-specific expertise requires that mental health professionals have a working knowledge of their own cultural frame of reference and the clients they serve. Gaining culturally specific knowledge about clients is necessary to meet clients where they are instead of making them fit within the therapist's culturally specific worldview and lifestyle. For example, mental health professionals need to be aware of the influence of clients' culture on their psychosocial development and to have the prerequisite skill needed to work within their cultural framework. We use three factors as exemplars that may influence the assessment and treatment process and require culture-specific expertise when working with ethnic and racial minorities: (a) symptom presentation, (b) cultural presentation, and (c) communication styles.

Symptom Presentation   Culture influences how clients describe their symptoms to mental health professionals. For example, Asian American clients may report somatic symptoms, such as dizziness, while neglecting to report emotional difficulties. However, if Asian American clients are questioned further, they do acknowledge having emotional difficulties (Lin & Cheung, 1999). Culture also has an influence on the way that clients make sense of their subjective well-being, which, in turn, influences whether they view mental illness as "real" or "imagined." For example, having a working knowledge of the experiences of Native Americans may aid the helping professional to accurately discern whether a client's mistrust is a culturally appropriate response or indicative of paranoia as a sign of a mental disturbance. For example, the second author observed an interaction in which a Native American woman described a bad experience with the mental health system that led her to question the therapist's motives throughout therapy. This bad experience reinforced other experiences she had in accessing the system for appropriate care. The client would make sweeping comments about the actions of others and wondered if they were intentional. The client's experiences and persistent concerns were reflected in her voicing an increased level of anxiety. Her previous therapist had diagnosed her as paranoid and in need of medication. Many therapists usually accept the diagnosis of other therapists, which under some circumstances may result in the client's mental state worsening instead of improving. In this case, the second author encouraged the therapist to contextualize this client not based on etic (an outsider's view) norms but emic (an insider's view) ones. Was this client operating differently from other Native American clients who had interacted with the mental health system in this community? What would be a normal reaction to her stated experiences?

Cultural Presentation   Everyone uses categorization to manage the enormous amount of information they are exposed to and must process. An easy form of categorizing and stereotyping is an individual's appearance (e.g., age, sex, social status, sexual orientation, and race–ethnicity). Categorization and stereotyping are established at a young age and are automatically activated unless an explicit effort is made to control the process (Devine, 1989). Even if cultural stereotyping is controlled, assessing the saliency of clients' culture and its role in their psychological functioning is vital to providing effective treatment. One way to go beyond the phenotypic expression of culture is to assess the saliency of a client's culture, also called social or cultural identity. Social identity refers to an individual's identification to and membership in a specific social group (Tajfel & Turner, 1979). Cultural identity is a term used to describe the social affiliation because of specific cultural attributes, such as race, ethnicity, gender, sexual orientation, and religion. Research on Black racial identity since the 1970s has had a significant impact on the conceptualization and understanding of cultural identities, resulting in models of racial identity (W. E. Cross & Vandiver,

2001; Helms, 1995; Sellers, Rowley, Chavous, Shelton, & Smith, 1997), sexual orientation (e.g., Cass, 1984; McCarn & Fassinger, 1996), and gender (e.g., Downing & Roush, 1985; Moradi, Subich, & Phillips, 2002), just to name a few. Research has advanced in this area, but application of it has lagged. Helms (1984) theorized the dyadic interaction of racial identity—providing a template of what interactions would look between a White counselor and a Black client with comparable racial identities and uncomplimentary ones. Little research has been conducted on dyadic interaction between various ethnic/racial identities of clients and counselors to advance specifically how to evaluate and use such a model. However, this information could be incorporated into the clinician's decision tree to evaluate and ask about. Thus, individuals' cultural identity has value, and asking and probing about cultural beliefs and behaviors is a way to assess how important culture is to them. Thus, the presentation has less to do with the phenotypic expression than it has to do with how culture is manifested in the person's life.

Communication Style   The mental health profession puts a premium on verbal communication. Therapy is often referred to as the "talking cure." A key to accurately assessing a client's problem is the ability to verbalize one's discomfort. Such emphasis on verbal communication creates situations in which the potential for miscommunication is enhanced when clients are culturally different from the mental health professional. Subtle miscommunication and misunderstandings can lead to an inaccurate assessment of the client's problem (DHHS, 2001). When the first author was working with a diverse group of Native American college students, understanding their communication style was important. As a group, the students' style was quieter, low key, and less animated than other racial/ethnic minority students, but was still dynamic. Being with them required the counselor to change not only her expectations about how to interact with the group, but also her communication style. Thus, the goal was to parallel the counselor's communication style to theirs and pay close attention to the nuances in words and actions. What did excited look like? What did sad look like? What was the difference between frustration and general concern? A good assessment required that a baseline of normative behavior be established for the communication style of the group. The normative standards of a community of people need to be known first before drawing conclusions about a client's functioning. Knowing the style of communication of a client will help in facilitating a better relationship. The goal of counseling should not be to change the communication style of a client to make it easier for the clinician. Altering the communication style of clients needs to be the focus of therapy when it is fundamentally interfering with functioning in their community, in the workforce, and social agencies. Helping them to code switch or to become bicultural also needs to become the goal of the practitioner. Thus, modeling a style is a great way to facilitate the adoption of a style.

Components of Assessment

We view assessment as made up of three primary components: (a) the interview, (b) psychological tests, and (c) diagnosis and treatment planning. Much has been written about all three and our goal is not to repeat what is known about the components of assessment (see Cuellar & Paniagua, 2000, and Suzuki, Ponterotto, & Meller, 2008, for extensive coverage of cultural assessment). Our focus is on how clinicians can assess the role of culture in the client's functioning. One word sums up how culture can be assessed: ask. How clinicians conduct the assessment process tells more about who they are as cultural beings than the clients. Many clinicians are uncomfortable in explicitly asking clients about cultural issues. If they are, then racial/ethnic minority clients will know that, possibly increasing their suspicion and distrust of the counseling process as well as the clinician. Some clinicians dismiss the importance of cultural issues, believing that individual difference is the only thing that matters. Again, the clients will sense this, resulting in their questioning themselves or feeling unimportant to the clinicians. In both cases, the likelihood is high that premature termination will occur. Asking about cultural issues is the simplest route to knowing, and most times racial/ethnic minority clients welcome the inquiries if the asking is set up well.

Pretherapy orientation provides an excellent opportunity to establish an open avenue of communication and to prepare the client for not being surprised about the myriad of questions that will be asked, including cultural ones. Once an orientation has been given to the client, then asking cultural questions becomes all about timing. Normally, it can be explored when inquiring about interpersonal and intrapsychic issues. For example, a clinician could ask the questions in numerous ways: (a) "You indicate on your intake sheet that you identify as 'biracial' (identify as Black), how important is your cultural background to you?" (b) "You mentioned that your parents are first-generation immigrants from India and you are second generation. Has that presented any challenges for you?" (c) "You have openly acknowledged being lesbian with me, but are you out in the Black community?" (d)

"I noticed that you left your religious affiliation blank on the intake sheet. What are your religious beliefs?" At some point or another, we have asked all of the questions and the clients' responses have been numerous. There is no set response. However, each response is illuminating about the idiographic nature of the client's functioning in relation to the larger cultural community to which they may or may not belong. By asking direct questions about cultural issues, clients will take the asking as a sign that the clinician is interested in getting to know them. It also empowers the client to feel in control of treatment and equally responsible for the outcome.

Based on the need for additional information, the clinician may use other methods of assessment beyond a clinical interview. Answers to each set of questions as well as other assessment methods will lead to the use of inductive and deductive reasoning. Clinicians' observations and experience will lead them to draw conclusions about possibly what is going on with the client (inductive reasoning). At the same time, general laws about the nature of human functioning and dysfunction must also be applied (deductive reasoning). Using both types of reasoning is critical to understanding the functioning of a client. Thus, the clinician must "split hairs" and reconstitute the hairs, ruling in as many possible problems underlying the client concerns as well as ruling out as many possible problems. This process of thinking is effective for all clients. What makes it even more effective for culturally diverse clients is that it requires the clinician to not operate from the "familiar," meaning the personal worldview individuals have about what is "normal" or "appropriate." Imposing guidelines on conducting an assessment allows for a more objective process, which means a less biased and a more fair assessment of the client. This process is the integration of cultural competence into the assessment process in the broadest way. Cultural competence must also be integrated into the process in specific ways. That is, the clinicians must infuse culture into their process of thinking and needs to be evidenced in their decision tree. No matter what question is asked or no matter what area is explored, an overarching question that clinicians need to ask themselves is, "Is there a culturally specific element to the issues?" or "How does culture influence the client's functioning in this area?" This internal process of infusing culture into the assessment must occur and requires practice until it becomes an automatic process of clinicians' mindsets.

We have three primary comments about using psychological tests with racial/ethnic minority clients. First, clinicians need to know the normative data on the psychological tests. Are the norms representative of the clients seen in the agency? Test scores are only valid and reliable for the community they represent. If there are no test norms for the client being seen, then don't use the protocol. This issue may come up for clients with English-language proficiency or recent immigrants who have not assimilated the cultural norms of the United States. The use of intelligence and achievement tests with African American children has been controversial since *Larry P. v. Riles* (1972), which challenged the use of standardized intelligence tests for placement of Black children in educable mentally retarded (EMR) classes that contained a disproportional enrollment of Black children in comparison to the number of Black children in the state school population.

Although there are varying opinions about the cultural biases of objective tests, especially intelligence tests (Flynn, 1980; Graves, 2004; Jensen, 1998; Montagu, 1999; Reynolds, 2000; Sternberg, 2000), our second comment is that the most compelling implication is that no one clinical tool should be used in making decisions about a person's mental health state. Psychological tests are only as good as the users and when used only in conjunction with a confluence of evidence from other evaluative sources such as interview, observations, and interviews with significant others. If there is a lack of consistent findings across sources, then further evaluation is needed before determining a diagnosis and disposition.

Our final comment is that if clinicians administer a psychological test and are unsure of the accuracy or stability of the results, then is it important after the standardized test has been given for the clinician to query about unclear answers and increase structure of the task/question or ask the question/task differently to determine whether clients know the material within a different context. "Testing the limits" after the test has been given may not change the standardized score, but it may provide insight into (a) how the person approached the task, (b) how the person was feeling during test taking, and (c) what the person actually knows or can convey about the self.

The Case for Culturally Sensitive Practice

The need to consider cultural and contextual variables when intervening with clients has been echoed by many in the helping profession (Alvidrez, 1999; Bernal & Sáez-Santiago, 2006; Miranda et al., 2005) and has been reinforced by the adoption in psychology of the multicultural guidelines on education, research, training, practice, and organizational change (American Psychological Association, 2003) and the inclusion of cultural competence in the ethical guidelines of all major helping professional organizations. However, there still is a void in adapting evidenced-based treatments (EBTs) and interventions to be culturally sensitive (Miranda et al., 2003). Lack of evidence to support the use of specific therapeutic outcomes for racial/ethnic minorities does not mean that empirically supported treatments would be ineffective with such clients. Most likely, even without evidence, many EBTs would probably be effective with racial/ethnic minority clients. In essence, without evidence stating that they do not work, by default the assumption is that they will work. This premise led Miranda et al. (2003) to conclude that there is need for clear evidence on when and how EBT interventions should be altered to make them acceptable and accessible to racial/ethnic minority clients. Also, when, why, and how are interventions more likely to fail? This type of knowledge would assist the helping professionals in intervening better as well as furthering research on best practices.

One promising study captures the possibilities of science and practice working as one in developing culturally effective interventions. Miranda et al. (2003) developed culturally and linguistically sensitive interventions for primary care clinicians to use with 1,269 patients (398 Latino/a, 93 African Americans, and 778 European Americans). This study was designed to test whether EBTs for depression, which involve the use of psychotherapy and medication, could improve the therapeutic conditions equally for Euro-American patients as well as racial/ethnic minority patients. The interventions consisted of three components, of which two are described here. One component involved training local expert leaders to implement quality improvement onsite at the mental health agencies. At each site, the expert leaders (a primary care provider, a nursing supervisor, and mental health specialist) participated in a 2-day workshop on a culturally specific depression treatment model and collaborative care principles. The training entailed providing written manuals, monthly lectures, and monthly meetings using intervention staff records as a method to provide feedback on treatment patterns. The second component was training local staff nurses in a 1-day workshop to serve as depression specialists. The nurses provided brief critical assessments to patients who screened positive for depression and then used material developed by the researchers to educate the patient and help motivate them to engage in treatment. The intervention materials were available in English and Spanish. Information regarding cultural beliefs and ways of overcoming barriers to appropriate treatment for Latino and African American patients were included in the provider training materials. Additionally, racial/ethnic minority investigators provided direct supervision to the local experts throughout the intervention. (The third component involved providing the cost to implement the study, which is self-explanatory and therefore is not summarized here.)

Miranda et al. (2003) found that when racial/ethnic minorities received appropriate interventions, their clinical outcomes were better than those of Euro-American clients. Minor modifications (i.e., including experts on treating ethnic minorities on the intervention team, making information relevant to the treatment of ethnic minorities available for providers, and translating patient materials into Spanish) of the empirically established treatment for depression exponentially improved the outcomes for racial/ethnic minorities. This study serves as an exemplar of the need for more systematic research on the factors that lead to effective, culturally sound treatment as well as its relevance to the practice of helping professionals. Being culturally sensitive means attending to the minor everyday details that tell clients they matter. It is highly recommended that practitioners review Miranda et al.'s (2003) study for best practices.

Recommendations for Culturally Sensitive Interventions

Providing quality culturally sensitive interventions for traditionally underserved populations can be a daunting task for those in the helping profession because of personal limitations and lack of experience with certain groups, the middle-class bias in training, and systemic bias in agencies in which helping professionals work. However, those in the helping profession can actively work to overcome the aforementioned barriers. We recommend three specific practices that will aid helping professionals gain the skills to provide culturally sensitive interventions when working with racial/ethnic clients. These recommendations are grounded in the idea that there is no substitute for experience. Becoming culturally competent requires the helping professional to engage racial/ethnic minority clients on all levels of difference. How individuals become engaged into their culture is based on the experiences that have shaped their lives. Other variables such as poverty, lack of educational opportunities, gender, family constellation, and religious beliefs can have a profound impact on how a person expresses his or her culture. We have worked extensively with clients from diverse backgrounds and offer the following suggestions in aiding helping professionals to move from having only a philosophical understanding of cultural competence to the actual practice of cultural competence.

1. *Find a culturally sensitive mentor.* Counselors need to resist falling into a rut of complacency and apathy in their practice. Gaining skills and comfort in working with clients requires more than eating lunch with the resident racial/ethnic minority therapist. Although the resident therapist may be representative of a group the counselor is interested in, the therapist in question may be just as unsure about how to work with people from his or her identified group. For the interested helping professional, it may be more beneficial to find a mentor or clinical supervisor who can give the helping professional the type of constructive feedback and dialogue that is needed for critical skill development. The helping professional should contact agencies, community centers, and places of worship to find an appropriate mentor. The authors have found that these are great resources and the people at these places are interested in sharing their wisdom and expertise.

2. *Engage in cultural didactical activities.* No one person should be solely responsible for strengthening the cultural skills of another. Thus, it is important for practitioners to engage in cultural didactical activities to increase their overall knowledge of a particular racial or ethnic group. The authors recommend joining culturally focused book clubs, where the content of the books and discussions is about the life experiences of various racial/ethnic minorities. These books can be either fictional or nonfictional. One excellent nonfictional book is *Willow Weep for Me: A Black Woman's Journey through Depression* (1999) by Meri Nana-Ama Danquah, which highlights the struggles and cultural issues surrounding African Americans dealing with depression. Another excellent practice book is *The First Session with African Americans: A Step-by-Step Guide* (2000), by Janis Sanchez-Hucles, which describes how to engage African American clients in therapy. Also Fouad and Arredondo's (2007) book titled *Becoming Culturally Oriented* and *The Lakota Way* (2001), by Joseph Marshall III, are excellent resources. Fictional books that may give the helping professional some insight include the following: (a) any book from the Walter Mosley's Easy Rawlins Series (e.g., *Devil in a Blue Dress* [1990]), (b) *Faces of an Angel* (1994) by Denise Chavez, and (c) *The Fifth Sun* (2004) by Mary Lagasse. Occasionally a walk through the aisles of university bookstores will easily keep practitioners current on required cultural readings professors in the humanities, literature, history, sociology, anthropology, and cultural studies have ordered for their classes and may prove to be useful in learning more about diverse clients.

3. *Perform regular counselor–client evaluations.* Besides getting experience in working with a diverse clientele, learning from the work
requires that the helping professionals engage in a regular and systematic client evaluation of all of their work, specifically with racial/
ethnic minority clients. The helping professionals should use informal as well as formal tools to examine client outcomes and the therapeutic process. These outcomes should be used to help the therapist
to assess what interventions have facilitated the therapeutic process
and those that have not. Many formal measures assess symptom
reduction as a sign of effectiveness; however, the helping professional
who is interested in increasing his or her cultural competence should
examine the therapeutic process more comprehensively. After establishing a therapeutic relationship the helping professional should ask
the clients questions about the effectiveness of interventions.

For example, we have asked clients on a regular basis the following questions: (a) What was helpful in this session? or (b) Was there
anything that was particularly troublesome during this session? It is
also important for the helping professional to pay attention to nonverbal cues. The second author's experience has been that racial/ethnic
minority clients will communicate their comfort level either verbally or
nonverbally. Phrases like, " I do not know if counseling is for me," or
"How much longer do we have?" may be indications that the counseling process is not going well. The author has also noted that clients'
utilizing a lot of formal language may indicate a level of discomfort
in the therapeutic process. It is important to observe the racial/ethnic
minority client in the waiting room when talking with family and close
friends, paying attention to communication style and lingo, and assessing if there is a difference in how the client speaks in counseling. The
second author had an experience in which he was engaging with an
African American client in a very spirited conversation. In the course
of this conversation a White person entered into the room and the client's tone and casual style of conversation became formal and distant.
Upon the person leaving the room, the second author inquired about
the change in tone and style of conversation. The client disclosed she
was uncomfortable around White people.

Summary Developing culture competency is multilayered. For the new
practitioner, learning to be an effective provider takes time. As the person
gradually gains more experience, it is equally important to understand the

cultural worldview of the mental health agency, other social service agencies and programs, and the local community. Becoming culturally competent is hard work. There are no shortcuts, as becoming competent is a lifelong cultural experience. It is important that helping professionals establish annual goals and specific plans to work at cultural competency. It is impossible to know and learn everything at once. Finding a culturally sensitive mentor to meet with on a regular basis, at least monthly, will assist in allaying fears and worries about the therapeutic process and content while at the same time increase the counselor's self-efficacy about cultural practice. Reading may be the last thing a counselor wants to do, but doing so is a powerful antidote to not understanding racial/ethnic minorities. It won't be surprising that "aha moments" will occur, as books, fiction or nonfiction, that tell a story make it easier to identify with the protagonist. For example, in the book *A Time to Kill* (1989) by John Grisham, the defendant's attorney is giving his closing argument about why the Black father should not be convicted for killing the two young White males for raping his daughter. He asked the jurors to close their eyes as he asked them to imagine the trauma that the young Black girl experienced. However, he unexpectedly switched perspectives on them. Instead of taking an etic perspective, what must the Black father feel, he asks that the jurors take an emic perspective—what would you do if this girl were White? Numerous books exist that provide a beginning path to take different cultural perspectives. Asking bookstore staff about possible books is a start. Finally, getting formal and informal feedback about the counseling from clients is incredibly important to ensure growth across all spheres of functioning. People work hardest about being better when there is concrete information to facilitate the improvement. Most clients want to have an effective and caring being working with them. Thus, they will give good and perceptive feedback. Seeking it will be the hardest part for counselors, especially if the relationship is cross-cultural.

Psychotropic Medication

Psychotropic medication is a key issue in the treatment of mental health problems. Many mental health professionals work with clients who receive counseling as well as take medication. However, the use of medication has been deemed in some instances a barrier and a concern for ethnic minorities receiving mental health services. Many minority clients are concerned about the side effects and addiction potential of psychotropic medication. Additionally, there is evidence to suggest that racial/ethnic minorities are often overmedicated as well as metabolize medication differently than White clients. Both issues may increase the number of side effects and difficulties of racial/ethnic minorities taking and trusting the use of psychotropic medications (DHHS, 2001; Lin, Poland, & Nakasaki, 1993; Pi & Simpson, 2005).

Ethnopsychopharmacology is the study of ethnic variations in medication dosing, examining how medications are metabolized across ethnic populations. After a drug is taken, it is circulated in the liver and metabolized by enzymes. Genetic variations that affect the functioning of these enzymes are more common in some ethnic or racial groups. These variations can have an impact on the rate at which medication is metabolized in the body. African Americans and Asians on average are more likely than Whites to slowly metabolize several medications used for psychosis and depression (DHHS, 2001; Lin et al., 1993). Being unaware of these differences may mean that clinicians have racial/ethnic minority clients who have been prescribed higher doses, who experience more medication side effects, and are at a greater risk for more long-term severe side effects (Lin et al., 1993). Findings about the differential metabolic rates by race are based on group averages and may be not applicable to all racial/ethnic minorities. Nevertheless not knowing this information, mental health professionals may overlook the symptoms reported by some racial/ethnic minority clients, which may result in discouraging these clients from taking the medication and ultimately may lead to their premature termination from treatment. Thus, it is critical that counselors specifically ask clients (a) what are their beliefs and values in taking medications and (b) whether they are adhering to taking the prescribed dose. It is equally important to query specifically about typical and unusual side effects.

Cultural Competence in Training and Supervision

Training

Most mental health professionals at the master's and doctoral levels who provide mental health services continue to be European Americans and are primarily female (Arredondo, 1998; Hays, 2001). Research on counselor preparedness to work with diverse clientele suggests that European Americans are less multiculturally aware and knowledgeable than racial minority mental health professionals (Hays, 2001; Sodowsky, Kuo-Jackson, Richardson,

& Corey, 1998; Yeh & Arora, 2003). Holcomb-McCoy and Meyers (1999), in a national survey, found that counselor trainees had low levels of multicultural competence. Additionally, Steward, Boatwright, Sauer, Baden, and Jackson (1998) reported that 33 percent of the counselors they surveyed had negative reactions to discussions and guest speakers that discussed and focused on multicultural issues. Other research has shown that many counselors continue to feel discomfort when working with an ethnically diverse caseload with negative feelings ranging from anxiety to increased irritation (Bimrose & Bayne, 1995; Sanchez-Hucles, 2000). Difficulties in working with racial/ethnic clients may be exacerbated when these clients report experiences of racism or express different values than those of the therapists (Bimrose & Bayne, 1995). Thus, the availability of trained professionals to work effectively with diverse clients continues to be limited (Bernal & Castro, 1994).

To meet the growing demand for mental health providers who can respond to the challenge of serving a more diverse population, many training programs have mandated that their trainees receive training through cultural course work and clinical practicum that involve working with diverse clients. This emphasis on improving multicultural education has resulted in the majority of mental health programs providing at least one course on multicultural counseling (Abreu, Gim Chung, & Atkinson, 2000). However, a number of studies have shown that most students in counseling programs require at least two or three courses over a period of a year to learn about and appreciate differing worldviews (Abreu et al., 2000).

Research has identified six multicultural counseling training (MCT) models or schemes that have been utilized by mental health training programs: (a) traditional program, (b) workshop design, (c), separate course, (d) interdisciplinary cognate, (e) subspecialty cognate, and (f) integrated program (Ridley, Mendoza, & Kanitz, 1994; Ridley, Mendoza, Kanitz, Angermeir, & Zenk, 1994). The traditional approach assumes homogeneity in treatment and that no modification of treatment is necessary for racial/ethnic minority clients. Trainees are encouraged to attend diversity workshops, but these workshops are not integral to the training program. Generally, programs that ascribe to this model are seen as inadequate and evasive when it comes to a commitment to multicultural training. A related approach is the separate course model, which involves adding multicultural courses to the program curriculum. These courses are designed for trainees to develop competence. The interdisciplinary and the subspecialty cognates are extensions of the separate course model in which the trainees are encouraged to iden-tify several courses that would serve as a specialization or cognate. These courses are in sociology, anthropology, and other disciplines where the study of culture is primary in their mission. This approach requires substantial program commitment to diversity training. The integrated approach is the most comprehensive approach to multicultural training. It involves integrat-ing multicultural training in all course work offered by the counseling pro-gram. Programs that utilize this approach would probably have the option to specialize in certain areas based on interest.

Although the integrated approach is the most desirable, most programs approach multicultural training utilizing the separate course model (Hills & Strozier, 1992; Ponterotto, 1997). This model does provide some exposure to cultural issues, but the exposure is cursory at best. Many of the programs squeeze large amounts of information into one or two courses, which makes it difficult for the students to process the information in any meaningful way. Potentially, students leave these courses overwhelmed and resistant to multicultural counseling (Arredondo & Arciniega, 2001). The separate course approach is also lacking in the area of experiential learning. Many of the courses are didactic in nature and may not have as a requirement that students actually work with diverse clients.

The effectiveness of these approaches to multicultural training has yielded few empirical studies as to which approach is most effective. However, studies on the overall effectiveness of multicultural training have shown a decrease in negative racial attitudes and overt racist behavior, increases in self-perceived multicultural competency, and increased ability to concep-tualize clients in a multicultural context, particularly White trainees in higher stages of racial identity (Brown, Parham, & Yonker, 1996; Butler & Constantine, 2006; Constantine, Warren, Milville, 2005; Neville et al., 1996). Additionally, research found that trainees reported higher levels of cultural competence when supervised by an ethnic minority as opposed to a White supervisor, and supervisors who had more developed racial identities were better at training their students to become multiculturally competent (Abreu et al., 2000).

Given the paucity of literature that establishes a strong relationship between receiving cross-cultural training and supervision, and that the majority of counseling programs only offer one course, it behooves those in the help-ing professions to find ways to increase their multicultural competence. The literature does support the general idea that cross-cultural supervision and training does increase self-perceptions of competency and does have an influence on racial attitudes. With this in mind we offer the following suggestions for helping professionals to enhance their cultural competence.

Practical Suggestions

1. *Set goals.* Setting goals to become culturally competent is similar to the call for counselors to become culturally aware, but involves clinicians making a deeper commitment to exploring the beliefs that may enhance their effectiveness and biases that may prevent them from doing so. This step would include identifying individuals who possess culture-specific skills that would be beneficial for the counselor to develop. We suggest that counselors set yearly goals with objectives and subgoals centered on cultural competence. The growth and use of the Internet have skyrocketed in the last 10 years. It has been a place where one can get connected to people all over the country and the world, and contains numerous cultural and mental health resources. Thus, the Internet may be an excellent platform for counselors to develop cultural skills. With technological advances such as webcams, webinars, and videoconferencing, counselors can gain valuable skills and engage other professionals all over the world. The second author has been a part of webinars sponsored by the National Center for Cultural Competence. These webinars connected the second author with other professionals who shared knowledge and expertise about a variety of techniques that were successful in working with racial and ethnic minorities. The Web also has a plethora of useful information related to a variety of racial and ethnic groups, including current information about research and best practices. Some recommended Web sites include: Transcultural Psychology Listserv, Asian American Psychological Association Listserv, Korean American Psychological Association Listserv, Student affairs.com, Centers for Disease Control and Prevention—Office of Minority Health & Health Disparities, Office of the Surgeon General—A Report of the Surgeon General, National Center on Minority Health and Health Disparities, and National Center for Cultural Competence.

2. *Become a good listener.* This suggestion involves the counselor actively developing a stronger cultural self. The second author has learned much from being a good listener and seeking out informal opportunities to receive impromptu supervision and training. Significant learning occurs when it is least expected. Listening is one of them.

3. *Practice.* This suggestion involves two components: putting into (a) practice the things that the clinician-trainee has (b) learned. Learning and practice cannot be separated. Experiential learning is the most effective way to gain a skill set that would allow counselors to work effectively in their community. No matter how much individuals explore their cultural beliefs and increase their cultural knowledge, few substantive changes will permanently occur until the behavioral risks are taken. Interacting with culturally diverse individuals in formal and informal settings provides opportunities for counselors to practice juggling being cultural observers of the self as well as others. The more counselors are able to manage their feelings and beliefs, the easier it will be for them to be more comfortable with themselves and be attentive and responsive to the unique cultural characteristics of the client.

Supervision

Mental health professionals spend many hours under supervision from a seasoned mental health professional in learning how to be an effective practitioner. With the focus on developing skills that will allow counselors to work effectively across a diverse clientele, supervisors have come under scrutiny in their ability to provide counselor trainees with the appropriate multicultural skills. The mental health profession has traditionally been conservative and supported by the values and beliefs of the dominant cultural groups in the United States and Europe (Butler, 2003). Within the context of a more diverse world, supervisors are required to be well versed in multicultural issues or at least have access to pertinent information about the various cultural groups that may populate a given region. However, many supervisors who received their training prior to the 1990s have had little training in providing clinical services to diverse populations (Ladany, Inman, Constantine, & Hofheinz, 1997). Constantine (1997) reported that 30 percent of interns and 70 percent of counseling supervisors had never completed a multicultural counseling course. If the majority of supervisors have had no formal training in providing services to diverse populations, then it would not be a stretch to assume that little to no time in supervision is devoted to addressing multicultural issues. This issue is even more troubling when coupled with the low number of racial/ethnic minority clinicians, further limiting the pool of supervisors who may be available to work with trainees on multicultural issues.

The infusion of multicultural issues into supervision improves the clinical training and cultural competence of the trainees. For example, a supervisor's willingness to engage and initiate conversations around diversity issues has been associated with trainees' satisfaction with supervision (Abreu et al., 2000). Ethnic minority trainees reported that being respected by supervisors enhanced their satisfaction with cross-cultural supervision. Furthermore, effective multicultural counseling supervision allows for new and creative supervisory interventions, which, in turn, allows for the supervisor to provide effective supervision of trainees with differing worldviews and values (Robinson, Bradley, & Hendricks, 2000). Thus, the increased repertoire of interventions utilized by the supervisor can serve as a model for the counseling trainee. According to Butler (2003), the culturally competent clinical supervisor (a) is flexible, (b) is a critical thinker, (c) is able to work across cultures, (d) has a working knowledge of the supervisory process, (e) creates a positive environment, (f) manages anxiety level, (g) has a well established sense of identity, and (h) is effective in the use of humor, humility, and patience. Most of these characteristics are reflective of the typical clinical supervisor, except for being able to work across cultures. Developing cultural skill means that the supervisor becomes better in the aforementioned characteristics.

As the helping professions continue to move toward more inclusive models of multicultural training, it is imperative that mental health programs continue to find ways of infusing cultural issues into existing curricula as one mechanism in increasing the viability of counseling for all. Supervision plays a major role in preparing all mental health professionals, and, as result, it is a critical aspect in training counselors to work effectively with diverse clients. Given the emphasis put on supervision, it is paradoxical that this area of professional development remains one of the least regulated areas of training (Abreu et al., 2000; Butler, 2003; Constantine, 1997). As cultural competence becomes a normative standard of mental health training, supervisors need to be held to a high standard and be accountable in providing culturally sound and effective supervision. For example, what clear expectations are in any of the helping professions' codes or guidelines about cultural competence? Do states' certification and licensure laws include any expectations about the expertise of supervisors to provide culturally sound training? Professional and state codes usually include a general statement about supervisors working in the area of expertise. As a result, it is left to the supervisors to regulate themselves about their level of competence. With the discomfort that many supervisors of the previous generations have in working with culturally diverse clients, it is unlikely that they would be effective observers of their level of cultural competence. Thus, the helping professions are at a critical juncture in determining how clinical training and supervision are conducted or in restructuring or forging a new path that lays out specific guidelines for supervisory skills, continuing education, and possibly additional certification in establishing that the requisite skills are continuing to be met.

Recommendations for Supervisors

Writing this section is difficult. At this point much has been said in previous sections about practical ways to increase one's cultural competence. On some levels those sections were easier to write because they involved direct service to clients in which implementing the ideas would allow helping professionals to get immediate feedback. However, supervisory relationships are in some part more authoritarian than the counseling relationships regardless of one's approach to supervision. There are limited areas in which a supervisee could complain about the supervision that he or she has received. The supervisee is at the mercy of his or her supervisor. It is the supervisor who defines competence as well as the attitudes and behaviors that demonstrate competence. Given these dynamics, supervisors, for the most part, are their own judges of what they need to do to be an effective supervisor. With that said, we offer these recommendations to increase the supervisor's cultural competence. As noted, there is great overlap with recommendations in other sections.

1. Like the trainee, supervisors need to find a mentor-supervisor who can assist in increasing their cultural competence. This mentor-supervisor should be competent, have knowledge of the necessary population(s), and can be trusted to give constructive feedback.

2. The helping professional should increase his or her knowledge on cultural issues by becoming a process observer of those mentor-supervisors who have developed more skills at providing supervision for those who work with culturally different clients. Practically, the helping professional should sit in with said supervisor and take process notes of the supervision session. The helping professional would then process these notes with the mentor-supervisor and get clarification on issues that seemed unclear. We would suggest that this relationship continue at least 3 to 6 months.

3. The helping professional should develop a checklist to ensure that he or she covers important cultural themes in supervision. This checklist may include items such as: (a) Are cultural issues openly discussed in

my supervision sessions?; (b) Do I openly discuss my cultural heritage in supervision and relate it to how I work with clients?; and (c) Do I encourage my supervisee to explore his or her cultural heritage and how it relates to his or her work with clients?

These recommendations assume that the helping professional is committed to becoming a better supervisor as it relates to gaining skills to effectively supervise novice counselors working with culturally diverse clients. To implement the suggestions one has to have some internal motivation. Having ethical codes and other external pressures are useless without an internal commitment. It is also requires helping professionals to reject the status quo and challenge their core beliefs on what it means to be a competent supervisor. Being a culturally competent supervisor is being a competent supervisor. Once this shift in thinking has occurred, then the helping professional has started the process of moving from stagnation to action.

Conclusion

Helping professionals who focus on cultural competence will guarantee that over time they will develop better skills in working with racial/ethnic minority clients. It requires counselors setting workable goals connected to realistic and concrete behaviors. It requires consultation with someone brave and kind enough to give sound, constructive feedback. It requires that counselors set their egos aside and acknowledge that they don't know it all about mental health treatment, especially with culturally diverse clients. It requires finding ways, first small steps, of being involved in culturally diverse communities, knowing that feeling out of place and anxious will be the norm. Being open and flexible are fundamental necessities. Finally, it requires that counselors take risks and do it.

References

Abreu, J. M., Gim Chung, R. H., & Atkinson, D. R. (2000). Multicultural counseling training: Past, present, and future directions. *The Counseling Psychologist, 28*, 641–656.

Adkison-Bradley, C., Johnson, D., Lipford Sanders, J., Duncan, L., & Holcomb-McCoy, C. (2005). Forging a collaborative relationship between the black church and the counseling profession. *Counseling and Values, 49*, 147–154.

Alegria, M., Canino, G., Rios, R., Vera, M., Calderon, J., Rusch, D., et al. (2002). Inequalities in use of specialty mental health services among Latinos, African Americans, and non-Latino Whites. *Psychiatric Services, 53,* 1547–1555.

Alvidrez, J. (1999). Ethnic variations in mental health attitudes and service use among low-income African American, Latina, and European American young women. *Community Mental Health Journal, 35,* 515–530.

American College of Physicians. (2004). Racial and ethnic disparities in health care: A position paper of the American College of Physicians. *Annals of Internal Medicine, 141,* 226–232.

American Psychological Association. (2002). Ethical principles of psychologists and code of conduct. *American Psychologist, 57,* 1060–1075.

American Psychological Association. (2003). Guidelines on multicultural education, training, research, practice and organizational change for psychologists. *American Psychologist, 58,* 377–402.

Anglin, D. M., Alberti, P. M., Link, B. G., & Phelan, J. C. (2008). Racial differences in beliefs about the effectiveness and necessity of mental health treatment. *American Journal of Community Psychology, 42,* 17–24.

Arredondo, P. (1998). Integrating multicultural counseling competencies and universal helping conditions in culture-specific contexts. *The Counseling Psychologist, 26,* 592–601.

Arredondo, P., & Arciniega, G. M. (2001). Strategies and techniques for counselor training based on the multicultural counseling competencies. *Journal of Multicultural Counseling & Development, 29,* 263–273.

Arredondo, P., Toporek, M. S., Brown, S., Jones, J., Locke, D. C., Sanchez, J., et al. (1996). *Operationalization of the multicultural counseling competencies.* Alexandria, VA: Association of Multicultural Counseling and Development.

Bernal, M. E., & Castro, F. G. (1994). Are clinical psychologists prepared for service and research with ethnic minorities? Report of a decade of progress. *American Psychologist, 49,* 797–805.

Bernal, G., & Sáez-Santiago, E. (2006). Culturally centered psychosocial interventions. *Journal of Community Psychology, 34,* 121–132.

Bimrose, J., & Bayne, R. (1995). A multicultural framework in counselor training: A preliminary evaluation. *British Journal of Guidance and Counselling, 23,* 259–265.

Brown, S. P., Parham, T. A., & Yonker, R. (1996). Influence of a cross-cultural training course on racial identity attitudes of White women and men. Preliminary perspectives. *Journal of Counseling and Development, 74,* 510–516.

Butler, S. K. (2003). Multicultural sensitivity and competence in the clinical supervision of school counselors and school psychologists: A context for providing competent services in a multicultural society. *Clinical Supervisor, 22,* 125–141.

Butler, S. K., & Constantine, M. G. (2006). Web-based peer supervision, collective self-esteem and case conceptualization ability in school counselor trainees. *Professional School Counseling, 10,* 146–152.

Cardemil, E. V., & Battle, C. L. (2003). Guess who's coming to therapy? Getting comfortable with conversations about race and ethnicity in psychotherapy. *Professional Psychology: Research and Practice, 34,* 278–286.

Cass, V. C. (1984). Homosexual identity formation: Testing a theoretical model. *Journal of Sex Research, 20,* 143–167.

Chavez, D. (1994). *Faces of an angel.* New York: Warner Books Edition.

Chow, J. C. C., Jaffee, K., & Snowden, L. (2003). Racial/ethnic disparities in the use of mental health services in poverty areas. *American Journal of Public Health, 93,* 792–797.

Constantine, M. (1997). *Facilitating multicultural competency in counseling supervision: Operationalizing a practical framework.* Thousand Oaks, CA: Sage.

Constantine, M. G., Warren, A. K., & Miville, M. L. (2005). White racial identity dyadic interactions in supervision: Implications for supervisees' multicultural counseling competence. *Journal of Counseling Psychology, 52,* 490.

Cooper-Patrick, L., Powe, N. R., Jenckes, M. W., Gonzales, J. J., Levine, D. M., & Ford, D. E. (1997). Identification of patient attitudes and preferences regarding treatment of depression. *Journal of General Internal Medicine, 12,* 431–438.

Cross, T., Bazron, B., Dennis, K., & Isaacs, M. (1989). *Towards a culturally competent system of care* (Vol. 1). Washington, DC: Georgetown University Center for Child and Human Development, CASSP Technical Assistance Center.

Cross, W. E., Jr., & Vandiver, B. J. (2001). Nigrescence theory and measurement: Introducing the Cross Racial Identity Scale (CRIS). In J. G. Ponterotto, J. M. Casas, L. M. Suzuki, & C. M. Alexander (Eds.), *Handbook of multicultural counseling* (2nd ed., pp. 371–393). Thousand Oaks, CA: Sage.

Cuellar, I., & Paniagua, F. A. (Eds.). (2000). *Handbook of multicultural mental health: Assessment and treatment of diverse populations.* San Diego, CA: Academic Press.

Danquah, M. N.-A. (1998). *Willow weep for me: A black woman's journey through depression.* New York: W. W. Norton.

Devine, P. G. (1989). Stereotypes and prejudice: Their automatic and controlled components. *Journal of Personality and Social Psychology, 56,* 5–18.

Diala, C., Muntaner, C., Walrath, C., Nickerson, K. J., LaVeist, T. A., & Leaf, P. J. (2001). Racial differences in attitudes toward professional mental health care and in the use of services. *American Journal of Orthopsychiatry, 70,* 455–464.

Downing, N. E., & Roush, K. L. (1985). From passive acceptance to active commitment: A model of feminist identity development for women. *The Counseling Psychologist, 13,* 695–709.

Duncan, L. E. (2005). Overcoming biases to effectively serve African American college students: A call to the profession. *College Student Journal, 39,* 702–710.

Flynn, J. (1980). *Race, IQ and Jensen.* London: Routledge.

Fouad, N. A., & Arredondo, P. (2007). *Becoming culturally oriented: Practical advice for psychologists and educators.* Washington, DC: American Psychological Association.

Freire, P. (1970). *Pedagogy of the oppressed* (M. B. Ramos, Trans.). New York: Herder & Herder.

Graves, J. L. (2004). *The race myth: Why we pretend race exists in America.* New York: Dutton.

Grisham, J. (1989). *A time to kill.* New York: Doubleday.

Hall, G. C. (2001). Psychotherapy research with ethnic minorities: Empirical, ethical, and conceptual issues. *Journal of Consulting and Clinical Psychology, 69,* 502–510.

Hargrove, B. K., & Sedlacek, W. E. (1997). Counseling interests among entering Black freshmen over a ten-year period. *Journal of the Freshmen Year Experience, 9,* 83–92.

Hays, P. (2001). *Addressing cultural complexities in practice: A framework for clinicians and counselors.* Washington, DC: American Psychological Association.

Helms, J. E. (1984). Toward a theoretical explanation of the effects of race on counseling: A black and white model. *The Counseling Psychologist, 12,* 153–165.

Helms, J. E. (1995). An update of Helms's White and people of color racial identity models. In J. G. Ponterotto, J. M. Casas, L. A. Suzuki, & C. M. Alexander (Eds.), *Handbook of multicultural counseling* (pp. 181–198). Thousand Oaks, CA: Sage.

Hills, H. I., & Strozier, A. L. (1992). Multicultural training in APA-approved counseling psychology programs: A survey. *Professional Psychology: Research & Practice, 23,* 43–51.

Hogan, M. F., Adams, J., Arredondo, R., Carlile, P., Curie, G. G., Fisher, D. B., et al. (2003). *Achieving the promise: Transforming mental health care in America* (Final report, DHH Publication No. SMA-03-3832). Rockville, MD: President's New Freedom Commission on Mental Health.

Holcomb-McCoy, C. C., & Myers, J. E. (1999). Multicultural competence and counselor training: A national survey. *Journal of Counseling & Development, 77,* 294–302.

Isaacs, M. R., Huang, L. M., Hernandez, M., & Echo-Hawk, H. (2005). *The road to evidence: The intersection of evidenced based practices and cultural competence in children's health* (draft paper). Washington, DC: National Alliance of Multi-Ethnic Behavioral Health Association (NAMBHA).

Ivey, A. E. (1995). Psychotherapy as liberation. In J. G. Ponterotto, M. Casas, L. Suzuki, & C. Alexander, C. (Eds.), *Handbook of multicultural counseling* (pp. 53–72). Thousand Oaks, CA: Sage.

Jackson, M. L. (1995). Multicultural counseling: Historical perspectives. In J. G. Ponterotto, J. M. Casas, L. A. Suzuki, & C. M. Alexander (Eds.), *Handbook of multicultural counseling* (pp. 3–16). Thousand Oaks, CA: Sage.

Jensen, A. R. (1998). The g factor and the design of education. In R. J. Sternberg & W. M. Williams (Eds.), *Intelligence, instruction, and assessment: Theory into practice* (pp. 111–131). Mahwah, NJ: Lawrence Erlbaum.

Johnson, J. L., & Cameron, M. C. (2001). Barriers to providing effective mental health services to American Indians. *Mental Health Services Research, 3,* 215–223.

Klonoff, E. A., & Landrine, H. (1994). Culture and gender diversity in common-sense beliefs about the cases of six illnesses. *Behavioral Medicine, 17,* 407–418.

Kung, W. W. (2003). Chinese Americans' help seeking for emotional distress. *Social Service Review, 77,* 110–133.

Ladany, N., Inman, A. G., Constantine, M. G. & Hofheinz, E. W. (1997). Supervisee multicultural case conceptualization ability and self-reported multicultural competence as functions of supervisee racial identity and supervisor focus. *Journal of Counseling Psychology, 44,* 284–293.

Lagasse, M. H. (2004). *The fifth sun.* Willimantic, CT: Curbstone Press.

Larry P. v. Riles, 343 F. Supp. 1306 (N.D. Cal. 1972).

Lasser, K. E., Himmelstein, D. U., Woohandler, S. J., McCormick, D., & Bor, D. H. (2002). Do minorities in the United States receive fewer mental health services than Whites? *International Journal of Health Services, 32,* 567–578.

LaVeist, T. A., Nickerson, K. J., & Bowie, J. V. (2000). Attitudes about racism, medical mistrust and satisfaction with care among African American and white cardiac patients. *Medical Care Research and Review, 57*(Supp. 1), 146–161.

Leong, F. T. L., Wagner, N. S., & Tata, S. P. (1995). Racial and ethnic variation in help-seeking attitudes. In J. G. Ponterotto, J. M. Casas, L. A. Suzuki, & C. M. Alexander (Eds.), *Handbook of multicultural counseling* (pp. 415–438). Thousand Oaks, CA: Sage.

Lim, R. F. (Ed). (2006). *Clinical manual of cultural psychiatry.* Washington, DC: American Psychiatric Association.

Lin, K.-M., & Cheung, F. (1999). Mental health issues for Asian Americans. *Psychiatric Services, 50,* 774–780.

Lin, K.-M., Poland, R. E., & Nakasaki, G. (Eds.). (1993). *Psychopharmacology and psychobiology of ethnicity* (Progress in Psychiatry Series, No. 39). Washington, DC: American Psychiatric Association.

Marsella, A. J., & Pedersen, P. B. (2004). Internationalizing the curriculum in counseling psychology. *Counselling Psychology Quarterly, 17,* 413–424.

Marshall, J., III. (2001). *The Lakota way: Stories and lessons for living.* New York: Viking Compass.

McAuliffe, G., & Associates. (Eds.) (2008). *Culturally alert counseling: A comprehensive introduction.* Thousand Oaks, CA: Sage.

McCarn, S. R., & Fassinger, R. E. (1996). Revisioning sexual minority identity formation: A new model of lesbian identity and its implications for counseling and research. *The Counseling Psychologist, 24,* 508–534.

Miranda, J., Bernal, G., Lau, A., Kohn, L., Hwang, W., & LaFromboise, T. (2005). State of the science on psychosocial interventions for ethnic minorities. *Annual Review of Clinical Psychology, 1,* 113–142.

Miranda, J., Nakamura, R., & Bernal, G. (2003). Including ethnic minorities in mental health intervention research: A practical approach to a long-standing problem. *Culture, Medicine and Psychiatry, 27,* 467–486.

Montagu, A. (1999). *Race and IQ.* New York: Oxford University Press.

Moradi, B., Subich, L. M., & Phillips, J. C. (2002). Revisiting feminist identity development: Theory, research, and practice. *The Counseling Psychologist, 30,* 6–43.

Mosley, W. (1990). *Devil in a blue dress.* New York: W. W. Norton.

Nadeem, E., Lange, J. M., Edge, D., Fongwa, M., Belin, T., & Miranda, J. (2007). Does stigma keep poor young immigrants and U.S.-born black and Latina women from seeking mental health care? *Psychiatric Services, 58,* 1547–1554.

Nadeem, E., Lange, J. M., & Miranda, J. (2008). Mental health care preferences among low-income and minority women. *Archives of Women's Mental Health, 11,* 93–102.

National Association of Social Workers. (2000). Cultural competence in the social work profession. In *Social work speaks: NASW policy statements* (pp. 59–62). Washington, DC: NASW Press.

Neighbors, H. W. (1991). Mental health. In J. Jackson (Ed.), *Life in Black America* (pp. 221–237). Newbury, CA: Sage.

Neighbors, H. W., Trierweiler, S. J., Ford, B., & Muroff, J. R. (2003). Racial differences in DSM diagnosis using a semi-structured instrument: The importance of clinical judgment in the diagnosis of African Americans. *Journal of Health and Social Behavior, 44,* 237–256.

Neville, H. A., Heppner, M. J., Louie, C. E., Thompson, C. E., Brooks, L., & Baker, C. E. (1996). The impact of multicultural training on White racial identity attitudes and therapy competencies. *Professional Psychology: Research and Practice, 27,* 83–89.

Office of Minority Health. (2000). *What is cultural competence?* Retrieved, November 13, 2005, from http://www.omhrc.gov/templates/browse. aspx?lvl=2&lvlID=11

Ortega, A. N., & Alegria, M. (2002). Self-reliance, mental health need, and the use of mental health care among island Puerto Ricans. *Mental Health Services Research, 4,* 131–140.

Pedersen, P. B. (1991). Multiculturalism as a generic approach to counseling. *Journal of Counseling and Development, 70,* 6–12.

Pi, E. H., & Simpson, G. M. (2005). Cross-cultural psychopharmacology: A current clinical perspective. *Psychiatric Services, 56,* 31–33.

Ponterotto, J. G. (1997). Multicultural counseling training: A competency model and national survey. In D. B. Pope-Davis, & H. L. K. Coleman (Eds.), *Multicultural counseling competencies: Assessment, education and training, and supervision* (pp. 111–130). Thousand Oaks, CA: Sage.

Reynolds, C. R. (2000). Why is psychometric research on bias in mental testing so often ignored? *Psychology, Public Policy, and Law, 6,* 144–150.

Ridley, C. R., Mendoza, D. W., & Kanitz, B. E. (1994). Multicultural training: Reexamination, operationalization, and integration. *The Counseling Psychologist, 22,* 227–289.

Ridley, C. R., Mendoza, D. W., Kanitz, B. E., Angermeier, L., & Zenk, R. (1994). Cultural sensitivity in multicultural counseling: A perceptual schema model. *Journal of Counseling Psychology, 41,* 125–136.

Rivera, T. E., Phan, L. T., Maddux, C. B., Wilbur, J. R., & Arredondo, P. (2006). Honesty in multicultural counseling: A pilot study of the counseling relationship. *Revista Interamericana De Psicología, 40,* 37–45.

Robinson, B., Bradley, L. J., & Hendricks, C. B. (2000). Multicultural counseling supervision: A four-step model toward competency. *International Journal for the Advancement of Counselling, 22,* 131–141.

Roysircar, G. (2005). Research in multicultural counseling: Client needs and counselor competencies. In C. Lee (Ed.), *Multicultural issues in counseling: New approaches to diversity* (3rd ed., pp. 369–387). Alexandria, VA: American Counseling Association.

Sanchez-Hucles, J. (2000). *The first session with African Americans: A step-by-step guide.* San Francisco, CA: Jossey-Bass.

Sellers, R. M., Rowley, S. A. J., Chavous, T. M., Shelton, J. N., & Smith, M. (1997). Multidimensional Inventory of Black Identity: A preliminary investigation of reliability and construct validity. *Journal of Personality and Social Psychology, 73,* 805–815.

Snowden, L. R., & Thomas, K. (2000). Medicaid and African American outpatient mental health treatment. *Mental Health Services Research, 2,* 115–120.

Snowden, L. R., & Yamada, A. M. (2005). Cultural differences in access to care. *Annual Review of Clinical Psychology, 1,* 143–166.

Sodowsky, G. R., Kuo-Jackson, P. Y., Richardson, M. F., & Corey, A. T. (1998). Correlates of self-reported multicultural competencies: Counselor multicultural social desirability, race, social inadequacy, locus of control racial ideology, and multicultural training. *Journal of Counseling Psychology, 45,* 256–264.

Speight, S. L., Myers, L. J., Cox, C. I., & Highlen, P. S. (1991). A redefinition of multicultural counseling. *Journal of Counseling & Development, 70,* 29–36.

Sternberg, R. J. (2000). *Handbook of intelligence.* Cambridge: Cambridge University Press.

Steward, R. J., Boatwright, K. J., Sauer, E., Baden, A., & Jackson, J. D. (1998). The relationships among counselor-trainees' gender, cognitive development, and white racial identity: Implications for counselor training. *Journal of Multicultural Counseling & Development, 26,* 254–272.

Sue, S. (2006). Cultural competency: From philosophy to research and practice. *Journal of Community Psychology, 34,* 237–245.

Sue, S., & Dhindsa, M. K. (2006). Ethnic and racial health disparities research: Issues and problems. *Health Education & Behavior, 33,* 459–469.

Sue, S., Fujino, D. C., Hu, L. T., Takeuchi, D. T., & Zane, N. W. (1991). Community mental health services for ethnic minority groups: A test of the cultural responsiveness hypothesis. *Journal of Consulting and Clinical Psychology, 59,* 533–540.

Sue, S., & Sue, L. (2003). Ethnic research is good science. In G. Bernal, J. E. Trimble, A. K. Burlew, & F. T. L. Leong (Eds.), *Handbook of racial and ethnic minority psychology* (pp. 198–207). Newbury Park, CA: Sage.

Suzuki, L. A., Ponterotto, J. G., & Meller, P. J. (Eds.). (2007). *Handbook of multicultural assessment: Clinical, psychological, and educational applications* (3rd ed.). San Francisco: Jossey-Bass.

Tajfel, H., & Turner, J. C. (1979). An integrative theory of intergroup conflict. In W. G. Austin & S. Worchel (Eds.), *The social psychology of intergroup relations* (pp. 33–48). Monterey, CA: Brooks/Cole.

U.S. Bureau of the Census. (2004). *Statistical abstract of the United States: 2004* (124th ed.). Washington, DC: Author.

U.S. Department of Health and Human Services. (1999). *Mental health: A report of the surgeon general.* Rockville, MD: Author.

U.S. Department of Health and Human Services. (2001). *Mental health culture, race, and ethnicity: A supplement to mental health; a report of the surgeon general.* Rockville, MD: Author.

Vega, W. A., Kolody, B., Aguilar-Gaxiola, S., & Catalano, R. (1999). Gaps in service utilization by Mexican Americans with mental health problems. *American Journal of Psychiatry, 156,* 928–934.

Vera, E. M., & Speight, S. L. (2003). Multicultural competence, social justice, and counseling psychology: Expanding our roles. *The Counseling Psychologist, 31,* 253–272.

Wells, K., Klap, R., Koike, A., & Sherbourne, C. (2001). Ethnic disparities in unmet need for alcoholism, drug abuse, and mental health care. *American Journal of Psychiatry, 158,* 2027–2032.

Wiggins, J. S. (1973). *Personality and prediction: Principles of personality assessment.* Reading, MA: Addison-Wesley.

Yeh, C., & Arora, A. (2003). Multicultural training and interdependent and independent self-construal as predictors of universal-diverse orientation among school counselors. *Journal of Counseling & Development, 81,* 78–83.

Zambrana, R. E., Carter-Pokras, O., Nunez, N. P., Valdez, R. B., & Villarruel, A. M. (2004). *Drawing from the data: Working effectively with Latino families. A guide for health and family support practitioners.* Chicago: American Academy of Pediatrics and Family Support America.

Zhang, A. Y., Snowden, L. R., & Sue, S. (1998). Differences between Asian and White Americans' help seeking and utilization patterns in the Los Angeles area. *Journal of Community Psychology, 26,* 317–326.

Index